George Weaver

**The Lives and Graves of our Presidents**

George Weaver

**The Lives and Graves of our Presidents**

ISBN/EAN: 9783743324725

Manufactured in Europe, USA, Canada, Australia, Japa

Cover: Foto ©ninafisch / pixelio.de

Manufactured and distributed by brebook publishing software (www.brebook.com)

George Weaver

**The Lives and Graves of our Presidents**

LINCOLN MONUMENT.

ENGRAVED EXPRESSLY FOR WEAVERS' LIVES AND GRAVES OF OUR PRESIDENTS.

# THE LIVES AND GRAVES

—— OF OUR ——

# PRESIDENTS.

—— BY ——

## G. S. WEAVER, D.D.

AUTHOR OF

"THE HEART OF THE WORLD,"
"AIMS AND AIDS FOR YOUNG MEN AND WOMEN,"
"HOPES AND HELPS FOR THE YOUNG,"
"WAYS OF LIFE," ETC.

Chicago:
ELDER PUBLISHING COMPANY.
1884.

## PREFACE.

By the great interest that attaches to our presidents, on account of their personal worth as well as high position, it is hoped to win the attention of the young, first to the fine likenesses presented, and then to the sketches of the lives of our rulers.

As the lives of the presidents so overlap each other, and so many lived contemporaneously, there must be not a little repetition, which the author has accepted without scruple as necessary to a fair presentation of each life.

The difficulty of reducing the great amount of material in the personal lives and historical relations of the presidents to the narrow limits of a moderate-sized book cannot be realized by any one till he undertakes a similar task.

The difficulty of reconciling the conflicting statements of different biographers and the differences of historians, and of supplying the deficiencies of their information, is greater than can be apprehended till one has had the experience of an effort of this kind.

The author's hope is to so win attention to the history and biography of the country that his readers will get a thirst for the larger works, and will so acquaint themselves with them as to become alive to the principles involved in our government and its history. Few things would be more beneficial than a general re-study of our national history. Patriotism is waning for want of it.

CHICAGO, January 2, 1884.   G. S. W.

# CONTENTS.

## CHAPTER I.

| | |
|---|---|
| THE BEGINNING OF THE REPUBLIC | 17 |
| The Quality of Colonial Men | 20 |
| Our Country the Outgrowth of Many Causes | 21 |
| The Cause of the Revolution | 21 |
| The Battles of Lexington and Concord | 26 |
| The Battle of Bunker Hill | 26 |
| The Taking of Fort Ticonderoga | 26 |
| The Evacuation of Boston | 27 |
| The Declaration of Independence | 29 |

## CHAPTER II.

### GEORGE WASHINGTON.

#### FIRST PRESIDENT OF THE UNITED STATES.

| | |
|---|---|
| Ancestry | 35 |
| Boyhood of Washington | 38 |
| His Education | 41 |
| His Youth | 43 |
| His Heart Sorrow | 44 |
| His Surveying Expedition | 45 |
| Coming Complications | 46 |
| Lawrence Washington's Sickness | 47 |
| A Perilous Mission | 48 |

An Expedition to the Ohio . . . . 51
Braddock's Campaign . . . . . 52
Washington's Courtship and Marriage . . . 54
Mount Vernon . . . . . . 56
Personal Characteristics . . . . . 59
Commander-in-chief . . . . . . 60
Boston Besieged . . . . . . 61
New York in Danger . . . . . 63
Philadelphia Captured . . . . . 66
The Campaign of 1778 . . . . . 68
The Campaign of 1779 . . . . . 68
The Campaign of 1780 . . . . . 70
The Campaign of 1781 . . . . . 71
Life at Mount Vernon . . . . . 74
The Confederation and the Constitution . . . 76
Washington Elected President . . . . 78
Washington's Administration . . . . 80
Washington's Death . . . . . 84
The Grave of Washington . . . . 85

## CHAPTER III.

### JOHN ADAMS.

#### SECOND PRESIDENT OF THE UNITED STATES.

Genealogy . . . . . . . 89
John Adams, a Teacher . . . . . 91
Law Practice in Braintree . . . . 94
Removal to Boston . . . . . . 97
Public Life Began . . . . . . 99
The Colonial Congress . . . . . 101
Correspondence with his Wife . . . . 102
His Election to the Provincial Congress . . . 102
The Second Continental Congress . . . 103
Minister to France . . . . . 105
Massachusetts Constitutional Convention . . 106

| | |
|---|---:|
| Commissioner for Peace | 107 |
| The New Commission | 108 |
| Adams' Publications in England | 109 |
| Made Vice President | 110 |
| Made Second President | 110 |
| Retirement to Braintree | 113 |
| The Graves of the Adamses | 115 |

## CHAPTER IV.

### THOMAS JEFFERSON.

#### THIRD PRESIDENT OF THE UNITED STATES.

| | |
|---|---:|
| Ancestry | 119 |
| His Education | 120 |
| Personal Appearance | 125 |
| Mr. Jefferson a Lawyer | 126 |
| Mr. Jefferson a Legislator | 127 |
| Jefferson Not a Speaker | 128 |
| Loss by Fire | 129 |
| Marriage | 130 |
| The Approaching Conflict | 132 |
| Nation Building | 139 |
| Mr. Jefferson Made Governor | 141 |
| Mrs. Jefferson's Death | 141 |
| Appointed to Negotiate Peace at Paris | 143 |
| Commissioner of Treaties of Commerce | 143 |
| Minister at the Court of France | 144 |
| Secretary of State | 146 |
| Resigns his Secretaryship | 150 |
| Vice President | 150 |
| The Third President | 152 |
| The Purchase of Louisiana | 154 |
| Jefferson's Religious Opinions | 156 |
| The University of Virginia | 157 |

## CONTENTS.

| | |
|---|---|
| Financial Misfortunes | 157 |
| Final Departure | 157 |
| The Grave of Thomas Jefferson | 158 |

# CHAPTER V.
## JAMES MADISON.
### FOURTH PRESIDENT OF THE UNITED STATES.

| | |
|---|---|
| Ancestry, Youth and Education | 163 |
| Entrance upon Public Life | 166 |
| Made a Member of the Continental Congress | 168 |
| Elected to the Virginia Legislature | 168 |
| A Constitutional Convention | 170 |
| The Federalist | 175 |
| A Member of Congress | 175 |
| Secretary of State | 176 |
| Fourth President | 177 |
| War with England | 178 |
| Retirement in 1817 | 179 |
| Mrs. Madison | 180 |
| The Grave of James Madison | 181 |

# CHAPTER VI.
## JAMES MONROE.
### FIFTH PRESIDENT OF THE UNITED STATES.

| | |
|---|---|
| Ancestry and Youth | 183 |
| A Soldier | 185 |
| A Legislator | 187 |
| A Minister Abroad | 188 |
| Governor of Virginia | 190 |
| Secretary of State | 191 |
| Fifth President | 192 |
| Domestic Relations | 196 |
| The Grave of James Monroe | 198 |

## CHAPTER VII.
### JOHN QUINCY ADAMS.
#### Sixth President of the United States.

| | |
|---|---:|
| Ancestry | 199 |
| The Time | 200 |
| His Boyhood | 202 |
| The Lawyer | 205 |
| The Writer | 205 |
| Foreign Minister | 207 |
| Begins Anew | 207 |
| Minister to Russia | 209 |
| Minister at the Court of St. James | 211 |
| Secretary of State | 211 |
| The President | 216 |
| Representative in Congress | 220 |
| The Grave of John Quincy Adams | 227 |

## CHAPTER VIII.
### ANDREW JACKSON.
#### Seventh President of the United States.

| | |
|---|---:|
| Ancestry | 229 |
| Andrew Jackson, Senior | 230 |
| Jackson's Boyhood | 231 |
| Jackson the Youth | 234 |
| Jackson the Lawyer | 237 |
| The Legislator | 239 |
| Judge Jackson | 240 |
| Business Embarrassments | 241 |
| Personal Complications | 241 |
| General Jackson | 243 |
| President Jackson | 249 |
| The Grave of Andrew Jackson | 253 |

## CHAPTER IX.

### MARTIN VAN BUREN.

#### EIGHTH PRESIDENT OF THE UNITED STATES.

| | |
|---|---:|
| Ancestry, Birth and Boyhood | 255 |
| Van Buren the Lawyer | 258 |
| A Politician | 259 |
| Secretary of State | 263 |
| Vice-President Van Buren | 266 |
| President Van Buren | 266 |
| The Grave of Martin Van Buren | 271 |

## CHAPTER X.

### WILLIAM HENRY HARRISON.

#### NINTH PRESIDENT OF THE UNITED STATES.

| | |
|---|---:|
| Ancestry | 273 |
| Birth and Youth | 274 |
| Opening Manhood | 275 |
| Governor Harrison | 281 |
| The Tecumseh War | 282 |
| Commander-in-Chief | 288 |
| The Grave of William Henry Harrison | 292 |

## CHAPTER XI.

### JOHN TYLER.

#### TENTH PRESIDENT OF THE UNITED STATES.

| | |
|---|---:|
| Ancestry | 295 |
| Birth and Boyhood | 296 |
| Political Career | 297 |
| Vice-President and President Tyler | 303 |
| The Grave of John Tyler | 308 |

## CHAPTER XII.

### JAMES KNOX POLK.

#### Eleventh President of the United States.

| | |
|---|---:|
| Ancestry | 312 |
| His Boyhood | 313 |
| Mr. Polk a Lawyer | 314 |
| Mr. Polk a Legislator | 315 |
| Mr. Polk the Congressman | 316 |
| Mr. Polk the Governor | 318 |
| Mr Polk as President | 321 |
| The Grave of James K. Polk | 325 |

## CHAPTER XIII.

### ZACHARY TAYLOR.

#### Twelfth President of the United States.

| | |
|---|---:|
| Birth and Boyhood | 328 |
| Zachary Taylor the Soldier | 330 |
| President Taylor | 340 |
| The Grave of Zachary Taylor | 342 |

## CHAPTER XIV.

### MILLARD FILLMORE.

#### Thirteenth President of the United States.

| | |
|---|---:|
| Birth and Early Life | 345 |
| Mr. Fillmore the Lawyer and Public Man | 346 |
| Vice-President Fillmore | 347 |
| Mr. Fillmore the President | 348 |
| The Evening Repose | 351 |
| The Grave of Millard Fillmore | 352 |

## CHAPTER XV.

### FRANKLIN PIERCE.

#### FOURTEENTH PRESIDENT OF THE UNITED STATES.

| | |
|---|---|
| Birth and Early Life | 353 |
| Mr. Pierce the Lawyer and Politician | 354 |
| President Pierce | 357 |
| The Grave of Franklin Pierce | 359 |

## CHAPTER XVI.

### JAMES BUCHANAN.

#### FIFTEENTH PRESIDENT OF THE UNITED STATES.

| | |
|---|---|
| Ancestry and Education | 361 |
| Buchanan the Lawyer | 362 |
| Buchanan the Legislator | 362 |
| Secretary of State | 364 |
| Minister to England | 364 |
| President Buchanan | 365 |
| The Grave of James Buchanan | 367 |

## CHAPTER XVII.

### ABRAHAM LINCOLN.

#### SIXTEENTH PRESIDENT OF THE UNITED STATES.

| | |
|---|---|
| Ancestry and Early Life | 370 |
| Early Manhood | 373 |
| Lincoln a Soldier | 375 |
| Lincoln a Surveyor | 377 |
| Lincoln a Legislator | 377 |
| Mr. Lincoln a Lawyer | 381 |
| Mr. Lincoln a Congressman | 385 |

Return to His Profession . . . . . 387
The Great Debate . . . . . . 391
The Coming Storm . . . . . 394
Mr. Lincoln President . . . . . . 399
The Grave of Abraham Lincoln . . . . 405

## CHAPTER XVIII.

### ANDREW JOHNSON.

#### SEVENTEENTH PRESIDENT OF THE UNITED STATES.

Ancestry . . . . . . . 407
Childhood and Youth . . . . . . 407
Early Manhood . . . . . . . 409
Johnson a Legislator . . . . . 410
Military Governor . . . . . . . 412
Mr. Johnson Vice-President . . . . 413
Mr. Johnson President . . . . . . 414
The Grave of Andrew Johnson . . . . 417

## CHAPTER XIX.

### ULYSSES S. GRANT.

#### EIGHTEENTH PRESIDENT OF THE UNITED STATES.

Ancestry, Birth and Boyhood . . . . . 420
Grant a Cadet . . . . . . 423
Lieutenant Grant . . . . . . . 424
Grant's Marriage . . . . 425
Captain Grant a Farmer . . . . . 427
Grant a Real Estate Agent . . . . . 427
Grant a Clerk in Galena . . . . . . 428

The Opening Rebellion . . . . 428
Brigadier-General Grant . . . . . 429
Lieutenant-General Grant . . . . 432
President Grant . . . . . . 436
President Grant the Traveler . . . . 438

## CHAPTER XX.

### RUTHERFORD BIRCHARD HAYES.

#### NINETEENTH PRESIDENT OF THE UNITED STATES.

Birth and Boyhood . . . . . . 442
The Youth and Student . . . . . 443
Mr. Hayes the Lawyer . . . . . 444
Mr. Hayes the Soldier . . . . . 444
Governor Hayes . . . . . . 446
Mr. Hayes as President . . . . . 449
Mr. Hayes' Marriage and Family . . . . 450
The Hayes Home . . . . . 452

## CHAPTER XXI.

### JAMES ABRAM GARFIELD.

#### TWENTIETH PRESIDENT OF THE UNITED STATES.

Ancestry . . . . . . . 453
Birth, Boyhood and Youth . . . . 455
Garfield's School Life . . . . . 460
Garfield a Teacher . . . . . 462
Colonel Garfield . . . . . . 465
Congressman Garfield . . . . . 467
President Garfield . . . . . . 468
Assassination . . . . . . 469
The Grave of Garfield . . . . . 470

## CHAPTER XXII.

### CHESTER ALLAN ARTHUR.

#### TWENTY-FIRST PRESIDENT OF THE UNITED STATES.

| | |
|---|---:|
| Ancestry and Boyhood | 473 |
| Mr. Arthur the Lawyer | 474 |
| Mr. Arthur the Politician | 475 |
| Vice-President and President | 479 |

## CHAPTER XXIII.

| | |
|---|---:|
| AN ANALYSIS OF THE AMERICAN GOVERNMENT | 481 |
| The Preamble | 482 |
| Article I | 483 |
| Article II | 485 |
| Article III | 485 |

### CONSTITUTION OF THE UNITED STATES.

| | |
|---|---:|
| Article I | 487 |
| Article II | 493 |
| Article III | 495 |
| Article IV | 496 |
| Article V | 497 |
| Article VI | 498 |
| Article VII | 498 |

#### AMENDMENTS.

| | |
|---|---:|
| Article I | 500 |
| Article II | 500 |
| Article III | 500 |
| Article IV | 500 |

## CONTENTS.

| | |
|---|---:|
| Article V | 500 |
| Article VI | 501 |
| Article VII | 501 |
| Article VIII | 501 |
| Article IX | 501 |
| Article X | 501 |
| Article XI | 502 |
| Article XII | 502 |
| Article XIII | 503 |
| Article XIV | 503 |
| Article XV | 504 |

# THE LIVES AND GRAVES OF OUR PRESIDENTS

## CHAPTER I.

### THE BEGINNING OF THE REPUBLIC.

I T is in the nature of men to honor and love their rulers; and from this impulse of their nature the people of all nations have not only magnified their rulers while they lived; but preserved their histories, and, in the olden time, deified them after they were dead.

No nation has had greater occasion to profoundly respect their rulers than the people of the United States, for no nation has ever had greater capacity and worth, nobler character and manhood in high places than this. From the beginning, the people have in the main selected great and true men for their public servants. Almost with instinctive knowledge have they put worth into power and honored with constant devotion the public service which deserved it. There is scarcely an instance in our national history which warrants the old slander that republics are ungrateful. On the contrary, this republic has gloried in its great and good men and sought them for places of public trust and honor. And as their names fall deeper into the shadows of the past, the more sacred do they become in the gratitude of the new generations. Even the new comers to our shores join in the grateful memories of the noble dead who served the republic in its early days and put something of their worth and power into its laws and institutions. The history of the respec'. that has been given to them through the successive generations since their departure is a quickening incentive to all aspirants for public favor to imitate their virtues and copy their devotion to the public good. Vigor of mind, high virtue, generous sympathy, manliness, private purity, domestic honor and unselfish devotion to the public good in men in high places, always have, and do now, command the deepest respect of the American people; they have been trained to this; it is in their blood. They came of good Anglo-Saxon stock. Our early English ancestors venerated great names and worth among the ruling classes. They profoundly honored the king and all royalty. They were slow to see any wrong in the king. His authority had sanctity in it in their mind. When, by the selfish greed of power and love of royalty, George III. disenchanted their minds of the glamour of royalty, they turned away from hereditary royalty with disgust, but soon learned to fix their loyal affections on royalty of mind in the noble rulers of their own choice, who answered infinitely better to their ideals of men in authority. From royal loyalists they changed to democratic loyalists. The seed of respect for "the powers that be," planted in the blood of their race by long obedience to "constituted authority," brought forth a full harvest in a republican government. The trained and christianized respect for rulers grew in due time into respect for the masses of men which republican rulers represent. In their minds their chosen rulers stood for the whole people. The president represented the whole people of the country, and was to be respected not only for his own worth as the head of the nation; but as the symbol of all the people and their rights and interests. He was more than a king; he was the *chosen* ruler of the people; chosen not to rule in any right of his own, but to rule as their voice and hand; not to enforce his own will, but to execute their laws, to enforce their will. By the change from a monarchical to a republican form of government, respect for rulers as persons was changed to respect for rulers as the embodiment of the people's will and worth. The president stood for the nation; not for states, but for the confederated embodiment of the whole people. In this new aspect of rulers they became objects of higher and deeper interest. They stood for the people who had chosen them; for the nation as an organized commonwealth, as well as in their own worth. This new dignity of rulership our forefathers realized in its full force.

The seeds of the republic were planted in a distrust of the king. As that grew, the necessity for self-government became more apparent. Slowly, but absolutely, at last, their loyalty and affection for the king died, and self-government was the one only form of national existence to adopt. They adopted it in solemn recognition of all that it meant, and so adopting it they realized the momentous significance and responsibility of the ruler of a free people who lived and acted for them, in the heart of a new continent, growing rapidly in every element of power and greatness, with the eyes of the world turned upon them, and in an age ripe for great revolutions. Their peculiar, and as they thought providential, history deepened the solemnity of what they did.

Then, their first president was as a man and a magistrate so almost infinitely above the king they once loved but now loathed, and had done so much, and with such singular devotion to the public good and every high obligation in securing their liberties, that all their old respect for rulers returned to their hearts with increased tenderness and force. The president became more to them than the king ever was. In his person there centered all the profound regard they had learned to cherish for the people, for republican institutions, and the humanity of which they formed a part. The baptism of suffering and sorrow through which they passed in the change from the king to the president gave them one of the great lessons that went deepest into their hearts, and started in the new nation a tide of profound respect for the chief magistrate who was the people's authority.

No other nation ever had so fortunate a beginning, or so rich a pupilage through an infancy abounding in lessons of wisdom and worth, or so grand an entrance into the manhood of national life. Such a beginning prophesied all the greatness, worth and power which have followed.

The colonial school of America was rough, but solid and genuine; and trained a people such as the world never saw before, as the seed of a new nation and a new era of mankind.

### THE QUALITY OF COLONIAL MEN.

In re-studying the lessons of that school nothing is clearer than that the men of the colonies were superior to the men of the British parliament with whom they contended. They were better students of English law and history, and especially better in the principles of the English constitution. They were better philosophers; more acute and comprehensive in their views of government; more loyal to reason and the lessons of human nature, and greatly more faithful in the application of christian principles to human affairs. The debates in parliament compared with the speeches in the public meetings in the colonies, indicate clearly that the leaders in thought in the colonies were the profounder and better men. And the people's appreciation and acceptance of that thought, compared with the prevailing style of thought among the English people, showed that the masses of the colonial people had gained upon the people of the mother country by their hard colonial school. They had a clearer hold upon principles and a greater loyalty to them; knew and appreciated human rights better, and were truer to them; carried with a heartier faith the teachings of the christian religion to their practical results, and believed more in individual responsibility and power. The result was, that both leaders and people became more assured in the righteousness of their convictions, and more positive in maintaining them. They became a people of thinkers who acted on their thoughts. Freedom, human rights, personal responsibility, the authority of rulers, the duties of people, were themes they studied and discussed. And this study had developed a power among the leaders able to cope with any in the English parliament, and among the people a stalwartness of conviction and will superior to what prevailed among the English people.

## OUR COUNTRY THE OUTGROWTH OF MANY CAUSES.

The establishment of our nationality was due to many causes. The church as the outgrowth of Romanism—absolute power—imperialism—had done its worst. With a cruel tyranny it had played lord of men and nations, of thought and conscience, of education and taxation, till it had produced more or less protestantism in all countries. And protestantism in conflict with Romanism had produced more or less liberalism. And protestantism and liberalism had both trained a great body of free thinkers in all the more advanced countries. In France liberal thought was very powerful. With much good it did much evil. It prepared the way to give much help to the English colonies. In England protestantism and liberalism had weakened the power of kingcraft and strengthened the power of the people. In the English colonies of America protestantism was of the freest and most personal kind, having no interest in kingcraft and great sympathy with popular faith and rights. Everywhere a great struggle was coming on between consolidated power and the power of the people—between kingcraft and popular rights. The struggle on the part of King George and his parliament was to sustain kingcraft against the growing doctrine of popular rights. The logic, philosophy and morality were all on the side of the colonies, and these were not slow to produce character and power to sustain them. The world was ready for a great change. Roman imperialism had run its course to its own ruin. Kingcraft must sink with it. The final struggle for these ancient powers came with the American colonies because they were most advanced in intelligence and moral character and most animated by the true spirit and power of the christian religion.

## THE CAUSE OF THE REVOLUTION.

The particular question at issue was the right of the English parliament to tax the colonies. The king and parliament claimed the absolute right, and to maintain it passed various kinds of tax laws and sought in arbitrary ways to enforce them; and in connection with them passed repressive laws against nearly all kinds of manufactures. They taxed all goods imported into the colonies, and forbade all manufactures. The colonies claimed that as British subjects they could not be taxed against their will, or by a parliament in which they had no representation. They said taxation without representation is against English law and the constitution of the realm, and also against right and natural law. And here they stood and for years argued this question in all the forms in which it was presented, quoting all the best English lawyers and statesmen, and claiming that the freedom of the British subject was invaded by the doctrines and practices of parliament. Every colony produced men equal to the occasion. In South Carolina Lynch, Gadsden and Rutledge with great clearness and power defended the colonial position. In Virginia Patrick Henry and Richard Henry Lee, and others, with logic and transcendent eloquence fired the hearts of the people with a knowledge of their rights and freedom as British subjects. In Pennsylvania John Dickinson, the farmer writer, wrote in vigorous articles the true doctrines of English freedom, which were published in all the colonial papers and read and studied by all the people; read in book form in England and translated into French, and won for the colonies great sympathy in France. Benjamin Franklin, philosopher, writer, practical statesman, friend of humanity, lent the energies of his great mind to maintain the colonial doctrine of English rights against parliamentary usurpation. William Livingston and many like him in New York; Roger Sherman in Connecticut; James Otis, Samuel Adams, John Hancock and Mayhew Thatcher, in Massachusetts, kept constantly before the people their charter as well as their natural rights. The world had never seen an instance of a whole people studying so profoundly their political and natural rights, and so peacefully and religiously maintaining them. The lawyers and people of England were in a large majority with their parliament, in favor of taxing the colonies and prohibiting their manufactures. The argument of the colonies, as stated by their public men, their press, ministers and legislative enactments, was about this, as stated by Mr. Bancroft in his history of the United States: "The law of nature is the law of God, irreversible itself and superceding all human law. It perfectly reconciles the true interest and happiness of every individual with the true interest and happiness of the universal whole. The laws and constitution of the English government are the best in the world; because they approach nearest to the laws God has established in our nature. Those who have attempted this barbarous violation of the most sacred rights of their country deserve the name of rebels and traitors, not only against the laws of their country and their king, but against the laws of Heaven itself."

But their arguments failed to stay the resolute wrong-headedness of the king and parliament, and law after law was enacted to tax and oppress them. These laws they resisted in every way open to an intelligent and resolute people. They thoroughly studied and discussed all questions relating to them; ministers preached about them; the press was full of them. They made common cause and formed a colonial congress. From South Carolina to New Hampshire they became of one mind. They closed their ports against English goods and wore homespun clothes, and did without the common comforts to which they had been accustomed. They made it uncomfortable for soldiers quartered upon them, and for oppressive colonial governors. While they kept the peace, they resisted and made ineffectual the unjust laws of parliament. Merchants suspended their lucrative calling to see the goods sent for their customers returned to England in the same vessels in which they came. The rich vied with the poor in their loyalty to their conviction that it was wrong to pay unjust taxes. They made every new law which embodied the unjust principle of taxation without representation inoperative, and all the while increased the determination in the king and parliament to enforce their laws with military power. At last the final test came on their determination to tax tea, just to maintain their right. So, while other tax laws were in the main given up, a tax was laid on tea, and ships loaded for Boston, New York, Philadelphia and Charleston. Three tea ships were sent into Boston harbor. The people, in mass meeting, urged their immediate return to England. The governor refused to give the shipmasters passes to go out of the harbor by the ports. A meeting of the people had been in session a long time, and it was an hour after dark when word came that the governor had refused the pass. Then Samuel Adams rose and said: "This meeting can do nothing more to save the country." Instantly a shout and a warwhoop was heard at the door. Forty or fifty men, disguised as Indians, rushed by toward Griffin's wharf, where the tea ships were fast. Hancock, Adams and the people followed in haste. Guards were posted to keep off spies. The men in disguise boarded the ships, and in three hours all the tea, three hundred and forty chests, was emptied into the sea. John Adams afterward, in a letter to Warren, said: "All things were conducted with great order, decency and perfect submission to government." The people on the wharf and in the streets were so still that every blow in breaking open the chests was distinctly heard.

New York heard of it before its tea ships arrived and was anxious to do likewise, but the ships returned to England at once. At Philadelphia five thousand people met and allowed the tea ship to come no nearer than Chester, four miles below the city, from which point it returned to London immediately with its tea and a new freight of wisdom on board to carry back to parliament and the king. At Charleston the tea was unloaded into a cellar where it rotted; no South Carolina tea drinker having any appetite for falsely-taxed tea. So ended the tea-taxing, but not the quarrel which it provoked.

Parliament closed the port of Boston, called the legislature to Salem, forbade all public carrying business in Boston, designated its principal citizens for trial in England on treasonable charges, quartered soldiers on the public common, ordered war ships and munitions of war into the harbor, made Boston the headquarters of the commanding general of all the forces in America, and him the governor of Massachusetts, who prorogued the legislature at his will and hindered legislation as much as possible. And yet Boston, with its harbor lined with war ships, its common covered with soldiers, its business paralyzed, its people threatened with severest punishment, stood firmly on its asserted doctrines that parliament was wrong and the colonists right in all their differences.

Old Faneuil Hall, the cradle of liberty, was kept warm with public meetings and discussions of the acts of parliament and measures of defense against its tyrannies. The first thing was to appeal to all the colonies to be united and of one mind about these oppressions, and the way to resist them. To secure this a congress was needed at once. After brief discussions the colonies agreed to the necessity and appointed delegates: Virginia and South Carolina being most heartily in sympathy with Massachusetts. The discussions in calling this congress, and in it, developed two parties very distinctly, the lovers of monarchy and the lovers of republicanism — the fearful and the brave. Dickinson and Franklin, of Pennsylvania, counseled moderation, yet were in sympathy with the people. Both parties were represented in the congress, but the overwhelming majority were with suffering Boston and against parliament. The tyrannical change made by the king in the charter of Massachusetts had aroused the people, and they said all government was at an end because the change was unconstitutional; and they forbade the king's judges from holding court in all the counties. The governor had seized by force the provincial stock of powder and established a fort on Boston Neck, which had so exasperated the people that his government was at an end everywhere out of Boston, and the people were being rapidly aroused to a general revolt. Men of military experience were being fired; farmers and mechanics were getting ready for desperate service. Congress was hearing almost daily of what was transpiring in and around Boston.

In this state of fearful ferment the men of that congress saw clearly that the king and his parliament meant subjugation of the colonies; yet with great moderation and profound sagacity they cemented more and more the bonds of union, fanned the flame of liberty, roused the courage of the weak and laid surely the foundation of a new nation.

### THE BATTLES OF LEXINGTON AND CONCORD.

On the nineteenth of April, 1775, the ever-memorable first skirmish between the British soldiers and the American minute men took place at Lexington and Concord, in which the Americans lost forty-nine killed, five missing and had thirty-four wounded, and the British two hundred and seventy-three in killed, wounded and missing. The British went to destroy stores and frighten the people; they returned a rout of frightened soldiers, leaving their dead and wounded along the way. "They were driven before the Americans like sheep," and when they met a large body of troops sent out to rescue them, "they lay on the ground for rest, their tongues hanging out of their mouths like dogs after a chase."

### BATTLE OF BUNKER HILL.

Two months later, on the seventeenth of June, 1775, the battle of Bunker Hill was fought, which was a battle, indeed, in which the British reported a loss of one thousand and fifty. Seventy commissioned officers were wounded and thirteen killed. The loss of the Americans was one hundred and forty-five killed and missing and three hundred and four wounded. The powder of the Americans gave out and they were obliged to leave their entrenchments on the third charge of the British. It was a dear bought victory, teaching them the wholesome lesson that the Americans would fight.

### THE TAKING OF FORT TICONDEROGA.

At day-break, on the morning of the tenth of May, 1775, eighty-three Vermont men, called "Green Mountain Boys," under the lead of Ethan Allen, surprised and took Fort Ticonderoga, on Lake Champlain. On the same day, Crown Point, a few miles away, surrendered upon summons to a detachment of Vermont minute men.

On the tenth of May, a few hours after the capture of Ticonderoga, the second continental congress met at Philadelphia.

It had such members as Benjamin Franklin, Samuel Adams, John Adams, George Washington, Richard Henry Lee, Patrick Henry, Peyton Randolph, Thomas Jefferson, John Jay, Robert R. Livingston, John Dickinson, John Hancock, and many more held as their peers, a galaxy of brilliant and grand men such as is seldom seen in this world.

On the fifteenth of June, two days before the battle of Bunker Hill, George Washington was elected commander-in-chief of the continental army. Yet all this time the colonists were seeking reconciliation with the mother country, and a settlement of all their difficulties on just and humane grounds. They were sending petition after petition to the king, asking for a redress of their grievances, and expressing in strong and even tender terms their loyalty to him, and their love of their mother country and her people and laws, only to be spurned from the throne and have their petitions responded to with increased outrages upon their property and rights. Franklin was for a long time kept in England as the agent of the colonies, to present their appeals and give parliament, the king and people of England the true state of their case.

While this effort at reconciliation was going on the king was sending troops to Boston to punish its independent spirit, trafficking with other kings for foreign troops, enlisting all he could at home, and threatening to turn the slaves and Indians upon the defenseless colonies.

### THE EVACUATION OF BOSTON.

Washington took his place at the head of the army a few days after the Battle of Bunker Hill, with his headquarters at Cambridge, Massachusetts. With a mob for an army, though composed of noble men, poorly armed and officered, with but little ammunition, little money, little of anything that makes an efficient army; annoyed, tried, hindered everywhere, he so hedged in and surrounded and pressed and frightened the British army in Boston as to force them to evacuate the place and take to their ships for safety. This was in March, 1776, nine months after he had been appointed commander-in-chief. It was done without a battle, simply by hedging in, cutting off supplies, taking possession of and fortifying strategic points and giving them a clear idea that in a few days they would be at the mercy of the rebels they had so abused and despised.

Three months after, the twenty-eighth of June, 1776, the battle of Fort Moultrie was fought in Charleston harbor, which ended in disaster to the British ships and arms, and proved that the South Carolinians were as able to defend their native soil as the men of Massachusetts.

Each colony was discussing in its Congress the question of independence, and every discussion carried it nearer that great event. One by one they began to declare for it. The first of July was set apart by the Colonial Congress for a discussion of this subject. The situation of the affairs of the colonies and their relations to Great Britain were thoroughly discussed. The great spirits argued with a mighty power for independence. On the second of July, with fifty members present, the great vote was taken by twelve of the colonies, New York being yet undecided, which resolved: "That these United Colonies are, and of right ought to be, free and independent states."

This resolution of congress made a new country, and created the necessity for presiding magistrates. No greater act had ever been done by any body of mortal men. It was as they believed to effect the whole world and revolutionize its governments. It remained for Congress to set forth the reasons for this act, then inaugurate the machinery for the new government and defend it against British arms.

A committee was appointed to draft a declaration of their independence, with the reasons therefor, and as Thomas Jefferson, of Virginia, received the most votes, he was designated to write the declaration. From the fullness of his own mind, without consulting one single book, Jefferson drafted this immortal state paper. In his first draft he made a severe indictment against King George for having forced slavery and the slave trade upon the colonies, and for having vetoed all their attempts to prohibit them. This indictment was "disapproved by some southern gentlemen, whose reflections were not yet matured to the full abhorrence of that traffic, and the offensive expressions were at once yielded." Such was the abhorrence and fear of slavery at that time in the colonies, that had not this been expunged from Jefferson's first draft, it is altogether probable that slavery would not have survived the establishment of the new government. No other so fatal mistake was made by the grand patriots of that great day. Slavery was the one root of evil left to grow on American soil, a great tree of oppression and wrong. The spirit of conciliation was so great in those noble men, that they yielded this point in the expectation that independence of British tyranny would put an end to slavery. Beyond this change no essential modification was made, save an improvement of some of its phraseology.

### THE DECLARATION OF INDEPENDENCE.

"When in the course of human events it becomes necessary for one people to dissolve the political bonds which have connected them with another, and to assume, among the powers of the earth, the separate and equal station to which the laws of nature and of nature's God entitle them, a decent respect for the opinions of mankind requires that they should declare the causes which impel them to the separation.

"We hold these truths to be self-evident, that all men are created equal; that they are endowed by their Creator with certain inalienable rights; that among these are life, liberty and the pursuit of happiness; that to secure these rights governments are instituted among men, deriving their just powers from the consent of the governed; that whenever any form of government becomes destructive of these ends, it is the right of the people to alter or abolish it, and to institute a new government, laying its foundations on such principles, and organizing its powers in such form, as to them shall seem most likely to effect their safety and happiness. Prudence, indeed, will dictate that governments long established, should not be changed for light and transient causes; and, accordingly, all experience hath shown, that mankind are more disposed to suffer, while evils are sufferable, than to right themselves by abolishing the forms to which they are accustomed. But when a long train of abuses and usurpations, pursuing invariably the same object, evinces a design to reduce them under absolute despotism, it is their right, it is their duty, to throw off the government, and to provide new guards for their future security. Such has been the patient sufferance of these colonies, and such is now the necessity which constrains them to alter their form of government. The history of the present king of Great Britain is a history of repeated injuries and usurpations, all having, in direct object, the establishment of an absolute tyranny over these states. To prove this, let facts be submitted to a candid world:

"He has refused his assent to laws the most wholesome and necessary to the public good.

"He has forbidden his governors to pass laws of immediate and pressing importance, unless suspended in their operation till his assent could be obtained; and when so suspended, he has utterly neglected to attend to them.

"He has refused to pass other laws for the accommodation of large districts, unless those people would relinquish the right of representation in the legislature; a right inestimable to them, and formidable to tyrants only.

"He has called together legislative bodies at places unusual, uncomfortable and distant from the depository of public records, for the sole purpose of fatiguing them into compliance with his measures.

"He has dissolved representative houses repeatedly, for opposing, with manly firmness, his invasions on the rights of the people.

"He has refused for a long time after such dissolutions, to cause others to be elected; whereby the legislative powers, incapable of annihilation, have returned to the people at large for their exercise; the state remaining in the meantime, exposed to all the danger of invasion from without and convulsions from within.

"He has endeavored to prevent the population of these states, for that purpose obstructing the laws for naturalization of foreigners; refusing to pass others to encourage their migration hither, and raising the conditions of new appropriations of lands.

"He has obstructed the administration of justice by refusing his assent to laws for establishing judiciary powers.

"He has made judges dependent on his will alone, for the tenure of their offices, and the amount and payment of their salaries.

"He has created a multitude of new offices, and sent hither swarms of officers to harass our people and eat out their substance.

"He has kept among us, in times of peace, standing armies, without the consent of our legislature.

"He has affected to render the military independent of, and superior to, the civil power.

"He has combined with others (that is, with the Lords and Commons of Britain), to subject us to a jurisdiction foreign to our constitution, and unacknowledged by our laws; giving his assent to their acts of pretended legislation: For quartering large bodies of armed troops among us: For protecting them by mock trial, from punishment for any murders which they should commit on the inhabitants of these states: For cutting off trade with all the world: For imposing taxes on us without our consent: For depriving us, in many cases, of the benefits of trial by jury: For transporting us beyond seas to be tried for pretended offenses: For abolishing the free system of English laws in a neighboring province, establishing therein an arbitrary government, and enlarging its boundaries, so as to render it at once an example and fit instrument for introducing the same absolute rule into these colonies: For taking away our charters, abolishing our most valuable laws, and altering, fundamentally, the powers of our governments: For suspending our own legislatures, and declaring themselves invested with power to legislate for us in all cases whatsoever.

"He has abdicated government here by declaring us out of his protection, and waging war against us.

"He has plundered our seas, ravaged our coasts, burnt our towns, and destroyed the lives of our people.

"He is at this time transporting large armies of foreign mercenaries to complete the work of death, desolation and tyranny already begun, with circumstances of cruelty and perfidy scarcely paralleled in the most barbarous ages, and totally unworthy the head of a civilized nation.

"He has constrained our fellow citizens, taken captive on high seas, to bear arms against their country; to become the executioners of their friends and brethren, or to fall themselves by their hands.

"He has excited domestic insurrections amongst us, and has endeavored to bring on the inhabitants of our frontiers the merciless Indian savages, whose known rule of warfare is an undistinguishable destruction of all ages, sexes and conditions.

"In every stage of these oppressions we have petitioned for redress in the most humble terms; our petitions have been answered only by repeated injuries. A prince whose character is thus marked by every act which may define a tyrant is unfit to be a ruler of a free people.

"Nor have we been wanting in attention to our British brethren. We have warned them from time to time of attempts made by their legislature to extend an unwarrantable jurisdiction over us. We have reminded them of the circumstances of our emigration and settlement here. We have appealed to their native justice and magnanimity, and we have conjured them by the ties of our common kindred to disavow these usurpations, which would inevitably interrupt our connections and correspondence. They, too, have been deaf to the voice of justice and consanguinity. We must, therefore, acquiesce in the necessity which pronounces our separation, and hold them, as we hold the rest of mankind, enemies in war; in peace, friends.

"We, therefore, the representatives of the United States of America, in general congress assembled, appealing to the Supreme Judge of the world for the rectitude of our intentions, do, in the name and by the authority of the good people of these colonies, solemnly publish and declare that these United

Colonies are, and of right ought to be, FREE AND INDEPENDENT STATES; that they are absolved from all allegiance to the British crown, and that all political connection between them and the state of Great Britain is, and ought to be, totally dissolved, and that as free and independent states they have full power to levy war, conclude peace, contract alliances, establish commerce, and to do all other acts and things which independent states may of right do. And, for the support of this declaration, with a firm reliance on the protection of DIVINE PROVIDENCE, we mutually pledge to each other our lives, our fortunes and our sacred honor."

This immortal state paper, which created a nation and startled the old nations with a proclamation of the enduring freedom and rights of all humanity, was an exact transcript of the mind and heart of the people of the colonies. Jefferson wrote it out of his heart, and it has immortalized his name; but he only wrote for the people, and it has given enduring fame to them and the work they did for themselves and humanity. There are no richer chapters in human history than those that record the inception and establishment of the United States government. Every youth in America, aye, in the whole world, should study them till he learns by heart the grand worth of the noble men and great deeds of those "times that tried men's souls." John Adams said, on the day the declaration was passed: "The greatest question is decided which ever was debated in America, and a greater perhaps never was, nor will be, decided among men. When I look back to 1761, and run through the series of political events, the chain of causes and effects, I am surprised at the suddenness as well as greatness of this revolution. Britain has been filled with folly, and America with wisdom. It is the will of Heaven that the two countries should be sundered forever, and it may be the will of Heaven that America shall suffer calamities still more wasting, and distresses yet more dreadful. If this is to be the case, the furnace of affliction produces refinement in states as well as individuals; but I submit all my hopes and fears to an overruling Providence, in which, unfashionable as the faith may be, I firmly believe."

It was the folly, selfishness and tyranny of Britain that separated the colonies from her. The colonies outgrew the mother country in mind and heart, in ideas and men, in conscience and character. A few in England kept abreast of American growth, but they were too few to repress the rising tide of venality and dominance of power. American youth should study those times. From 1761 to 1783 a series of events transpired more important to humanity than any ever seen in the same time, save at the establishment of christianity,—a series which need to be studied by our modern men to rekindle their patriotism, to quicken their respect for true men and righteous principles, and to revive in them the moral elements of personal and national freedom. Mr. Bancroft, in his history of the United States, has set these things in order with consummate fidelity and skill, worthy of the careful study of the best men. His great work should be in every American home, and be made to contribute to the education and growth of all American men.

In the stirring and prolific time from 1761 to 1783 the first presidents of this republic were made. Their characters cannot be understood except by a study of the times, men, events and principles that made them. They were exceptionally grand men, because they lived in times exceptionally charged with great principles, occasions and events. Our men of to-day perhaps need nothing more than a baptism in the spirit and power of the American revolution. It is the purpose of this review of the lives of our presidents to relight the old fires in the souls of our modern men, and invigorate our modern character with the mighty, manly and moral forces which gave the world such men as George Washington and his compeers.

## CHAPTER II.

## GEORGE WASHINGTON.

### First President of the United States.

#### ANCESTRY.

GENEALOGISTS have found no difficulty in tracing the line of the Washington ancestry back through six centuries of English history. It was a vigorous stock, and held its distinct place and power in the world by marked qualities of mind and body, which persisted in living and having and being known. Marrying into different families, serving different kings and governments, changing localities and countries, did not weaken the family qualities nor abate its force of character. It rather gained strength and improved in quality till it flowered in the transcendent opulence and excellence of our Washington, who made his name and time and country immortal.

The family was doubtless of Norman origin and served under William the Conquerer. Among the knights of the county of Durham, England, who held great landed estates and manorial privileges, in the twelfth century, was WILLIAM DE HERTBURN. It was the custom at that time for the owners of large estates, with castles and villages on them, to take the name of the estate. The records of the time show that William De Hertburn exchanged his village of Hertburn for the manor and village of Wessyngton, receiving the diocese with it. After that the De Hertburn family took the name of its new estates, and appears on the records as De Wessyngton. The De Wessyngtons appear at different times and always in important positions, till 1264 the name of William Weshington is recorded on the roll of loyal knights who fought for their sovereign in the battle of Lewes, when the king was taken prisoner. Here the *De* is left off and the name takes a new form.

In 1416 John De Wessyngton was elected prior of the Benedictine convent, with a cathedral attached. This was an ancient and honorable position, taking rank with a bishopric. There had been many disputes about the claims and privileges of this convent. John De Wessyngton took up the dispute in a tract, which thoroughly set forth the rights of the convent and settled the long controversy in its favor. It won him much renown in his time.

The De Wessyngtons separated and went into different countries, engaged in different pursuits, some in the learned professions, some as great land owners, some were knighted for valorous services, some associated with religious houses. Gradually the *De* was dropped from the family name, and in the later records it appears as it is now spelled, WASHINGTON.

The branch of the family from which our Washington descended, sprang from Laurence Washington, Esq., of Gray's Inn, son of John Washington, of Lancashire.

This Laurence Washington was for a time mayor of Northampton, and received in 1538 a grant of the manor of Sulgrave with other lands adjoining. Sulgrave remained the landed estate of the family till 1620, and was called "The Washington Manor." Several of the descendents of this family distinguished themselves in wars and public services. This branch of the family was always true to the king, and under the protectorate when the king was in exile, many of his faithful subjects sought homes in other lands, some of them in the new colony of Virginia, which, from its fidelity to the exiled monarch and the Anglican church, had become a welcome refuge to the cavaliers. Among those who came here were John and Andrew Washington, grandsons of the grantee of the Sulgrave estate.

The brothers reached Virginia in 1657 and made extensive

land purchases in Westmoreland county, between the Potomac and Rappahannock rivers. John made his home on Bridge's creek and married Miss Anne Pope of the same county, thus at once identifying himself with the interests and life of the colony. He entered largely into the agricultural pursuits of the county; became a magistrate; a member of the house of burgesses; a colonel in the military forces that operated against the Seneca Indians, and a tower of strength in the community of which he was an honored member. The parish in which he resided was named for him. He is buried in the family burial place on Bridge's creek.

His extensive landed estate and accumulations remained in the family. Augustine Washington, John's grandson, was the father of George Washington. Augustine was born in 1694, forty-seven years after his grandfather reached America. He was married April 20, 1715, to Jane Butler, daughter of Caleb Butler, of the same county. He had four children by her, but only Lawrence and Augustine survived the years of childhood; their mother died November 24, 1728. March 6, 1730, he married Mary Ball, a young and interesting girl, regarded as the belle of the neighborhood. Six children came of this marriage: George, Samuel, John Augustine, Charles, Elizabeth and Mildred. Mildred died in infancy.

George, the eldest, the great general, president, man, whom we can scarcely think of as a child, was born February 22, 1732, in the old home on Bridge's creek. This old family home of the Washingtons occupied a sightly position, overlooking a great reach of the Potomac river and valley. The house had four rooms on the ground floor, a high pointed roof with rooms in it, and immense chimneys at each end. The house is entirely gone. There is nothing there to mark it as once a home, but the inscription on a stone which tells the traveler that this is the birth-place of George Washington. The record of the Washington ancestry is a noble one, showing that the family through every variety of experience and trial had kept a high respectability, and met all the demands of noble life with ability, fortitude and success. There seems always to have been in the family a strong tendency to the independence of agricultural pursuits. They were lords of land. They were patriarchal men, and had large families, flocks and possessions. They seem through the whole six centuries of their known history, to have been loyal to their king, patriotic and devout. They were a large-minded, conservative, generous, devout race of men, abreast of their times, provident, broad-seeing, magnets around which property and men naturally gathered, centers of power which their communities always felt with confidence and respect.

### BOYHOOD OF WASHINGTON.

The trite saying that "the boy is father of the man," is seldom found truer than in the case of Washington. Our Virginia boy that we have found has twenty generations of good English blood running in his veins, and the strong minds and hearts of a long line of noble ancestors behind him, is favored with some excellent surroundings that are likely to do more and better for him than they would for many boys less thoughtful and sensitive to such surroundings. He had no village near him where the boys congregate often to amuse each other, dissipate time, originate nonsense, concoct mischief and create demoralizing tastes. He had no resort of evil associates, to counteract the good influences of his home and his neighbors. He had the open country which he early appreciated, the business of his father's plantation, his good home, his two older half brothers, who were high minded, and the strong interest of the family in the English church, which in Virginia was the prevailing church.

The tradition of the neighborhood represents his father, Augustine, as seeking in ways peculiar to himself to impress upon George the lessons of virtue and religion. The strong mother, who was always a woman of high force of character, did her full part in giving shape and force to the character of her first born.

Lawrence was fifteen years older than George, and was sent to England to be educated. He returned, an educated and accomplished young man, when George was seven or eight years old. He took a great interest in George and the two became fast and life-long friends. The stories of his school life, his teachers and friends in England, of English customs, manners, society, politics and men, which Lawrence told with youthful enthusiasm, to amuse and instruct George, were of immense importance to him. The educated thought, language and manners of Lawrence had their influence. Lawrence became the model man for George to imitate and grow up to. Few things, probably, in his boyhood did more to elevate and give character and cast to George's mind than this constant association with his educated and high-minded brother.

Soon after George was born, the family moved to an estate in Stafford county, opposite Fredericksburg. The house to which they went was similar to the one they left, and stood on rising ground overlooking the Rappahannock. There was a meadow in front of the house which was often George's playground. He was a robust boy, large of his age, tall, athletic, vigorous and fond of all athletic sports. He grew up among the fine horses of the plantation, their friend and rider. By the time he was twelve years old he felt himself equal to the management of any stalwart and spirited colt. In jumping, running, climbing, pitching quoits, throwing stones, lifting, wrestling, and all the active games of the youth of his neighborhood, he was equal to the best. He was so full of muscular activity that he delighted in these sports. It is said that his fondness for them continued far into his manly years. These things show that he was a wide-awake boy and must have been a great favorite among the boys of his neighborhood.

Lawrence had inherited much of the military spirit of his ancestors. His education in England had quickened it. His two voyages across the Atlantic had taught him to love the sea. Two or three years after his return from England, a difficulty with the Spaniards in the West Indies broke out. France lent aid to Spain. A regiment of four battalions was raised in the colonies and sent to Jamaica. There was a quick outburst of military ardor in Virginia. Lawrence Washington, now twenty-two, caught the spirit and enlisted. He obtained a captain's commission in the regiment and embarked with it for the West Indies. He served under General Wentworth and Admiral Vernon, and acquired the friendship of both. He served with zeal through that campaign, and returned to rehearse its vivid experiences in the ears of George.

George, too, had inherited the military spirit of his ancestors, and that spirit was easily aroused in him. The recitals of Indian wars, the stories of ancestral military exploits, Lawrence's observations in England, and now his actual experience in an army on sea and land, fired the military spirit in the boy's heart, and he became the military leader of the boys at school. He organized them, drilled them, fought mimic battles with them, and thus in his own and their hearts began that training which served them so well in after years.

Lawrence came back from the West Indies intending to seek promotion in the army and devote himself to military pursuits. But becoming acquainted with Miss Anne Fairfax and falling in love with her he changed his plan, married her and settled down on his estate which, in honor of his admiral, he named Mount Vernon.

Augustine, the father, died April 12, 1743, after a brief illness, aged forty-nine. He left large possessions, which he divided by will; giving Lawrence the estate on the Potomac, which he named for his admiral, and several shares in iron works; to Augustine the estate on Bridge's creek; to George the estate on the Rappahannock, when he should become of age; and to the rest their share of his property; but put all the property of the children under age into the mother's hands to manage till they should reach their majority. Augustine soon married an heiress of the same county of his estate, Miss Anne Aylett.

George was left fatherless at eleven years of age; so the responsibilities of the household and estate rested upon him and his mother. Thus at twelve he took up a man's cares and responsibilities in connection with his mother. Great school was this for such a boy.

## HIS EDUCATION.

Such a boy as George Washington is sure of an education, whether the schools provide for it or not. His own strong judgment will lead him to educate himself. Life around him will give him lessons. He will force circumstances to become his teachers. He will demand knowledge of the men and things about him, and they will grant the demand. His ancestry and his life make it certain that he was born to greatness. He was the child of a favoring Providence. The conditions of eminent usefulness were all fulfilled in the circumstances of his birth and life. While humanly speaking he was a self-made man, truly speaking he was divinely made. The history into which he is set as the most lustrous gem, bears to the man of faith undoubting marks of a divine procedure, of a purpose to lift the world to a higher life through America, and Washington appears as the chosen and prepared man to lead in the sublime enterprise. To one who has studied the whole matter profoundly, this seems clear. And this thought is the fitting one to preface a consideration of his education.

In those days the children of the Virginia planters were educated as they could be. The estates were large, and neighbors far apart. The schools were not plenty, nor of a high order. One Mr. Hobby, a tenant of George's father and sexton of the church which the family attended, kept a school in a humble building called "The old Field school-house;" here George got the rudiments of reading, writing and ciphering. Nothing but the beginnings of an education was attempted. But the helps which the boy got at school were so meagre that his parents joined their help with the teachers as much as they could. After his father's death he was sent to his brother Augustine, at Bridge's creek, where a more advanced and systematic school was taught by a Mr. Williams. His education here, where he remained the most of the time for four years, was of the plain and solid kind. His object seems to have been to fit himself for the practical business of a Virginia planter. He was fond of mathematics, and became quite proficient, not only in arithmetic, but in geometry and surveying. He practiced the art of surveying in the fields about the school, and made extensive and accurate drawings of them which are preserved. It is not known that he studied grammar or rhetoric, or any lingual or philosophical studies. His early attempts at composition, preserved at Mount Vernon, by their grammatical mistakes and inaccuracies indicate that all philological studies were neglected. He aimed at the practical. He has left a volume into which he had copied forms for most all kinds of business transactions, such as notes, bills of sale and exchange, bonds, deeds, wills, legal transactions of all kinds common in the colony. He had dealings with domestics, tenants, magistrates and every matter of business likely to occur in his life, set in form, and neatly and accurately written out. His manuscript school-books are preserved—models of painstaking neatness and precision. His field-books of surveying show proficiency in drafting, and that he studied order and accuracy as he would study a science. Even in these early days Mr. Irving, his most elaborate and accomplished biographer says: "He had acquired the magic of method, which of itself works wonders."

When about fourteen, a plan was concocted by Lawrence and Mr. Fairfax to get him a place in the navy. A midshipman's warrant was obtained, his mother's consent gained and his luggage taken aboard the vessel he was to go on; when his mother relented and he was retained at school a while longer.

It is recorded of his mother that at stated times she was accustomed to gather her family about her and read to them from her favorite book, "Sir Matthew Hale's Contemplations, Moral and Divine." And we may well suppose that her readings were selected with reference to the moral lessons they imparted, and were emphasized with a mother's wisdom and affection. The effect of this maternal instruction on such a thoughtful youth as George, must have been great. His biographers have taken great pains to trace his ancestry and to recount the surrounding influences that helped educate and make George Washington, and have spoken respectfully of his mother's part; yet it seems clear to the author of this sketch, that the mother's part in his education was the major part. She was a beautiful and good woman; he was her oldest child; she was yet young when left alone to care for the family and great estates. Many must have been the consultations which she and her son had over their affairs. The management of their property, domestics and their families; the care and education of the children, their discipline, health, manners and morals, all came often before the young mother and her thoughtful and considerate son. This education with and by his mother was more to him in making him the wise, great and good man he was, than all he got from schools and books.

This is one of those marked instances of what a good mother can do for her children when left to her sole care. Every country and age abounds with such cases.

### HIS YOUTH.

Lawrence Washington, living on his estate, which he called Mount Vernon, in close proximity to his father-in-law, William Fairfax, invited George to his home on leaving his school. George had now become a youth. Though only sixteen, he was tall, sedate, courteous in manners, more a man than a boy.

William Fairfax was a brother of Lord Fairfax, and had come to Virginia to look after the immense estates of his brother. Lord Fairfax had received grants of the land between the Rappahannock and Potomac rivers, and tiring of society at home on account of social disappointment, he came to Virginia and established his brother on his estate. Their elegant English home, near Mount Vernon, now became the frequent resort of George Washington. His frankness and modesty, and thoughtful, manly bearing won the cordial regard of all the family. The eldest son had just married and brought his wife and her sister home, adding much to the interest and sociality of the family. This educated circle of fine-bred people, old and young, and all older than he, did much to refine his manners and give him the appearance of being older than he was.

Lord Fairfax was a great rider and fox hunter, and kept horses and hounds for this old English sport. He found his match in young Washington, and in their frequent rides on the chase learned the young man's worth and attainments; and engaged him to survey his grant of lands. This exactly suited young Washington, as he had educated himself for it, loved the wild woods of the mountain and valley, and had in his heart an unspoken reason for craving just such an adventurous excursion away from society into the wilds of the forest.

### HIS HEART SORROW.

We have not been accustomed to think of George Washington as a lovesick swain, or ever having had those sorrowful experiences of the heart which unrequited love produces and which always bring bitter disappointment and often disasters. But it seems clear that when he went from school to Mount Vernon, he carried a poor aching heart smitten with an affection not reciprocated, or which, for some reason, he did not announce to its object. Who the young miss was who so filled his great heart with tenderness and pain is not known. He speaks of her in a letter to his "Dear Friend Robin," as "your Lowland Beauty." To different friends he wrote of his love sorrows. In his journal he wrote of it, and like other love-afflicted mortals, attempted to soothe his sorrows with poetic effusions. In these he speaks of his "poor, restless heart, wounded by cupid's dart, bleeding for one who remains pitiless of his griefs and woes." Some of his verses indicate that he never spoke his love to the ears that should have heard it, prevented, it may have been, by bashfulness:

> "Ah, woe is me, that I should love and conceal;
> Long have I wished and never dare reveal."

This experience, perhaps, should be set down as a part of his youthful education. It was not a loss. It softened his nature and manners. It revealed to himself the depth of his heart capacity. It awakened in him that deep respect for woman which he always felt, and might have been the secret of his studied courtesy of manner and gentleness of spirit toward all women. It is more than likely it was the experience of the tender passion that led him to write in his journal, " Rules for behavior in company and conversation." One of his lady friends in his youth, late in her life said of him: " He was a very bashful young man; I often wished that he would talk more." He also compiled in his journal a code of " morals and manners," that he might be guided by them in his conduct and intercourse in society. He was self-directing and self-educating, and so methodical that he set down in his journal his plans for self-improvement. His bashfulness, doubtless, made him feel that he must have rules of conduct, and enforce them upon himself. At this time he had had much experience of life; he had lost his father; had aided his mother in their extensive domestic and business affairs; had studied most of the time for four years; had listened much to his mother's reading and instruction; had associated intimately with his educated brother Lawrence, who was both father and brother to him and deeply loved him; had had his heart smitten with a great love; had had much intercourse with the eccentric, but strong Lord Fairfax, and with William Fairfax and his intelligent and refined family and visitors; had put in his journal his reflections and plans for self-improvement, and yet was but just entering his seventeenth year. It is clear, that, though not educated in any college of letters and science, he was educated and profoundly educated, for one of his age, in the school of life. A grand and broad foundation had been laid for the great manhood that was afterward built thereon.

### HIS SURVEYING EXPEDITION.

In the month of March, 1748, Washington, with George William Fairfax, son of William, with whom he had spent a happy winter, started on a surveying expedition to locate the boundaries of Lord Fairfax's grant of Virginia land. It was a rough, hard experience with rivers, forests, mountains, rain, Indians, squatters and mud; but it was satisfactorily completed by the twelfth of April. It gave Washington a clear knowledge of the Shenandoah valley and the mountains, rivers and lands about it, which was of great value to him in after years. Lord

Fairfax procured his appointment as public surveyor, and he spent the next two or three years mostly in the survey of Virginia lands. Lord Fairfax took up his residence on the Shenandoah, where Washington often tarried with him for a time on his surveying expeditions, and was largely profited by his great knowledge and extended acquaintance with the world.

#### COMING COMPLICATIONS.

The growing colonies were exciting ambitious schemes in the minds of peoples and kings. The great west was full of alluring prospects. Empires of land stretched away toward the setting sun. Something was known of the Ohio and Mississippi rivers and the immense territories they drained. Subjects of the French king had seen them and taken possession of them and all their tributaries and lands on them, in the name of their king. The English claimed that through the "Six Nations" they had acquired a right to all this territory. The people of both nations were full of colonization schemes. Virginia and Pennsylvania were interested and excited. It was not far to the head waters of the Ohio's tributaries. Their Indian traders were already trafficking with the Ohio tribes. Settlers were making their way through the passes of the mountains and great interest was felt to push the settlements forward.

Among the many enterprising men who were interested in these schemes of wealth and dominion was Lawrence Washington. He desired that Virginia should join with Pennsylvania and make large settlements on the Ohio under the liberal religious policy of Pennsylvania. He said: "It has ever been my opinion, and I hope it ever will be, that restraints on conscience are cruel in regard to those on whom they are imposed, and injurious to the country imposing them." Then he refers to the liberty of conscience enjoyed in Pennsylvania, and the restraint put upon conscience in Virginia by its one English church, and points to the much more rapid growth of Pennsylvania. He would have this liberal policy applied to the western settlements. His enlightened views on this subject were no doubt imparted to his younger brother and helped form his mind for the noble opinions and character which he afterward carried into his great career.

On the north, the French were equally active in pushing forward settlements, forts and possession. Both French and English were seeking alliance with the Indians, and the already disturbed borders indicated a coming clash of arms. In both nations, especially in the colonies, preparations were beginning. In Virginia the war spirit was aroused; the province was divided into military districts, each district having an adjutant-general with the rank of major, and pay of one hundred and fifty pounds a year. Lawrence Washington sought for his brother George an appointment to one of these offices. This indicates the maturity of mind he had already reached to have gained such confidence. The appointment was made and preparations were begun for a military campaign into the western wilds. George put himself under the military drill of the best instructors he could get, and Mount Vernon became the scene of military preparations and discipline.

## LAWRENCE WASHINGTON'S SICKNESS.

But these preparations were stayed by the ill health of Lawrence Washington. His constitution had never been the firmest, and now he was threatened with dangerous pulmonary symptoms. By the advice of physicians, it was determined that he should spend the next winter in the West Indies. It was not thought safe for him to go alone, nor did he feel like going without his favorite brother George with him, whose strength and wisdom he had already begun to lean upon. So the preparations for a military campaign were changed to preparations for the journey to the West Indies. The young military leader was changed to a fraternal nurse. On the twenty-eighth of September, 1751, Lawrence and George started on their tour in search of health for the invalid. George kept a journal with his usual exactness. They reached the West Indies on the third of November. Here were new things in the style of life—the people and natural productions—which interested George at once; but they had been there but two weeks when he was taken down with the small-pox, and had himself to be nursed by others. Good treatment and nursing carried him through with only slight marks left upon his face.

Lawrence's health not improving, in December George returned to Virginia for Lawrence's wife; but as she could not go immediately, he returned to his home in the early Spring. But nothing could stay the progress of his consuming disease, and on the twenty-sixth of July, 1752, he died, at the age of thirty-four. Now George, at a little past twenty years of age, had lost his father and his brother, who had been father and brother in one. Lawrence left by will his estate to his wife and daughter, and in case the daughter died without issue, to George at the decease of the wife. George was made one of the executors. The estate did at last come to George, and is now known as the sacred resting place of "The Father of his Country."

### A PERILOUS MISSION.

The difficulties about the western territories increased. The French on the north kept pressing forward their forts, settlements and claims. They sent commissioners among the Indian tribes to secure their coöperation. They made bold their claim to the whole Mississippi valley, even to the head waters of all the tributaries of the Ohio. The English from Pennsylvania and Virginia pressed their claims and sent envoys, traders and settlers among the Indians, and quickened their preparations to occupy the coveted territories.

It was needful to know the minds of the Indians, the purposes of the French, the condition of their forts and settlements, and what was needful to check their encroachments. This knowledge could be got only by a competent ambassador to the French commander on Lake Erie.

Governor Dinwiddie, of Virginia, looked about him for a man equal to this delicate and dangerous errand. He must meet and treat with Indians, friendly and unfriendly; transact business with white men who, while professing friendliness would plot his destruction and the defeat of his mission; traverse a dense forest of six hundred miles, in which were high mountains, large rivers, morasses, dangerous animals, and more dangerous savages who must be used as guides and for supplies. It needed great courage, sagacity, skill, tact, strength, health and self-sacrifice. Who was equal to such a mission? George Washington, a youth of twenty-one years, was suggested as the man with the requisite combination of qualities. After due consideration he was selected and invited to undertake the perilous mission. The ostensible object was to bear a message of the governor of Virginia, in the name of the king of England, to the commandant of the fort on French creek, fifteen miles south of Lake Erie, and to take back his answer. The real object was to reconnoitre the whole country and learn the condition, purposes and strategy of the enemy with whom they were likely soon to come into close conflict.

Washington undertook the mission, and set out from Williamsburg October 30, 1753. He left Wills' creek, Cumberland river, November 15, with Mr. Gist, an intrepid pioneer well known among the Indians; John Davidson, an Indian interpreter; Jacob Van Braam, a French interpreter, and four frontiersmen, two of whom were Indian traders.

After all sorts of difficulties with Indians, white deserters, French duplicity, rain, snow and mud, he reached the French fort December 11.

After much ceremony and parley, he got his reply and started on his return. Winter had set in. The streams and swamps were full. The French settlers, huntsmen, Indians and stragglers, were all made acquainted with the mission. Everywhere there was plotting to hinder, bewilder and lead astray the party. It had grown smaller till it was reduced to Washington, Mr. Gist and an Indian guide. The horses had been left and the luggage reduced to absolute necessities. Their direct course was through an unbroken wilderness of which they knew nothing. The conduct of the guide became so peculiar that their suspicions were awakened. He wanted to carry Washington's gun; led them as they believed the wrong way; became churlish; pretended that there were inimical Indians in the woods. At length, when some fifteen paces ahead, he turned suddenly, leveled his gun at Washington and fired. He missed his mark, ran on hastily a few rods behind a large tree and began to reload his gun. Finding that neither of them was hurt, they went to him and when his gun was reloaded took it from him. Mr. Gist wanted to dispatch the Indian at once; but Washington's scruples were too great. Then Mr. Gist said: "We must get rid of him;" so pretending still to have confidence in him they sent him to his cabin, which he said was not far away, promising to meet him there in the morning. When he was well out of sight they started and traveled all night. By the next night they reached the Alleghany river. It was frozen only along the shore. Great quantities of broken ice were floating in the stream. There was no way to get across but to make a raft; and only one poor hatchet for a tool. It was one whole day before they got a raft they dared venture upon. When in the middle of the stream poling it amid the ice floes as they could, a block of ice struck the pole with such force as to knock Washington from the raft into the deep stream. He saved himself by catching hold of a raft log. They had to let their raft go and get to an island by the help of the float wood, which now was near them. Here they spent the night and nearly perished with cold. But the cold which came near freezing them to death, made a bridge of the floating ice, so that they got off in the morning, and before night reached the comfortable quarters of an Indian trader. On the sixteenth of January they returned to Williamsburg.

Washington's journal of this mission was published and spread widely through the colonies and in England. It awakened England to the danger before it, and it fixed the eyes of all on young Washington as a remarkable youth, of prudence, sagacity and resolution far above his years. His admirable tact in treating with fickle savages and crafty white men; his soldierly eye to the true condition of the country, its exposures and defences, and his fortitude and faithfulness, all won for him the confidence and admiration of his countrymen. From this time he is a commanding figure in the colonies; the foundation of his great name and work is laid.

## AN EXPEDITION TO THE OHIO.

Washington was quick to observe that the fork of the Ohio, now the site of Pittsburgh, was the key to the country west and north of it, and suggested that it be occupied and well fortified, which was speedily done. Governor Dinwiddie made strenuous endeavors to raise a body of soldiers for that purpose. Three hundred were enlisted and other colonies were asked to share in the expedition. Washington was offered the command, but declined on account of his youth and inexperience. It was given to Colonel Fry, an English officer, who made Washington his lieutenant-colonel.

After great efforts the little army started on its hard march, half supplied and half paid, and with almost insurmountable obstacles before them. Recruits came in slowly and some of them under separate commands. They had not been many days out before friendly Indians brought them word that the French in strong force, had possession of the fork of the Ohio and were building a fort; and were soon to be reinforced by Indians and more French. Washington had started with his command in advance of Colonel Fry, who was to follow with artillery. With infinite trouble with his raw recruits on account of insubordination, poor pay, poor rations and supplies, rivers, swamps, defiles and mountains, Washington pushed on as fast as possible, expecting every day to meet advance parties of the enemy. Reaching a place called Great Meadows, he cleared a field of brush, and began a fort. While at this work word came of a party of the enemy but a few miles away. With Indian allies who had joined him, Washington took such men as could be spared from his camp, and started for the enemy hovering about him, with a view to surprise them. They soon came upon them unawares and a sharp conflict ensued. The French leader, a young officer of merit, Jumonville, was killed at the onset. The action was short and sharp. The French losing rapidly, gave way and ran. They had ten killed and twenty-one taken prisoners. This was Washington's first battle He led it in front of his men and was in the thickest of it. Bullets whistled about him, but he was not harmed. He had one killed and three wounded.

Washington's situation was now most perilous. Colonel Fry had not yet come with his forces. The French were increasing their numbers from the north and from the Indians. They were strongly fortified in their fort, and had large scouting parties all about him.

Colonel Fry died on the way. More recruits came, some of them independents, which proved of little service. But Washington pushed on toward the enemy. His hope was to make an army road, get recruits from the colonies, allies from the Indians and hold the enemy at bay till his own army was large and strong enough to take the fort at the fork of the Ohio. But the enemy was reinforced faster than he was; better armed and supplied; met him on the way in great force, and compelled him to retreat to Fort Necessity, which he had made as a refuge. There he was surrounded with such numbers that he capitulated, but marched his army off in order, with his stores, leaving only his artillery. It was a disastrous attempt to gain possession of the Ohio, poorly supplied and supported; but it was a training school for a great general. Washington's courage, zeal, fortitude and military capacity were all recognized by the country. His conduct was so much above his years that it prepared the way for the colonies in their great emergency, years after, to look to him to lead their armies. Without this disastrous campaign the world might never have had the great General and President Washington. This is an instance of defeat working victory of another kind. Seldom do we see the Providential hand working its great affairs till long after the work is done.

### BRADDOCK'S CAMPAIGN.

England now saw that something vigorous must be done or the French would make good their claims in the northwest. So a grand army of regulars in the service was sent over under command of General Braddock, which was increased by Virginia levies to four thousand, to cross the mountains and take Fort Duquesne, at the fork of the Ohio, and possess that territory. Washington was invited by Braddock to accompany him on his staff. He had resigned his commission, and was attending to his affairs at Mount Vernon. His military enthusiasm was enkindled by this grand display of England's best troops, such as had never been seen before on American soil, and he accepted the invitation and volunteered in the service. It was a tiresome, long and disheartening journey they had over the mountains and through the gorges. Braddock was a trained British officer; believed in British order, drill, authority, tactics and success. He would march, drill, pitch his tents, call his rolls, picket his camp, send forward his scouts, move his artillery, order his battle and proceed with it, according to English rule or not at all. He despised the Indian allies, the Virginia levies and everything not in the king's regular service. He was conceited, vain, pompous, self-willed and absolute. He was slow to take advice of Washington, refused to learn of the new circumstances, and was sure of victory. The army toiled from April to July on its weary drag through the wilderness, only to get a most ignoble defeat just before reaching the fort. It was surprised and nearly surrounded by French and Indians who, from behind trees, logs, stones and knolls, poured into it fearful showers of well-aimed bullets, and filled all the region with unearthly whoops and yells. The regular British platoons broke like fog before a gale and scattered everywhere, fired at random, wounded the trees, killed each other, became a mass of panic-stricken confusion, and took the back track, leaving everything behind them, not having seen their enemy at all. Braddock was wounded and died at Great Meadows on his retreat. This disastrous campaign and battle have gone into history as "Braddock's Defeat." The only men under Braddock who did good fighting were the despised Virginia levies. They made the best of their opportunity, and though terribly thinned, so stunned the enemy as to prevent a chase after the retreating army.

This was another school for Washington. He learned regular English warfare, the value of camp order, discipline, drill; and learned also that British regulars were a poor match for American hunters, woodsmen and levies, in border warfare.

This defeat alarmed the colonies and they put themselves in order for defense. Militia companies were raised, military equipments procured, money was promptly voted and a small home army provided for and officered. Washington was appointed commander-in-chief of the Virginia forces. Notwithstanding he had been the leader of one disastrous campaign, and on the staff of the commanding officer of another, he had not lost, but rather gained, popularity. He was the only man the people would think of to command their defense of their homes. He had been in the thickest danger of two fights and had come out unharmed. Rev. Samuel Davies spoke of him at that time, as "that heroic youth, Colonel Washington, whom I cannot but hope Providence has hitherto preserved in so signal a manner for some important service to his country."

The next year a great campaign against the French all along the line of their defenses, was more successful. On Lake Champlain, at Lake George, Oswego and Niagara, British arms were successful. Washington, in correspondence with the northern commanders, was working up his Virginia forces, people and house of burgesses, to join in the final reduction of Fort Duquesne. But after laborious preparation and toiling to reach it with an army competent to its reduction, it was found nearly deserted and was taken without resistance. All hope of success had been cut off from the north, and the garrison had mostly departed. The next season the war closed and gave England Canada and the great west, which a French statesman predicted would be a dear possession to England, as her colonies, now grown strong, when oppressed with taxation would resist it with *independence*.

### WASHINGTON'S COURTSHIP AND MARRIAGE.

In working up the final expedition against Fort Duquesne it became necessary for Washington to go in haste to Williamsburg. In crossing the Pamunkey river in a ferry boat, he fell in company with a Mr. Chamberlayne, who lived in the neighborhood, and who in true Virginia hospitality, invited him to dine with him. Washington urged the necessity of haste on his mission, but was prevailed on at last to accept the invitation. Among the company who dined there that day was a young widow, Mrs. Martha Custis, daughter of Mr. John Dandridge, whose husband had been dead some three years. She was yet youthful, small in stature, but well-formed, of a fresh, blooming complexion and engaging manners. Washington was the best known young man in Virginia—perhaps in America—the defender of the colonial homes against the savage Indians, the commander-in-chief of the Virginia forces, the intimate friend of Lord Fairfax and his brother William and his accomplished family—himself the flower of an honored Virginia family, wealthy in his own right and already greatly distinguished for public services. Mrs. Custis had been well reared, was of a good family, accustomed to good society, had been the wife of an honorable gentleman who had left her rich, and the mother of two children, twice as rich as she. There is every reason for supposing that the dinner and the occasion were full of interest for them both, and that both were at their best. As it turned out, Braddock's army was not taken more by surprise near Fort Duquesne, than was the young commander-in-chief of the Virginia forces at Mr. Chamberlayne's dinner table.

When the servant brought the young soldier's horse to the door, according to order, he was in no mood for departing. He who was in great haste before dinner, was now more than willing not to go at all, and ordered his servant to take back the horses to the stable. So the afternoon and evening were spent in the genial company of his new made friends and the next morning he went on his way quite full of other thoughts than those which took him to Williamsburg. But he had learned that Mrs. Custis' home was not far from Williamsburg, and that she would soon be at the "White House," as her home was called.

Military duties pressed, and he had not long to stay at Williamsburg; but he made the most of his opportunity and before he left, the young couple had plighted their faith in each other The affairs of the campaign went on as already rehearsed: Fort Duquesne was taken, the war ended, peace was restored, and on the sixth of January, 1759, George Washington and Martha Custis were married at her home in the good old Virginia way, in the midst of a joyous assemblage of mutual friends, to them the happiest result of the campaign against the French fort at the fork of the Ohio.

## MOUNT VERNON.

For three months after their marriage the young people lived at the White House, her home. While there he took his seat in the house of burgesses at Williamsburg. By a vote of the house previous to his coming it was agreed to give him a signal welcome through an address by the speaker. The speech was hearty and eulogistic, and recounted his distinguished services to his country. Washington attempted to reply, but only blushed, trembled and stammered. "Sit down, Mr. Washington," said the speaker; "your modesty equals your valor, and that surpasses any language I possess."

Mount Vernon, his estate, was on the Potomac river, beautifully situated on a bluff of land which gave a wide view of the river and surrounding country. He described it in a letter to a friend thus: "No estate in United America is more pleasantly situated. In a high and healthy country; in a latitude between the extremes of heat and cold; on one of the finest rivers in the world, a river well stocked with various kinds of fish at all seasons of the year, and in the spring with shad, herring, bass, carp and sturgeon in great abundance. The borders of the estate are washed by more than ten miles of tide-water; several valuable fisheries appertain to it; the whole shore, in fact, is one entire fishery." Here on this rich estate George and Martha Washington lived in old Virginia style, with many colored domestics, in a large house for those times, with many outbuildings, in the midst of care, plenty, hospitality, carrying on a great business, and having the oversight and conduct of so great an agricultural establishment. Among his slaves were men of nearly all trades then in use. Almost everything needed was produced on the estate, and the owner had need to be versed in the business of every department. It was Washington's ideal of a true manly life. He loved the country, the soil, agricultural pursuits; he loved the independence, isolation, dignity, plenty of the planter style of life. After he had taken his wife to his home, he wrote to a friend: "I am now, I believe, fixed in this seat, with an agreeable partner for life, and I hope to find more happiness in retirement than I ever experienced in the wide and bustling world." His wife brought him over a hundred thousand dollars in money and property, and her two children—a boy six and a girl four years of age—double that amount to care for; so that his retirement to a private and domestic life meant business, care and responsibility on a large scale. The last year of his military service had quite impaired his usually robust health, which now rapidly improved.

Washington was an Englishman, at this time, of the truest type, loyal to the king and constitution, customs, laws and church of England. There was no country like England; no people like Englishmen; no other government so genuine, strong and noble. He had much intercourse with England; had his agents there to whom he consigned the products of his estate and through whom he made purchases. Ships plied directly between England and the Potomac river. There was considerable travel between Virginia and the home country. Many young men were sent to England to be educated, and they kept up a fresh importation of English customs, tastes and style of life.

Virginia was the most English at this time of any of the colonies, and prided herself on this distinction. She made the least departure from the opinions and life of aristocratic England. Such homes as Washington's were conducted, as much as they could be, as were the wealthier homes of the mother country. And the expectation, no doubt, was that more and more American society would take the form of English society. The war that had been just fought with the French and Indians was in part to get more room for the English government to spread out its people, laws and power.

But how often are human calculations thwarted. Washington, now called to serve in the legislature of his State, in the civil service of his country, began to feel the greed, and injustice and tyranny of the English government. Her laws for the colonies were restrictive; often entrenched upon their rights; shut up their trade to her ships and ports; her governors in the colonies often vetoed the most wholesome laws, and, like Braddock with his regulars, seemed to forget the new circumstances of a new people. As he learned of Braddock that the English army, conducted on the home system, was an unwieldy, slow and expensive thing in an American border warfare; so he learned in the civil service that King George and his parliament, and the governors and judges they sent over, were as incompetent to conduct the civil service of America. Little by little he was learning England's faults; learning that one people cannot legislate for and rule wisely another people far away and living under essentially different circumstances.

Washington was a devoted English churchman, was a vestryman in the church at Alexandria, and also at Pohick, and always attended church with his family when the weather favored, and, Mr. Irving says, was a communicant. This consecrated his devotion to England and its government and order of life. He was in the House of Burgesses when questions of difference came up with the governor and home government; understood, both as a legislator and a business man; how the restrictive navigation and trade and anti-manufacturing laws hindered the business of the colonies; heard the arguments *pro* and *con*; heard the vehement and powerful eloquence of Patrick Henry, as he set forth the natural rights of men and the injury to those rights in the colonies, by the unnatural and oppressive measures of the mother country. Notwithstanding his great love of England, he could not be blind to her faults. He loved the colonies and saw the great prospects before them. His quickest, deepest sympathies were for humanity.

In Washington's quiet and careful life at Mount Vernon, he studied, as they came up one after another, the great questions at issue between the colonies and the king and parliament, and his clear judgment favored the colonies all the time. As a private citizen he studied the great questions of statecraft; of natural and colonial rights; of the English constitution and law; of navigation and commerce; of taxation and representation; of the rights of the people; as they were discussed by the great minds of the colonies and England as they never had been before. It was the maturing period of his thoughts and principles, which was preparing him for public action on that grand scale and in those stirring scenes which made him "The father of his country" and one of the world's most illustrious of men.

## PERSONAL CHARACTERISTICS.

It is pleasant to think of great men as natural men; and such was Washington. He was intensely interested in human things; in human ambitions and pleasures; in human loves and affairs. He was careful in his dress; circumspect, polite and deferential in his manners; prudent in his speech; usually self-governed, yet of strong passions; was a good hunter; enjoyed duck-shooting; entered heartily into social intercourse; was a good horseman, and took pride in his horses; relished jokes; with all his dignity and aristocratic associations, was democratic in his sympathies. He loved women and children; was a thoroughly domestic man; he loved the stir and show and power of military combination and movement; loved the drill, promptness and obedience of a good soldier. He was an exact and methodical business man; kept his accounts with punctilious accuracy; wrote in a clear, round hand; kept his clothes, books, tools, affairs in complete order; was a good correspondent, warm in his friendships, severe in his censures of wrongdoing; courageous, yet prudent; kept a diary and preserved much of his personal history; was bashful and modest; not given to public speech, yet never fell into the mistake that he was not of much account; was a reader of good books; an accurate observer of men and things; was very practical, and of wide and varied wisdom; was large-hearted and public-spirited.

In his full manhood he stood six feet high; was broad-shouldered and full-chested; was erect, stately; moved with grace and dignity. He was of robust constitution, invigorated by outdoor occupation, rigid temperance and orderly habits. Few men equaled him in strength and endurance. His hair was brown, eyes blue, complexion florid, head round, face full, expression calm and serious.

### COMMANDER-IN-CHIEF.

While Washington was quietly attending to the affairs at Mount Vernon and occupying his seat in the house of burgesses at its sessions, the disturbed affairs of the colonies moved rapidly on from bad to worse to an open rupture with the mother country, as related in the first chapter of this book. At the suggestion of John Adams, in the general Congress, seconded by Samuel Adams, he was nominated and unanimously elected commander-in-chief of the army of the united colonies. It was an office unsought and undesired. He accepted it to serve the distracted colonies and the suffering people, and with the conviction, as he said to Patrick Henry on the day of his election, that "This day will be the commencement of the decline of my reputation." He refused all pay, asking only that his expenses be provided for. No man in America was more honest and earnest in the position the colonies had taken, and he cast all he had and was into the cause, believing it would be of little worth if the cause was not sustained.

Mr. Bancroft, in his history of the United States, says: "Never in the tide of time has any man lived who had in so great a degree the almost divine faculty to command the confidence of his fellow men and rule the willing. Wherever he became known, in his family, his neighborhood, his county, his native state, the continent, the camp, civil life, the United States, among the common people, in foreign courts, throughout the civilized world of the human race, and even among the savages, he, beyond all other men, had the confidence of his kind."

Washington was elected commander-in-chief on the fifteenth of June, 1775. He accepted the office with great diffidence, believing himself not equal to its great duties. He started as soon as he could set his affairs in order; not stopping to visit his family at Mount Vernon. He met everywhere on the way the acclamations of the people. Confidence and enthusiasm were inspired at once in many who had been distrustful and disheartened.

On the third day of July, at Cambridge, Massachusetts, under an elm tree on the common, attended by great numbers of the best citizens, Washington assumed the command of the continental army. It was a great day for America; a great day for England also, for the liberties of her people were to be preserved and developed, as well as of those of the colonies; a great day for the world, for Washington's sword was unsheathed for the rights of humanity.

Governor Trumbull, of Connecticut, wrote him: "Be strong, and very courageous." Washington replied: "The cause of our common country calls us both to an active and dangerous duty; Divine Providence, which wisely orders the affairs of men, will enable us to discharge it with fidelity and success."

### BOSTON BESIEGED.

Washington found Boston in the hands of a British army of some ten thousand men, well equipped, and supported by ships and munitions, under command of General Gage. It was a pretentious, self-assured army, confident of an easy victory over the rural rebels who had come down from the hills and shut them in. Their British conceit had been a little punished by the frays at Lexington and Bunker Hill, but a little of the art and power of English war, it was expected, would send them flying to their hills and homes again.

About three fifths of the citizens of Boston were remaining in their homes, suffering many indignities and deprivations.

The army which Washington had come to command was a mixed multitude, gathered from the ships, shops and farms, under very little discipline, order, or government. It was poorly officered and armed, with but little ammunition and a poor prospect of getting supplied. It lacked everything which makes an efficient army, but high principles and manly courage; but perhaps never so large a body of men in an army knew better what they wanted and were resolved to have. It was stretched in an irregular semi-circle, a distance of nine miles, around Boston from Dorchester to Malden. Its immediate business there was to keep the British lion in the den into which he had crept from the sea; its real and ultimate purpose was to tell King George and his parliament that the American colonies would not pay taxes without representation, nor submit to unjust laws.

Washington immediately set about making this intelligent, strong-willed, high-principled rabble into an army; learning the exact situation of things in and about Boston, and quickening congress and the several colonies to supply the wants and increase and make permanent the force of the army. The summer and autumn were spent in making the girdle about Boston stronger, in hedging up the highways in and out; in sweeping the surrounding islands of stock and supplies; in getting horses, cattle and supplies back into the country; in entrenching, throwing up breastworks, planting batteries, gathering arms, ammunition, tents, wagons; in drilling, picketing, skirmishing and capturing squads of the enemy.

This spade and pickaxe warfare by the close of the year had planted batteries on all the near heights around Boston, guarded with entrenchments all the outlets and waterways, built forts where these would best serve the siege operations, and made the British lion's palace a prison with short rations and a good prospect of none at all in a little while. In the way of military glory the British lion had got Lexington and Bunker Hill; in the way of luxury and booty it had got a military prison without supplies. In February, Washington entrenched himself strongly on Dorchester Heights, which commanded the city and the harbor. Early in March he was well entrenched on Nook's Hill, which commanded Boston Neck. And now the roaring lion became a frightened sheep, and took to his swift feet and ran into his ships and set sails for the open sea. Evacuated, Boston was the proud old city again, and her citizens flocked home with great joy. The colonies were glad, and praised the Lord. Washington had gained a great victory in his first campaign without fighting a battle.

On the twenty-ninth of March both Houses of the Massachusetts Legislature made a joint address of congratulation to Washington, in which they said: "Go on; still go on, approved by heaven, revered by all good men and dreaded by tyrants. May future generations, in the peaceful enjoyment of that freedom which your sword shall have established, raise the most lasting monuments to the name of Washington."

The Continental Congress voted him thanks and a commemorative medal of gold, in reply to which he gave all the credit of the great triumph to his soldiers, saying: "They were, indeed, at first, a band of undisciplined husbandmen—but it is, under God, to their bravery and attention to duty, that I am indebted for that success which has procured me the only reward I wish to receive—the affection and esteem of my countrymen."

### NEW YORK IN DANGER.

Where had the frightened enemy gone? His multitude of ships, loaded with his army and all his munitions of war, had put out to sea. Where would they land? Washington feared that New York was his coveted prey, so the next day he started five regiments for the defense of that city, and sent letters and swift messengers to awaken Congress, the governor and the people to their danger.

The enemy landed on Staten Island, and soon crossed to Long Island. The severe battle of Long Island followed, which was disastrous to Washington's too-weak line of defense, and he had to fall back into the city, and finally to the higher ground in the rear of the city. The many water ways about the city gave the enemy opportunity to use his ships and their heavy armament against the colonial forces. Now began one of the severest campaigns of the revolution. Heavy reinforcements had come from England, with hired soldiers from the continent. A strong army had been sent up the St. Lawrence into Lake Champlain and Lake George, to cut its way down to Albany, and so down the Hudson to New York, and meet with the army in New York, which was expected to break through Washington's line and go up the Hudson, thus cutting turbulent New England off from the rest of the colonies. In the meantime Philadelphia and Charleston were to be threatened and attacked, if possible, to keep the southern colonies busy in their own defense. So it was to be war all around.

Lord Howe, who now commanded the British armies in America, was a wary and strategic commander. He was full of feints. If he thought to break his way round the east side of New York, he would make a great demonstration into New Jersey, as though to force his way round west, to draw the American forces as far away from his intended course as possible. If he purposed to move by land, he would make a great parade of ships lading for a sea movement. The whole spring, summer and autumn were spent in attempts in different directions, skirmishes here and there, pushing for the Hudson at one time, up the sound for Newport at another, sending Cornwallis with a strong army late in the fall making toward Philadelphia. Washington, full of every care, pacifying his disaffected officers, struggling to retain his homesick soldiers in the field and to recruit his thinning ranks; instruct Congress in the facts and needs of the army, and inspire the disheartened colonies, had his wary and powerful enemy to watch and head off in every direction. By the first of December it became apparent that the main body of the British army under Lord Cornwallis were aiming at Philadelphia. The British were jubilant. Proclamation was made to the people of New Jersey to surrender and accept of pardon or meet the consequences of destructive war. Many surrendered; nearly all were dismayed.

Washington put himself and his small army in front of Cornwallis' jubilant legions and fought them, retreating himself the length of the state. He destroyed bridges, hedged up their way and hindered them in every way possible, all the time urging his commanders elsewhere to hurry to his help. He appealed to Congress, to Pennsylvania and New Jersey to rally now in this darkest hour of freedom's cause. His army was weakening every day by the expiration of the term of service. Some of his generals were churlish and fretful and did not try to get forward to his help. That December was a fearful month to the colonies,

"Poor Washington," as some spoke of him, was left largely to his own great wisdom, and courage. Mr. Bancroft says: "Hope and zeal illuminated his grief. His emotions come to us across the century like strains from that eternity which repairs all losses and rights all wrongs; in his untold sorrows his trust in Providence kept up in his heart an undersong of wonderful sweetness." Congress was alarmed and fled to Baltimore. Philadelphia was in a panic and deserted by great numbers. Distress was everywhere. The British believed the colonies were just about conquered. Yet Washington was firm and was making plans for next year's campaign. As he approached the Delaware, he secured all the boats up and down the river for seventy miles, and prepared for resistance at all the crossings. Here he determined to make a stand. Militia were recruited. Help came from other sections of the American army. The enemy had become confident and careless.

On the night of the twenty-fifth of December, 1776, Washington had arranged to recross the Delaware and attack the enemy at three points. The plan was to cross in three places, some miles apart, and make the attack in three places simultaneously. Washington led the left and uppermost division. The night was fearfully cold and stormy. The river was running with heavy ice-floes. The lower divisions of the army both failed to cross. Washington and his forces, after almost superhuman efforts, got across; marched down several miles to Trenton, attacked the British army a little after daylight, won a brilliant victory, and sent its scattered remains flying backward toward New York. Now the tide was turned. The best skill of the enemy was needed to save an utter defeat. He was punished in many a skirmish and soon learned that the colonies were not conquered. So inspiring was Washington's success at Trenton and in the movements following, that the colonies were soon making ready for another campaign.

Washington crossing the Delaware has gone into history, poetry and painting, as one of the master strokes of military courage and genius, by which the world's destinies were grandly affected. It is hoped that the readers of this too brief sketch will read the grand and thrilling accounts given by Mr. Bancroft in his history of the United States, and Mr. Irving in his unequaled biography of Washington. Every American should be familiar with those stirring times that tried men's souls.

### PHILADELPHIA CAPTURED.

The campaign of 1777 opened slowly. Burgoyne had received command of a large British army to open its way from Lake Champlain down to Albany, and so on down the Hudson to New York.

Lord Howe was in New York; with a part of his army in New Jersey, a part on Long Island, and a part at Newport. In the early summer he made some movements in New Jersey, but on the thirteenth of June left that state to return to it no more.

In July, Lord Howe embarked his whole army on board his transports and put out to sea. Washington had no doubt he was aiming at Philadelphia. In August, the British fleet appeared in Chesapeake bay and landed with a view to a direct march to Philadelphia. Washington was soon before him to retard his progress as best he might. The battle of the Brandywine was soon fought; but it only checked the progress of the enemy. In September, the British army reached and entered Philadelphia; but Washington gained one of his purposes which was to hinder Howe from reaching Philadelphia in season to form a junction with Burgoyne from the north. He detained him thirty days in a march of fifty-four miles.

Burgoyne had an army of ten thousand troops, well equipped, to break his way from Lake Champlain through to Albany and down the Hudson. Washington had spared all the men he could to oppose Burgoyne. He had weakened his own army to make strong that of the north. Burgoyne's success would be a fire in the rear, which must not be allowed if it could be prevented.

This was one of Washington's most trying times. Several of his generals were complaining of him, and plotting either for independent commands or to supplant him. Some leading congressmen, and even John Adams, were severe on his excessive prudence and disposition to avoid a general battle with Howe. Some of the earliest and noblest patriots, like John Dickinson, were disheartened. Some said, if we only had some strong mind to lead us we could drive the British from our shores.

Yet the people loved and confided in Washington; and congress always, in emergencies, gave him full power and asked him what the civil arm should do.

In a few days after Lord Howe entered Philadelphia, and the cause of the colonies seemed as dark as it did the year before when Washington was flying before Cornwallis in New Jersey. General Gates surrounded, fought and captured Burgoyne's army. It was one of the grandest victories of the Revolution, and taught England what the colonists would do with her armies when well back in the woods.

The winter of 1777 and 1778 Washington and his army spent at Valley Forge, watching Howe in Philadelphia and suffering untold hardships of cold, hunger, nakedness, sickness, short pay, neglect and exposure of every kind. Washington himself was fearfully harrassed by dissensions among his leading generals, intrigue, opposition and faction in and out of congress, which threatened more evil to the country than the British army. It was a terrible winter. But the effect of the capture of Burgoyne was doing much for the cause of the colonies in Europe. France acknowledged their independence, and formed a treaty of alliance with them. England sent commissioners to treat for peace with them, but they would not receive them till she would withdraw her armies or acknowledge their independence. Washington saw clearly the certain triumph of the American cause if only the people would hold out and Congress and the army officers would work in harmony. His great endeavor was to encourage the people, harmonize Congress and his officers, secure obedience to his orders and coöperation in his measures. Never was great wisdom more tried and a great heart more tortured. But slowly and surely he silenced his enemies in the camp and in Congress, kept the heart of the people warm toward himself and the cause, and won the admiration of the watching world.

## THE CAMPAIGN OF 1778.

Lord Howe's ill success lost him the confidence of his government, and Sir Henry Clinton was appointed to the command of the English armies in America. As soon as spring opened the way he evacuated Philadelphia, sending his ships and stores to New York, and marching his army across the Jerseys to join all his forces in that city. Washington was immediately hounding his slow footsteps, harrassing his flanks, attacking his advance and rear, and preventing him from doing mischief on his march. Clinton had not more than got into New York when a strong French fleet appeared at the mouth of the Delaware with four thousand men to coöperate with the Americans. The rest of the summer was spent in forays, attempts and failures, and the next winter set in with Clinton's forces scattered along the coast from Rhode Island to Florida, and Washington's at stations back in the country from Connecticut to Georgia, with the French fleet in the West Indies.

## THE CAMPAIGN OF 1779.

Washington spent the most of the winter of 1778 and 1779 in Philadelphia preparing for the next campaign. It was another anxious winter with him. The French army and fleet which had come to our help had done us no good, but had created a feeling among the people that France was going to fight our battles now, and we could let the war take care of itself. This feeling had lulled the people into what Washington feared was a fatal sense of security. The most of the great minds of the earlier Congress had left it for posts abroad, in the army, in state affairs or private business, so that it had lost much of its former power. It had dissension and irresolution. The belief had become general that the English people were becoming tired of fighting their own children, and so would soon give it up. Our people had suffered much, and while they had no disposition to surrender, they had become indolent in duty to the great cause. Many of them had become interested in the state governments and had not become accustomed to a double form of government and loyalty to both. All these things had created a stupor which pained and alarmed Washington.

Sir Henry Clinton seemed, by his movements all summer, to have no general plan in view, but to content himself with doing mischief in every direction, in destruction of property, burning buildings and spreading desolation. Late in December, he left New York with all the ships and troops which could be spared from its defense, to attempt the capture of Charleston and the submission of South Carolina.

Washington, during the year, had to be governed by the movements of his wary adversary, and so nothing especially decisive was accomplished by this campaign of 1779. The country had suffered much by the losses and destructions of the war. The productive interests had languished. Food and forage were short and dear; business paralyzed; the currency at a discount; everything in a state of ferment. The courage of many was faltering; many who began the war with zeal had grown half indifferent; yet Washington's high courage was steadfast, and though he did not know it, he was building the monuments of his world-wide fame higher and higher. It was this year that he received men of high standing from France and treated them with the greatest consideration, though his dinner was the plainest and simplest that could be served. When ladies dined with him he was especially polite and considerate, no matter how little he had to offer them. While the British officers were supplied with every luxury and spent their winters in riotous luxury and indolence, the Americans were often nearly destitute of the common comforts. Severe indeed were the hardships of the men who won the independence of America.

The winter of 1779 and 1780 was spent at Morristown; a fearfully cold and suffering winter. Washington's army, perishing with cold and hunger, could be kept together only by enforcing food from the counties as a military necessity. To add to the horrors of the winter, Sir Henry Clinton took his fleet, with several thousand men, to Charleston and forced a capitulation of that city, and as he believed, the conquest of South Carolina. In the mean time, the army left in New York made raids into

New Jersey, and an attempt on Morristown, when Washington and a part of his army were absent toward the Hudson. In these raids villages, farm houses and churches were destroyed.

In June, Sir Henry Clinton returned with his ships and as much of his army as he dared take from Charleston to New York. But before this, Lafayette had returned from France and privately informed Washington that a fleet and army were on the way from France to help.

### THE CAMPAIGN OF 1780.

The summer of 1780 opened with difficulties of every kind increased. The American army was small and scattered; the currency had sunk more than sixty per cent in value; General Arnold had fallen into difficulties which threatened his further usefulness; General Greene, Washington's most trusted and efficient general, had incurred the displeasure of congress and nearly lost his commission; Georgia and South Carolina were under British dominance; New Jersey had been swept over by the opposing armies and the people everywhere were worn and weary with the destructive war. Besides these troubles, every community had more or less tories, who were aiding the enemy in every possible way. Yet, at the bottom, people, army and officers, except the tories, were for fighting and suffering on.

On the tenth of July a French fleet of seven ships of the line, two frigates, with bombs and transports and five thousand men, landed at Newport. This help in a time of need brought the promise of more. But on the thirteenth came reinforcements to the British. General Gates was appointed to the command of the southern department of the American forces, and began with such confidence as to lead a strong force into the very embrace of the enemy and bring on a great disaster. Washington had but just heard of this, when Major Andre, the British spy, was caught with the evidence of Arnold's treason on his person. "Whom can we trust?" was Washington's first remark on receiving the intelligence. Troubles thickened on every side. But he immediately fortified West Point, which Arnold had attempted to sell to the enemy, and put General

Greene, his most trusted officer, in its command with a strong force. By a kind of rigid justice, grateful to every American, West Point has become the seat of the national school for training the defenders of American nationality and liberty; while Arnold's name is coupled with that of Judas.

The season closed with skirmishes north and south, and with many intimations that the British commander inclined to carry the war more forcibly into the south; as Georgia and South Carolina had not offered so much resistance as the northern states. Nothing marked was done in this campaign.

## THE CAMPAIGN OF 1781.

The sufferings of the army were so severe this winter, that there were several mutinies, and on one occasion quite a body of soldiers organized to march to Philadelphia and compel Congress to supply their wants and make sure their pay. This was a new trouble.

But the invasion of the Carolinas by Cornwallis aroused the people; and Sumpter, Marion and Morgan gathered the militia to the help of Greene, who had now been appointed to the command of the American army in the south. The invaders were severely punished. The tide of the conflict was various, but the British were the greater losers. The tories did not render them the help they expected, while the resistance was greater than they had provided for. They found that the open country in the south was scarcely more hospitable to them than in the north; and that nowhere in America were they safe out of the reach of their protecting ships of war.

The tide of war now set rapidly southward, as Washington expected it would. Both the British and the French fleets went to the Chesapeake bay and came into a sharp conflict which injured both; but gave neither a victory. Washington had sent Lafayette south with all the force he could spare. Lafayette had charge of the forces in Virginia, which were managed with great judgment and skill, according to Washington's plan of avoiding battles only when sure of favorable results. Greene commanded in the Carolinas and Georgia, on the same plan and with excellent results.

In July, Washington led all the forces he could spare from before New York, and the French forces also, toward Virginia, with a view to the capture of Cornwallis and his army, now at Yorktown. Their passage through Philadelphia was hailed by the people with great enthusiasm. The French army, neatly uniformed, well drilled, officered and supplied with bands of music and rich flags, made an appearance dazzling to American eyes.

About the first of September, Count De Grasse came into the Chesapeake with heavy reinforcements of war ships and land forces. In conjunction with these, it was Washington's plan to make Yorktown a coop for Cornwallis. Forces were marching from every quarter with the greatest speed. The French army from Newport; the new French forces landed from De Grasse's fleet; Washington with all he could rally from New York, Pennsylvania and New Jersey; Lafayette with his forces; the governor of Virginia with such militia as he could muster; were all hurrying toward Yorktown, while the fleet waited at the mouth of York river. Greene was left to threaten Charleston and hold the attention of the British in that region.

Early in October the great girdle began to draw around Cornwallis. He expected naval help from New York, but he did not see his danger soon enough to get it. His only resource was to entrench and defend. All Washington's plans carried. Armies from afar reached Virginia in time. The French fleet was but a few days behind the anticipated time for its arrival. The Virginia militia were gathered in season. Cornwallis had chosen a favorable spot for Washington at this opportune moment. Providence seemed helping the Americans in the fortunate combination of circumstances. When Cornwallis saw his danger he attempted a night escape across the York river, but a fierce storm scattered his boats and defeated the attempt. Officers and soldiers of all arms of the service were of one mind and worked with one will. All saw that the wary Cornwallis was cooped in a place of his own selection, and only some strange chance of war could save him. Enthusiasm such as our poor soldiers had never known fired their hearts. Every man felt himself freedom's king. They made short work with their wily foe, whom they had got at last at a great disadvantage. They saw Washington's prudent plan of warfare ripening at last in a great and almost bloodless victory. Cannon from every quarter played upon the enemy's works and beat them down. The spade and pick opened a safe way to a close encounter with the caged lion. Seeing his certain fate, he surrendered, and in due time marched out into an open field and laid down his arms. This unequaled victory was the great ripe fruit of all their sufferings. It enheartened the whole country and gave it name and credit abroad. The whole world was watching this American conflict. If the new nation maintained its independence, a new era was to open to mankind. The nineteenth of October, 1781, which brought Cornwallis' surrender, made sure this opening future.

Washington visited Mount Vernon, and after a few days repaired to Philadelphia where he spent the winter months of 1781 and 1782 with Congress, counseling in relation to both the civil and military affairs of the country. The army's suffering condition bore heavily on his generous heart.

A treaty of peace between Great Britain and the United States was signed at Paris, January 21, 1783. A letter from Lafayette to Congress, bearing the intelligence, reached that body March 23. Sir Guy Carlton informed Washington a few days after that he was ordered to proclaim a cessation of hostilities by land and sea. On the seventeenth of April Washington made a similar proclamation to his army by order of Congress.

On the eighteenth of the following October Congress discharged the army, many of whom had already gone to their homes on furloughs.

On the second of November Washington made his farewell address to the soldiers who had won the independence of America.

Thus closed the great Revolutionary War, the most important and justifiable of any that the world had then known; as important, perhaps, in securing the liberties of the English as the American people. Now that it is so far in the past, all true men can unite in tributes of praise and honor to the people who so nobly sacrificed for their convictions; and to Washington, their great leader, who, under Providence, became truly the "Father of their country," and, perhaps, the most fortunate and truly great man, taken all in all, in the history of the world.

## LIFE AT MOUNT VERNON.

Washington now retired to Mount Vernon to take up again those rural pursuits so congenial to his retiring and domestic nature. He at once set about improving his estate, embellishing his home and its surrounding and reviving his former pleasures and associations. But he could not forget the country he had helped to bring into being. His wide acquaintance with the resources of the country and its great possibilities, and his intimate knowledge of the people, filled his mind with speculations on the settlement of the wilderness, the means of land and water communication with the fruitful regions which he saw must soon be settled. His correspondence and his conversation with visitors were filled with these thoughts, which reached far away from Mount Vernon.

In December, 1784, he was invited to Annapolis, by the Virginia Assembly, to consider with other public spirited gentlemen, the best ways of improving inland navigation. The meeting resulted in the formation of two navigation companies, for opening the navigation of the Potomac and James rivers, under the coöperation of the assemblies of Virginia and Maryland. He was made president of both. It was a part of the plan to open a communication with western waters and facilitate the movements of settlements into those inviting regions. The Assembly of Virginia, as a mark of respect and in recognition of his great services given without remuneration to the country, voted one hundred and fifty shares in these companies as a gift to General Washington. This generous proposal puzzled and troubled him. It was one of his settled purposes not to accept public gifts, because of their tendency to swerve the private judgment and put one under purchased obligation to the public. He had given eight years of the best of his life to fight for personal freedom, and now he would not accept a gift which might in any way act as a bribe upon that freedom; and yet he did not desire to seem not to appreciate the generous sentiments of his fellow-citizens. After much consideration he concluded to accept the gift, if the assembly would allow him to hold it in trust for some public institution. Later in life he applied it to public education.

It is the testimony of those who knew much of him that his character in private life was as free from guile and blemish as in public positions. His secretary, Mr. Lear, after two years residence in his family on very intimate relations, says: "General Washington, is, I believe, almost the only man of an exalted character, who does not lose some part of his respectability by an intimate acquaintance. I have never found a single thing that could lessen my respect for him. A complete knowledge of his honesty, uprightness and candor in all his private transactions, has sometimes led me to think he was more than a man."

Bishop White says of him: "I know no man so carefully guarded against the discoursing of himself or of his acts, or of anything that pertained to him, and it has occasionally occurred to me when in his company, that if a stranger to his person were present, he would never have known from anything said by him that he was conscious of having distinguished himself in the eye of the world." His wife's grandchild who lived in his family, Miss Custis, has written of him: "He spoke little, generally; never of himself. I never heard him relate a single act of his life during the war."

He was social, fond of company, of children and youth; loved their laughter and gaiety; laughed himself sometimes immoderately; yet was usually calm and benignant. His friendships were very strong. Many of his companions in arms became very dear to him; General Greene, Lafayette and Hamilton in particular. To his early friendships he was always steadfast. The little excellencies of spirit and conduct, like the little touches of the painter's brush, gave the last and delicate finish to the solid and grand character which made him the wonderful man he was.

## THE CONFEDERATION AND THE CONSTITUTION.

When Washington returned from the army to Mount Vernon, he went to spend the rest of his life in retirement. But the troubles of the country he had called into being would not let him rest. The debts incurred in the war; the settlement of claims and differences; the need of money that could not be furnished, of laws that in many places would not be accepted, of authority with force behind it; the general distraction, and in some places actual rebellion, convinced him that the confederation of the states under which the war had been fought out, was but a rope of sand. He saw, and urged in letters and in private conversation, the need of a strong central government, a league of all the people which should be a power over the states, which should make a nation in which the states should exist as local bodies. With these thoughts in his mind, he read much of the ancient republics and of those nations which had existed without kings. He made known his views all over the Union in correspondence with the leading minds. He wrote: "I have ever been a friend to adequate powers in Congress, without which it is evident to me we shall never establish a national character, or be considered as on a respectable footing by the powers of Europe. We are either a united people under one head for federal purposes, or we are thirteen independent sovereignties eternally counteracting each other. If the former, whatever such a majority of the states as the constitution points out conceives to be for the benefit of the whole, should, in my humble opinion, be submitted to by the minority. *I can see no evil greater than disunion.*" Again he writes: "I do not conceive we can exist long as a nation without lodging somewhere a power which will pervade the whole Union in as energetic a manner as the authority of the state governments extends over the several states. To be fearful of investing Congress, constituted as that body is, with ample authorities for national purposes, appears to me the very climax of popular absurdity and madness."

The people were drifting into anarchy. The states were selfish and jealous. Washington felt that they were rejecting his counsel, solemnly given in his farewell address to the soldiers and people. He was alarmed and troubled and asked, "What, then, is to be done? Things cannot go on in this strain forever." There are many letters extant, written about this time, full of the sorrow of his great heart and the fear that the war had been in vain. He did not dream it, though these letters, and a plan of federate organization started at Mount Vernon by the commissioners appointed by the assemblies of Maryland and Virginia, the year before, had given hints of the remedy needed for the prevailing disasters and dangers. These great matters were being considered in the state assemblies and resulted in a proposition for a convention of delegates from all the states, to meet in Philadelphia, for the purpose of revising and correcting the federal system; the action of the convention to be reported to congress and the state legislatures for their approval.

Washington was put at the head of the Virginia delegation. The convention was appointed for the second Monday in May, 1786; but enough delegates to form a quorum did not get there till the twenty-fifth. Washington was unanimously elected president of the convention. The convention continued in session four months. It was a great deliberative body. It came together thoroughly alarmed for the safety of the new country. It worked in earnest and with a will, and produced the great constitution under which the United States have become a great country and lived a hundred years—the greatest compend of deliberative wisdom, perhaps, which has been produced in this world.

The constitution was sent to Congress, and by that body to the state legislatures, which appointed state conventions to consider it. It must be accepted by nine before it became the fundamental law of the land. On the thirteenth of September, 1788, Congress, the constitution having been ratified by a sufficient number of states, appointed the first Wednesday in January,

1789, for the people of the United States to choose electors of a president, and the first Wednesday in February for the electors to meet and make a choice. The meeting of the government was to be on the first Wednesday in March following in New York city.

Concerning it, Washington wrote to a friend: "We may, with a kind of pious and grateful exultation, trace the finger of Providence through those dark and mysterious events which first induced the states to appoint a general convention, and then led them, one after another, by such steps as were best calculated to effect the object, into the adoption of the system recommended by the general convention; thereby, in all human probability, laying a lasting foundation for tranquility and happiness, when we had too much reason to fear that confusion and misery were coming rapidly upon us."

### WASHINGTON ELECTED PRESIDENT.

As the time for the meeting of the electors drew nigh Washington's personal friends became satisfied that he would be elected the first president of the United States, and so informed him in their letters. It was painful to him to think of re-entering public life. He loved agricultural pursuits, and craved a peaceful afternoon of life on his estate. His letters at this time are full of anxiety and fear, lest he should be elected. He dreaded the weight of care attending such an untried position, and feared the loss of his good reputation. When he was elected commander-in-chief he thought his reputation would decline from that day; so now he feared his evil day would begin with this new position.

In a letter to Lafayette, after expressing his extreme reluctance in accepting the place and his diffidence in his own capacity to fill it properly, he says: "If I know my own heart, nothing short of a conviction of duty will induce me again to take an active part in public affairs; and in that case, if I can form a plan for my own conduct, my endeavors shall be unremittingly exerted, even at the hazard of my former fame and present popularity, to extricate my country from the embarrassments in which it is entangled through want of credit; and to establish a general system of policy which, if pursued, will ensure permanent felicity to the commonwealth. I think I see a path clear and direct as a ray of light which leads to the attainment of that object. Nothing but harmony, honesty, industry and frugality are necessary to make us a great and happy people. Happily the present posture of affairs and the prevailing disposition of my countrymen, promise to coöperate in establishing those four great essential pillars of public felicity."

His fruitful mind at once formed plans and provided ways to national prosperity.

In due time he was elected; and on the sixteenth of April, 1789, started for New York to assume his high office. At once his course began to be an ovation. Meetings, speeches, masses of the people, music, cannon, bells, triumphal arches, soldiers, citizens, women, girls, children, met him everywhere, in every possible expression of gratitude, honor and joy. Over the places where he had fought and toiled and suffered, he now went amid the huzzas and shouts of the whole population. Each place seemed to have some new device to express the people's love and joy. It was one long way of triumphal popular joy, from Mount Vernon to New York, such as king never knew and no other human being ever experienced. It humbled, subdued, saddened, overcame him. He felt himself unworthy of it, feared it could not last, dreaded the danger of mistake which might break the spell of this tumultuous congratulation, and bring harm to his now happy country.

After he had reached New York, and all was ready for his inauguration in the presence of a vast multitude of people, when he moved forward to take the oath of office, he was so overcome as to be unable to stand, and stepped back to a chair and sat down for a few moments to recover strength. A breathless silence prevailed. Not a word was spoken. All seemed to know that the great bosom was overshaken with inward tumult. After a few moments he rose and went forward. The secretary of the senate held up the bible and Washington laid his hand upon it. The chancellor of New York read the oath of office to him; he responded: "I swear—so help me God," bowed reverently and kissed the bible. The chancellor then stepped forward, waved his hand and exclaimed: "Long live George Washington, President of the United States!" At this moment a flag swung from the cupola, the bells in all the city sent out their clangor, and the cannon in all the forts and ships pealed their thunderous joy while the people joined in long and rapturous shouts.

Bowing to the people, he went into the senate chamber and delivered his inaugural address. After this he, with the whole assembly, went on foot to St. Paul's church, where prayers were read by Bishop Prevost, of the Episcopal church.

Through it all he was deeply stirred and inexpressibly anxious lest he might fail to do what was expected of him, and turn this whirlwind of praise into a storm of reproach. How little did he foresee that his future course was to be as fortunate as his past, and that this beginning of praise was to go on increasing with the ages.

## WASHINGTON'S ADMINISTRATION.

Nothing could be conceived more difficult than Washington's new position. He had been made president of a government yet to be organized and that government new in the world, having not even an ideal in any one's mind. What sort of a court should it have? What formalities and dignities should it assume? How near the people and how far away should the president be? Should he be approached only through a line of officials as were the rulers of Europe, or should he be open as any citizen to the people? After his inauguration everybody wanted to see him and counsel him. The first week's experience taught him that his privacy must be guarded in some way or he could do no business. Then what about the social life of this republican court? There was no model for it in the world. Franklin, Adams and Jefferson had represented the colonies at foreign courts, but they could not outline a republican court. All Washington's intimate friends had suggestions. Adams and Hamilton inclined to much imitation of royalty to secure the respect of foreign courts and people; as well as our own people who had always profoundly respected the English royalty and its form of government. Others leaned to almost no formalities.

The constitution provided for the different departments of the government; these must be provided with official heads and so set to work as not to hinder each other; and all must work in harmony.

A currency must be provided for the business of the country; the debts of the war must be paid, and there was nothing to pay them with; domestic and foreign credit must be secured; a system of taxation provided; differences between the states settled; international intercourse provided for; and postal, judicial, military and naval affairs arranged. Indeed, there was no end to the new things to be done. It is wonderfully interesting to read of the details of Washington's new work and of the skill and wisdom with which he put together the scattered materials for this new government. There seemed to be every possible conflict of opinion to settle, and everything to be made anew from raw materials, to set up this wonderful machine — a republican government. But Washington led in this new and difficult work with a marvelous capacity for invention and adjustment.

People now, who only hear Washington's praises, can scarcely comprehend his trials. His cabinet was divided, and at length so divided as to break up. Thomas Jefferson, his secretary of state, had been much in France and become strongly interested in the revolution going on there. He sympathized with the radical element in opposition to the throne and its adherents. He favored the Jacobin clubs and excused the bloody excesses of the reign of terror, and favored the formation of similar societies in America. He, therefore, favored the most popular and radical measures in the administration of our government and opposed the more conservative which aimed at solidity and stability. Alexander Hamilton, his secretary of the treasury, on the contrary, feared the fury and passion of the French mobs, as the excited masses looked to him, and favored a government in America which should avoid all popular extremes, and be well ballasted with the weight of the well-tried and conservative principles of the British constitution. The throne and all its appendages, of course, were set aside by our constitution, and he hated them as did the American people, but there remained the essential form of the English government in our executive, legislative and judiciary departments which he wished to carry into harmonious and stable operation.

Washington was devoted to both of these men, and both were devoted to him. They each had a wide following in the country, and became the head of a party. Washington was non-partisan and sought to administer the government in the interest of the whole country, and in fidelity to the principles of the American revolution which had been incorporated in the constitution. In doing this he was often assailed by both parties, and bitterly assailed by the French party, who were coming more and more to hate everything English and love everything French.

The fact that the French had helped us in the revolution won the popular heart of America, which did not stop to weigh well the passion and recklessness and want of wisdom and principle which led on the French revolution. Indeed many thought the French revolution was the American revolution over again, whereas there was but little similarity between them. And yet the French revolution shook the new American government to its center, and had it not been for the strong hand at the helm it would have gone to pieces and been as short-lived and disastrous as was the French republic. A rebellion was started in western Pennsylvania. "The factious and turbulent opposition to the collection of duties on spirituous liquors," as Washington called it, was the occasion of this outbreak, but it was really promoted by the French sympathies and the "democrat clubs," in imitation of the "Jacobin clubs" which were formed all over the country. These clubs gave Washington immense trouble. for they promoted the dissenting, querulous, rebellious spirit against his administration and the unmeasured abuse that was heaped upon him by their papers and public speakers.

The French republic soon got itself into a war with England. Then it demanded that the United States should join it in that war, because France had helped the colonies to get their liberties. The French sympathizers, who had already done so much to paralyze Washington's government and abuse him, now sought to revive the old hatred of England and force America to join France in the bloody conflict. It required all Washington's sagacity and moderation to avoid this wreck of his new nation, and when he secured a treaty of peace and intercourse with England through Mr. Jay, the very best that could be got for this country, and which resulted in immense and permanent benefit, he was more violently abused than ever before, even the House of Representatives unconstitutionally and insultingly demanding his reasons for signing the treaty.

There was from the beginning much difference between the northern and southern states in their business and social life. It was with difficulty that this difference could be adjusted in the constitution. Slavery was dominant in the south, and grew more so. It waned in the north, and soon departed. The south inclined to looser and less scrupulous exactness in morals and social life, and to less devotion to business. The north was exacting, organizing, thrifty and more devoted to constituted forms and the instituted customs of society, and hence moved more in masses, more by the rules of combination and law.

This general difference soon developed a prevailing sympathy with Jefferson and his free views in the south, while in the north the more conservative views of Hamilton, who was anxious that the government should be strong and united—a firm nationality—a power to be feared and honored, prevailed. In the south this free spirit which magnified the individual and the state at the expense of the nation soon showed itself in individuals and also in states, and developed a disloyal and arrogant notion of individual and state rights. The *nation* was never so much prized in the south as in the north, simply because the individual and the state were more prized. In the south individual and state rights were supposed to be dominant in the American idea. In the north the nation and its rights were supposed to be dominant in the American idea. In the north Hamilton's teachings have prevailed; in the south, Jefferson's. At last, after more than a hundred years of jar and conflict, the north and south are likely to come to a better understanding and thoroughly respect the individual and at the same time magnify the nation.

In the second administration of Washington the spirit of this difference was rampant, fanned into a flame by French zealots and radicals and made more demonstrative by hatred of British tyranny, which it was restrained by Washington's strong and wise hand from fighting. Grandly now does Washington's commanding figure rise up against the black and fierce cloud of those early and troublous times.

When Washington made his final address to Congress, December 5, 1796, the Senate heartily approved it; but in the House there was dissension. Mr. Giles, of Virginia, made a strong speech against approval, and when the vote came to be taken twelve names were recorded against it and stand there yet, among them the name of Andrew Jackson, then a young man of twenty-nine years of age, just admitted from the new state of Tennessee.

### WASHINGTON'S DEATH.

At the close of his second term as president, March 3, 1797, Washington repaired to Mount Vernon, grateful for his release from public duty. John Adams was his successor, who very soon found himself threatened with a war with the French republic, and he looked at once to Washington to lead it, should it be forced upon the country. He had had but a few month's peace when this war cloud rose in the east. He at once set about the plans for organizing an army, but before the settlement of the difficulties he died from the effects of a severe cold, on the night of the fourteenth of December, 1799, in the sixty-eighth year of his age.

Thus closed unexpectedly the earthly life of one of the greatest and best of men, who, while he was subject to all human frailties, was not brilliant or specially endowed with any marked power above many, was yet one of the greatest men that has ever lived in the soundness of his judgment, strength of his fortitude, self-control, patience and persistence under difficulties, and in the power to combine and control great affairs and great bodies of men and bear them on to a triumphant issue of great and good purposes. Jefferson said of him: "His integrity was most pure; his justice the most inflexible I have ever known,—no motives of interest or consanguinity, of friendship or hatred, being able to bias his decision. He was in every sense of the word, a wise, a good and a great man."

Adams, in his inaugural address, spoke of him as one "who by a long course of great actions, regulated by prudence, justice, temperance and fortitude, had merited the gratitude of his fellow citizens, commanded the highest praises of foreign nations and secured immortal glory with posterity."

## The Grave of George Washington.

The sacred enclosure which holds the dust of George Washington is at Mount Vernon, near the mansion in which he lived and died, and which has now become a shrine visited, probably, by more people than the resting place of any other mortal man. It is on the west bank of the Potomac river, seventeen miles below Washington. The mansion and tomb are some two hundred feet above the river and afford a fine outlook over water and land.

The original Washington estate was eight thousand acres. In 1856 the state of Virginia passed an act authorizing the purchase of Mount Vernon by the ladies of the Mount Vernon Association. The ladies purchased two hundred acres, for which they paid two hundred thousand dollars, since which great improvements for preserving and beautifying the place have been made. The worn and decayed parts of the buildings have been renewed; the grounds are being made more beautiful every year.

Mr. Lossing has dedicated his book entitled "The Home of Washington":

TO HIS

PATRIOTIC COUNTRYWOMEN,

BY WHOSE EFFORTS

THE HOME AND TOMB OF WASHINGTON

HAVE BEEN

RESCUED FROM DECAY.

The tomb of Washington is in a quiet, secluded place, but a short distance from the mansion. It is made of brick according to his will, though it was not made till thirty-eight years after his death. Till then his body rested in the old tomb. The new tomb is in a small ravine coming down from a well-wooded hillside. The place abounds with sweet-briar, trailing arbutus and other flowers.

The front of the tomb is plain, with wide, arching gateway and double iron gates, above which, upon a plain marble slab, is this inscription:

WITHIN THIS ENCLOSURE

REST THE REMAINS OF

General George Washington.

The ante-room in which are the sarcophagi, which hold the remains of George and Martha Washington, is about twelve feet square. Behind this room is the vault in which repose the remains of about thirty members of the family. For a time, through fear of disturbance, the sarcophagi were kept in the vault; but on the seventh of October, 1837, they were placed where they now rest, in the ante-room, the vault closed and locked and the key thrown into the river.

The right-hand sarcaphagus, as seen from the gate, holds the remains of the "Father of his Country"; the one on the left, those of his wife.

On a tablet over the door of the tomb, are these words of the Great Teacher:

> "I am the resurrection and the life.
> He that believeth in me,
> though he were dead, yet shall he live."

The sarcophagus of Mrs. Washington is without ornament or symbol; and has on it these words:

> **Martha,**
> CONSORT OF WASHINGTON,
> DIED MAY 21ST, 1801; AGED 71 YEARS.

The sarcophagus of Washington is ornamented with the United States coat of arms upon a draped flag.

It has this one word on it:

> **Washington.**

Near the entrance to the vault are four white marble monuments with inscriptions commemorating the lives and deaths of the members of the family whose forms rest there.

Everything is being done, and will continue to be done, to make Mount Vernon and its sacred tomb one of the most marked and hallowed mausoleums in the world. Its great sleeper there is a mighty magnet drawing all the world reverently to his resting place.

In 1833, Dr. Andrew Reed, an English philanthropist, wrote at the grave of Washington, this tribute to his memory, and left it in the family:

WASHINGTON,
The Brave, The Wise, The Good;
WASHINGTON,
Supreme in War, in Council and in Peace;
WASHINGTON,

| Valiant | Discreet | Confident |
| without | without | without |
| Ambition; | Fear; | Presumption; |

WASHINGTON,
In Disaster, Calm; in Success, Moderate; in All, Himself;
WASHINGTON,
The Hero, the Patriot, the Christian;
The Father of Nations, the Friend of Mankind;
who
When he had Won all, Renounced all
and sought
In the Bosom of his Family and Nature,
Retirement,
And in the Hope of Religion,
Immortality.

## CHAPTER III.

### JOHN ADAMS.
#### SECOND PRESIDENT OF THE UNITED STATES.

##### GENEALOGY.

JOHN ADAMS is a representative name in the annals of New England. It stands for the average man — for the hardy, strong middle class, which made up the great body of the early New England society. It belonged to a family that for several generations escaped poverty but did not attain riches; who were of strong sense, but did not become great; who were virtuous, but not marked with ability for leadership and supremacy. The ancestors of John Adams, the second president, were men of plain common sense, with virtue which often rose into rugged strength. They were of that stock which makes up the anatomy and muscle of strong society. Away back from the beginning of the colony; they were hard-working, good-sensed, solid-charactered men, who added force and stability to the new colony. As they approached his time they rose in their community; more of them sought a liberal education; more of them entered the ministry and served in public trusts; more of them gave evidence of the character-developing effects of the Puritan style of thought and life. His father's oldest brother, Joseph, was a Harvard scholar, and a minister for more than sixty years, in Newington, New Hampshire. His father intended that he should follow his uncle's example. Men of the Adams stamp in the Massachusetts colony believed in education and religion. They founded schools and colleges and supported them. They believed in an educated ministry and public service. Their state of society was largely the product of university culture in England. There were not many of them university men, but they read the books and were nourished by the thought of university scholars.

The father of John Adams was a small farmer, as the most of his ancestors had been. He was a deacon of the church, while many of his name had served their towns as selectmen and recorders, indicating the range of their place in society.

The subject of this sketch was born in that part of Braintree, Massachusetts, now called Quincy, some ten miles southwest of Boston, October 30, 1735. Little is known of his boyhood, more than that he worked on his father's farm, fished, hunted, played and went to school as other country boys of his time did, till he neared his sixteenth year. About this time his father told him his serious and ambitious intentions concerning him. The boy did not relish the thought of exchanging the free and cheery life of the farm, with the woods and brooks and not-far-off ocean, for the confinement and rigid rules and close study of the college, and told his father that he wanted to be a farmer. "Well, then," his father said, in substance; "if you want to be a farmer it is time you were at it in earnest. It will take all your time from now till you are twenty-one to learn it well. So you can give up play and go to work." John went to the field and plied the heavy implements in thoughtful meditation till weariness was in all his muscles. A little steady toil, a little sacrifice of pleasure to a purpose in his doing, a little serious thoughtfulness of life and its use and outcome, led him to conclude that he would like to try his father's plan for him, at least so far as a college course of study was concerned. His father was pleased, and put him at once upon his preparatory studies. At the age of sixteen he entered Harvard and graduated when he was twenty, esteemed for his integrity, energy and ability. He was one of a class of twenty-four, several of whom became distinguished men, but none so much so as he. Though among his farm-boy associates no one dreamed of his superior capacities, he had not got through his college course before he was recognized as one of the three strongest scholars in his class; and the two who were classed with him became noted men, one of them a president of the college, the other a distinguished divine. The sharpening and developing effect of the college study soon began to show the quality and strength of the coming man.

### JOHN ADAMS A TEACHER.

Now that he was through college by his father's aid, he must at once do something for his own support. He soon got a position as teacher in a grammar school in Worcester, for such meager pay as to barely meet his wants. But he made it help him in other ways. The minds of his school children became studies. The government of his school taught him law, jurisprudence, executive order. He had a miniature republic before him, with each individual's rights claiming place in connection with the general good, each limiting the other. The subject of government had at this time become a great study in all the colonies. Everybody was a politician. All theories of government were studied and discussed. Every town was a sort of public lyceum for the study and discussion of government. Many were reading history to find philosophy and example to help them to true opinions and right conclusions. People can now scarcely realize the interest then felt in all that pertained to social order and well being. They were a new people on a new continent, crystalizing into a new order of society; what was it likely to be or to attain? Young Adams was studying these problems while he was teaching the Worcester children the rudiments of an education. From a letter written to his kinsman, Nathan Webb, and published by Mr. Webb's son fifty years after, take the following as a sample of the young man's thinking at this time: "Soon after the reformation a few people came over into this new world for conscience's sake. Perhaps this apparently trivial incident may transfer the great seat of empire into America. It looks like it to me; for if we can remove the turbulent Gallicks, our people, according to the exact computations, will in another century become more numerous than England itself. Should this be the case, since we have, I may say, all the naval stores of the nation in our hands, it will be easy to obtain the mastery of the seas, and then the united force of all Europe will not be able to subdue us. The only way to keep us from setting up for ourselves is to disunite us. *Divide et impera.* Keep us in distinct colonies, and then some great men in each colony, desiring the monarchy of the whole, they will destroy each other's influence and keep the country *in equilibrio.*" This was written just before he was twenty years of age. This was twenty years before the revolution; and yet this youth was computing the growth and resources of America, the probable time before it would hold the balance of power against all Europe; the importance of the colonies being united, and, if united, the certainty that they would by and by set up for themselves. Here was the great statesman beginning to develop the philosophy of his statesmanship, while yet a youth teaching the children of a country village for his daily bread. How little he foresaw the outcome of his thinking, and yet how true to the common law that the character of the man is given shape before the boy is out of his teens. Washington at nineteen was a military leader; John Adams at nineteen was a political philosopher. The boy is the type of the man inwardly as well as outwardly. Immensely important is this truth to know and act upon in the training of youth.

In this same letter there are some noble sentiments on friendship. He says: "Friendship, I take it, is one of the distinguishing glories of man; and the creature that is insensible to its charms, though he may wear the shape of man, is unworthy of the character. In this, perhaps, we bear a nearer resemblance to unembodied intelligence than in anything else. From this I expect to receive the chief happiness of my future life." This indicates that he was as great in heart as he was in intellect. A biographer says of this letter: "It was a letter of an original and meditative mind; a mind as yet aided only by the acquisitions then attainable at Harvard college, but formed by nature for statesmanship of the highest order."

Very soon the political part of it began to be fulfilled. Its fulfillment is not complete yet, but as a nation we are marching in the line of his foresight.

In a letter to his classmate, Charles Cushing, written the next April, he writes: "Upon common theatres indeed the applause of the audience it more to the actors than their own approbation. But upon the stage of life, while conscience claps, let the world hiss. On the contrary, if conscience disapproves, the loudest applauses of the world are of but little value.

"We have, indeed, the liberty of choosing what character we shall sustain in this great and important drama. But to choose rightly, we should consider in what character we can do the most service to our fellow men as well as to ourselves. The man who lives wholly to himself is less worthy than the cattle in his barn."

Here is a recognition of conscience in the conduct of life which would be creditable to any divine in any age. Indeed, it was written in reply to his friend's counsel that he should enter the ministry for his life's work. His father desired it; his own heart almost persuaded him to it; yet he had become such an original thinker on all questions, and so profoundly believed in the mind's liberty and power and duty of choice that he finally decided in favor of the law as the field in which he could be most useful to himself and the world. In this letter to Charles Cushing there is this postscript: "There is a story about town that I am an Armenian." Those were the days of dominant Calvinism. In this same letter he had indicated that the divine "should revere his own understanding more than the decrees of councils or the sentiments of fathers," and "should resolutely discharge the duties of his station according to the dictates of his mind." This power and necessity of original thinking on all subjects that was so imperious in him led him to turn from the ministry, though as he said in his diary: "My inclination, I think, was to preach." Under the same date he says: "Although the reason of my quitting divinity was my opinion concerning some disputed points, I hope I shall not give reason of offense to any of that profession by imprudent warmth."

On the twenty-first of August, 1756, he arranged with a Mr. Putnam to study law two years in his office. The next day, in noting this in his diary, he said: "The study and practice of law, I am sure, does not dissolve the obligations of morality and religion." A few days after he wrote to his friend Cranch of his "hard fortune:" "I am condemned to keep school two years longer. This I sometimes consider a very grievous calamity, and almost sink under the weight of woe." He was to teach school while he studied law. The hours out of the school-room were to be given to the study of law. The school-room was to board and clothe him, while the law office was to prepare him for his future profession. But checking his complaint about his hard fortune in having to continue teaching, he goes forward in a long letter recounting in fervent eloquence the blessings he is receiving from his Maker, and his multiform reasons for gratitude and praise. In all the literature of religion there are few finer things than this sweet outpouring of intelligent and even poetic gratitude, in this letter to his young friend, and written two months before he was twenty-one. After enumerating in fine and fervent language his blessings in this life, he points to the richer ones in the realm of the future, and then asks: "Shall I now presume to complain of my hard fate? God forbid. * * * I am happy, and shall remain so while health is indulged to me after all the other adverse circumstances that fortune can place me in." He then speaks of teaching school and studying law at the same time, and says: "It will be hard work, but the more difficult and dangerous the enterprise a brighter crown of laurel is bestowed on the conqueror." He persisted in his double work till he carried through his law studies and was admitted to the bar.

### LAW PRACTICE IN BRAINTREE.

Mr. Adams was now a lawyer by profession; the next thing was to be a lawyer by practice. He could not very well teach school and practice law. Clients would not seek him in the school-room, so he left the school-room to take his chances at earning a living in his profession. He was poor. Where should he go? There seemed but one place for him, which was Braintree, where his father's roof and table gave him what he had not money to buy. So here he began his professional career. But he had no prestige. His greatness was not yet known. It had not been published that he would sit in kings' courts, help create and then rule a great nation—that he was to enter the the ranks of the greatest men of the world and was to go into history as one of the luminaries of humanity. His old neighbors did not know, or dream these things of him; so they did not go much to him with business. He sat lonely hours in his office waiting for clients that did not come, wondering how he should ever get clients and business. He was anxious, sad and full of questionings as to what to do and what he could do. His coming greatness did nothing for him, and he had to plod and work, and worry and wait, as nearly all young professional men have to do. These were the gloomy days of his life. It was long an anxious question as to what he should do in life—what profession he should adopt. So now it was an anxious question as to how he should get anything to do in his profession. But he did not give up in despair, nor waste his time in idle sorrow. He renewed his zeal in the study of law. His diary indicates the great amount of study, speculation and investigation, which he gave to the broad fields of natural, statute and constitutional law, as well as the law of nations. In this lonely and unenlivened work of legal research, he laid the foundations of his future greatness. If clients did not bring him cases, he found them in the books. If his neighbors did not consult him, he consulted the law as it had been adjudicated in the practice of the past. To this uncheered study he devoted several years.

On the twenty-fifth of May, 1761, his father died, after nearly three years of this much study and little practice. He remained with his mother, caring for her business, three years longer, when he married Miss Abigail Smith, daughter of Reverend William Smith, a Congregational clergyman of Weymouth, a town adjoining Braintree. Mrs. Adams was a woman of rare ability and worth. She was connected with several of the best families in the colony. She was herself a rich flower of her rich family tree. By this marriage, after six years of weary plodding and studying and waiting, his business prospects brightened. The many family connections on his wife's side began to employ him, and by their influence put business into his hands. His acquaintance enlarged. Influential friends suggested, here and there, his employment in important cases. By the time he was thirty years old he seemed to have got well started in his profession, largely through the influence which came to him through his marriage with Miss Smith.

The troubles between the British parliament and the colonies began to foment about this time, which led to public meetings, to addresses, resolutions, and much private and public discussion of the relations of the colonies to the mother country. A society of lawyers had been formed in Boston for extended study of, and dissertations on, important legal questions. Mr. Adams, though living ten miles away, was invited to join this association. It did much to sharpen and broaden the legal talent of Boston and vicinity; and his participation in its discussion brought him to a more intimate acquaintance with the bar of Boston. He had, some years before, heard James Otis, in an argument on writs of assistance, go to the bottom of their danger as instruments of tyranny, and written out the argument in his diary, which led him to a profound study of human rights. All these things were schooling him for the great work that was before him, and acquainting him with the men to be joined with him. The Stamp act was passed by the British parliament in March, 1765, and was to go into operation November 1. The Massachusetts Colonial Legislature took decisive action, in June, to resist that act, which proposed to tax the colonies without their representation. James Otis proposed that all the colonies should be invited to join with Massachusetts, and that to this end a representative meeting of delegates from all the colonies be held in October, in New York city.

This was the initiatory movement to a union. It was due to James Otis, at that time one of the most powerful and patriotic orators of Massachusetts. The public meetings held in Boston that summer to resist the Stamp act were addressed by Mr. Adams, by invitation of the citizens.

When it became clear that the people would not permit the use of stamps, the Governor announced that all business would be suspended, especially of the custom-house and courts. Mr. Adams had now got a good start as a lawyer, had a thriving business, a large acquaintance and a growing popularity. It seemed to him as though this Stamp act was sure to ruin it. If the courts were closed, his occupation was gone. He expressed his gloomy fears in his diary. The very next day he received a letter, sent by express, from the town clerk of Boston, asking his aid as counsel for the town, in connection with James Otis, Jeremiah Gridley and William Cooper, to secure the continuance of the courts without the use of stamps. The proposition was to be argued before the governor and his council. Nothing was effected by this hearing, only to make more vigorous and popular and intelligent the opposition to the tyrannical act.

### REMOVAL TO BOSTON.

So much had his business increased in Boston, and all his interests become identified with that town, that in 1768 he took up his residence there. The events in England and America were tending rapidly to revolution. Question after question was being discussed. The conflict between the governor of Massachusetts and the town of Boston grew more and more complicated and determined. The best legal talent was in constant service. Mr. Adams was one of the most active, and was always unswerving in the interests of justice and the people. The front of the conflict was between the governor, England's servant, and the legislature — the servant of the people. For several years this conflict raged with all the force that craft and power and money could apply on the part of the governor, and the honest skill and patriotic zeal of the people, defending their rights and resisting tyranny on the part of the legislature. Mr. Adams, through these years of intellectual encounter, was the patriotic lawyer, the people's counsellor, the sharp, strong, zealous advocate of American rights and principles. He, with his patriotic coadjutors, won victory after victory in these legal and moral encounters, till the people were so fired and the king and his parliament so resolved on the forced submission of the colonies that the civil power retired and the military arm came into rule by might. Now courts were suspended, legislatures were at an end, and Mr. Adams realized what he feared when the Stamp act was passed—the loss of all business. With the coming of General Gage, commander of all the British forces in America, and the occupancy of Boston by his troops, the lawyers' business ceased. Cases were not to be tried in the presence of cannon. Arguments were not to be made to regiments in arms.

At this gloomy time, when his wife was on a visit to Braintree, he wrote to her as follows:

BOSTON, 12 May, 1774.

My own infirmities, the account of the return of yours, and the public news, coming all together, have put my philosophy to the trial.

We live, my dear soul, in an age of trial. What will be the consequence I know not. The town of Boston, for aught I can see, must suffer martyrdom. It must expire, and our principal consolation is, that it dies in a noble cause—the cause of truth, of virtue, of liberty and of humanity, and that it will probably have a glorious resurrection to greater wealth, splendor and power than ever.

Let me know what it is best for us to do. It is expensive keeping a family here, and there is no prospect of any business in my way in this town this whole summer. I don't receive a shilling a week. We must contrive as many ways as we can to save expenses, for we may have calls to contribute very largely, in proportion to our circumstances, to prevent other very honest, worthy people from suffering for want, besides our own loss in point of business and profit.

Don't imagine from all this that I am in the dumps. Far otherwise. I can truly say that I have felt more spirits and activity since the arrival of this news than I have done for years. I look upon this as the last effort of Lord North's despair, and he will as surely be defeated in it as he was in the project of the tea.

His letters, diary and public addresses all indicate that he had a profound philosophy of the triumph of liberty and justice. However dark the present, he saw light in the future. If Boston shall be laid in ashes, a new Boston will rise therefrom more glorious and powerful. If America shall suffer from misgovernment and oppression, she shall come from her sufferings renewed in spirit for a grander career. He had read history to learn that truth, right and virtue, in the long run, prevail; and that wrong and injustice turn upon and devour their propagators at last. He had rejected the prevailing theology because of its despair of human nature and its distrust of the Divine goodness. He had adopted a generous and hopeful philosophy of humanity. All this now came to sustain him in his own and his country's peril and distress; and not only to sustain him, but to make him a great leader, through darkness and war, to the light and peace beyond. It was not simply his intellectual strength and furnishing that made him the power he was in his times, but those great and humane, and hopeful, moral and religious convictions which almost led him into the ministry, and would, but for his rejection of some of the dogmas of the prevailing church, and which he carried into all the work of his life. He was a lawyer, and believed in law; a philosopher, and believed in truth; a moralist, and believed in virtue; and a religionist, and believed in God. All these combined made the basis of his statesmanship and the ruling power of his private and public life.

The opening of the war scenes of the revolution changed the course of Mr. Adams' life. He was a lawyer, and sought only to magnify his calling. He had ambition, but it was in the line of his profession. He saw an ample field for all his power; but now his occupation was gone. Boston, his chosen home, was a camp of war. The rights of his countrymen were trampled under invading feet. There was but one course for him to pursue; that was to put himself and all he had into the defense of the rights of America.

### PUBLIC LIFE BEGAN.

Mr. Adams was now thirty-nine years old. General Gage, now acting in the double capacity of military commander and civil governor, had ordered the meeting of the legislature of the colony at Salem, instead of Boston. An effort was made to put John Adams on the council of the governor, but Gage, hearing of it, negatived it at once. The legislature met in Salem, June 7, 1774. Its members began at once the most active secret measures to defeat the plans of the governor. On the seventeenth of June, a motion was made that the doorkeeper keep the door closed against all passage in or out. One hundred and twenty-nine members were present. At once a resolution was offered in approval of the meeting in Philadelphia on the first of September, of the committees from the several colonies of America—the Colonial Congress, in fact,—according to the suggestion of James Otis nine years before, in relation to the Stamp act. The object of the meeting as stated in the resolution was: "To consult upon wise and proper measures to be recommended to all the colonies for the recovery and establishment of their just rights and liberties, civil and religious, and the restoration of union and harmony between the two countries, most ardently desired by all good men." This bold resolution, with others, was taken up at once. It was a surprise to most of the members. It was a move toward union, and dictation to England. They were consulting in defiance of their governor. There were spies in the assembly. One of them evaded the vigilance of the doorkeeper and carried intelligence to the governor. The governor immediately sent a messenger to prorogue the legislature. But the doorkeeper's orders were absolute and he would not admit him, but sent in word of his mission. The legislature took no notice of it. A few idlers and members had gathered on the steps outside, and to them the messenger read the governor's proroguing message; but the work inside went on. The resolutions were discussed and passed—one hundred and seventeen for, and twelve against them. James Bowdoin, Thomas Cushing, Samuel Adams, John Adams and Robert Treat Payne, were appointed to serve Massachusetts in the congress. When this great initiatory step was taken, the legislature dissolved according to the governor's order, never more to meet under royal authority.

## THE COLONIAL CONGRESS.

The Colonial Congress was called to meet September 1, 1774. It was for consultation. It had no authority; it was simply a meeting of delegated citizens to talk over their grievances; to get acquainted with each other and the condition of the colonies, and try to act together in their endeavors to bring England to a better mind toward them. Massachusetts had asked for this meeting to get the other colonies to make common cause with her, to sympathize with, and share her oppression.

The first things considered were non-importation, non-consumption and non-exportation acts. It would hurt England to refuse to buy her goods, to cease to consume anything she made, to cease to sell her anything the colonies produced.

But their consultation produced quite other results than their acts! It stimulated their courage. It led them to speak out their feelings. "What is a king's promise?" asked young Rutledge, of South Carolina, in a defiant tone. "A constitutional death to Lords Bute, Mansfield and North!" cried Harrison. And so by brave words which the world did not then hear, as their consultations were secret, they opened their hearts to each other. On the seventeenth of September Adams wrote in his diary: "This day has convinced me that America will support Massachusetts, or perish with her." Yet the delegates were far from being agreed on anything. Many of them were fearful of offending the king and his governors. They generally loved and honored England. With patience, forbearance and wisdom they talked over their differences of opinion, and yet gave out to the world that unity and harmony prevailed among them. The unity was in their mutual desire to allay the lion's anger, and their wise readiness to stand by each other in their efforts to do it.

The Congress continued two months. It prepared with great care a petition to the king, and the acts of non-intercourse as threats and proofs of their resolution; but the greatest benefit of the Congress was the acquaintance of the leading men of the colonies with each other, and the preparation for the final union made by this acquaintance.

### CORRESPONDENCE WITH HIS WIFE.

This journey to Philadelphia was Mr. Adams' first visit out of New England. It was full of interest to him in many respects. During this journey began that correspondence with his wife on political matters, which has been of great interest to the world since their day. Mrs. Abigail Adams was a woman of rare mind who entered into all the great interests of the colonies with judgment and enthusiasm. He wrote to her of the questions discussed in Congress, and she to him of the stirring events going on in Boston and the colony.

The correspondence on state matters thus begun, was kept up through all their separation. After his public life began they were much separated, and the history of that life was largely written in his letters to her.

### HIS ELECTION TO THE PROVINCIAL CONGRESS.

He had been at home but a few days, before he was called to Watertown to give his counsel in the Massachusetts Provincial Congress, then in session. A few days later he was elected by Braintree, a member of that Congress, and continued so till the end of its career. He was thus in the heart of the activities of the time in Massachusetts. At this time some leading tory in Massachusetts, who called himself "Massachusettensis," wrote a series of able articles in a Boston newspaper, on the British view of the situation and in defense of the course of King George.

Mr. Adams wrote a series of articles for the Boston Gazette in reply, over the name of "Novanglus." Both series were widely read and studied in the colonies. The articles of Mr. Adams were afterward published under the title of "A History of the Dispute with America." They now appear permanently as a part of the history of the times in his works. His grandson and biographer, Charles Francis Adams, says of them: "No publication of the times compares with them in extent of research into the principles of the ancient law, and in the vigorous application of them to the question at issue."

By the Massachusetts congress Mr. Adams was appointed to

### THE SECOND CONTINENTAL CONGRESS.

The winter of 1774 and 1775 was a fearful one to the people of Massachusetts. In April, 1775, the battles of Lexington and Concord were fought, which brought almost all the male population of the colony under arms to defend their homes against the soldiers of their king. Fearful was the agitation over the whole country. In the midst of this agitation Mr. Adams set out for the second Continental Congress at Philadelphia. The delegates were everywhere hailed with delight. Their journey was made an ovation. In New York, almost the whole city came out. The whole of the militia were in arms. This day's ovation settled it that New York would go into the confederation of the colonies. They hastened on. The Congress met in a very different mood from that in which it parted the fall before. Lexington and Concord had united them. The spirit of the men of Massachusetts was now in the people of all the colonies.

Early in June Mr. Adams moved that Congress adopt the army around Boston as its own, and proceed to officer and supply it, and, in making the motion, said that though it was not time to name a commander yet, "I have no hesitation to declare that I have one gentleman in my mind for that important command, and that is a gentleman from Virginia, who is among us and very well known to us all; a gentleman whose skill and experience as an officer; whose independent fortune, great talents and excellent universal character will command the approbation of all America and unite the cordial exertions of all the colonies better than any other person in the Union."

On the fifteenth of June the army was adopted. Immediately after George Washington, whom Mr. Adams a few days before had pointed out as the proper man, was elected commander-in-chief. Two days after, June 17, perhaps at the very time the battle of Bunker Hill was being fought, he wrote to a friend: "This appointment will have a great effect in cementing and securing the union of these colonies; the liberties of America depend upon him, in a great degree."

The work of this Congress was great, and it was greatly done. It had to provide an army and a government, unite and consolidate the people—in a word, it had to create an empire, and it did it. It had every difficulty in the way, but by a marvelous wisdom it got over and around them all.

While Mr. Adams was at this work he was receiving letters from his wife in Braintree, with her four little children exposed to the horrors of war, her home but a little way from the sea, in a region swept over and over again by the marauding British soldiers, and visited often by our own soldiers in their needs. Under anxiety for his family, and for the whole country, he and his coadjutors from Massachusetts had to perform their great duties. These were indeed "the times that tried men's souls."

After the battle of Bunker Hill, Mr. Adams saw clearly that all talk of reconciliation was vain, and he shaped his course accordingly; he did all he could to strengthen, officer and support the army, and he began to forecast a constitution, laws, a system of finance, a naval defense and whatever must enter into a nation's necessities. While he did not break with the timid and halting, like John Dickinson, he yet planned in his mind for what actually came.

About this time two of his private letters—one to his wife and one to General James Warren—were intercepted by the British and published in Boston. They were so radical and vigorous for independence, and spoke with such disrespect of all conciliation, that he became a marked man in the king's hatred. Parliament talked much of arresting him, and the king's friends in America made their dislike of him conspicuous. Many of the timid friends of the colonies shunned him. It is said that John Dickinson became his enemy for the rest of his life, and that even John Hancock drew away from him and became cautious of intercourse with him. This made it necessary for him to use every argument, public and private, to make his views known and understood by the people. In Congress and out, he grew more and more influential, and he reiterated more and more his strong opinion that peace was possible only at the arbitration of the sword. Sink or swim, survive or perish, we must fight, was his burning conviction.

The course of the British government more and more convinced the people that John Adams saw the alternative offered to the colonies, to fight for their independence or be permanently oppressed. Every month made it clearer to some of them, and when the summer of 1776 made clear to the people that our soldiers could match the red-coats, and that the decision must be made by the fierce onslaught of war, they were ready for the declaration of independence. There were still many for begging and cringing and waiting,—many who so believed in the infallibility and omnipotence of England, that it seemed like resisting the Almighty to lift the feeble hand of the colonies against her; but John Adams' strong voice rang out for freedom or death; and Patrick Henry responded with matchless eloquence to the mighty appeal. At length the die was cast, and the country committed to freedom or death.

### MINISTER TO FRANCE.

In the last part of the year 1777, Mr. Adams was appointed by congress minister to France. He accepted the dangers, and set sail on the thirteenth of February, 1778, and reached Paris the eighth of April, after having been chased by British cruisers, encountered a severe storm in the gulf-stream, met and captured a British letter-of-marque, and passed safely the exposure in the British channel. He found affairs in a better condition than was expected. His predecessor, Mr. Deane, had arranged a treaty that gave reasonable satisfaction to the country. Mr. Adams found the French people in full sympathy with America, and in the belief that the war would soon close. Indeed, it has been since learned that the capitulation of Burgoyne convinced the English government that it could not conquer her vigorous colonies in America; but the dogged stubbornness of the British spirit would not yield till the capture of Cornwallis at Yorktown. Mr. Adams put the affairs between France and America in a satisfactory condition, and returned in about seventeen months.

## MASSACHUSETTS CONSTITUTIONAL CONVENTION.

In two days after his return to his home, Mr. Adams was elected by Braintree to serve in the convention which was to form a constitution for Massachusetts. In this commonwealth there were three interests to be conciliated and combined — the extreme democracy of the rural districts, the extreme property interests chiefly of the seaport towns, and the middle class of trading and professional men. They were each clamoring for supremacy. If they could be happily combined, the great question of popular government in America would be favorably solved. The convention met. As though by a good Providence, the best-read constitutional lawyer of America, John Adams, had returned and been elected to this convention. He was no partisan; he served no faction; he had no interest of his own to serve; he was simply the ripe man of the times prepared to serve the new nation being born and the new era of constitutional law for the world. As Washington was the providential man to lead the armies to victory, so was Adams the providential man to lay the foundation of the new government in constitutional law. At the opening of the convention, his pre-eminent abilities and service to his country pointed to him to open an outline of the work to be done, which he did in a speech of such commanding clearness and force that it became the fountain of unity for all adverse interests. Personal rights, property rights, state rights and national rights, were so disentangled and classified that the convention was enabled to give them all their proper place in the constitution, and thus set before the world an outline of constitutional law in which all rights are protected, and a government by the people made possible and powerful.

The true aim of government, in his idea, was to establish upon the firmest footing the rights of all who live under it, giving to no one interest power enough to become aggressive upon the rest, and yet not denying to each a share sufficient for its own protection. The convention at once announced its object in two propositions: first, "to establish a free republic;"

second, "to organize the government of a people by fixed laws of their own making."

### COMMISSIONER FOR PEACE.

Mr. Adams was not through with the work of the convention when he was appointed commissioner to treat for peace and commerce with Great Britain. On the thirteenth of November, 1779, he sailed for Paris on this mission, and reached the French capital on the fifth of February, 1780. But difficulties arising between him and Count de Vergennes, he had less to do on this mission than was expected. While remaining at Paris he used his pen freely in enlightening Europe on American affairs.

During his stay in Europe he visited Holland and effected a treaty of amity and commerce with that country which he always regarded with as much satisfaction as any service he ever rendered his own country.

Here, in the "Gazette" of Leyden, he published twenty-six letters on the revolution in America, which are now published in his works by his grandson.

With Holland he arranged for a loan of money for the United States, which was a great help to them in their financial stress.

Now France, Spain and Holland had become friendly and helpful to the United States.

In October, 1782, he returned to Paris, and after much diplomatic manœuvering, met the other commissioners from America and those from England, and arranged for a treaty of peace with England, which was signed at Paris on the twenty-first of January, 1783.

Soon after this, Frederick the Second, of Prussia, made overtures to Mr. Adams for a treaty of amity and commerce with his country. After some correspondence, he agreed upon a treaty to offer to Congress; by this time he received authority, in conjunction with Dr. Franklin and Mr. Jefferson, to negotiate treaties with any European power desiring such treaty.

This opened a prospect of a much longer stay in Europe, and Mrs. Adams, with their only daughter, went to France to join him in his lonely life abroad. This was a comfort and help he greatly needed. His health had become impaired by the strain upon him in the last ten years. He needed her society. His country was now free, and though yet in many trials, he believed would maintain and justify itself before the world

Paris was in a stage of transition from what it had been to something yet to be determined. Philosophy and literature had become the rage of a class of brilliant and fashionable people. Religion was, in the main, scouted by them. The flippant ridicule of all things sacred, in which Voltaire was the brilliant and easy-virtued leader, had a great following. Old France was despised; new France, under philosophy and popular leadership, was hailed with hurrahs. Mr. Adams was in the midst of this society. They had only congratulations for him and his happy country. But he knew how little they understood his country, and the profound respect of its people for all that is sacred in religion, and severe and self-sacrificing in virtue. Through a casting down of religion and all the old notions of government, the French looked for a government of the people; while America looked for a republic through an elevation of religion, and a practical respect for whatever has been found useful in constitutional government.

With the French, freedom was a frenzy of the passions; with the Americans, it was a principle of the conscience. Not understanding it, the French gave the Americans great joy over their success, and thought they were about to copy the example; but they gave, at last, so much of their distraction to America, that they much endangered the liberties of the new nation.

### THE NEW COMMISSION.

On the thirtieth day of August, 1784, Mr. Adams, Dr. Franklin and Thomas Jefferson met in Paris to begin their work of forming treaties of amity and commerce with the countries of Europe. But no country came forward but Prussia, which had already a well-considered plan. In due time this was completed and signed.

On the twenty-fourth day of February, 1785, Congress elected Mr. Adams to the post of envoy to the court of St.

James; and accordingly in the May following he went to reside in England. This appointment to the court of George III. made necessary a presentation to the king in person. It was probably as profoundly cool a meeting as two strongly self-willed and high-positioned persons ever had. Each did his part as well as he could under the circumstances. But so solid was the king's hatred of the rebels whom he could not conquer, and so heartily did his government and people sympathize with him, that no satisfactory treaty of commerce could be made with them. At that time, in England, the prevailing opinion was that the United States was a union of sand and would soon fall apart. The first flush of enthusiasm in Europe over the American war, soon turned into a distrustful waiting to see what would be the result. All the ancient republics had been short-lived. European intelligence generally supposed this would be. The poverty of the American people after the war; the general distraction of society; their difficulty in paying foreign debts; the fierce opposition of many to Washington as president; the organization of Jacobin or democrat clubs; the tendency in many places to rebellion; the prevailing sympathy with revolutionary France; the sectional jealousies; the distrust of the national government in many minds, and the general irritability of the popular nerves, made European monarchists generally distrust the capacity of America to make successful the experiment of self-government; and in England this conviction amounted almost to a certainty, that in a very few years the conquering rebels would call upon their mother country to take them back. And there was much in America to awaken distrust of them. Why, then, should they make treaties with such a body of anarchy? Mr. Adams was full of anxiety, and often wished he was at home to assist in making general the principles he had put into the constitution of Massachusetts.

### ADAMS' PUBLICATIONS IN ENGLAND.

From his long residence in France, Mr. Adams became deeply convinced of the dangerous fallacies that were leading the French people into irreligion and anarchy, which fallacies he feared were misleading many Americans and endangering their attempt at self-government. So to rectify European and American mistakes together, as far as he could, he prepared and published, while in England, a work of three volumes, entitled, "A Defense of the Constitution of the United States of America against the Attack of M. Turgat." It gave an analysis of all ancient free governments, and summarized their histories and results in the main. It stated and enforced his ideas of the American system. The first volume was published and sent to this country in season to be republished, circulated and read, before the meeting of the convention which made the constitution under which the United States have had a century of unexampled prosperity. It was an antidote to the French ideas and influence which were then prevailing. It was a help to the members of the constitutional convention, to the state legislatures and people at large. Perhaps it was this great work published abroad, which made possible to America the inimitable constitution under which, in one hundred years, it has become the first nation in the world.

### MADE VICE-PRESIDENT.

Mr. Adams took leave of the Old World on the twentieth of April, 1788. He reached America in the midst of the excitement over the acceptance of the constitution. In the formation of the government under the constitution, he was elected the first vice-president to serve under Washington. The office usually is not very important, but at this beginning of the government it was important in settling usage and defining important principles; for no less than twenty times during the first administration did he cast the deciding vote in the senate, and sometimes explained the reasons for his vote, to set the principles involved clearly before the people.

### MADE SECOND PRESIDENT.

At the close of Washington's second term of office as president of the United States, John Adams was elected as his successor, with Thomas Jefferson as vice-president.

At this time, political partisanship had grown to be strong. The federalists were those who had promoted the adoption of the constitution; had favored a strong government fashioned after the English model, in which the legislative, judicial and executive departments held checks over each other, and all had their source in the people. Washington and Adams were of this party, though neither of them were strong partisans. Thus far it had been the dominant party, though the influence of French opinions and politics had grown much of late among the rural people, and the influence of Jefferson, the leader of democratic ideas, had come to be strong. The democratic party was rather organizing than organized. It was composed largely of those who sympathised with the lovers of freedom in France, and had an intense hatred of everything English. Its whole stock in trade was a splendid theory, and the enthusiasm of many of its devotees was very great. Mr. Adams was a leader in founding the government, in constitution-making, in putting great practical principles into working forms; but not a leader in organizing men into party activities.

At that time the greed for office had not grown much among the strong men of the new nation, and Mr. Adams found it difficult to fill the leading places in his government with first-class minds. He was obliged to take such as would serve, and in the end the weakness of some of his cabinet filled his way with difficulties. The country was divided chiefly over its foreign policies. The federalists, in the main, approved of Mr. Jay's treaty with England, which Washington had signed, and lost many friends by doing so, while the opposition party approved of a close sympathy with the new things in France and called the federalists tories. The strong French party in America led many unscrupulous French managers to attempt to carry America into the French war with England, and then their conduct was so false to treaty obligations as to come near causing a war between France and America. All preparations were made, even to raising an army and appointing its leading officers; but before declaring war, Mr. Adams thought some further effort should be made to avert it, and when the French leaders found what resentment they had stirred up in America, they were as anxious to allay it as were the friends of peace in America to have it allayed. It was an over-interest in French and English affairs which led different classes in America into foreign sympathies and entanglements, that caused the government much trouble and came very near wrecking the new ship of state.

It has since become pretty clear that Mr. Hamilton, the leader of the federalists, was in league with ambitious schemers in England and elsewhere to secure large portions of the Spanish possessions in America for the United States, and as an entering wedge to this scheme, a war with France would raise a large army which he would lead, and once raised he thought to make it necessary to keep it large and active in promoting his ambitious schemes of empire. A country without an army was not known in the world, and Hamilton believed an army was needed in America. It looks as though he would have been glad to play a Napoleonic part on the American continent.

To inaugurate his plan, Mr. Hamilton worked secretly, through Mr. Adams' cabinet and the friendship of Washington, neither of whom mistrusted his ambitious designs. But Mr. Adams' aversion to war, only as a last resort, and his personal resolution against his cabinet, to make still further overtures to France, consumed time for France to see some of her mistakes and to make clear a way of adjustment. So war with France was averted; Hamilton's schemes of an empire in the Spanish possessions were frustrated, and the young American ship of state was tided over the most dangerous shoals it has yet encountered.

It was, perhaps, some knowledge of these growing "foreign entanglements" which led Washington in his farewell address to solemnly warn his countrymen against them, and to charge them to be loyal to the development of their own affairs. A tolerably full account of these troublous times and their intrigues and dangers, is to be found in "The Life and Works of John Adams," by Charles Francis Adams. A knowledge of these things is necessary to an understanding of the political issues of that time, and the strong parties that proceeded therefrom.

In due course of time Mr. Adams' intelligent and faithful administration came to its close. As it is looked to now, his part in it is regarded as one of great purity and integrity. The policies and schemes of France and England had been forced upon this country. The people had not learned that they should be wholly separate from foreign entanglements. Some individuals in Mr. Adams' party schemed with parties abroad, which brought him and his party into great and undeserved odium. The truth of this scheming was then only partially understood, and the bitterness engendered by it was all the greater on this account.

### RETIREMENT TO BRAINTREE.

On the fourth of March, 1801, Thomas Jefferson was inaugurated as Mr. Adams' successor, with Aaron Burr as vice-president. Mr. Adams retired at once from the scene, not waiting even for the ceremonies of inauguration. He was sensitive and passionate to a high degree, even dictatorial and absolute when aroused. He had been level-headed and just-minded through all the differences, and had actually saved his country from war, and perhaps from an early death, and yet was rewarded for it by seeing his most bitter opponent, and the man that had done most to bring in foreign ideas, raised to his place. But far wiser would it have been for him to have mastered his resentment and gone calmly from what he thought the scene of his defeat. In reality he was victor. Posterity has done him justice. He now stands as more nearly the peer of Washington than any other of the great revolutionary patriots. He was greatest of all as a constitutional lawyer and statesman. His purity and integrity were equal to Washington's, but he lacked the fine poise, the discretion, the quick insight into men and occasions, the ability to put himself aside and see as an outsider, and act accordingly. He lacked the reserve of speech, the prevailing modesty and overmastering serenity which did so much for the great father of his country. He was too out-spoken, self-asserting, and too separate from common men, and so was never popular—was always unfortunate with the masses.

After the presidency, he retired to his farm and followed that early inclination which wanted to be a farmer.

He at once set about his private and domestic affairs, and spent the remainder of his life in retirement from public interests. Twenty-six years he had spent in the heart of his country's affairs, after Washington, the most useful man in founding our institutions. This great country owes much to the genius of his great mind in harmonizing and adjusting the principles and powers put into it. It has worked a hundred years with but little change, and may work on as long as its people shall be loyal, intelligent and virtuous.

In his retirement, Mr. Adams read extensively—more extensively than ever before. He restudied the great questions of religion, and finally settled nearly upon the general ideas of the unitarian theology, and lived and died in great peace of mind touching those matters.

After years of estrangement, through mutual friends, ne came into amicable relations with Mr. Jefferson. With the decline of that rancorous party spirit that was so savage at the close of his administration, returning friendship for him showed itself in many ways, and his, at first, embittered life in retirement, became cheerful and beautiful. His son, John Quincy, came into public notice as a rising man of his time, and he felt a renewed interest in the affairs of government, and the general interests of the public.

On the twenty-eighth of October, 1818, his wife died in the eighty-third year of his age. This cast a deep shadow over his life. They had lived in great peace, mutual helpers to one another.

When about eighty-five years old he wrote a series of letters to Judge Tudor, detailing with great definiteness the early movement of the people of Massachusetts in defense of their rights — giving in minute detail the parts enacted by Otis, Hawley and Samuel Adams. This series of letters has been the source from which nearly all we now know of those events, was drawn.

On the fifteenth day of November, 1815, he was elected by Braintree to the state convention called to amend the constitution on the creation of the district of Maine into a separate state; and so he helped amend the constitution he assisted in making forty years before. In this convention he received great testimonials of respect. It was a fitting close of a great public career. His declining years grew more and more tranquil. He enjoyed the rising recognition of his son's worth, and lived to see him elected president of the government he had done so much to found. He died on the fourth of July, 1826, just fifty years after the declaration of independence. His last words were, "Thomas Jefferson still survives." But it was soon learned that Jefferson had died an hour before. So these great compatriots were called home almost together, just when the nation was rejoicing in the first semi-centennial of its existence.

## The Graves of the Adamses.

There is something touching in the contemplation of the graves of two presidents, father and son, who sleep side by side, with their companions, in the town where they were born and which always held their homes, and under the church built by the congregation with which they worshiped. So sleep the two Adamses. At the death of John Adams in 1826, his son, then president, secured from the trustees of the new church about to be built, a deed to "a portion of soil in the cellar, situated under the porch, and containing fourteen feet in length and fourteen feet in breadth," with the privilege of affixing tablets with obituary inscriptions, in the walls of the church. In this crypt was deposited, in 1828, the bodies of John and Abigail Adams; and in 1848, those of John Quincy Adams and his wife. The tomb is in the front part of the cellar and is made of large blocks of granite, slightly faced. A granite slab, seven feet by three, hung on strong iron hinges, and fastened with clasp and padlock, is the door. The bodies are inclosed in leaden caskets, placed in stone coffins, each hewn from a single block of granite.

In the church above, at the right of the pulpit, as seen from the pews, is the memorial tablet of marble, seven feet by four, surmounted by a life-size bust from Horatio Greenough. Below the bust is the Latin line:

*Libertatem, Amicitiam, Fidem, Retinebus.*

Above the tablet are the words: *Thy will be done.* The inscription upon the tablet is in two columns; the first is as follows:

D. O. M.

Beneath these walls

Are deposited the mortal remains of

**John Adams,**

Son of John and Susanna (Boylston) Adams,

Second President of the United States:

Born 19–30, October, 1735.

On the Fourth of July, 1776,

He pledged his Life, Fortune and Sacred Honor

To the

INDEPENDENCE OF HIS COUNTRY.

On the Third of September, 1783,

He affixed his seal to the definitive treaty with Great Britain,

Which acknowledged that independence,

And consummated the redemption of his pledge.

On the Fourth of July, 1826,

He was summond

To the Independence of Immortality,

And to the

JUDGMENT OF HIS GOD.

This House will bear witness to his piety;

This Town, his birthplace, to his munificence;

History to his patriotism;

Posterity to the depth and compass of his mind.

ENGRAVED EXPRESSLY FOR WEAVERS' LIVES AND GRAVES OF OUR PRESIDENTS

## CHAPTER IV.

## THOMAS JEFFERSON.

### THIRD PRESIDENT OF THE UNITED STATES.

#### HIS ANCESTRY.

THE common maxim, that "blood will tell," is as well enforced in the case of Thomas Jefferson as of George Washington, or any other conspicuous character. Though it must never be forgotten that some other things "will tell," also. Work will tell; virtue will tell; persistent effort will tell; manhood, worth, courage will tell; all good qualities have a telling force. Not all good blood tells for great character. In families of the best blood, only a few become conspicuous. Though good blood is a good thing, there are better things — strong mind ; noble will; virtuous heart ; resolute high-mindedness.

The ancestors of Thomas Jefferson, on his father's side, were of good Welsh stock, occupying good places in society in the mother country, and exhibiting strong force of character and rightness of purpose. They did not deteriorate in their change of home. The forest did not hurt them; the new experiences rather developed their power.

Virginia was begun as a settlement as early as 1607, thirteen years before the Mayflower reached Plymouth Rock. The ancestors of Jefferson were some of the early comers. They took up large landed estates, and became thrifty and influential.

Peter Jefferson, the father of Thomas, was born February

29, 1708. His early education was neglected, but he made it up as well as he could, by much reading and intelligent observation. He learned surveying, and did much good service in that line in the early days of Virginia. He was the intimate friend of William Randolph, of Tuckahoe, and the preferred suitor for the hand of the oldest daughter of Isham Randolph. Three years before he was married he "patented," as it was called, a thousand acres of land on the James river, which included the tract and hill since called Monticello, and went about preparing for a home. He was married to Jane Randolph in 1738. The Randolphs were English people of opulence and high standing. They were educated and influential; had large landed estates; kept up old English customs prevalent among the gentry, and did what they could to renew old England in America. It was their expectation to see great estates and rich scenes of opulence and taste all over the rich Virginia lands.

Peter Jefferson was a strong, large, independent, honest and warm-hearted man. He had cultivated a strong taste for literature, and read many of the old poets with hearty appreciation.

Thomas Jefferson, the subject of this sketch, was born April 2, 1743, and was the third child, Jane and Mary being older. Six other children constituted the family group.

### HIS EDUCATION.

At five years old he was sent to an English school, in which he learned the rudiments of an education. An evidence of an early activity of his mind is given, of his remembering when two years old of being handed up on a pillow to a slave and being carried on horseback when the family moved to Tuckahoe for a time. A year or two later he remembered, when his dinner was delayed, of going out and repeating the Lord's prayer, in the hope of sooner getting his dinner. Few memories go back even to the third year.

At nine years old, on the return of the family to Shadwell, their home, he was placed in the school of Mr. Douglas, a Scotch clergyman, who taught him in Latin, Greek and French. While here his father died, leaving him at fourteen years of age to the sole care of his mother. This is another instance of a widow's son rising to greatness and worth, by the inspiration and help of a mother's wisdom and love. It is recorded of her that she was a beautiful and accomplished woman; cheerful, with a fund of humor and fond of writing letters. Well educated as she was for her time, with these things related of her, it is evident that the literary talent was in her, though developed only in her friendly letters. As both father and mother gave evidence of literary taste, and both belonged to strong families, and the mother especially to one of the most intellectual and vigorous families in the colony, it is clear that on grounds of heredity it would be reasonable to expect good literary abilities in their children. Thomas showed a combination of the physical and intellectual qualities of both parents. His father was large and muscular; his mother slender and fine-fibered. He was tall, slender, agile and closely made. He had his father's strength and his mother's fiber and endurance. From the accounts given of the two, Thomas was a genuine combination of the leading qualities of both.

Added to this favorable heredity bias toward literary pursuits, there was the early training in language, having begun Latin, Greek and French as early as nine years of age. To his susceptible and imaginative nature, this early training in language must have given a strong bent toward a close observation of the elegance and finish and force of complete forms of speech, and an appreciation of the thought couched in what he read. Books early became his boon companions. Their thoughts became his thoughts. The humor, piquancy, liveliness of his mother, must have acted on the strong talent received from both parents, as yeast in bread, to give it ferment, stir and uplift. He drew nourishment from her brain as well as breast. Brainy forces went into his original make-up, and brainy influences were about him from the beginning.

Still more: when his father died, he left the request that Thomas should be sent to college, so that from that time the boy's mind began to shape itself to this course, and familiarize itself with its coming career.

With his strong and delicate nature, and the early influences that educated him, it is easy to see that he must grow up to be a sort of natural harp through which the winds of a revolutionary period would blow to make strong and stirring music. He was born to be a force in the world.

His father was a surveyor, and traversed all the valleys and hills of that fine country on foot. He became a footman of the woods, and learned to love their wild retreats. He had, too, the hunter's eye and taste, and led his son to find health and delight in the woods and on the mountains. This gave him an intimate acquaintance with nature, and filled his mind with figures and forces which much enriched his literary and intellectual work in after years.

The loss of his father, doubtless, deeply impressed his young mind, and the intimacy with his mother after he was thrown wholly upon her for counsel and guidance, further deepened his thoughtfulness, and ripened and enriched his character. With such a constitution, the circumstances which surrounded his early life did much to educate and develop him.

In 1760 he entered William and Mary college at Williamsburg. This town was then the capital of the colony, the seat of learning, and the gathering place of the dignity, learning, and worth of Virginia. It gave him an opportunity to be for awhile in this center of the leading men of the times in this oldest English colony in America and to form the acquaintance of some of them. The educating influence of great men on susceptible and ambitious youth, is very great.

On his way to Williamsburg he spent a few days at the residence of Colonel Nathan Dandridge, and made the acquaintance of Patrick Henry, then a young man who had failed as a merchant and was idling away his time in the vicinity of his home in the frolics and dances of the young people, and in fishing, hunting and story telling. "His passion," said Mr. Jefferson of him afterward, "was fiddling, dancing and pleasantry." Jefferson was fond of the violin, the dance, and every social pleasantry. Now, at seventeen, the quaint, piquant, brilliant, half-philosopher, half vagrant young man Henry, had many charms for him. They were much unlike, but there were deep points of similarity, which made them friends for life. Not many months afterward, Mr. Henry called on Jefferson and informed him that he had studied law, and was at the capital to obtain a license to practice, indicating the quickness with which great things were done in those early days.

Jefferson was admitted to an advanced class in college and continued there two years. Williamsburg had many attractions for him the first year which interfered somewhat with his study; but the second year he gave himself to unremitting work, studying fifteen hours a day and making rapid progress.

As a student he was about equally fond of mathematics and the classics, both of which branches of learning he continued to pursue, more or less, through life. He became a good Latin and Greek scholar, and read many ancient works in these ancient languages. He became familiar with written French; learned something of Anglo-Saxon, Spanish and German. His early literary inclinations became more and more established, till early in his life he became a general scholar for his times, and a devoted friend of books as well as men.

His mathematical professor in college was Doctor Samuel Small, who soon conceived a great interest in young Jefferson, and not only instructed him with great care, but made him a personal friend and companion, and did much to shape his life. Indeed, Mr. Jefferson said, late in life, that the instruction and intercourse of Doctor Small "probably fixed the destinies of his life."

In his youth he was away from home and among strangers, with none to guard or counsel him, and late in life he wrote of of this to a young relative similarly situated: "I had the good fortune to become acquainted very early with some characters of very high standing, and to feel the incessant wish that I could ever become what they were. Under temptations and difficulties, I would ask myself: What would Doctor Small, Mr. Wythe or Peyton Randolph do in this situation? What course in it will insure me their approbation? I am certain that this mode of deciding on my conduct, tended more to correctness than any reasoning powers I possessed. Knowing the even and dignified line they pursued, I could never doubt for a moment which of two courses would be in character for them." \* \* \* "Be assured, my young friend, that these little returns into ourselves, this self-catechising habit, is not trifling nor useless, but leads to the prudent selection and steady pursuit of what is right."

Here is a hint at the shaping influences of his early life; they came from men whom he knew to respect and honor, from teachers whom he loved, from characters whose course of life had the approval of the good and true. In the same letter, he says: "I was often thrown into the society of horse-racers, card-players, fox-hunters, scientific and professional men, and of dignified men; and many a time have I asked myself, in the enthusiastic moment of the death of a fox, the victory of a favorite horse, the issue of a question eloquently argued at the bar, or in the great council of the nation: Well, which of these kinds of reputation shall I prefer? That of a horse-jockey, a fox-hunter, an orator, or the honest advocate of my country's rights?" Here was the young man settling his own destiny, in the midst of all sorts of characters which he might choose for models. He loved the fleet horse, the chase, the social pleasantry? He was fond of physical sports, the dance, the wild-wood ramble. He saw men before him giving their lives to such things. Should he do likewise? He loved books also, and saw the glory of a noble life, and men about him who were examples of right living and manly dignity. Should he follow them? When a young man seriously debated such questions in his mind, could there be much doubt as to which way he would decide to go?

This was the formative period of his character. He had been well reared and instructed in his home and church, which was the church of England; he was warm-hearted, enthusiastic, social, imaginative; he was healthy, strong, buoyant in spirit; now he had met the world in all its characters, and the question had come to him: With what class shall I identify myself?

After leaving college, through the aid of Dr. Small he entered the law office of George Wythe, and became the acquaintance and friend of Governor Fauquier, one of the ablest men of that time. He mentions in his memoir, that he and Wythe and Doctor Small often dined with the governor, forming a social quartette, and that "to these habitual conversations he owed much instruction." It seems clear that to good books and good men, Jefferson was much indebted. They did much to make him. Yet he had the wisdom to choose to be educated and directed by them.

Governor Fauquier made him a companion of all hours; they practiced on musical instruments together and talked on gay and serious subjects as though equals,—one the acknowledged great man and gentleman of the state, the other a youth of twenty-one. This intimacy indicates an early developement of talent and manly power, and a personal magnetism above his years, in young Jefferson.

George Wythe was one of the most erudite and accomplished lawyers of his day, and young Jefferson felt himself happy in enjoying his instruction and companionship. Jefferson's extensive reading of the best authors; his fine manners, and cheerful, social enthusiasm, won such friends for him. And there can be no doubt but the bright promise of his coming career was reflected to these men, in his unusual wisdom and brilliancy.

To the study of law he gave five years. If his college course was short, his law course was long, and he made it a thorough study. The summers he spent at Shadwell, his home, and the winters at Williamsburg; and at both places kept up his rigid college habits of studying fifteen hours a day. No native talents, no brilliancy of mind or favoring opportunity, made him the man he came to be without hard study. Till he was twenty-four he plied the work of his education with diligence and plodding fidelity.

### PERSONAL APPEARANCE.

He was tall and slender in comparison, standing six feet two inches in height. His face, though angular and far from beautiful, beamed with intelligence, with benevolence, and with the cheerful vivacity of a happy, hopeful spirit. His complexion was ruddy and fair; his hair was chestnut, of a reddish tinge, fine and soft; his eyes of a hazel gray. He was lithe, active, graceful. His manners were simple and cordial. In conversation he was peculiarly agreeable, so much so, that in later years his enemies attributed to him a seductive influence through his art and charm of speech. Possessing the accomplishments, he avoided the vices of the young Virginia gentry of the day. He did not gamble; or drink; or use tobacco; or swear. He had an aversion to strong drink, and was temperate at the table. With frankness, heartiness, humane sympathies and sanguine hopefulness, he had strong personal influence over those who came near him. This was Thomas Jefferson at twenty-four, when he entered upon the practice of law.

### MR. JEFFERSON A LAWYER.

In 1767, Mr. Jefferson was admitted to the practice of law at the bar of his native state. He was well prepared for his profession and met with success at once. His excellent connection with the good families of Virginia, his inherited fortune and his good personal bearing, gave him his business. His register of cases shows sixty-eight for 1767; one hundred and fifteen for 1768; one hundred and ninety-eight for 1769; one hundred and twenty-one for 1770; one hundred and thirty-seven for 1771; one hundred and fifty-four for 1772; one hundred and twenty-seven for 1773; twenty-nine for 1774. It is probable that the troublesome times affected all business. These were his cases in the general court. He had much other legal business, according to the records left in his own writing. He had a strong legal mind which was recognized at once. While in the study and practice of law he made a collection of most of the early statutes of Virginia, and preserved them for later uses.

It was a habit of his to classify his knowledge, his business, and multitudes of little matters that most men would not think worth the time of writing. His account books, keeping the items for different articles separately, as for meat, bread, etc.;

his expenses, the number of persons in his family, the details of all his business — agricultural, legal, domestic — show a mind wonderfully given to a close observation of little things. He left an account carefully arranged and kept, of the earliest and latest appearance in the Washington market of thirty-seven different kinds of vegetables, during the whole eight years of his presidency. His garden book, farming book, weather record, expense accounts, notes on natural history, on Virginia, on reading, on legal study, and on almost everything that passed before him, show a remarkable interest in details. Had it not been for a fire which consumed his library and many of his private records, it is supposed he would have left almost his whole life in minute details. This not only indicates close powers of observation, but readiness to labor industriously to keep such extended accounts.

## MR. JEFFERSON A LEGISLATOR.

In 1769, Mr. Jefferson was elected a member of the House of Burgesses. Lord Botetourt had now become governor. He opened the House with the customary address. Mr. Jefferson, at the request of some of the older members, drew the responding resolutions.

The House passed spirited resolutions on the action of Parliament in relation to Massachusetts. It reasserted the exclusive right of taxation in the colonies, their right to petition for a redress of grievances, and to procure the concurrence of the other colonies therein. The House also remonstrated against the proposition in Parliament to transport to England for trial persons in the colonies charged with treason.

The governor, on hearing what the House had done, without waiting for official statements, dissolved the assembly. The following day the members met at the Apollo, the large hall of the Raleigh tavern, and entered into an association, pledging themselves during the continuance of the act for raising revenue in America, not to import or purchase or use British merchandise; and they recommended their constituents to join them in this pledge.

Mr. Jefferson was one of the largest slave owners in Virginia, yet among the earliest movements he made was a proposition for the gradual emancipation of the slaves, but it was voted down by a strong majority. His humanity and political wisdom were manifest in this proposition. He had many sympathizers in Virginia at that time, in his disbelief in slavery. Washington was one of them. From that time on this began to be a subject of serious thought with many just minds.

### JEFFERSON NOT A SPEAKER.

Though a fluent, graceful conversationalist, and believed by his political enemies, later in life, to have almost seductive charms in this way, and though a most accomplished and vigorous writer, he yet was not a public speaker. It is said that some defect in his vocal organs made his throat dry and husky after a little while, so that his speaking became painful to him as well as to those who heard him.

It is not often that the talent for speaking and writing is found in any marked degree in the same individual. They are separate talents, and for their marked expression require very different powers. Writing is a work of seclusion, done with deliberation, care, precision, with the mind bent upon accuracy, detail, elegance, finish, completeness. It depends solely on the power, furnishing and taste of the writer. He writes out of himself. His inspiration is in his theme and his own soul. If he is full of and on fire with his subject, he writes to instruct, warn and captivate his reader.

Speaking is a public act, in which the occasion, the audience, the voice, the face, the whole physical man, enters in to form a part of the moving power. Often passion commands the hour, and summoning all the powers to its service, moves upon its point of attack with a sort of dashing, stunning, overwhelming force.

Mr. Jefferson was the careful student, the close, painstaking thinker, who, from wide observation of facts, drew his conclusions and arranged them into orderly systems.

Had his voice been all right, it is not likely he would have spoken with great power. His mind was organized to express itself with the pen rather than with the tongue. And had his mind been formed for the orator, it is altogether likely that his voice would have responded loyally, and his parched throat would have been oiled and active in the service of his mind.

No contrast between the speaker and writer was ever more sharply drawn than between Mr. Jefferson and his friend, Patrick Henry.

### LOSS BY FIRE.

On the first of February, 1770, the family mansion at Shadwell, "with every paper he had in the world and almost every book," and all his father's papers and books, was consumed by fire. Had it been their cost-value in money, he said, "it would not have cost me a sigh."

Later in life he was wont to have his facetious story over this fire, as the news was brought to him by one of his negroes.

"But, were none of my books saved?" he asked. "No, massa," was the doleful reply; "but," with a quick brightening face, he said, "*we saved de fiddle.*"

The fiddle was dear to Mr. Jefferson, not only because he loved its music, but because it was intimately associated with his sister Jane, the eldest of the family who had died some five years before, at about twenty-five years of age. He regarded her as a person of a very superior mind and of great excellence of character. She was almost his constant companion in the later years of her life. She shared much of his study and reading, held similar opinions and had kindred sentiments. She was devout and loved her church, the church of England in which they were brought up, and was an excellent singer. He was a good bass singer, and entered heartily into much of the music of his church, which he believed was the best in the world. This music they sang much together accompanied with his violin. It was their practice to go often into some grove, or quiet natural retreat, and sing their favorite pieces, enjoy together the natural scenery, and what was more to them, enjoy each other's society. This violin saved from the fire, was a perpetual reminder of his sister and those halcyon seasons of sacred affection and communion.

The year before the loss of the old family mansion, Mr. Jefferson had begun to build a residence for himself on Monticello, a portion or wing of what was afterward his famous house. Into that a part of the family went, and the rest into the overseer's house.

## MARRIAGE.

New Year's day, 1772, was made memorable to Thomas Jefferson and Mrs. Martha Skelton, by their marriage. She was the youthful widow of Bathurst Skelton, Esq., and daughter of John Wayles, a lawyer of eminence in his time. She is represented by the annalists of the time as beautiful, accomplished and sensible; as being a fine singer, and playing skillfully on the spinet and harpsichord; as joining her voice with Jefferson's and her instruments with his violin to produce the music in which their souls flowed together; as having many suitors and great wealth, bringing to him a fortune fully equal to his own. On the day of their marriage there was a snow storm which thickened as they went, so that the last eight miles of their journey had to be made on horse-back, after dark and alone. They reached Monticello through two feet of snow, after the servants were all abed and the house cold, to find no supper, no welcome, no light or fire, and only such cheer as their young hearts could produce. But chilly and forbidding as was the beginning of their wedded life, they turned it all into the joy of triumph and made a world for each other that was full of sunshine and success. Such is the mystery of young love.

Their united fortunes made them wealthy. His estate was five thousand acres and hers forty thousand acres; but hers was so encumbered with debts that he had to sell much of it to own it clear. He had forty-two slaves and she one hundred and thirty-five. He had an income, before his marriage, of five thousand dollars a year. His income after was uncertain till he had cleared her estate of its indebtedness. This condition of his affairs for a few years, gave opportunity for his political enemies to make capital against him as a bad financier. He seems to have been a sagacious business man; orderly in his habits; prompt and exact in his dealings; careful in expenditures, yet generous according to his circumstances; keeping always exact records of all his affairs to the smallest details.

It is clear to see from the style of life in which he and his associates were reared, that colonial Virginia, and that whole sections of America, was looked to from England as a new and ample field for the extension of the great English estates; for the broadening and enriching of the English aristocracy; for an increased support of the English crown, and a safe depository of English power. Mr. Jefferson's debts to be paid were chiefly in England; his business was largely with England; and so was that of all the great southern estates. The people got their styles of life from England. Society in Virginia was a transcript of society in England.

Under these circumstances, it was not to be expected that democracy would spring up in Virginia; that popular government would find its stout advocates in the House of Burgesses and on the great estates of the Old Dominion; that the representatives of the old and wealthy families of England settled in America would dissent from the English view of government, and become the enthusiastic leaders of a republican order of society. But so it turned out. The newness and freedom of American life gave a new order of manhood; produced new thinkers and actors; developed a new philosophy of society and humanity, and led American intelligence and justice to see the defects in the English society and administration of government. And these men of the largest calibre, like Washington and Jefferson, though inheriting most from England, were among the first to see the English faults.

Among the things they first deprecated in their new society was human slavery. They felt its injustice and foresaw its direful evils, and they sought its gradual abolition, but were overruled. Had Jefferson's proposition in the House of Burgesses to that effect been accepted, and slavery in Virginia gone out as

it did in New York and New England, the United States would
have been double gainers by their independence; the great
hindering evils of slavery would have been avoided; the sectionalism of our experience would not have been known; and the
great civil war and its terrific loss of property, energy and life,
would not have been. Jefferson was called the philosopher in
his day; and the worth of his philosophy is far clearer now than
it was to most people then.

He is a proof that men do sometimes rise above their circumstances; that humanity may grow to be a powerful and con-
trolling sentiment in the midst of slavery; that democracy may
have a vigorous development in the midst of aristocratic
surroundings.

### THE APPROACHING CONFLICT.

The House of Burgesses met in the spring of 1773. An event
had just occurred to arouse such alert souls as Jefferson's to a
sense of danger to come. The Gasper, a British vessel, stationed in Narraganset bay to enforce the obnoxious revenue laws,
had been decoyed aground, and burned. Parliament immediately passed an act "for the better securing of His Majesty's
ships, docks, etc.," which made punishable with death the least
harm done to anything pertaining to the British marine service,
and the transportation for trial of any one accused of such
harm. Against such transportation Jefferson had offered a
resolution in 1769. Now he joined with Patrick Henry, the
Lees and Mr. Carr, his brother-in-law, to offer a series of resolutions against the injustice of such transportation, and against
all laws "tending to deprive the colonies of their ancient, legal
and constitutional rights," and in favor of seeking the earliest
information of what parliament should do, and of appointing a
committee of correspondence with the other colonies, to act in
unison in opposition to British aggression, and especially
instructing the committee of correspondence "to inform themselves particularly of the principles and authority on which was
constituted a court of inquiry, said to have been lately held in
Rhode Island, with powers to transport persons accused of

offenses committed in America to places beyond the seas to be tried." The resolutions are supposed to have been drafted by Mr. Jefferson, offered in a very telling speech by Mr. Carr, and adopted without a dissenting vote by the House. This was one of the first movements for a committee of consultation from all the colonies. It was one of the seeds which ripened into a Colonial Congress.

The governor immediately dissolved the House. But the committee met the next day and prepared a circular to the colonies containing a copy of the resolutions, with a request that they might be laid before their assemblies, and asking them to appoint "some person or persons of their respective bodies to communicate from time to time with the Virginia committee."

Mr. Jefferson is said to have believed that this was the germ of colonial union. But whether it was or not, it is proof of a kindredness of sentiment, and a preparedness for union and action in Virginia and Massachusetts. And this sentiment soon reached all the colonies.

During the spring session of the Burgesses in 1774, the news of the Boston port bill reached Virginia. Mr. Jefferson, believing that something startling should be done to arouse the people to a sense of the danger to their liberties, gathered about him a few kindred spirits in consultation. They agreed upon a resolution appointing a day of fasting and prayer. And as the Boston port bill was to go into operation the first of June, they fixed upon that day for a public fast day. They consulted with some of the older and more religious members, and got such a good understanding that it was agreed to without a dissenting vote. So on the day that the port of Boston was blockaded by British assumption of power, the people of Virginia were praying for the people of Boston and the preservation of their liberties. Mr. Jefferson said: "If the pulse of the people beat calmly under such an experiment by the new and until now unheard of executive power of the British Parliament, another and another will be tried, till the measure of despotism be filled up."

The governor dissolved the assembly the next day after the

passage of this resolution. And the next day the members met at the Apollo hall and talked freely of English tyranny and what should be done about it; and they talked of a congress of the colonies for mutual consultation. They further agreed that a convention should be held at Williamsburg, August 1, to learn the result of the proposed colonial congress, and if such a congress shall be held, to appoint delegates to it. Here was the spirit and intelligence of Massachusetts in the Old Dominion.

When the members of the assembly returned to their homes they invited the clergy to address the people in all their churches on fast day; and they generally did so, awakening a profound interest. Mr. Jefferson said: "The effect of the day through the whole colony was like a shock of electricity, arousing every man and placing him erect and solidly on his center."

The freeholders in all the counties held meetings to appoint delegates to the coming convention and express their views in resolutions.

Mr. Jefferson, on account of sickness, was unable to attend the August convention, but sent in "a summary view" of the situation in a long document, which Edmund Burke, in England, styled "A Summary View of the Rights of British America." It contained the most of the statements afterward put into the Declaration of Independence, only more radically stated; and denied that the British crown had any rights on American soil, because the people of America, without the king's help, have made it what it is. It was a document probably more radical than anything Otis, Adams, or Henry had ever said. In it, he said: "The God who gave us life, gave us liberty at the same time; the hand of force may destroy, but cannot disjoin them."

The Colonial Congress met in Philadelphia on the fourth of September. Peyton Randolph, one of Virginia's most accomplished and honored citizens, was made its president.

In the mean time nearly all the counties of Virginia organized committees of safety. On the twentieth of March, 1775, a second Virginia convention was held at Richmond. Mr. Jefferson was a member from his county. This was one of the most memorable assemblies ever held on this continent. It had many of Virginia's best men, such as Richard H. Lee, Pendleton, Bland, Wythe, Nicholas, Harrison, Mason, Page, Henry, Jefferson. It was composed of the conservatives and radicals. The old men of wealth and dignity were there, and the young men who were for forward movements. The old men spoke softly of England, praised the British constitution, and talked in conciliatory words, which were as "wormwood and gall" to Patrick Henry, who rose and moved that "the colony be immediately put in a state of defense, and that * * * be a committee to prepare a plan for embodying, arming and disciplining such a number of men as may be sufficient for that purpose." This startling proposition was most painful to the old conservative members. It sounded like rebellion. The young members, Lee, Jefferson, Mason, Page, were quick in its support. It was on this occasion that Patrick Henry made the flaming speech which has immortalized him. It was in support of his resolution. He said, "war is inevitable; we must fight." The story of that speech has thrilled Americans for a hundred years. Wirt, in his life of Henry, has given a graphic picture of the scene and the speech. Many eye-and-ear witnesses have described it. Mr. Randall, in his life of Jefferson, gives this account as related to him by an old Baptist clergyman who heard it. "Henry rose with an unearthly fire burning in his eye. He commenced somewhat calmly — but the smothered excitement began more and more to play upon his features and thrill in the tones of his voice. The tendons of his neck stood out white and rigid 'like whipcord.' His voice rose louder and louder,—until the walls of the building and all within them, seemed to shake and rock in its tremendous vibrations. Finally his pale face and glaring eye became terrible to look upon. Men leaned forward in their seats, with their heads strained forward, their faces pale and their eyes glaring like the speaker's. His last exclamation, 'Give me liberty or give me death,' was like the shout of a leader which turns back the rout of battle!"

The old clergyman said when Mr. Henry sat down, "he (the auditor) 'felt *sick* with excitement.' Every eye gazed entranced on Henry. It seemed as if a word from him would have led to any wild explosion of violence. Men looked beside themselves." Wirt in his account of it, says: "Richard H. Lee arose and supported Mr. Henry with his usual spirit and elegance. But his melody was lost amid the agitations of that ocean which the master spirit of the storm had lifted upon high. That supernatural voice still sounded in their ears and shivered along their arteries. They heard in every pause the cry of liberty or death. They became impatient of speech. Their souls were on fire for action."

Mr. Henry's resolution for arming the colony was passed by a decided majority; and he, George Washington and Thomas Jefferson were put on the committee, with others, to carry out its provisions. The committee reported a plan on the twenty-fifth of March, and the convention accepted it.

The convention chose Mr. Jefferson to fill the place of Peyton Randolph in the next Colonial Congress.

On the night of the twentieth of April, 1775, a British armed vessel lying in the James river, by order of Governor Dunmore, entered Williamsburg and carried off all the powder in the magazine. This awakened much feeling. It was done two days after the battle of Lexington, the news of which soon came, to verify Henry's speech and to call many Virginians to arms.

On the first of June, the House of Burgesses was convened to consider Lord North's "conciliatory proposition." Peyton Randolph returned from the Colonial Congress to preside, and Mr. Jefferson had been elected to supply his place; but Mr. Randolph was anxious that Mr. Jefferson should draft a reply to Lord North. This reply rings with the spirit of all Mr. Jefferson's great state papers of that great period.

The eleventh of June, 1775, Mr. Jefferson took his seat in Congress. He was greeted with great cordiality. He was then but little past thirty-two years of age. His fame as a writer had gone before him. His "Summary of the Rights of British America," the "Albemarle Resolutions," and other convention papers, had stirred the whole country; and now he brought with him his reply to Lord North, more full than anything he had written. All the most advanced members received him with open arms. John Adams said of him: "Mr. Jefferson had the reputation of a masterly pen"; and again, "he brought with him a reputation for literature, science, and a happy talent for composition." Of him, as a member, Mr. Adams says: "Though a silent member in Congress, he was so prompt, frank, explicit, and decisive upon committees and in conversation—not even Samuel Adams was more so—that he soon seized upon my heart."

Five days after Mr. Jefferson took his seat, he was appointed on a committee to draft a declaration of the causes of taking up arms. He made a draft, but it was too radical to please John Dickinson, also a member of the committee. So Mr. Dickinson recast it, making it new with the exception of the last four paragraphs. Mr. Jefferson was one of the most advanced thinkers and actors, while Mr. Dickinson was very conservative; and yet they were intimate friends to the close of their lives.

Lord North's "conciliatory proposition" came before Congress for its answer. A committee was appointed to draft an answer July 22. Benjamin Franklin, Thomas Jefferson, John Adams and Richard H. Lee were made that committee. The committee chose Jefferson to draft the answer. It constitutes another of his great state papers, and was the last great statement of the differences between America and England by way of conciliation. Up to this time, and after, all the great leaders, the Adamses, Jay, Washington, Jefferson, desired to remain in union with England. They craved for England a great empire, and wanted to be a part of that empire. They saw, far better than English statesmen, the possibilities of that empire, and yielded this dream of British greatness, only from stern necessity. They regarded themselves as forced to an unnatural and cruel divorce.

On the ninth of November, 1775, a letter was received in Congress from Richard Penn and Arthur Lee, who had carried the second petition to the king, that "no answer would be given to it." This made the prospect of conciliation most dark. From this time the leaders were compelled to face the probability of a final separation. The dream of a great British empire must vanish. Little by little they began to talk about the almost certain separation.

The king opened the next Parliament with bitter denunciation of the colonists as rebels, and determinatoin to punish them into submission. News of this reached America in the spring of 1776. From this time it became a question of whether the colonists could stand more punishing than the irate mother could give.

About this time Paine's "Common Sense" was published, and did much to convince many that separation and war for independence were absolute necessities. Public sentiment began to set strongly in this direction. Congress kept up with public sentiment.

On the tenth of May, John Adams offered, and on the fifteenth Congress passed, a resolution advising all the colonies to form governments for themselves. On the eleventh of June, 1776, congress resolved to appoint a committee of five to prepare a declaration of independence. Thomas Jefferson, John Adams, Benjamin Franklin, Roger Sherman and Robert R. Livingston were that committee, chosen by ballot. John Adams says Jefferson had one more vote than any of the rest, and on that account, he thought, he was made chairman of the committee.

Mr. Jefferson, at the instance of the committee, and, as Adams suggests, because he was the best writer, and probably because he had written several papers covering the general subject; and, still further, because he was connected with no clique, wrote the declaration. Dr. Franklin and Mr. Adams made a few verbal changes; and it was read in Congress June 28. July 2, it was taken up for discussion, and two days were spent over it, according to Randall, Jefferson's biographer. The censure of the people of England and the rebuke of slavery were taken from it; and it was passed on the evening of July 4. Mr. Bancroft says the vote on it was taken July 2. At any rate, July 4 has been fixed upon as the day of its passage.

On the day of the passage of the declaration, Franklin, Adams and Jefferson were appointed to prepare a seal for THE UNITED STATES OF AMERICA.

Henceforth, a new name and a new nation are in the world. The declaration was the turning point in the great struggle. The advanced patriots were stirred to greater confidence; the moderate men were advanced to patriots; the cool were warmed; the tories were marked and silenced; the people at large were kindled to enthusiasm; foreign nations were made friendly, and France a genuine friend. It set before the armies and the people a definite object. It began the apprenticeship of a people in nation-making and defending.

### NATION-BUILDING.

Now began everywhere the great work of nation-building. In every state there were to be constructed state, county, town and city governments, according with the great principles of the declaration. It was an era of education in this work. The people were obliged to study the new work of government-making. It was practical study. There were no models for the government they had to make. They had started a nation on a new plan; and they were to build it by the principles of righteousness and common sense, recognizing every man's place and right in the new structure.

Mr. Jefferson went home to Virginia to engage at once, and with all his might, in the reconstruction of Virginia. In no state was the work more radical. Virginia was thoroughly English. Its land, for the most part, was divided into large estates, which were entailed and descended to the oldest son. All the laws and usages conformed thereto.

The Church of England was the same "establishment" in Virginia as in the British isle. To reconstruct such a state on republican principles required a re-making of all the laws and all the usages of society. To such a work there was great opposition. The old property-owners, the oldest sons, the old lawyers, the conservative people generally, were against such a reconstruction as the principles of the declaration required. To carry all the people peacefully forward into the new order of things was an almost infinite task. To conquer a peace with

England was the smallest part of the work of our revolutionary fathers. From end to end of the new nation had to begin this process of reconstruction; and this while the war was going on, and the business and the growth of the country were almost stopped. It makes one almost dizzy just to read the titles of the bills which Jefferson introduced into the House of Burgesses at the session after the declaration of independence. But he had such suavity and good will, and such strong following among the younger members, that the state at once took its place by the side of Massachusetts, and held it till the nation was organized and on its feet among the great nations of the earth. Massachussetts in the north and Virginia in the south were the two arms of the new nation, and they worked together and with equal efficiency.

In 1776, Mr. Jefferson gave as one reason for declining the French mission, that he saw "that the laboring oar was really at home."

In 1777 he wrote to Dr. Franklin: "With respect to Virginia. * * * The people seemed to have laid aside the monarchical and taken up the republican government, with as much ease as would have attended their throwing off an old and putting on a new garment. Not a single throe has attended this important transformation. A half dozen aristocratic gentlemen, agonizing under the loss of pre-eminence, have sometimes ventured their sarcasm on our political metamorphosis. They have been fitter objects of pity than of punishment."

He took a roseate view of the difficulties he had met, because he had been successful.

Before his state was reconstructed the tide of war had swept that way. Massachusetts was first attacked, but with such ill success that it was soon determined to attack New York, and with a foothold there, break New England from the southern colonies by a blow from the north through Lake Champlain. Burgoyne's defeat frustrated that plan. Then the destruction of the south became the British object, and the armies by sea and land were pushed that way.

## MR. JEFFERSON MADE GOVERNOR.

On the first day of June, 1779, Mr. Jefferson was elected governor of Virginia. Patrick Henry was governor before him. These two men, who had been most active in the cause of republican government in Virginia, were the first and second to occupy the chair of state under the new form.

This was the gloomiest time of the war. France had declared for America and promised help. The alliance gave the Americans a fatal sense of security. The army was decreasing and it was difficult to renew. The whole tide of war was setting southward, and Virginia was selected for the severest punishment. Georgia had been, for the most part, subjugated. The Carolinas were crippled, and armies moving upon Virginia. The most of her regular soldiers were in defeated divisions of the general army. There was no outlook for Virginia but that she must fight. Henry's words, "We must fight," had come true. The people must fight. The British were at their doors and coming with fire, and rapine and ruin, as well as with sword. They were vieing with the red savages of the forest in their cruelty. The word went out among the people of the Old Dominion, and they came from their homes to meet the coming foe. Washington hastened home with his northern army; the French came with their ships, and help from all around, and Cornwallis was cooped in Yorktown, so it turned out that the war which began in Massachusetts, with Virginia's sympathy, ended on Virginia's soil. Governor Jefferson did everything in his power for the defense of his state and conquering a peace for the nation. Governor Jefferson's home was a mark for the enemy. His stock, slaves, crops and lands were wasted; yet he pushed on the war by every force he could raise in his state.

Brief must be the reference to the important events of these great times.

## MRS. JEFFERSON'S DEATH.

On the fifteenth of June, 1781, Congress associated Mr. Jefferson with Adams, Franklin, Jay and Lawrens, to settle the terms of peace with Great Britain, at Paris. But the sickness of his wife prevented him from going. Her health had declined through several years. He had several times returned from the legislature and from congress on account of her failing health. On a number of occasions he had refused to accept important public trusts, because he could not force himself from her in her feebleness. Their union was one of mutual affection and honor. They had a pride as well as a pleasure in each other. Their home had become a center of the great and good of Virginia. They had six children born to them, and the children of his widowed sister, Mrs. Carr, lived with them almost as though their own. Mrs. Jefferson grew feebler through some years. Her constitution seemed slowly to give way. When she came to require constant care, her husband spent his entire time with her. For weeks he sat by her bed, administered to her her medicine, and every care. She died September 6, 1782, in the thirty-fifth year of her age.

Mrs Randolph, his eldest daughter, many years after wrote of her mother's sickness and death, and her father's care and sorrow, as follows: "For four months that she lingered, he was never out of calling; when not at her bedside, he was writing in a small room which opened immediately at the head of her bed. A moment before the closing scene, he was led from the room almost in a state of insensibility, by his sister, Mrs. Carr, who, with great difficulty, got him into his library, where he fainted, and remained so long insensible that they feared he would never revive. The scene that followed I did not witness; but the violence of his emotion—when almost by stealth I entered his room at night—to this day I dare not trust myself to describe. He kept his room three weeks, and I was never a moment from his side. He walked almost incessantly night and day, only lying down occasionally when nature was completely exhausted, on a pallet that had been brought in during his long fainting fit. When at last he left his room, he rode out, and from that time he was almost incessantly on horse-back, rambling about the mountain in the least frequented roads, and just as often through the woods."

After Mr. Jefferson's death, forty-four years later, were found in one of his private drawers, locks of hair, and other little souvenirs of his wife and each of his children. They were done up in separate envelopes, "with words of fond endearment written on the mementos."

Very tender was the heart of this great man.

### APPOINTED TO NEGOTIATE PEACE AT PARIS.

After the death of his wife Mr. Jefferson was again appointed by Congress minister plenipotentiary to negotiate peace with Great Britain. He proceeded to Philadelphia and then to Baltimore; but the dangers of capture were so great that it was not thought best for him to sail till news of a provisional treaty came, and so he did not go, but returned to Monticello. After the war of the revolution there was a call for the best talent of every colony for the state and national legislatures. Mr. Jefferson labored industriously in both. He was kept a member of Congress and did excellent service in it till he was again appointed to a foreign mission.

### COMMISSIONER OF TREATIES OF COMMERCE.

May 7, 1784. Mr. Jefferson was appointed minister plenipotentiary with Mr. Adams and Doctor Franklin, to negotiate treaties of commerce with the nations of Europe. Taking his oldest daughter with him, he proceeded to Boston, through New Jersey, New York, Connecticut and Rhode Island, and also visited New Hampshire and Vermont, to learn as well as he could the commercial condition of the country. On the fifth of July he sailed from Boston, and reached Paris the sixth of August, having stopped a few days in England.

He immediately joined the other ministers; and they prepared their plan for treaties. Frederick of Prussia, through his ambassador, was quick to enter into a treaty. Denmark and Tuscany also came forward and made treaties; but the other nations of Europe knew but little of America, and cared less.

Americans were rebels, and they wanted nothing to do with them. So not much came of this appointment, though it began the work of commercial treaties.

### MINISTER AT THE COURT OF FRANCE.

On the tenth of March, 1785, Congress appointed Mr. Jefferson minister at the court of France, in the place of Doctor Franklin. Doctor Franklin had won the favor of the French as a great statesman, philosopher and man. He was well stricken in years, yet well preserved and ripe in every manly grace. "You replace M. Franklin, I hear," said Count De Vergennes to him. "I *succeed*, no one can *replace* him," was the ready reply. This was a good beginning with the count, who was a great admirer of Franklin. Jefferson had a profound respect for Franklin, and Franklin a tender regard for Jefferson. Differing much in age, they were yet most intimate friends. They agreed in their general principles and philosophy. In nature they were quite similar. They were equal advocates of human rights, and had like views of the new government in America. Jefferson's early manhood, yet ripe mind, agreeable manners and ready adaptation to circumstances, soon won for him the confidence of the government circles and the intelligent and influential of Paris. America was then all the rage in France. She had cast off and driven back England, the old foe of France. She had achieved liberty. She had set up a government of the people. There were many in France to rejoice in this. The representative of such a people had the enthusiasm of Frenchmen to begin with. But he was, as De Chastelux called him, "the young senator," the musician, the geometrician, the astronomer, the philosopher, the statesman, the polite and solid scholar, and the elegant gentlemen in society. These accomplishments made him the rage as well as his country.

France, by war, tyranny and taxation, had impoverished and degraded its people. Long abuse of power and privilege had corrupted its ruling classes. The better thinkers had come to see the evils upon them, and to dream of possible release from them. The example of America made many believe freedom was possible to France. All such gathered around Jefferson, received inspiration from him, and poured out their hopes to him. It soon became the fashion to talk liberalism; and fashion rules in Paris. All classes soon took up the talk, and an era of enthusiasm for liberty in France came rushing on. Jefferson's presence and conversation, no doubt, stimulated the democratic sentiment.

The beginnings of the revolution came while Jefferson was in France: the assembly of the notables; the meetings of the commons; the consultations about the forms of the new government; the rising of the people against the king's soldiers; the submission of the king to the popular will, and the great opportunity for a peaceful change from a monarchical to a republican government. He was much consulted by the patriots of a new France.

His business as minister was thoroughly attended to; and all done for the commerce of America that could be done.

On the twenty-sixth of September, 1788, on leave of Congress, he left Paris to bring home his daughters, and look after his affairs. Another man was temporarily appointed in his place; but as events moved on, he was so employed in the home interests of his country that he never returned to France. On leaving France, he made this record of his impressions of that country: "I cannot leave this great and good country without expressing my sense of the pre-eminence of its character among the nations of the earth. A more benevolent people I have never known; nor greater warmth and devotedness in their select friendships. Their kindness and accommodation to strangers is unparalleled, and the hospitality of Paris is beyond anything I had conceived to be practicable in a large city."

His welcome at Monticello by his slaves, who unhitched his horses from his carriage and drew it to his house; and then received him from it into their arms, and "toted" him into the house, covering his hands with kisses, and pressing his person with embraces, is told by his eldest daughter.

### SECRETARY OF STATE.

Mr. Jefferson had come home to look after his business and home interests; but, before he reached Monticello, he received a letter from General, now President, Washington, appointing him secretary of state. He would gladly have been excused from this duty. The government was starting anew. He had been away three years, and knew his foreign duties. He distrusted his ability to put the domestic affairs of the new government in order. He craved the domestic quiet of Monticello with his children, relatives and neighbors. Yet he was loyal, and said to Washington: "You are to marshal us as may be best for the public good."

On the twenty-third of February, 1790, his daughter Martha was married to Mr. Thomas Mann Randolph, Jr., of Tuckahoe, a second cousin and a young man of excellent connection, education and promise.

On the first of March Mr. Jefferson left home for New York, but tarried a little at Richmond and Alexandria. He went in his own carriage, making three miles an hour in the day time and one mile an hour at night. At Philadelphia he visited Dr. Franklin, now aged and in his last illness. He was deeply impressed with the visit.

He reached New York on the twenty-first. Congress was in session, and much business awaited him.

He was singularly and sadly affected by New York society. He had come from Paris, where America and republicanism were enthusiastically extolled. He believed in the right of the people to govern themselves; that kingcraft was a delusion and a sin; that monarchy was a rock of offense to humanity; and yet in New York society it was common to hear England and its government lauded above all others. He says: "I cannot describe the wonder and mortification with which the table talks filled me. Politics were the chief topic, and a preference of kingly over republican government was evidently the favorite sentiment!" New York city was in British hands during the revolution. Many of its old families were tories at heart after independence was secured. As a colony and state, New York was slow to accept republican teachings. Jefferson had never lived in such an atmosphere. It was stifling and offensive to him. It, no doubt, intensified his republicanism.

Very soon after peace was declared, there came to be a divided political sentiment in the country. The old love of the English style of government was very strong in many minds. All admitted that it was the best model yet known; so the question was: How closely shall America follow the model? Alexander Hamilton would follow it very closely. He was, no doubt, the strongest and clearest political thinker of his time. The world hardly had a superior. He was an ardent friend of Washington and America; had put all his hopes into the revolution; and after the constitution was adopted, wrote in the "Federalist" some of the ablest articles in its defense ever written. He probably paved the way to its acceptance more than any other. Mr. Jefferson, who at first was opposed to the constitution in many particulars, though he said the convention that made it was a "convention of demi-gods," acknowledged his indebtedness to Mr. Hamilton for so enforcing its provisions that he saw it in a new light and came to be its friend.

Governor Morris, of New York, was even more in favor of a monarchical form of government. Some, no doubt, would have been glad of the English government with the king left out. There grew up a party of this class of political thinkers, who accepted the constitution, but some of whom thought, perhaps, it would be modified more in favor of monarchy. The difficulties and occasional discontent and outbreak among the people; the lawlessness engendered by the long war, doubtless frightened some of republican ways of thinking, and turned them back toward monarchical views. Hamilton himself grew more monarchical with his experience of the many defects in the first attempts of government by the people.

On the other side were strong believers in the capacity of the people for self-government. This class had more confidence in human nature, more trust in fair treatment and just laws, a greater readiness to think well of mankind generally. And this class, too, were more out with the old forms of government generally. They were political reformers willing to take the risk of something new. They hated King George, and all kings. They hated Parliament as a tool of the king; hated the lords and peers, and all the titled nobility; even hated England for sustaining such a tyrannical crew. Jefferson, a man of the people for many years, grew more and more in sympathy with these radically republican views. His experience in France helped them on. When he returned he was shocked by the monarchical and English opinions of many Americans. He was repelled by them, and soon began to resist them, and with so much energy and honest fervor that he, in due time, without intending it, became the leader of that party.

Mr. Jefferson and Mr. Hamilton, personal friends, co-workers in the revolution, now became members of Washington's cabinet, the first cabinet of the kind ever formed. The other two heads of the cabinet were General Knox and Edmund Randolph. Knox sympathized with the federal views, Randolph with the republican. Washington was elected by the whole people; he sought to make his administration serve the whole. It was as he intended it should be, a no-party administration. But this mixing opposites in the same body did not work as Washington hoped. These leaders of contrary views, Hamilton and Jefferson, were too much opposed to coalesce. And instead of nearing each other they constantly separated. They were able men and each filled his office with great ability; and each had a great following. The sharp division between them gradually came to be a sharp division between two great political parties. Perhaps it was inevitable. Republican government was a new thing in the world. It was a new thing for the people to administer their own government. Leaders of popular parties had as much to learn as the people. Neither of these men were as perfect, or as wise or great as their followers thought them. The principles of neither were so bad as the opposite party thought. Successful governments could have been run by either.

Mr. Jefferson opposed Mr. Hamilton's paper-money schemes.

At first they seemed to work well; money was plenty; the public debts cared for; the national credit established; the spirit of trade and speculation awakened; the stock in the United States Bank went up to almost one hundred per cent above par. Then Hamilton was regarded as a broad-seeing and wonderful man. Jefferson regarded all this with distrust; pronounced it false in principle—demoralizing; claimed that it was corrupting the government, had already done it, and was leading to moral and financial ruin. A few years brought the very results Jefferson had predicted. The stock in the bank went down nearly one hundred and twenty-five per cent. Financial disaster was general. This gave great currency to Jefferson's wisdom and political philosophy.

A war between France and England came on, in which Spain was embroiled. Popular enthusiasm went with France. The French Minister, Genet, through popularity with the people, sought to carry the United States with France. For a time with a high hand he pushed his plans, and at length became embroiled with our government, which asked France to recall him. Jefferson's strong French sympathies drew him to Genet; but in the end he disproved his course, and set himself right in the very general estimate of his countrymen. Hamilton, on the other hand, sympathized with England, and all the more in consequence of his opposition to Jefferson and his followers. It was a critical time for the United States government, on account of its real dangers, but more on account of its divided counsels.

Hamilton's English leaning and opposition to France, to Jefferson and to the public sympathies, made strong inroads upon his popularity, and also upon his party, the federalist. By Washington's steady-going wisdom, neutrality was observed and war escaped. But very intense political feelings, even animosities, were engendered, which projected themselves through nearly three generations, and are scarcely ended yet. The old men of this age remember much of them and feel something of them yet. Jefferson's generous sympathies, hatred of kings and tyrannies, generally sound philosophy of human life, with his strong felicitous way of stating his views, put him into his age as a mighty personal power. Yet it seems clear to the riper thought of this age that he *leaned* to an extreme democracy; while Hamilton and his confreres *leaned* as much to an overstrong monarchical government; and they each, probably, leaned the more by their mutual repulsion. Left to themselves, they would both have grown up erect and giant oaks in the new republican forest. Such are the misfortunes of partisanship.

The essential principles of both the parties of that time have gone into the constitution and administration of the American government. The federalists gave the anatomy and solid structure, and the republicans, afterward called democrats, the blood and muscle and broad human sensibility. The two together have made it what it is, the joy and glory of the whole world.

### RESIGNS THE SECRETARYSHIP.

On the fifth of January, 1794, Mr. Jefferson resigned his place in the cabinet. A year later Mr. Hamilton resigned. Jefferson retired to Monticello and busied himself with his domestic affairs with zeal and satisfaction. His daughter, Mrs. Randolph, had two children in whom he found great pleasure. He and his daughter became almost inseparable, so much so, that she took her family home to Monticello, that she and her children might be constantly with him. Three years were spent in this way, most grateful to this man of rural and domestic tastes.

### VICE-PRESIDENT.

February 8, 1797, Mr. Jefferson was elected vice-president of the United States, under John Adams as president. Here were president and vice-president politically at variance, yet both high-minded, patriotic men. The government was new. Under Washington it had run largely by the influence of his great name. Now it had gone into other hands, and had opposite political sentiments in its president and vice-president. It had had serious troubles under Washington from opposing members of the cabinet.

Now, a war was threatened from France. President Adams and his government prepared for it. An army was raised; Washington appointed commander, with Hamilton the second in command. Stringent laws against foreigners were passed. Sedition laws were enacted and somewhat enforced, obnoxious to the spirit of the government. Great excitement was occasioned among the people. They were unused to their own institutions, and were experimenting in relation to them. There was much distrust and excitability.

There is now but little doubt but that at about this time, one Don Francisco de Miranda, of Caracas, who had been a literary traveler, and had figured as a military man in France, had conceived the idea of the independence of the Spanish-American states; had planned with Pitt for the coöperation of the British government in his scheme, and was now scheming with Hamilton to involve the United States in the project; and that this anticipated war with France, and these war measures in which Adams and Washington were innocently involved, were a part of the ambitious scheme. A few of Hamilton's special friends were his coadjutors, and probably some of Mr. Adams' cabinet. Those involved were all federalists. The discovery of something of their plot brought condemnation and retribution to that party. The most of the party were among the best men of the nation. And those involved in this scheme may have regarded it as a legitimate way of carrying the independence enjoyed by the United States to the central and southern states of America. It was an age when military schemes abounded. Bonaparte had begun his career. The American continent was regarded as a great field for the future. The principles of civil liberty were not well established. In the disturbed and demoralized condition of the times, this scheme took shape in Miranda's ambitious brain, and came near wrecking in foreign and intestine broils this new government by the people.

Those who speak of the early times of the republic, as its *good old* times, speak without knowledge. The truth is, its early days were its worst days. They were days of experimenting and blundering; of hard criticism and relentless partisanship; of distrust, accusation and recrimination. For twenty-years the government hobbled along. And why should it not? Its people were learning the great art of self-government. It may truly be attributed to the good Providence over them more than to their own wisdom and virtue, that they learned to walk at all. Everybody now ought to know the facts of those days and the whole history of this incomparable country, so as to properly appreciate the inestimable worth of this century-grown fabric of human wisdom and experience, under Divine guidance, which we call "our government."

Mr. Jefferson had no part or lot in these schemes and no knowledge of them at the time. No man of his party was approached by the foreign schemers. Only such were approached as were supposed to have English sympathies and French hatred. There were to be four nations involved in the scheme; to make several more new nations out of Spanish territory, and add to the United States the Spanish territories of Florida and on the Mississippi river. The federal party were not in the least to blame for the scheming of a half a dozen of its members, but the punishment came upon the whole party.

### THE THIRD PRESIDENT.

On the fourth day of March, 1801, Thomas Jefferson was inaugurated president of the United States, and Aaron Burr vice-president. His election had been stoutly opposed, but at last was cheerfully acquiesced in by the moderate federalists. There had come to be a very general fear that the republic was endangered by the fierce broils that were disturbing it; that the hot partisan spirit kept up might prove the ruin of the country and this experiment in popular government. This led the moderate federalists not only to acquiesce in the election of Mr. Jefferson, but to really feel like helping him to give the country a good administration. By the very fury of the canvass, peace came to the country.

Mr. Jefferson selected a cabinet of strong men who were in sympathy with himself. Washington's cabinet was oil and water that would not mix. Adams' cabinet was weak, subject to strong men outside who had personal schemes to carry out. Now there was a strong and united cabinet, interested only in giving the people an administration which should promote the welfare of the whole country.

At that early day there came up the question of civil service. Mr. Jefferson found all the offices in the gift of the government in the hands of the federalists, with a single exception. Mr. Adams had continued to make appointments up to the last day of his time, and always of federalists. Now came the question to Mr. Jefferson, shall these all remain, or shall a portion of them be dismissed to give place to friends of the new administration? He decided that all faithful and efficient servants of the public should remain, but in a few cases of inefficiency and unworthiness in office he would make changes, and so continue to change for good cause till the ratio of republicans in office should be about equal to the ratio of republicans in the country, and so at length have both parties fairly represented officially, according to their strength.

Mr. Jefferson's theory was that the great body of federalists as well as republicans were loyal to the republic and the principles on which it was founded, and that the fearful disturbances which came so near wrecking the new nation, were occasioned by scheming leaders and the arts and cabals of other nations. Washington's counsel to keep clear of foreign entanglement, was doubtless made because it was needed. Jefferson now hoped to have this counsel regarded.

In his public appointments he had three rules: first, to treat as nullities the appointments of the former administration, made after his own election; second, to ask, "Is he honest? Is he capable? Is he faithful to the constitution?" and third, to refrain from appointing relatives. He said: "The public will never be made to believe that an appointment of a relative is made on the ground of merit alone, uninfluenced by family ties. It is true, this places the relations of the president in a worse situation than if he were a stranger, but the public good, which cannot be effected if its confidence be lost, requires this sacrifice." Washington had adopted the same rule. Mr. Adams made the mistake of appointing a relative in one instance, but the Senate rightly refused to confirm it.

The population of the United States in 1800, on the eve of Mr. Jefferson's election, was 5,305,925. It had about doubled since the declaration of independence.

### THE PURCHASE OF LOUISIANA.

The Spanish possessions on the South and Central American coast, then reached as far north as South Carolina, so that the United States joined territory on the south, with Spain. In the settlement of the war between France and Spain, France became the possessor of Florida and Louisiana. This aroused the United States to the possible danger of future and not far off complications with France. Mr. Jefferson counseled France against the possession of this Spanish territory, as threatening the peace of the United States. But France was dreaming of colonial schemes. Bonaparte conceived of a French empire in America with its capital and great commercial outlet at New Orleans. But so stout was the resistance of the United States, and so threatening its attitude, that he began to think it might cost more than it would be worth. Mr. Jefferson had charged Mr. Livingston, our minister in France, to use every endeavor to purchase the territory of France. Then to press the matter still further, he sent Mr. Monroe to France on this special mission. The result was that on the thirtieth of April, 1803, the purchase was made. Sixty million francs was the price; twenty millions to be paid to citizens of the United States due from France for supplies and prizes at sea.

The territory was an empire of itself. It was in the heart of the American continent. It held the great rivers. After the declaration of independence, this was the greatest event that had transpired in America. It opened the valley of the Mississippi to the freedom and civilization of the United States. And it only cost a little money, easily paid in the growth of the country. And yet it was by some denounced at the time as a reckless waste of a nation's money. But it made the administration immensely popular, as it removed one great source of danger and was a peaceful settlement of a difficult problem.

Mr. Jefferson was inaugurated for his second term, March 4, 1805, in the sixty-second year of his age. The rapidly growing country, the developing principles of republicanism, the enlarging sphere of the nation's intercourse with the world, made his administration important in many respects. The development of Aaron Burr's plot for a western empire and his treasonable purposes, and his trial, came in Mr. Jefferson's time. So did the duel between Burr and Hamilton, and the death of the latter.

Mr. Jefferson grew in popularity and influence during his whole administration. He served as president in stormy times; but carried the ship of state into peaceful waters. Even a hasty study of his, and the earlier administrations, shows how much the people had to learn to be self-governing. They felt their way blindly—even those who governed for the most part. The people were sensitive, critical, suspicious, excitable. Little evils portended destruction; trifles were likely to upset the government; a new idea startled many; the faces of many were always turned backward for examples, and if any took a forward look it frightened them. Mr. Jefferson looked forward, and hoped for better things in the future than the past had known. He was constitutionally a reformer. He tried experiments and took new ways of doing things. He was no worshiper of the past. When he looked back he saw so many horrible things in the oppressions and sufferings of humanity that he shuddered. He was humane, and believed in humanity; in the equal rights of men; in fair dealing, and the helpfulness of governments and the higher classes of men. He honored human nature, and believed the natural order of things was good. He wanted to abolish slavery, and caste, and titles, and official dignities, and recognize plain worth and true merit only as conferring the dignity worth knowing. If he had been born among the Friends he would have been a zealous disciple of their principles. As he said in a letter to Mrs. Adams in explanation of the differences between him and the federalists: "One fears most the ignorance of the people; the other the selfishness of rulers, independent of them. Which is right, time and experience will prove." The federalists feared the ignorance of the people, he would say, while he feared more the selfishness of rulers.

Added to these constitutional qualities and opinions a strong imagination, a fervent temperament, high spirit, intensity of nature, an ability to talk and write with power, and a disposition to call things by the names most befitting his views of them, and we have Thomas Jefferson—not a model man, by any means; over fervent often; over severe sometimes; suspicious of the motives of those who sharply differed from him; over-generous to those he liked, and yet a good man; great, honest, hearty, brilliant, powerful; who could not help making a strong impression on his age, and having a wide following—a king among men, as royal in heart as in mind.

### JEFFERSON'S RELIGIOUS OPINIONS.

It was common in those high calvinistic times for his bitter political enemies to denounce him as an infidel, an atheist, a despiser of religion. And it must be said that the language of denunciation among those of different opinions was common then. It was common to be unjust and unfair to those of the contrary opinion. The most religious people were not wanting in hard terms to apply roundly to those whom they censured.

Mr. Jefferson was baptized and reared in the Episcopal church, and through his life contributed to its support. His wife and daughters were attached to it. Its ministers were often his friends. Had he lived in this time he would perhaps have been a broad churchman, or a Unitarian, or a friend, or a new orthodox, or a left-wing friend, of some church. At heart he was a religious man, but his religion was not the orthodoxy of his time. He always spoke and wrote reverently of God in all his state papers, as in the Declaration of Independence, recognized the just and good providence of God over men. In letters to friends he has occasionally spoken believingly of a future immortal life. To Mrs. Adams, he wrote: "Perhaps, one of the elements of future felicity is to be a constant and unimpassioned view of what is passing here. If so, this may well supply the wish of occasional visits." And to Mr. Adams, after the death of his wife, he speaks of ascending "in essence to a meeting with the friends we have loved and lost, and whom we shall still love and never lose again."

In a report concerning the religious instruction in the university of Virginia, he said: "The relations which exist between man and his Maker, and the duties resulting from those relations, are the most interesting and important to every human being, and the most incumbent on his study and investigation."

## THE UNIVERSITY OF VIRGINIA.

As early as 1816, Mr. Jefferson was instrumental in converting Albemarle academy into Central college. The scheme of a college grew in his mind into the University of Virginia. He gave much interest to this for many years. It was the initiatory movement for state universities. It did not realize his hopes, but became an efficient institution.

## FINANCIAL MISFORTUNES.

During the last years of his life, a crushing financial depression made the values of property uncertain and caused many failures. Mr. Jefferson's constant attention to public business had prevented his attention to his own affairs, and they suffered by this neglect. He got somewhat involved in debt, and just at this time Governor Nicolas failed for whom he had given his name as surety to the amount of twenty thousand dollars. It was a great trial for his declining years, but he bore it with cheerful fortitude. But when it became known to the country that his affairs were thus involved, personal gifts of gratitude and love from all parts came in to relieve his estate and give him great peace. He accepted them as tokens of affection from his children.

## FINAL DEPARTURE.

The robust frame of the great patriot at last began to give way to age. It is pleasant to read the correspondence between him and John Adams, in their declining years. In their early manhood they were compatriots and personal friends and served their country in mutual affection. But in the sharp division of parties they became estranged, and lived as strangers for many years. When the heat of political misunderstandings passed away, they became reconciled, and ever after they were like two loving brothers in their correspondence. As they grew old they told of and inquired after their infirmities. They kept each other informed of their conditions. When Adams came to die, his last words were: "Thomas Jefferson still survives." His last thought seemed to have been on his old friend.

It was on the fourth of July, 1826, fifty years after they had enacted the declaration of independence, when the whole nation was jubilant in their praises of what they had done, at fifty minutes after twelve o'clock noon, that Thomas Jefferson died. A little before he had taken affectionate farewells of members of his family, and when the last was said, he audibly murmured, "Lord, now lettest thou thy servant depart in peace." An hour later and John Adams followed. Earth sees them no more, save in their great works. Their love is complete in the light in which they dwell.

## The Grave of Thomas Jefferson.

The grave of Jefferson is at Monticello, the place of his residence, which he chose for its beautiful situation, and wide and grand views over a great sweep of valley and hills and richly wooded mountains in the distance, forty miles away. He made the selection while yet a young man. There he took his young wife in the midst of a great snow-storm and in the dead of night. There he lived his great life. It was the dearest spot on earth to him, and the most beautiful. There he died; and there reposes his dust. What associations cluster around this now lonely and neglected place! What characters once came here for counsel and high converse! What throngs from all the states and over the sea! What letters were here written and read; what words and works that live! How much for the young republic was here thought and done. Now how sadly lonely!

On the fly-leaf of an old book of accounts for 1741, was found, after Jefferson's death, the following in his hand, which was supposed to refer to the place where he would have his body sleep in peace. "Choose some unfrequented vale in the park, where is no sound to break the stillness, but a brook that bubbling winds among the woods—no mark of human shape that has been there, unless the skeleton of some poor wretch who sought that place out of despair to die in. Let it be among ancient and venerable oaks; intersperse some gloomy evergreens. Appropriate one half to the use of my family; the other to strangers, servants, etc. Let the exit look upon a small and distant part of the blue mountains."

A little way from his old residence, which crowns Monticello, and a little to the right of the Charlotteville road, in a thick growth of woods, still and lonely as he could wish, is Jefferson's grave. There is no vale, no brook to murmur, no sound but the soughing of the wind in the evergreens. There are some thirty graves in a space about one hundred feet square, which was enclosed by a brick wall, ten feet high. On the south side, this wall had fallen into a ruin. On the north and west sides it yet stood. The iron gates on these two sides were locked in rust. Virginia creepers adorned the west wall. The ground of the enclosure was neglected, grown up to grass, shrubs and weeds. Loose bricks and stones, and vegetable decay and growth marked the place as a solitude, if not a ruin. The tombstones were generally defaced and broken,—many of them fallen and overgrown with weeds and moss. About the middle of the northern side, is the grave of Jefferson, precisely where he had often told Wormley, his old servant, he desired to have it. The mound is trodden even with the ground. At the head of the grave was placed a coarse granite obelisk, nine feet high, which rested on a base three feet square. The monument was beaten and battered into a ruin by relic-hunters; even the inscription was beaten off, except the part that tells his birth and death.

After Jefferson's death, a rough sketch of an obelisk was found, after which this was patterned. Under the design was this inscription:

> HERE WAS BURIED
> **Thomas Jefferson,**
> AUTHOR OF THE
> DECLARATION OF INDEPENDENCE,
> OF THE
> STATUTE OF VIRGINIA FOR RELIGIOUS FREEDOM;
> AND
> FATHER OF THE UNIVERSITY OF VIRGINIA;
> BORN APRIL 2, O. S. 1743;
> DIED JULY 4, 1826.

Even this inscription, which was put upon the obelisk, is beaten off by the sacrilegious horde who have thronged the sacred place in idle curiosity, except the words that give the birth and death.

This was the condition of Jefferson's grave until very recently. In 1878 a movement was made in Congress to remove this battered and disfigured monument and to put in its place one which should properly recognize the great sleeper underneath. That movement failed because of objections by the owner of the place, who claimed ownership of the grave and the right of way to it. Arrangements were finally made, and last year a resolution was passed by Congress appropriating ten thousand dollars for erecting a suitable monument. During the pending of this resolution, Miss Sarah N. Randolph, a descendant of Jefferson, made to a member of Congress a full statement of the condition of the graveyard and the title to it by the family. The following is a part of this statement:

"The little graveyard at Monticello — only one hundred feet square — is all of the ten thousand acres of land owned by Jefferson when he entered public life, which is now left in the possession of his descendants. He sleeps amid scenes of surpassing beauty and grandeur, on that lovely mountain side, surrounded by the graves of his children and grandchildren to the fifth generation. At his side lies his wife whom he loved with singular devotion. A few feet from him rests the cherished friend of his youth — young Dabney Carr — whose motion in the Virginia House of Burgesses, to establish committees of correspondence between the sister colonies, leading as it did to the meeting of the First Congress, has given his name an enviable place in American history. A little farther off lie the remains of another devoted and distinguished friend, Governor Wilson Cary Nicolas, of Virginia; while at his feet sleeps another governor of the old commonwealth, his own son-in-law, Thomas Mann Randolph. The modesty of the spot is in striking contrast with the celebrity of its dead; and there are, perhaps, few in America of greater historic interest, or more deserving of the nation's care. Soon after the appropriation was made by Congress, Mr. W. W. Corcoran, the distinguished philanthropist, with characteristic munificence, endowed a professorship of natural history in the University of Virginia, on condition that the institution should take care of the graveyard at Monticello, thus very appropriately placing the care of Jefferson's tomb in the hands of this child of his old age and the last creation of his genius."

Congressman Manning said: "In God's universe there perhaps never lived a man who could point to grander and more glorious 'testimonials that he had lived.' He was, indeed, tenacious of living among men 'as one that serveth,' and 'Heaven, that lent him genius, was repaid.' He was sure of his reward through all succeeding generations."

The monument was erected last year, and inscribed, as was the old one, according to his direction. The three things for which Jefferson cared most to be known, were those he named for his monument. It is hoped they will stand perpetual monuments of his genius and humanity.

At last a fitting monument marks his resting place, erected as it should be, by the nation he did so much to create. A fitting enclosure is also made of the sacred place, and a suitable provision for its care.

The old Jefferson mansion, on the summit of Monticello, once so brilliant and hospitable, is now in desolate and ruinous decay. Thriving trees embower it. Living vegetables and animals are making inroads upon it. Ruin is seeking it for its own. Unless arrested, the decay will before long become complete. It is a brick structure which the tooth of time is gnawing at effectually.

There is much that is saddening at Monticello, the contrast between the past and the present is so great. It was once so much to the country and the world; now it is so little save in memory.

If Monticello, like Mount Vernon, were in the hands of some patriotic national association, or were owned by the national government, it could be so cared for as to invite visitors from every part of the world, and would still speak to the world of the great principles for which Jefferson lived. Jefferson dead would be as real and powerful as Jefferson living. It is more than likely that something of this kind will be realized by and by, and Monticello will rise from the dead.

ENGRAVED EXPRESSLY FOR WEAVERS' LIVES AND GRAVES OF OUR PRESIDENTS

# CHAPTER V.

## JAMES MADISON.

#### FOURTH PRESIDENT OF THE UNITED STATES.

So rich was the character and so valuable is the example of James Madison that the opening sentence of this sketch of his career must express the regret that so little can be given of him for want of space. The fineness and finish of his character, the harmony, intelligence and elevated moral tone of the man were such as put him among the choice spirits who have so lived as to bless their kind in simply living. Simply to be such a man as he is to leave a benediction behind as a legacy for after years.

He was the fourth president; he had been much associated with the three who had gone before him; had affiliated more or less with them all; was the personal friend of all, yet was a new character in the exalted position of chief magistrate of a great nation, and brought a new personality and spirit to adorn and honor the dignified place. No human position can give honor to such a man. He is himself honorable above all offices or places. He honors the highest place more than it honors him.

#### ANCESTRY, YOUTH AND EDUCATION.

Like the other great Virginians of his time, James Madison was of good English stock. He was a descendant of John Madison, an Englishman, who settled in Virginia in 1635, twenty-six years after the settlement of Jamestown, and fifteen years after the landing on Plymouth Rock. His father was James Madison, of Orange, a planter of a large estate and ample fortune. His mother's maiden name was Eleanor Conway.

James Madison, the president, was born March 16, 1751, at King George, Virginia. He was the eldest of seven children. His boyhood was spent on his father's estate, in the midst of the cares, duties, joys and business of such a family so environed. He was born into good educational surroundings for such a boy. Being sensitive, impressible, quick of mind, tender of heart, conscientious, he was quick to take the lessons of such a home and its affairs. It was a school to him from the beginning.

His father's home was at Montpelier, in Orange county, which became his in due time, and his permanent home. The school education of the boy was such as he could get in the rude schools of his time, till he began to be specially prepared for college at a school in Kings and Queens county, taught by a Scotchman by the name of Robertson. A portion of the time he had a private tutor in his home.

In 1769, his eighteenth year, he entered Princeton college, New Jersey, presided over by Doctor Witherspoon, for whom young Madison conceived a strong interest, and by whom he was much quickened and benefited. He always retained many of the wise sayings and fine thoughts of his college president. It is one of those cases in which the student absorbs from the teacher much of his mental and moral life, to be improved upon and reflected through another life. He never tired of quoting Doctor Witherspoon. He graduated in 1772, taking the degree of A. B. in his twenty-first year. He was but two years at college, indicating that he was so thoroughly fitted as to have entered an advanced class, or that the course of study was not so thorough as in all good colleges now. His biographers all speak, however, of the intensity of his devotion to his studies while in college, for he allowed himself only three hours sleep out of every twenty-four, at least for a portion of the time. This heavy work and little rest, even in two years, so impaired his health that for the most of his after life he suffered from the strain and over-taxation. It doubtless did much to subdue and restrain his native powers, and give him a more placid and submissive temperament than he otherwise would have had. His force of character was abated, his will enfeebled by this over-taxation in college. More time, and more consistent use of it, might have given the country quite a different fourth president.

After his graduation, he remained at Princeton till the next spring to pursue a course of reading under the direction of Doctor Witherspoon. This gave him the best part of another year, in connection with the college and its president and their stimulating associations. Take it all in all, his college life gave a commanding direction to his career. It put his thoughts into the line of scholarship, philosophy and religion. It made him a thinker, a peer of the great minds who think the way for the world to pursue.

In the spring of 1773 young Madison returned to his home in Virginia and began a course of legal reading to fit himself for the bar. During the time of his legal study, he did a large amount of general reading. He read works on philosophy, on belles-lettres, and general literature. He made a special study of the subject of religion, and satisfied himself upon the evidences of the christian religion. His nature would almost of necessity lead him into sympathy with christianity, his soul was such easy soil for its doctrines to plant themselves in; especially after his course at college had so quickened his mind to such studies and meditations. The study of christian evidences and doctrines, was a part of his education, and by that study he was not only established in the christian faith, but in that judicial way of thinking which fitted him for the stirring times in which his manhood was spent and the noble and helpful part which he took in them. Just such careful, passionless, clear-seeing thinkers, are the men who open the way for the on-moving march of great events, and who smooth that way also for the feet of the coming generations of men. Endowed with a mind singularly free from passion and prejudice, naturally religious and liberty loving, sincere and hearty in every emotion and thought, he came to every subject to be honest and faithful with it and with himself. Quiet, meditative, refined and peaceful in nature, he was unconsciously fitting himself for a place and work which providence was preparing for him.

Later in life, and after much of his fine and discriminating work was done for the help and admiration of men, Mr. Jefferson gave a classic pen-picture of him which may well be hung in this porch of his early manhood, that all who enter may be able to see beforehand something of the fineness and power of the man whose life they are about to become acquainted with.

"Trained in these successive schools, he acquired a habit of self-possession which placed, at ready command, the rich resources of his luminous and discriminating mind and of his extensive information, and rendered him the first of every assembly afterward of which he became a member. Never wandering from his subject into vain declamation, but pursuing it closely in language pure, classic and copious; soothing always the feelings of his adversaries by civilities, and softness of expression, he rose to the eminent station which he held in the great national convention of 1787; and in Virginia, which followed, he sustained the new constitution in all its parts, bearing off the palm against the logic of George Mason and the fervid declamation of Patrick Henry. With these consummate powers were united a pure and spotless virtue, which no calumny has ever attempted to sully. Of the power and polish of his pen, and of the wisdom of his administration in the highest office of the nation, I need say nothing. They have spoken and will forever speak for themselves."

### ENTRANCE UPON PUBLIC LIFE.

Mr. Madison did not complete his legal studies, partly because his tastes led him to such a wide range of reading in other directions, and partly because an opportunity to serve an oppressed party awakened his sympathies.

At that time the church of England held as absolute sway in Virginia as ever it did in England. It was the established church, sustained by a tax upon property which was collected by the officers of the law, the same as other taxes. Its ministers were legal officers and drew their support alike from church members and non-church members, alike from Episcopalians and believers in other creeds and churches.

After a while, believers in other churches began to increase in Virginia, among them Baptists, who supported their own churches by voluntary contributions and then were forced to pay taxes for the support of the Episcopalian church, in which they did not believe. The Baptists claimed that they ought to be relieved from this forced Episcopalian tax, that it was an intolerant oppression unworthy of free America. In due time this Baptist claim raised a warm debate. It was sometimes fierce, and the Baptists had to learn by experience the full meaning of religious intolerance. Young Madison took the side of the Baptists in the debate, not from sympathy with them in religious opinions, but because he regarded religion as a matter of conscience in which every man should be free. His honest and zealous advocacy of a cause in which his family and class associates were against him, attracted much notice and put him conspicuously before the public as a young man who had voluntarily adopted an unpopular cause in his first public act. Of course he won friends among the persecuted Baptists at once, and among all right thinking people at last.

In the spring of 1776, in the twenty-sixth year of his age, he was elected to serve in the convention to form a constitution for the state of Virginia. This was the year of the declaration of independence, just when the principles of civil liberty, national life, and local and general law were being discussed. With his training in study and observation, he was fitted to get the greatest possible personal benefit from this practical application of all he had learned to the actual business of forming the fundamental law of a state. It brought him into daily association with the best minds of Virginia and to a daily discussion of the principles of statecraft, a school of itself of magnificent instructive power. He was timid and retiring; said but little, but studied and thought much.

The next year, 1777, he was a candidate to the state assembly. He refused to treat the whisky-drinking voters, and some said he was not a public speaker, because he had kept so silent in the constitutional convention, and so he was not elected. But those who had served with him in the convention, and had witnessed the talents, energy, learning and fidelity of the modest young man, interested themselves in securing his ability in the public service, and obtained his appointment as a member of the executive council. In this capacity he served under Patrick Henry and Thomas Jefferson who, learning his great worth, became his powerful friends for the whole of their lives.

### MADE A MEMBER OF THE CONTINENTAL CONGRESS.

In the year 1780 Mr. Madison was elected to the Continental Congress, in the twenty-ninth year of his age. He was yet a young man and had given three years to the service of his native state in the organization and admistration of its government. Now he was in the great council of the forming nation, among its greatest men, and having a share in the conduct of its greatest affairs. The war had so far proceeded that it must be pushed through to final victory or defeat. America must be a country of freemen or slaves. With such young men as Mr. Madison, the question had but one side: America must be free. So their minds were occupied with plans for the government of the new nation. This was especially so with young Madison. He had a constructive mind. He saw that the old forms of government had gone to pieces, and new ones must be put in their places. To this constructive work he bent all his energies. Reared in the most aristocratic society in America, such was the freedom and originality of his mind that he adopted the broadest and most humane ways of thinking. He went to every question as to a fresh study, with little reference to what had been the prevailing opinion upon it. He served three years in Congress, which included the close of the war and the treaty of peace.

### ELECTED TO THE VIRGINIA LEGISLATURE.

In 1784 Mr. Madison was elected a member of the Virginia Legislature. Now that peace and freedom were secured, the work of government construction was fairly begun. To this work he carried all his power. Virginia was English to the core; it must be made American and republican to the core. He advocated such a thorough revision of the old statutes as would make them conform to the new republican order of society. It was hard for the tories to submit to these radical changes; and every change had to be secured by a hard battle of words and votes. The war of swords and cannon had been changed to a war of arguments and ballots. The war was not over by any means. The tories, who had lost all in the field, now meant to gain what they could in the legislatures. Into this legislature came the final settlement of the question of religious freedom in Virginia, which brought Mr. Madison, as a young man, into public notice. He published a "Memorial and Remonstrance" against a general and legal assessment for the support of religion, which was so able and exhaustive that it essentially settled the matter, and religion became as free in Virginia as elsewhere. Church and state were separated, to coalesce naturally and freely in their inner principles and life, and become mutual supports to each other.

He served in the legislature three years, during which time Kentucky was separated from Virginia and erected into a state by his aid. He opposed the introduction of paper money; favored the legal code proposed by Jefferson, Wythe and Pendleton; and supported the recovery of debts due to British creditors.

In January, 1786, Mr. Madison offered a resolution inviting the several states to send delegates to a convention to meet at Annapolis, to consider a reorganization of the general government of the country. Such a convention was held, but only five states sent delegates. But though the number was too small to act authoritatively for all the states, the delegates present discussed the condition and needs of the country and resolved upon a movement for a convention the next year to form a constitution. The proposition was generally accepted by the states.

## A CONSTITUTIONAL CONVENTION

was called for May, 1787. The convention met in Philadelphia. Mr. Madison was chosen as one of the delegates from Virginia. Washington was another, and was elected president of the convention. It met at the appointed time—one of the most able, earnest, conscientious and dignified bodies of men ever assembled. It was an assembly of giants—"of demigods," as Jefferson said. Nor were the men greater than the occasion The old confederation of states had proved itself inadequate in many particulars. It was a body without a head. It was a government by congress, in session only a part of a time, a government without system or fundamental law. So poorly did it work that many were losing confidence in popular government. In many of the best minds there was a turning back to monarchy as the only hope of stability and peace. Those of tory proclivities were beginning to say: "I told you so; the people are too unstable to know what they want." The call for a stronger government was getting loud. The time had fully come when something must be done, or the fruits of the long war might be lost in anarchy and disunion, and the hope of free government postponed for a long time. The great men who met in that convention realized the importance of their work. They were the patriots, who, for country and humanity, had staked everything in resistance of British tyranny and who now were in danger of losing everything in popular incapacity and anarchy. And yet the difficulty was not in the people, but in their having no systematic way of conducting their government.

Mr. Madison, probably more than any other man, realized the importance and greatness of the work of this convention. He had conceived and proposed it. It had struck the popular heart from the beginning. The people hoped for relief and safety from it. From the moment of its conception, the study of a plan of a constitution, became a profound meditation with Mr. Madison. For two years he studied and sketched and consulted other minds and wrought at his plan.

Among General Washington's papers was found one, after

his death, in his own writing, purporting to be the substance of a constitution, which Mr. Madison conceived to be about what was needed, and had written to him in a letter some time before the convention. Mr. Madison's letter has never been found. The portion of it which Washington transcribed is as follows:

"Mr. Madison thinks an individual independence of the states utterly irreconcilable with their aggregate sovereignty, and that a consolidation of the whole into one simple republic would be as inexpedient as it is unattainable. He therefore proposes a middle ground, which may at once support a due supremacy of the national authority and not exclude the local authorities whenever they can be subordinately useful.

"As the groundwork, he proposes that a change be made in the principle of representation, and thinks there would be no great difficulty in effecting it.

"Next, that in addition to the present federal powers, the national government should be armed with positive and complete authority in all cases which require uniformity; such as regulation of trade, including the right of taxing both exports and imports, the fixing the terms and forms of naturalization, etc.

"Over and above this positive power, a negative, *in all cases* whatever, on the legislative acts of the states, as heretofore exercised by the kingly prerogative, appears to him absolutely necessary, and to be the least possible encroachment on the state jurisdictions. Without this defensive power, he conceives that every positive law which can be given on paper will be evaded.

"This control over the laws would prevent the internal vicissitudes of state policy and the aggressions of interested majorities.

"The natural supremacy ought also to be extended, he thinks, to the judiciary departments; the oaths of the judges should at least include a fidelity to the general as well as local constitution; and that an appeal should be to some national tribunal in all cases to which foreigners or inhabitants of other states may be parties. The admiralty jurisdictions to fall entirely within the purview of the national government.

"The national supremacy in the executive departments is liable to some difficulty, unless the officers administering them could be made appointable by the supreme government. The militia ought entirely to be placed, in some form or other, under the authority which is entrusted with the general defense.

"A government composed of such extensive powers should be well organized and balanced.

"The legislative departments might be divided into two branches, one of them chosen every —— years, by the people at large, or by the legislatures; the other to consist of fewer members, and to hold their places for a longer term, and to go out in such rotation as always to leave in office a large majority of old members.

"Perhaps the negative on the laws might be most conveniently exercised by this branch.

"As a further check, a council of revision, including the great ministerial officers, might be superadded.

"A national executive must also be provided. He has scarcely ventured as yet to form his own opinion, either of the manner in which it ought to be constituted, or of the authorities with which it ought to be clothed.

"An article, especially guaranteeing the tranquility of the states against internal as well as external dangers.

"In like manner the right of coercion should be expressly declared. With the resources of commerce in hand, the national administration might always find means of exerting it either by sea or land; but the difficulty and awkwardness of operating by force on the collective will of a state, render it particularly desirable that the necessity of it might be precluded. Perhaps the negative on the laws might create such a mutual dependence between the general and particular authorities as to answer; or perhaps some defined objects of taxation might be submitted along with commerce, to the general authority.

"To give a new system its proper validity and energy, a ratification must be obtained from the people, and not merely from the ordinary authority of the legislatures. This will be more essential, as inroads on the existing constitutions of the states will be unavoidable."

Probably no other man in the country made such preparation for the convention as did Mr. Madison. He gave the many subjects to be considered careful and earnest study. He made, at least, this outline of what he thought should go into the constitution. Anyone who will compare this outline with the actual constitution will see how much of Mr. Madison's suggestion went in. Some of his suggestions were left out, that perhaps would better have gone in. It is clear that he wanted a strong government, a supreme government over the states in all that pertained to its functions. He did not intend to have secession, or disunion, possible by any of the states.

The great question of the time was, how much of the general power of government shall be given to the states, and how much to the general government. The federalists wanted a strong central government; the high federalists wanted it absolute. The republicans wanted to keep the power near the people, in the states as much as possible and not have a general government at all. Washington, Madison, Adams, and especially Hamilton and Morris, wanted strength in the general government. The two latter were high federalists of the strongest type. Madison was a moderate federalist, at this time. Later, he inclined more to trust the people, and became a moderate republican. Whatever partisan he was, he was moderate. He had a cool, judicial, constructive mind, which kept him from party extremes and usually on the middle ground of moderation. He was in close sympathy with Washington. Their spirits were in accord, only Washington was more a man of action, while Madison was more a man of meditation. In the formation of the constitution he sought to put strength into the general government over the states, in all that was peculiarly national. He wanted a nation, a union that was indissoluble — not only a union of states but of all the people. For national purposes, he would have state lines in abeyance. The old confederacy was too weak as a national compact. It was too much subject to state dictation. All the wise men were feeling this; so much so that many were beginning to swing back toward monarchical institutions. The states were jealous of their rights, and in the convention sought to keep them strong. Under the confederacy, they had been almost supreme. They were slow to give up prerogatives to the general government. This, then, was the great thing to adjust, the proper balance between the state governments and the general government. Mr. Madison did not secure all he desired for the general government. And the experience of a hundred years has proved that the general government has been often put to the strain in just those places where he wanted it stronger. Its weakest place was against the states. And it was just at this point that the rebellion of 1861 came in. Here too was where South Carolina nullification set up its claim in the administration of Andrew Jackson. It was over this that the great arguments of Haynes and Webster were made. There has always been a class of politicians who have claimed more for the states than the general government could safely grant. This weakness in the constitution, allowed against Mr. Madison's judgment, has always been a bone of contention and cost us one great civil war. Our experience has proved how wise was the great original outliner of the constitution. Gradually its special amendments have fortified its original weakness. Experience has proved that the moderate federalists were essentially right in their notion of the necessity of strength in the general government, and that our danger has come from a too little governed democracy. As between the dangers of monarchy on one side and democracy on the other, America has been most exposed to the latter. Her chief danger still lies in that direction. A strong and just government usually makes a happy people, just as a well-governed family or school is usually happy. So essential was the part that Mr. Madison acted in the constitutional convention that he has been called "The Father of the Constitution." He seems to have been raised up for this special work as Washington was to lead the armies, and Jefferson to draft the declaration of independence and Adams to argue the way to its adoption. And of all the work done by the founders of this great nation, nothing ever has been more important than the constitution of the United States. It is the great charter of our nationality, the most magnificent work of human wisdom yet done in this world. The nations have not yet sufficiently appreciated it; nor have our own people yet done full justice to the mind, character and life of James Madison, who is as literally the father of the constitution as Washington is of the country.

### THE FEDERALIST.

After the constitution was formed, a series of state papers was written in its explanation and defense, and published all over the country, and read and studied with more profound interest, than any such papers ever put forth in this country. After their first publication, they were gathered into a book entitled: "The Federalist." They became authority for the meaning and philosophy of the constitution. Their intellectual power, their clear elucidation of the intent and scope of the constitution, were so marked that they have always been held as master pieces of political philosophy. They were produced by Alexander Hamilton, James Madison and John Jay. Hamilton is supposed to have made the first draft of more of them than either of the others, and Madison next. But none of them went to press till the three had agreed in all their statements. They were thus the joint product of the three minds. As Mr. Madison was the mover in and originator of more of the constitution than any other, his part in "The Federalist," is apparent.

No thoughtful young American should consider himself equipped as a citizen, till he has not only read, but studied, "The Federalist."

### A MEMBER OF CONGRESS.

In 1789, the time when the constitution went into operation, Mr. Madison was made a member of Congress. He thus began with Washington the conduct of the new government. Mr.

Hamilton was Washington's secretary of the treasury. The country was in a bad financial condition; debts everywhere, and nothing to pay them with. Mr. Hamilton was a bold operator and full of great schemes. His financial plans did not meet Mr. Madison's approval; so he was forced into the attitude of opposition to many of the things of Washington's administration; but his opposition was so tempered with friendly consideration, that it did not disturb the good relations between the father of his country and the father of the constitution. He served in Congress eight years. During Mr. Adams' administration, "The alien and sedition laws" were passed, and other high federalist measures, which became unpopular. Mr. Madison drafted two series of resolutions against them, one as a private citizen in 1798, and one as a member of the Virginia legislature in 1799, which had a powerful influence against the federal rule and for the speedy triumph of the democratic party under Jefferson.

### SECRETARY OF STATE.

Thomas Jefferson was elected president of the United States in 1801. He appointed Mr. Madison secretary of state, which office he held during the eight years of Mr. Jefferson's service. Scarcely could Mr. Jefferson have made a wiser choice. Mr. Jefferson was a man of strong impulses and radical action and speech. He was liable, under provocation, to be an extremist. He was elected as a radical democrat; whom the high federalists regarded as a leveler, a Jacobin, a contemner of law and religion. They dreaded his election as they would that of Lucifer. Extreme feelings were in the ascendant. Mr. Madison had all along been a moderate federalist; was a moderate man always; was profoundly respected by all parties; was one of the authors of "'The Federalist," which was that party's political bible. His appointment to the first office in the cabinet was an assurance of moderation in the democratic president, and encouraged the federalists to hope that all was not lost. And this, which worked so well in the beginning, worked equally well through the whole administration.

# JAMES MADISON.

### FOURTH PRESIDENT.

Mr. Madison succeeeeded Mr. Jefferson as president, in 1809, being the fourth to hold that high office. He went in with a strong majority, having one hundred and twenty-two votes out of one hundred and seventy-six.

He took the great office at a gloomy period. The domestic affairs of the nation were getting more peaceful. The people were learning self-government, and learning to have more confidence in each other and their government. They were learning too not to see ruin in each others' opinions; not to see a throne in a federalist's opinions; nor a French revolution in a democrat's. But there was trouble brewing with England. She had never been satisfied with the result of the revolution; had been sulky and sour ever since, and making herself disagreeable to her former colonists. She deemed herself mistress of the seas, and that other nations, especially her old colonists, had no rights that she was bound to respect. So she infringed on American rights on the high seas; went aboard American merchant vessels, when she pleased, and took off such of the crews as she thought would make good soldiers, and forced them into her army and navy to fight her battles; and did all such things as she chose, without any respect for her treaty obligations.

Various appeals and measures were adopted to rectify these grievous wrongs; but all to no effect. With a high hand, England kept going on her own way; impressing our seamen into her service whenever it suited her necessities; and doing many other unworthy acts. Mr. Madison was peaceful, and dreaded war; and so went on a couple of years, bearing and persuading; but all to no purpose. By this time his party had a strong majority in Congress. Among the leaders were such men as Henry Clay, John C. Calhoun, Crawford, Lowndes, and others like them. They said: "We must fight the old oppressor. She will never do right till we compel her to." So they began a movement for creating an army and navy, and getting ready the munitions of war; and pushed it on till they felt the time had come to begin to strike again military blows for our rights.

## WAR WITH ENGLAND.

In June, 1812, Congress declared war against England.

President Madison gave a message to Congress and the country, detailing at length the belligerent course of England for years toward the United States, while the United States had remained at peace toward her.

Under pretence of searching for British subjects, she had impressed thousands of our seamen, transported them to other and deadly climes; had compelled them to expose their lives in battle and endure every hardship in foreign services; had subjected them to the severest discipline; her cruisers had violated the rights of peace on our coasts, by harrassing our outgoing and incoming vessels of commerce; had wantonly spilt American blood within the territory of our jurisdiction; had blockaded ports without the presence of adequate force, cutting off our markets and injuring our commerce; had invaded the rights of neutrals; and rendered all trade on the seas precarious and dangerous. To all our appeals for redress she has only returned insult. The message was long and able, and summed the whole cause of war.

It was thirty years since the revolutionary war; the old warriors were dead. No new ones had been made in their stead. None of the living generation knew much about war.

The first campaigns, therefore, were only defeats; or perhaps schools of discipline for the final victory. Then, as in our late war, our soldiers and officers had to be made. The first battles went against us. The first campaigns gave encouragement to the enemy; but as soon as time and necessity could drill our soldiers, and select well our officers, England found that the sons of her colonies were as hard to conquer, as were their fathers.

The war was pushed on vigorously for nearly three years, when a treaty of peace was signed at Ghent, on the twenty-fourth of December, 1814. On the eighth day of January, 1815, General Jackson gained his decisive victory, over the British, at New Orleans. In February, 1815, news of peace reached Washington. Great was the rejoicing all over the country. The war was strongly opposed by the federalists, who did many things in opposition to it, which rendered them unpopular; and brought utter defeat upon their party.

Early in 1815, a treaty of commerce was signed at London, by Messrs. Adams, Clay and Gallatin, which restored friendly intercourse between the two countries, never, we may hope, to be broken up again by the barbarous scourge of war.

Mr. Madison's administration went on satisfactorily through his two terms. After the war, a national bank was established with a capital of thirty-five millions; a tariff for the promotion of manufactures was adopted, and the country well started on that tide of prosperity that has not yet abated.

### RETIREMENT IN 1817.

Mr. Madison retired to Montpelier, his home, in March, 1817, at sixty-six years of age. Twelve years later he served in the Virginia convention for the revision of the constitution. With that exception the rest of his life was spent in the quiet of his home, in the enjoyment of his friends, his books, and the national life and peace he had spent so much of his life to secure.

Like Jefferson, he was interested in the University of Virginia, and was for a time its rector.

He died June 28, 1836, eighty-five years and three months old.

He was never of robust health, which made his life less robust and influential than it would have been if he had had the physical stamina that was needed to work up to its best his fine mind.

He was of moderate stature; moderate of speech; of serious, but mild expression; his head was bald on the top; he was modest, but companionable; made many friends; a few, if any, enemies. He went into retirement in the universal respect of his countrymen, and bore that respect ever after.

## MRS. MADISON.

Mrs. Madison's maiden name was Dolly Payne. She was born in North Carolina, of Quaker parents, and educated strictly in their faith and ways of life. When about eighteen she married a young lawyer by the name of Todd, and moved to Philadelphia. There she laid aside the Quaker garb and became a fashionable young woman of city society. Her husband lived but a little while, and she was left in the morning of her life a widow.

When Mr. Madison was attending Congress in New York city, in the forty-third year of his age, he met the blooming and somewhat gay Mrs. Todd. Like many others, he was taken with her fascinations. In his early years he had an unfortunate love experience, and had supposed himself proof against cupid's darts from every quarter; but now he was struck, and badly so, by a dart from this young widow's quiver. In due time he won the coveted prize, and was married to her in 1794. And she proved a prize indeed. She is spoken of by those who knew her as elegant and queenly in person and manner; as beautiful, sprightly, intelligent, and every way worthy. Her peculiar power was in social life. She was the beau ideal of a court lady of the time, genial, kindly, the grace and warmth and sprightliness of society. She was peculiarly thoughtful to the timid, young and unfortunate; was as warm of heart as sprightly in spirit. While Mr. Madison was secretary of state under Mr. Jefferson, she did the honors of the president's house, as he was without a wife. Then, as Mr. Madison came in, she was already installed in her place of honor and helpfulness, and continued through his two terms, making sixteen years as the lady of the executive mansion—the longest term that any lady has occupied that place. And none has more graced it, or rendered herself more helpful in it. In their retirement at Montpelier Mr. and Mrs. Madison tasted all the sweets of their well-earned honors. Happy in each other, and necessary to each other; they were rich in money, goods and friends; had both their widowed mothers and two orphan sisters of Mrs. Madison in their household, all in t e enjoyment of comfortable health. Their home was the resort of the wisest and best, whom they received with grace and hospitality.

Take them all in all, few lives of men present better models for men and women to copy than Mr. and Mrs. Madison. They were delightful people, lifted high up in the world, yet humble; intellectual and in many ways brilliant, yet in sweet sympathy with all common people; rich, yet they gave their lives to the world in a cheerful and laborious fellow service; brought up in wealth, yet never proud; official partisans, yet honored and loved by all parties; devoted to an established church, yet the ardent friends of religious liberty; descendants of an ancient aristocracy, yet democrats in life and spirit. The author of this too hasty sketch can scarcely refrain from asking the readers of this to seek Mr. Madison's life and works and make them a study.

It ought to have been said, in its place, that Mr. Madison kept a full record of the proceedings of the constitutional convention, the only one ever kept and preserved, and that after his death Congress purchased it of Mrs. Madison, paying her thirty thousand dollars. She survived Mr. Madison thirteen years. She died July 12, 1849, in the eighty-second year of her age.

## The Grave of James Madison.

Four miles from Orange, Virginia, is Montpelier, the home of James Madison, which he inherited when a child from his father. It is in one of the most picturesque and softly beautiful regions of this state. Gentle undulations of hill and dale, and wavy outlines of low mountain ranges, surround it. Lawn, tree and shrubbery, field, wood and hillside, give softness and diversity to the scene. Here lived and died the fourth President and his beautiful and accomplished wife, and here rest their mortal forms.

The mansion is large and plain, though beautiful. It is built of brick and is more extensive than most of the noted

Virginia residences. It is well preserved, and everything in and about it is cared for with excellent taste and conscientious regard for its history. Around it is a beautiful lawn of some sixty acres, surrounded by a variety of large trees, many of them planted, it is said, by the hand of Mrs. Madison. Somewhere near the center of this open field or lawn, in an enclosure of about a hundred feet square, surrounded by a brick wall about five feet high, is the grave of Madison. All about it is peaceful and harmonious like Madison himself. Four graves occupy this quiet enclosure. Over the grave of Madison, is a mound of earth, from the top of which rises a granite obelisk some twenty feet high. Near the base is the inscription:

**Madison,**
Born March 16, 1751.

By its side rises a smaller marble shaft with this inscription:

In Memory of
**Dolly Payne,**
WIFE OF JAMES MADISON.
Born May 20, 1768;
Died July 8, 1849, O. S.

ENGRAVED EXPRESSLY FOR WEAVERS LIVES AND GRAVES OF OUR PRESIDENTS.

# CHAPTER VI.

## JAMES MONROE.

### FIFTH PRESIDENT OF THE UNITED STATES.

#### ANCESTRY AND YOUTH.

JAMES MONROE was of Scotch descent, having come from a family of Scotch cavaliers, who were descendants from Hector Monroe, an officer of Charles I. He was born April 28, 1758. Coming from such a stock, he started life with an amount of brain and blood force that was quite likely to make itself felt in the new country in which it had taken form. Spence Monroe, of Westmoreland county, Virginia, was his father, and Eliza Jones, of King George county, was his mother. She was sister of Joseph Jones, who served Virginia twice in the Continental Congress, and as district judge in his own county. The measure of her force may be known somewhat by her brother and her son. It has passed into a common remark that great men are the sons of strong mothers. His father and mother were both Virginia born. So he was well born as to parentage, the best fortune that can befall one at the beginning of life.

The locality where he was born and reared was Westmorland county, between the Potomac and Rappahannock rivers, a region of great fertility, finely watered, of varied and beautiful scenery, which had attracted the attention of the most intelligent settlers from England, on account of its many advantages. It was between two grand rivers; but little above tide-water; originally heavy-timbered; bearing a great variety of natural products; in a mild climate; with rock and mineral in abundance. So he was well born as to place.

This county and vicinity was settled by some of the best comers from England. Lord Fairfax and his brother and fine family made their wilderness home here. Lawrence and George Washington and the other Washingtons grew up here. Thomas Jefferson, James Madison, Patrick Henry, Peyton and John Randolph, Richard Henry Lee and Henry Lee (Light Horse Harry, as he was called), John Marshall, Pendleton, Wythe, Nicolas, Dabney Carr, and many more worthy to be their associates, were the products of this vicinity. So numerous were its great and patriotic men, that some of their biographers have called it "The Athens of America." It is not without reason that Virginians of this region, so fruitful of historic men, have had a pride in Virginia society. In this society, in its best days, James Monroe was born and reared. So, as to society, he was well born.

At Williamsburg, in this vicinity, the seat of the colonial government, was founded and flourished William and Mary college, which at this time had an annual income of some twenty thousand dollars, and had been in operation over a hundred years; next in age to Harvard college. It had had a good history as to professors, classes and work, and had done much to fill that community with a class of educated men. Albemarle academy was located at Charlotteville, a village in this vicinity, which was converted into Central college and then into the University of Virginia, of famous history. Other academies and private schools did good work for education in all this region.

The *Phi-Beta-Kappa* society, so noted among college men, the chapters of which are connected with so many modern colleges, was formed at William and Mary college, December 5, 1776. Its first meeting is said to have been held in Apollo hall of the old Raleigh tavern, which was a kind of Virginia "cradle of liberty," like Faneuil Hall of Boston. The names of John Marshall and Bushrod Washington appear in the list of the first members. Many excellent libraries were founded here; books abounded; classical literature was common. So James Monroe was well born as to education and its influence in the community.

Nearly this entire vicinity was occupied by families who held large estates, and who came here with means to establish themselves in good old English fashion. They were large agriculturists who made their calling independent and honorable. It was a community of few dangers to young men. The church of England held its strong influence over all. So as to the moral tone of the community, James Monroe was well born.

Little has come down to us of the boyhood of James Monroe. No early biography was written of him. He has gone into history as lacking brilliancy of character action, and so has had no biographical limner to draw carefully the outlines of his early life. Fifty years efficient public service; fifty years intimate association with and confidence of many of the greatest men of his time; eight years of the conduct of the chief magistracy of the nation in such a way as to destroy all enemies, all opposing parties, and bring in "the era of good feeling," as his administration was called; it would seem ought to bring for a man some appreciative biographers, but in his case it did not; so the details of his early life are left in that obscurity which shrouds "the simple annals of the poor."

## A SOLDIER.

The third Virginia regiment, under Colonel Hugh Mercer, appeared at Washington's headquarters at Harlem, New York, in 1776. James Monroe, eighteen years of age, was a lieutenant in that regiment. He was a student in William and Mary college when the war broke out. As a youth he had heard all about the British oppressions of the colonists; the taxation without representation; the "Stamp act;" the Bostonians pitching the tea into the sea; the British possession of Boston; the Lexington, Concord and Bunker Hill fights; the calling of a Continental Congress; the appointment of Washington commander-in-chief; the declaration of independence; the pushing forward the war, and now, as the call for soldiers came, he shut up his books, and, with other students, joined the third Virginia regiment; was elected to a lieutenancy and marched off to headquarters, two or three hundred miles away. His election to the important office of lieutenant of the regiment indicates the estimate his associates put upon him.

After reaching the army he soon found himself in active service. He was in the skirmish at Harlem, which followed right on September 16; the battle at White Plains, October 28, and then the long retreat through New Jersey, fighting all the way, ending with the battle of Trenton, in which he received a severe wound in the shoulder. Captain William Washington and Lieutenant Monroe led the left wing of the American forces in that battle, and did good service in making complete the British rout, and reviving the American cause.

After recovering from his wound, he served as a volunteer aide, with the rank of Major, on the staff of the Earl of Stirling, and took part in the battles of Brandywine, September 11; of Germantown, October 4, and of Monmouth, June 28, 1778. This temporary promotion lost him his regular place in the continental army, so he was detailed to return to Virginia and raise a new regiment, with letters from Stirling and General Washington. But the exhausted state of the country prevented this, and the effect of his failure to raise a new regiment, and his loss of place in the line, for a time almost completely disheartened him. He was modest and self-deprecating, and the closing up of the military way before him, threw him into such a state of self-distrust that he thought to hide from society and become a recluse.

But Jefferson, then governor of Virginia, was his friend, and invited him into his office to study law and assist him in such ways as he could. His uncle, Judge Jones, favored his acceptance of the invitation, and so he joined his fortune with Jefferson's thus early, and the two became life-long friends. This decision was perhaps the key that unlocked to him the gate to that fortunate way that he pursued through the whole of his life. The closing of the military way before him he thought had ruined his prospects, and defeated his young life, and yet, more than likely it was the "blessing in disguise" which turned his feet into the way of greater usefulness and honor.

## A LEGISLATOR.

In 1782, when twenty-three years of age, Mr. Monroe was elected to the Assembly of Virginia. The next year, when twenty-four, he was elected to Congress and served three years. During this time Washington resigned his commission and Mr. Monroe was present. In Congress he was an active and working member, young as he was. He was in Congress three years. The next year he was elected to the Virginia Legislature. He was a member of the Virginia Convention which accepted the United States Constitution. He was opposed to it. He was afraid it was too monarchical; that it conferred too much power on the executive; that he might make himself a king; that the friends of the constitution secretly cherished purposes of making it still more monarchical. He made speeches against it, and it was adopted against his influence. The strong democrats of the time found great fault with the constitution. It was really a federal document; it embodied federal doctrines; was an epitome of modern federalism. Twenty-eight years afterward, in a letter to Andrew Jackson, he explained some of his reasons for opposing it. They grew chiefly out of his distrust of some of the federal leaders. Like Jefferson, who at first opposed it, he became a strong friend of it.

December 6, 1790, he took his seat in the United States Senate, under the constitution which he opposed, and took his oath to sustain it.

He was not conspicuous as a debater; nor noted as a great constitutional statesman; nor as a leader in the philosophy and principles of government; but as a practical, considerate, business legislator, faithful, hard-working, pains-taking. His distrust of the federal leaders, and especially of Hamilton, made him generally unfriendly to Washington's administration, though he was always on terms of personal friendship with Washington. The political feud of the times was a strong one, and he shared much of its one-sidedness and bitterness.

Virginia, an aristocratic, slave-holding state, produced many radical democrats, who sympathized intensely with the French cry of "Liberty and equality." Mr. Monroe was among them.

### A MINISTER ABROAD.

May 28, 1794, when thirty-six of age, Mr. Monroe was commissioned minister to France. His opposition to Washington's administration and to the federalists who had a strong influence with Washington, would have unfitted him for such an appointment, according to modern party politics. But Washington had confidence in Monroe, and his strong interest in the French cause of liberty would make him acceptable to the party in power in France. Mr. Monroe reached Paris just as Robespierre's career had closed. He was introduced into the French convention of citizens, as it was called, as "Citizen James Monroe, minister plenipotentiary from the United States near the French republic," August 15, 1794, and made a written address which was read in French by the secretary. It abounded in expressions of sympathy for the cause of liberty in France. This gave offense to many of the administration officials at home, and he was lectured for his over-warm sympathy with the popular party in the French republic. He went to France to prevent a war with France. Mr. Jay had been sent to England to prevent an embroilment with England. Monroe found it difficult to get a hearing in France. The new government was not receiving ambassadors, and had only coldness for him. He went outside of all routine and got a hearing in the popular convention. It seemed to those who had sent him, a partisan, over-hasty and ill-advised movement, liable to make trouble in England. His warmth for France made enemies at home who were very severe on his course. Mr. Jay made a treaty with England which displeased Monroe and the French. He called it hard names, and was called hard names in return for doing so. The French became warlike again. Mr. Monroe quieted them by sympathy with them and urging them to moderation, and to wait the end of Washington's administration. Just at this time he was recalled; he came home cut to the quick, and passed by Washington without giving him a call. He published a volume of five hundred pages in self-defense. The party critics against him, devoured it in piecemeal. His party friends defended him. A great newspaper war raged for a time. About as much fault was found with Jay and his treaty with England and with Washington for recommending its acceptance. But it turned out that there was no war with France or England and good treaties of amity and commerce were made with both nations, indicating that both men understood the situation in hand better than their critics at home. The war of words against them was carried on more with party gall than with common sense or patriotism. This country was a caldron of hot misunderstandings at this time.

In 1801, Spain ceded Louisiana to France. At once there sprang up a fever of anxiety in the United States as to what France was proposing to do with it. "We must have it," was the common saying among the people. Some one in Congress proposed to purchase it? Congress appropriated two millions of dollars for that purpose; and Mr. Jefferson, then president, appointed Mr. Monroe a special minister to France on this mission. Mr. Robert R. Livingston was already our minister in France, and was moving as he could in the same matter. In a few weeks after Mr. Monroe's arrival in France, they succeeded in making the purchase, which was ratified by Napoleon Bonaparte in May, 1803. The price paid was fifteen million dollars,—the grandest bargain ever made by any nation. It was a peaceful purchase of an empire, as one farmer would buy a farm of another.

Four nations were interested in this transaction—Spain, England, France and the United States. Six individuals were chiefly instrumental in it—Jefferson, Livingston and Monroe for the United States, and Bonaparte, Talleyrand and Marbois, for France. When it was accomplished, the plenipotentiaries rose and shook hands; and Livingston said: "We have lived long, but this is the noblest work of our whole lives."

Mr. Monroe proceeded at once to England as minister to St. James, leaving France this time in a more satisfactory frame of mind than he left it before. He soon returned to France as envoy to Spain, and in this mission he was to treat with the Spanish minister in Paris, concerning the purchase of Florida. But after several months' effort he returned to England, without accomplishing his object.

While in England, Mr. Monroe, in connection with Mr. Pinkney, conducted a long series of interviews with special English ministers, Lords Auckland and Holland, concerning English impressment of seamen, and other unwarrantable transactions on the high seas. They succeeded at last in forming a treaty, but it was so unsatisfactory to President Jefferson that he refused to offer it to the Senate for consideration, and so the long efforts at diplomacy failed, and things went on from bad to worse between the two nations, till the war of 1812 brought its bloody arbitrament.

Lord Holland, in his history of the whig party, speaking of this treaty, which he helped to form, says: "Mr. Jefferson refused to ratify a treaty which would have secured his countrymen from all further vexations, and prevented a war between two nations whose habits, language and interests should unite them in perpetual alliance and good fellowship."

President Jefferson did in haste, and doubtless in no good temper, take upon himself to decide what belonged to the Senate to decide, and the failure to ratify the treaty, left the ill temper between the two nations to rise to war heat, and the second war with England was the result. It looks now as though Mr. Jefferson's responsibility in that war was great, if his act was not the fatal failure to avert it.

Late in 1807, Mr. Monroe returned to America, having accomplished but little with Spain and England; and at once published an elaborate defense of his well-meant endeavors.

### GOVERNOR OF VIRGINIA.

The Virginia of the olden time was usually prompt to recognize the talent and worth of her sons.

When Mr. Monroe returned from France the first time under the cloud of a peremptory recall from the secretary of state, and felt himself obliged to defend himself in a published volume, his native state promptly elected him her governor, which position he held for three years.

Again, when he returned from England, at the next gubernatorial election, she honored him in the same way, believing he had been faithful in his foreign trust. But he soon resigned the place, being called by President Madison, in 1811, to the office of

## SECRETARY OF STATE.

He had been much talked of as a candidate for the presidency, in opposition to Mr. Madison, many of the same party preferring him. He took this important place at a period of great anxiety and danger. Our minister in England, Mr. Russell, had just written to our government that the insolence of England in relation to the impressment of our seamen, the search of our vessels for British seamen, and all the differences between the two governments, was so offensive and dictatorial, that war could not be honorably avoided. This soon became the conviction of President Madison's government; and war was declared June 18, 1812. The declaration of war was drawn by William Pinkney, and communicated to England by James Monroe; the two men who, a few years before, as our ministers to England, had labored so hard to convince England of her bad faith and her unjust treatment of our ships and seagoing countrymen. Then came right on the second war with England. It opened with a series of disasters to our arms. War is a trade and a science — a trade with the soldiers, a science with the leaders. We had neither trained leaders or soldiers. The revolutionary leaders and soldiers were too old. The mantles of their experience had not fallen on the shoulders of their sons. The new generation had to learn war the same way their fathers did—in the midst of its havoc and horror.

England sent against us her best trained officers and soldiers. She remembered the revolution, and knew she had a foe worthy of her best forces. They had their own way for awhile. Our government was poorly prepared for the onslaught. Our navy was almost nothing; our army was a shadow. There was much opposition to the war among our people. It put a stop to much New England business, and jeopardized much property and life. The old federalists aroused themselves and called it a democratic war, a party war. In New England a strong body of the wealthy, conservative, influential men, opposed it. This made the equipping of an army all the more difficult. But the trailing of the stars and stripes in the dust, the presence of British red-coats on our soil, as enemies, soon stirred patriotic blood, and money, and soldiers, and experience, came in due time; the opposition subsided, and victory came in the end; and an end of war with our mother country, it is hoped.

As secretary of state, Mr. Monroe had a more difficult task, because of the inefficiency of General Armstrong, who was secretary of war. After many failures, Armstrong was removed, and Mr. Monroe was entrusted with the double duties of secretary of war and secretary of state. He prosecuted his duties with great vigor, and in due time brought the war to an honorable close.

Toward the close of 1814, Mr. Monroe saw the exposure of New Orleans and its vicinity, and resolved to defend it. The finances of the country were at a low ebb, and to raise the necessary money he pledged his private property in addition to the pledge of the government, and so obtained the money; defended New Orleans; conquered the enemy, January 8, 1815, under General Jackson; and closed the war.

### FIFTH PRESIDENT.

On the fourth of March, 1817, Mr. Monroe was inaugurated president of the United States, with Daniel D. Tompkins, vice-president, in the fifty-ninth year of his age. Washington was made president at fifty-seven; John Adams at sixty-one; Jefferson in his fifty-eighth year, and Madison in his fifty-eighth. Mr. Monroe received one hundred and eighty-three electoral votes; Rufus King, the federalist candidate, received thirty-four. His vigorous conduct of the war had made him popular, and nearly destroyed the federal party. He made John Quincy

Adams, his secretary of state; John C. Calhoun, secretary of war; W. H. Crawford, secretary of treasury; and William Wirt, attorney-general. They were among the strongest men of the time. They were younger than Monroe; Adams being fifty; Calhoun, thirty-five; Crawford, forty-four, and Wirt, forty-five. They all remained in their places during the eight years of Mr. Monroe's administration. It was a strong and harmonious administration, and especially strong in its cabinet.

Mr. Monroe went into the presidency on the popular tide given him by his successful conclusion of the war; and he sought to keep the good favor of the people he had won, by journeys among them. Under the plea of looking after the fortifications on the coast and frontier which Congress had resolved to establish, he traveled through the east, north, west and south, stopping often to receive the salutations of the people, to make and hear speeches, sit at great dinners, and participate in the pageant of great demonstrations. The war was over; the old enemy conquered a second time; peace was in all the land, and the president who had done so much to bring about these happy results, was out shaking hands with his rejoicing people. Well might his administration be called "the era of good feeling." There were important things to be done; but it was easy to do them when many helped and few hindered. The divided, bickering, suspicious, crotchety, ungovernable people of John Adams' time, had now become a happy family, perfectly assured in its ability to govern itself; confident that it had a nearly perfect constitution, and the best government and country and people on earth. At Mr. Monroe's second election there was but one vote cast against him; the federal party was dead; the political millennium had come. Happy president! Happy America!

In 1818 a war broke out with the Seminole Indians in the extreme south. General Jackson was entrusted with its conduct. He never did anything by halves. The Floridas were then territories of Spain. He followed the Indians into the Floridas; established military posts there; approved the summary execution of two British subjects charged with inciting the Indians against the Americans, and by these high handed proceedings came near involving his country in a war with both Spain and England. But the conciliatory spirit of the administration prevailed, and war was avoided.

Perhaps this experience incited a greater desire in our country to possess the Floridas, and a greater willingness in Spain to part with them; for a movement was soon made in which Mr. Adams, the secretary of state, made a purchase of Florida, February 22, 1819, thus securing the last of the Spanish territories adjacent to our settlements. No transactions of that generation were wiser than these purchases of Louisiana and Florida. They were peaceful, commercial, satisfactory and immensely important to our country and humanity. Florida has now became the fruit garden of the country.

Another subject of great interest came up in this administration. It was the admission of Missouri into the Union. Missouri was a slave territory. The extension of slavery had become an ambitious scheme of southern politicians. The differences between the South and North had not grown less under the constitution.

Slavery, which at first extended over all the states, had retired from all the northern communities. It had become a southern institution, and grown up a state of society peculiar to itself, in which aversion to labor, class distinction, personal ease, dislike of all other forms of society, came to make a sort of oligarchy, distinct from the society the constitution was expected to foster.

The North objected to receiving Missouri as a slave state; the South insisted upon it. A great discussion arose, the beginning of the "irrepressible conflict" that came so near destroying the Union. At length a compromise was agreed upon, which was called "The Missouri Compromise," which agreed that Missouri should come in as a slave state, but that no slave territory should extend north of the line of thirty-six degrees thirty minutes. So the great settlement was effected, as the most of the people believed; and there was much rejoicing. But there were those who thought they knew it was only postponed to some future day, as it proved. This compromise dates March 1, 1820.

Still another great question came to the front in Monroe's time — that of "Internal Improvements." It came up on the proposition to establish a great central national road from the east westward, to be extended as fast as settlements were extended. The bill brought before Congress was called "The Cumberland Road Bill." The friends of a strong government, preparing for war in times of peace, cementing its bonds by great arteries of travel and trade, assisting the people in affairs of national interest too great for individual enterprise, moved strongly for this project. It was a Federalist idea.

The opposers of a strong government, who believed more in state governments, who feared central power and government monopolies, and were of the Jefferson school of thinking, opposed it. But the bill passed Congress, notwithstanding the federal party was dead. Its spirit still lived.

But Monroe had been trained at the feet of Jefferson. He scented danger in such a great road, owned and controlled and travel-taxed by the general government; so he vetoed it, and in a long message gave his reasons; but his veto only put off the measure. This veto was given May 4, 1822.

An event of very great interest to the whole people occurred in Monroe's administration. Congress invited Lafayette to revisit America. On May 10, 1824, he accepted the invitation, and came early in the fall. His journey through the states was an extended ovation. He and Monroe began their acquaintance and friendship in the revolutionary army. Now it was a joy to both to meet again in the midst of the grand fruits of their early labors and dangers. The people, the visitor, and the government joined to make the occasion one for cementing good feeling and giving strength and gladness to the whole country.

That which marks Mr. Monroe and his administration more than anything else, is his official enunciation of what may properly be called "The American Doctrine," but which, on account of his explicit statement of it, has ever since been called "The Monroe Doctrine." In his message, December 2, 1823, in consequence of Russian and other European overtures to our government touching matters in different parts of the American continent, he spoke at length of our isolation from Europe and the sentiment that had grown up among us, that we must not entangle ourselves with foreign alliances nor *permit European interference in American affairs, either in our own or other American republics.* The enunciation of the doctrine is interwoven with the whole message; but a few passages pretty clearly state it: "That the American continent, by the free and independent condition which it has assumed and maintains, is henceforth not to be considered as a place for future colonization by any European powers." Again: "We owe it, therefore, to candor and to the amicable relations existing between the United States and those powers, to declare that we should consider any attempt on their part to extend their system to any portion of this hemisphere as dangerous to our peace and safety." It is further elucidated and applied in the message. The doctrine is, European hands off from American nationalities; we avoid foreign entanglements; we do not permit foreign meddling. It does not seem that Mr. Monroe thought he was saying anything singular or of marked significance; but because thus authoritatively said, it has gone into history as the Monroe doctrine. It was the common sentiment of the American writers and statesmen put forth in a presidential message.

### DOMESTIC RELATIONS.

When Mr. Monroe was a member of Congress in New York, and about twenty-eight years of age, he married Miss Eliza Kortwright, daughter of Lawrence Kortwright, a respectable gentleman of that city who had lost his fortune in the revolution. He made his home in Fredericksburg, Virginia, with a view to go into the practice of law; we have seen with what success.

They had two daughters, Eliza, who married Judge George Hay, of Virginia, and Maria, who married Samuel L. Governeur, of New York. When her parents were in Paris, Eliza was a schoolmate with Hortense Beauharnais, daughter of Josephine, and step-daughter of the Emperor Napoleon, who became queen of Holland, and their teacher was the celebrated Madam Campan. The acquaintance of these school girls ripened into a life-long friendship. Eliza named a daughter Hortensia for Queen Hortense, who always retained a strong interest in her American namesake, and sent to her rich portraits of herself and sister, and Madam Campan.

Mr. Monroe had a tender interest in his family and his relatives. He was a modest, kindly, plain man; considerate of all; simple and polite; a little awkward in manner; in stature about six feet; compact, a little angular and bony in features and build; in youth and middle age strong and enduring. He made many friends and kept them. He served his country with a single purpose through more than five decades. He was often censured and sometimes publicly humiliated by his superiors in office, yet in the long run he has gained the approval of his countrymen. He is a standing proof that plain common sense, with good purpose and hearty industry, may serve the republic of a just and loyal people in its highest offices.

In his later years Mr. Monroe served with Mr. Jefferson and Mr. Madison as regent of the Virginia university. His declining years were harrassed with inadequate income. He gave his life to his country and was poorly paid. He was honored most by those who knew him best. In his life-time, his lack of brilliancy prevented him from being generally estimated at his real worth; but as the years pass away his record brightens and his solid merits came to be more appreciated. Mr. Daniel C. Gilman gave to the world, only last year, an appreciative sketch of his life, and predicted that some future biographer would do him ample justice.

The last years of Mr. Monroe's life were spent chiefly with his daughter, Mrs. Governeur, in New York. He died the fourth day of July, 1831, making the third president that died on that memorable day, about a year after the death of his wife. He was buried in New York. But the state of Virginia, on the one hundreth anniversary of the day of his birth, removed his remains to Richmond, that they might rest permanently in the soil of his native state which he had so signally honored with a patriotic and self-sacrificing life.

## The Grave of James Monroe.

After resting in its grave twenty-seven years in New York, where Mr. Monroe died, his body was removed to Richmond, Virginia. It was received with great demonstrations of respect in the capital of his native state. The removal was made July 4, 1858, and the re-interment July 5. Mottos expressive of the most loyal patriotism and the heartiest devotion to the union and liberty were hoisted over the streets. A vast procession moved slowly out to Hollywood cemetery bearing reverently and tenderly the honored dust of the fifth president of the United States, and the fourth from Virginia. To an eminence overlooking a long reach of the James river and its beautiful valley and a wide circuit of delightful country, in the southwestern and much-frequented part of the lovely cemetery, the sacred relics were borne and buried five feet under ground in a brick and granite vault. The vault was covered with a large, polished block of Virginia marble, eight feet long and four feet wide. On this, as a pedestal, rests a large granite sarcophagus, cut in the shape of a coffin. On the northern side of the sarcophagus is a brass plate, now dark with age, bearing this inscription:

### James Monroe.

BORN IN WESTMORELAND COUNTY, 28TH OF APRIL, 1758.
DIED IN THE CITY OF NEW YORK, 4TH OF JULY, 1831.
By Order of the General Assembly,
His Remains were Removed to this Cemetery 5th of July, 1858,
As an evidence of the
Affection of Virginia for her Good and Honored Son.

The ends and sides are filled in between the pillars with ornamental cast-iron grating, made so compact as to be difficult to look through the interstices. This unique monument will always mark, to every visitor, the grave of President Monroe from every other.

J. Q. Adams

## CHAPTER VII.

### JOHN QUINCY ADAMS.
#### SIXTH PRESIDENT OF THE UNITED STATES.

##### ANCESTRY.

THE name of John Quincy Adams is an inspiration to those who are in sympathy with the great men and deeds of the great ages of mankind. He was the product of an ancestry and period, both of which put their forces into him in strong measure. He was born in stirring times, when men were earnestly considering the rights of man and conscience, and were profoundly moved by the questions of duty and life.

John Quincy Adams was born July 11, 1767, in Braintree, Massachusetts, now Quincy, ten miles from Boston, when his father John Adams, second president of the United States, his neighbors, and the thinking men of the American colonies, were agitating the question of British oppressions and American rights. The Adamses were a vigorous race, solid and hardy in mind and body. They were of the genuine Puritan stock, strong-thinking, muscular, resolute, independent. They were descended from the hardy middle class of English society, which in those times craved better fortune and a freer life than were open to them in England. In this new country they rose gradually to better and better conditions. More of them sought education, and were sought for places of public trust. Henry Adams was the first of the family in this country, who fled from religious persecution in Devonshire, England, soon after the

Mayflower landed her freight of pilgrims. Then Joseph, and Joseph his son, and deacon John Adams and his son John and John Quincy, furnish the succession. Through the whole line they were noted for "piety, humility, simplicity, prudence, patience, temperance, frugality, industry and perseverance,"— the virtues that make genuine men.

The mother of John Quincy Adams was Abigail Smith, daughter of Rev. William Smith, who had descended from the Quincys. He received his name Quincy from his great-grandfather, on his mother's side. In a letter he once wrote, he said: "He was dying, when I was baptized; and his daughter, my grandmother, present at my birth, requested that I might receive his name. The fact recorded by my father at the time, has connected with that portion of my name, a charm of mingled sensibility and devotion. It was the name of one passing from earth to immortality. These have been among the strongest links of my attachment to the name of Quincy, and have been to me, through life, a perpetual admonition to do nothing unworthy of it."

John Quincy was a gentleman of wealth, education and influence. He held many places of public trust and honor. Exemplary in private life, and earnest in piety, he enjoyed the public confidence through a civil career of forty years duration. Josiah Quincy, a gentleman of great attainments, who has lately passed away, wrote an excellent biography of John Quincy Adams. The blood and the name of the Adamses and Quincys were thus mingled in him.

Abigail Adams, his mother, was a woman of great personal ability and worth. Scarcely a woman of her time was her superior. Her letters constitute an interesting feature of the literature of her time, and show how, with less opportunity than the men of their time, the women nobly did their part in laying the foundations of American society.

### THE TIME.

Times, as well as ancestors, have to do in the make-up of men. In 1761 there arose, in the Supreme Court of Massachusetts, a question as to the constitutionality of the laws by which England was systematically taxing her colonies. The cause was argued for the king by the attorney-general, and, against the laws, by James Otis. The question involved was the very one which at last was settled by an appeal to arms. John Adams, then a young lawyer, was present. He recorded his opinion of Otis and the question at issue in these emphatic statements: "Otis was a flame of fire! With a promptitude of classical allusion, a depth of research, a rapid summary of historical events and dates, a profusion of legal authorities, a prophetic glance of his eyes into futurity, a rapid torrent of impetuous eloquence, he hurried away all before him. *American independence*, was then and there born. Every man of an unusually-crowded audience, appeared to me, to go away ready to take up arms against writs of assistance." On another occasion he said: "James Otis then and there breathed into this nation the breath of life." This was six years before John Quincy Adams was born.

In 1765 the British Parliament passed the Stamp act, which made all transactions in the colonies illegal not recorded on stamped paper, which stamps must be bought of the crown. James Otis and John Adams argued against the constitutionality of the law before the governor and council of Massachusetts. This was two years before the birth of John Quincy Adams.

John Adams was so wrought upon by these things that he wrote a dissertation on the canon and feudal laws, which showed the democratic spirit then active in him, and his ideas of the rights of the people.

The colonies were so aroused by the Stamp act that it was repealed in 1766, one year before the birth of the younger Adams. In the year in which he was born, 1767, a law was passed taxing glass, paper, paints and tea. This roused the spirit of opposition to British oppression still more. John Adams was one of the leaders in that opposition in Boston, and his wife was joined with him in his stout determination to stand for the rights of the colonies. Of such parents and in such times was John Quincy Adams born.

The next year Boston held a meeting to instruct the Provincial Legislature to oppose the British usurpations, and John Adams was on the committee to prepare the instructions, with Richard Dana and Joseph Warren—the same Warren who fell on Bunker Hill, seven years later. On the fifth of March, 1770, a collision occurred between British soldiers and some citizens of Boston, in which five citizens were killed and many wounded, which was called "Bloody Massacre." The excitement grew more and more intense every year, and the Adams family was in the heat of it.

In December, 1773, the tea was destroyed in Boston harbor, and the harbor closed soon after. On September 5, 1774, the first American Congress met in Philadelphia, with John Adams as a member. In 1775, at his suggestion, George Washington was appointed commander-in-chief of the American army, and on June 17 the battle of Bunker Hill was fought, with Mrs. Adams and her children looking from the summit of Penn's Hill, not far from their home, at the burning of Charlestown, and hearing the distant roar of battle. The mother and children entered into the life of the times just as did Mr. Adams himself. During the siege of Boston, which followed right on, Mrs. Adams kept her house open to the soldiers in their needs, and often gave them food, shelter and sympathy. Her letters to him abound with descriptions of the fearful times, the sleepless nights and anxious days they were passing through, and the scenes in which she and her family had a part. The life, spirit and grandeur of those "times which tried men's souls" were felt by the Adamses as forcibly as by any who then lived. And it was in the midst of those times that John Quincy Adams came into being, charged with the life of the mighty period; and its scenes, deeds and forces were among his first teachers. It can not be otherwise than that he was made in part by these things. His soul was of his times—a product of the American revolution.

### HIS BOYHOOD.

Usually boys are boys the world over; but John Quincy Adams was an exception. Edward Everett Hale said of him:

"There seemed to be in his life no such stage as boyhood." When about nine years old he wrote to his father in Congress this letter:

BRAINTREE, June 2, 1777.

DEAR SIR,—I love to receive letters very well, much better than I love to write them. I make a poor figure at composition. My head is much too fickle. My thoughts are running after bird's eggs, play and trifles, till I get vexed with myself. Mamma has a troublesome task to keep me a studying. I own I am ashamed of myself. I have just entered the third volume of Rollin's History, but designed to have got half through it by this time. I am determined to be more diligent. Mr. Thaxter is absent at court. I have set myself a stint this week, to read the third volume half out. If I can but keep my resolution, I may again, at the end of the week, give a better account of myself. I wish, sir, you would give me, in writing, some instructions with regard to the use of my time, and advise me how to proportion my studies and play, and I will keep them by me and endeavor to follow them. With the present determination of growing better, I am, dear sir, your son, JOHN QUINCY ADAMS.

P. S.— Sir, if you will please be so good as to favor me with a blank book, I will transcribe the most remarkable passages I meet with in my reading, which will serve to fix them upon my mind.

Very little of the boy in that. The first sentence or two is a little boy-like. The reference to the bird's eggs and play indicate that the boy was in him, but suppressed, and he was bound to crush him out. A nine-year-old reading Rollin's History and transcribing the most remarkable passages to fix them in his mind!

February 13, 1778, John Adams started on a mission to France to which he had been appointed by Congress. He took his son, then not quite eleven, with him. In a note he sent to his wife just as they were to enter the frigate to depart, he said: "Johnny sends his duty to his mamma, and his love to his sisters and brothers. He behaves like a man."

"He behaves like a man!" Glad was the father no doubt to write that; but it indicates that the man was already getting the mastery of the boy, that the training he was receiving from his parents and the times was rapidly developing the man.

He learned the rudiments of an education in the village school of Braintree. In after life he often playfully boasted that the dame who taught him to spell flattered him into learning his letters by telling him he would prove a scholar. A student in his father's office instructed him in the elements of Latin.

Mr. Adams remained in Paris till June, 1779, when he and his son returned. In November, 1779, he went again to France to meet commissioners from England to negotiate a treaty of peace. Young Adams went again with his father.

In July, 1780, Mr. Adams was appointed ambassador to the Netherlands, and his son was removed from the schools of Paris to those of Amsterdam, and later to the University of Leyden. There he studied till July of the next year, when, at the age of fourteen, he was invited by Francis Dana, minister from the United States to the Russian court, to become his private secretary, and he accompanied him through Germany to St. Petersburg. Beyond his official duties he found time to continue his Latin, French and German studies, together with English history, until September, 1782, when he went to Stockholm and passed the winter. The next spring he went through Sweden to the Hague, where he met his father and went with him to Paris. He was present at the signing of the treaty of peace in 1783. He went with his father to England visiting eminent men and noted places; after which he returned to Paris and his studies, till May, 1785, when both father and son returned to the United States. He was now eighteen years old. His father had just been appointed minister to England. Should he go with his father, or go to college? Here was a great temptation. He saw the glittering prospects of a life at the court of St. James; he knew he needed the drill and discipline of a college and professional course of study. His father's finances had suffered by his public service. The boy chose to go home to study and become an independent worker-out of his own fortune. Wise choice, showing that the man and not the boy had control of him. After reviewing his studies under an instructor, he entered the junior class in Harvard college in March, 1786, a little before he was nineteen years of age. He graduated in 1787 with the second honor of his class, and gave an oration on "The Importance of Public Faith to the Well-being of a Community," which was published on account of the interest felt in it.

### THE LAWYER.

Now, at twenty years of age, young Adams entered upon the study of law, in the office of Theophilus Parsons, afterward chief justice of Massachusetts, at Newburyport. He was admitted to the bar in 1790. He at once opened an office in Boston. He was a stranger there, though born within ten miles. He afterward said of his practice. "I can hardly call it practice, because for the space of one year it would be difficult for me to name any practice which I had to do. For two years, indeed, I can recall nothing in which I was engaged that may be termed practice, though during the second year, there were some symptoms that by persevering patience, practice might come in time. The third year, I continued this patience and perseverance, and having little to do, occupied my time as well as I could in the study of those laws and institutions which I have since been called to administer. At the end of the third year I had obtained something which might be called practice. The fourth year, I found it swelling to such an extent that I felt no longer any concern as to my future destiny as a member of that profession. But in the midst of the fourth year, by the will of the first president of the United States, with which the Senate was pleased to concur, I was selected for a station, not, perhaps, of more usefulness, but of greater consequence in the estimation of mankind, and sent from home on a mission to foreign parts."

### THE WRITER.

While waiting for clients and continuing the active study of his profession, Mr. Adams was not a careless spectator of national affairs. He was an intense patriot. His travels abroad had made his patriotism broader, richer, more intelligent. He had been so thoroughly trained by his mother and the community in which he was born, in the morals of life, which he had been taught to apply to political and national affairs, that it was difficult for him to separate his personal life from the life of the nation. About this time Thomas Paine's "Rights of Man" was published in this country, with the approval of Thomas Jefferson. Both Paine and Jefferson had been much in France, and much influenced by the radically democratic, or as we would say now, communistic views of the French leaders in their revolution. Mr. Adams saw clearly the "political heresies" of Mr. Paine's pamphlet, and the mischief it was likely to do among the American people, who sympathized intensely with the French in their struggle for liberty, and exposed those heresies, and explained the difference between the French struggle and our own, in a series of articles which he published in the "Columbia Centinel," over the signature "Publicola."

In April, 1793, Great Britain declared war against France. Such was the sympathy for France in this country, that multitudes were ready to make our republic a French ally against our old enemy.

Mr. Adams published another series of letters, over the signature of "Marcellus," in which he advocated with great ability the neutrality of the United States. He enlarged upon the necessity of our keeping clear of all foreign entanglements.

A little later he published another series, over the signature of "Columbus," severely criticising citizen Genet, whom France had sent here to arouse America in her behalf. These several articles were republished in pamphlets and other papers and widely read. They were published also, in England and held as among the ablest political writings from America. Washington and his cabinet read them with great interest. They advocated in the main the doctrines Washington was trying to enforce in his administration. They did not suit either party, but were broader and wiser than either. They tended greatly to establish an American course of conduct, and fix many things on solid bases, which were then unsettled. They threw light, and much of it, into the gloom of that most doubtful period of our national history.

In these papers there was not only shown great political and literary ability and moral character of a high order, but a clear knowledge of foreign countries, and of the language and etiquette of courts and diplomacy. All this pointed out to Washington's quick and most accurate judgment, the man he wanted for a foreign minister; and when he found it was his vice-president's son, who was yet but a young man, who had written so wisely, he did not hesitate on account of his few years, but appointed him minister to the Netherlands. His commission was given him July 11, 1794, the day he completed his twenty-seventh year.

### FOREIGN MINISTER.

Mr. Adams left Boston in September, and reached London in October, where Messrs. Jay and Pinckney were negotiating a treaty between England and the United States. After fifteen days in London he sailed, October 30, for Holland. Holland almost at once fell into the hands of France, and his intercourse was about as much with the conquering as the conquered country.

In October, 1795, he was directed by the secretary of state to repair to England, where he found he was appointed to ratify Jay's treaty with the British government. After fulfilling this mission he returned to Holland.

In August, 1796, he received the appointment of minister to Portugal, but his credentials did not reach him till his successor came, the next July. He at once repaired to London, to find that an appointment to the court of Berlin had superseded the other. While waiting for instructions, he fulfilled an engagement of marriage with Miss Louisa Catharine Johnson, daughter of Joshua Johnson, American consul at London. The marriage took place July 26, 1797. They proceeded to Berlin where Mr. Adams faithfully discharged the duties of his high office till 1801, when they returned to the United States.

### BEGINS ANEW.

Mr. Adams returned to Boston and to the bar, but without practice. When he left the bar, seven years before, his practice had just become assured. But now, after seven years abroad, he must begin anew. He had now a family to support; his finances had suffered by the failure of foreign bankers; but, nothing daunted, he again sought practice. He applied himself diligently to read up the new statutes and to acquaint himself with the new conditions of law and society in his own country. He was but started in this study when the Boston district elected him to the Senate of Massuchesetts.

In Massachusetts the federalists were in the majority. While he had been absent his father had been president, and lost his re-election by the division of his party and the rise of the democratic party, under Mr. Jefferson. Mr. Adams was not a politician by nature, and had had no part in the party differences of the time. His first public act as a senator was one of political justice and conciliation. He was elected by federalists, but when the governor's council was appointed he moved that a portion be appointed from the minority party, on the ground that the minority had rights that the majority were bound, in justice, to respect.

In 1803 Mr. Adams was elected to the Senate of the United States by the Massachusetts legislature. He was now thirty-six years of age. The country, at this time, was fearfully embarrassed, both by home distractions and foreign complications. Party spirit was almost a craze; one party affiliated with France, the other with England; the people had not learned to be stable citizens, nor what belonged to good citizenship; many of their leaders were distracted by foreign theories and Utopian schemes; war was appealing to the belligerent spirit of the young nation. The president, Mr. Jefferson, was dreaded and hated by many of the federalists as a French Jacobin.

When these perils and embarrassments were thickening in and about the young republic, Mr. Adams took his seat in Congress, elected by federalists. The next year, 1804, Bonaparte became emperor of France. All Europe seemed falling under his sway. England alone withstood him. In 1807 England issued the "Orders in Council," which forbade all trade with France and her allies. Bonaparte replied with the "Milan Decree," which prohibited all trade with England and her colonies. American commerce became a prey to both these belligerent nations. As a last resort, Mr. Jefferson determined on an embargo to save the remnant of American commerce. Massachusetts opposed the Embargo act; Mr. Adams supported Mr. Jefferson, for which he was roundly abused by his constituents. It was a characteristic of his whole life not to be a partisan. He was a national man and could not step to party orders. As a result, he was often charged with corrupt affiliation with the opposite party. He was often the best abused man in the whole country. For the several things which he did contrary to the will of his federalist constituents, a small majority elected another person to be his successor at the close of his term, so in March, 1808, he resigned his seat in the Senate.

In 1805 he sought to have Congress levy a duty on the importation of slaves, and thus began his strong public opposition to slavery, which ended only with his life.

In 1804 he was urged to accept the presidency of Harvard university, which he declined, but, instead, accepted the chair of rhetoric and belles-lettres, which he filled to great acceptance. His lectures were very popular and attended by large crowds from Boston. They were afterward published in two volumes.

### MINISTER TO RUSSIA.

In March, 1809, Mr. Adams was appointed minister to Russia. It was a critical and important time. The republic was drifting toward a storm with England; and the president, Mr. Madison, was preparing for the worst. It had demanded the abrogation of the "Orders in Council" and the "Milan Decree." France complied; but England hesitated, haggled, put off, and although she finally complied, she did not do it till the embroilment was on the verge of war, which Congress had declared before the news of England's compliance reached this country. It was important that a strong man had charge of our affairs with Russia. Washington had predicted that the younger Adams would in due time be at the head of our foreign ministry. That time was now approaching.

Mr. Adams was received with marked respect at the court of St. Petersburg. His familiarity with the French and German languages—the former the diplomatic language of Europe—his literary acquirements; his perfect knowledge of the political relations of the civilized world; his plain appearance and republican simplicity of manners, in the midst of the gorgeous embassies of other nations, enabled him to make a striking and favorable impression on the Emperor Alexander and his court. The emperor, charmed by his varied qualities, admitted him to terms of personal intimacy, seldom granted to the most favored individuals.

Twenty-eight years before, when a boy of fourteen, he was there as Mr. Dana's private secretary; now he had returned in the prime of manhood, a diplomat of his nation.

While there, the aged Russian minister of the interior estimated the value of all the gifts he had received while in office; and paid the sum into the national treasury. It was an act which Mr. Adams greatly honored. About this time, a Russian bookseller sent him an elegant copy of the scriptures. He kept the copy, but returned the full price of it in money. He believed that public officials should be free from bias, and so should refuse all presents.

While at St. Petersburg, Mr. Adams wrote a series of letters to a son at school in Massachussetts, on the bible and its teachings, which after his death were published in a volume. Through his life, he was a careful and devout student of the bible. Its precepts of wisdom and morality were always the guide of his life. He took great pleasure in studying the scriptures in the different languages he had learned; and held them in profound respect.

While Mr. Adams was at his court, the emperor proposed to mediate between England and the United States, to secure a cessation of hostilities. England refused the emperor's offer, but proposed to meet American commissioners at London or Gottenburg. Mr. Adams, and Messrs. Bayard, Clay, Russell and Gallatin were appointed. In conducting the negotiations which followed, the American commissioners, with Mr. Adams at their head, displayed a knowledge of national rights and laws, a justice, firmness and magnanimity, which was profoundly respected by the nations of Europe; and which led the Marquis of Wellesley to say in the House of Lords that, "in his opinion, the American commissioners had shown the most astonishing superiority over the British, during the whole of the correspondence."

After six months of negotiations, the treaty of peace was signed at Ghent on the twenty-fourth of December, 1814.

The commissioners proceeded to London, where on the third of July, 1815, they signed a treaty of commerce with England. Thus was effected permanent relations of good will between these two great nations.

## MINISTER AT THE COURT OF ST. JAMES.

Before going to London as a commissioner, Mr. Adams had been appointed resident minister at the court of St. James. He remained here till 1817, attending faithfully to the duties of his high position; and reflecting great honor to his country, by his learning, wisdom and exalted character.

## SECRETARY OF STATE.

On the fourth of March, 1817, James Monroe was inaugurated president of the United States. He came into office when party spirit had for a long time run high. It was somewhat abated by the war, but was still in the way of a proper demonstration of the principles on which the republic was founded. It was his great purpose to conciliate the parties and bring domestic peace to his country. He looked about for the most able and acceptable men for his cabinet officers, who were most pronounced for their non-partisan patriotism and their broad wisdom. He fixed on John Quincy Adams for his secretary of state—the man of all others who could give the most commanding dignity to his administration, in the foreign world's estimation.

As soon as Mr. Adams received his appointment, he closed his affairs in England and took passage for New York, where he landed August, 1817. A great public dinner was given him in

Tammany hall, at which Governor Clinton, the mayor of the city, and some two hundred of the best-distinguished citizens gave expression to their profound regard for the great diplomat. He went immediately to Boston where a like reception awaited him, at which his aged father was a guest.

The next month Mr. Adams removed to Washington and entered upon the duties of his office.

During the eight years of Monroe's administration, Mr. Adams remained faithful to the duties of the secretary of state. He had entire charge of the foreign department of the government, and did much to establish, on just principles, the good relations our government has since maintained with countries abroad. He carried out the principles he had, in his early manhood, formulated in his papers in the "Columbian Centinel," and which so pleased Washington that he adopted them in his farewell address to the people of the United States.

It was during Mr. Adams' term of office as secretary of state, that the Greek revolution broke out, in 1821. Greece had for a long time been subject to the Ottoman power, which was a cruel oppression. She resisted it and took up arms for independence. The American people sympathized deeply with the Greeks. Meetings were held all over the country to express that sympathy. Resolutions were passed. The press was ablaze with Greek sympathy. Money, clothing, provisions, arms, were collected and sent to Greece. Men volunteered to go into her service. The Greek cause was immensely popular. The struggling Greeks appealed to the United States for assistance; but Mr. Adams remained true to his principles, and in his correspondence with the Greek minister, said: "But while cheering with their best wishes the cause of the Greeks, the United States are forbidden, by the duties of their situation, from taking part in the war, to which their relation is that of neutrality. At peace themselves with all the world, their established policy and the obligations of the laws of nations, preclude them from becoming voluntary auxiliaries to a cause which would involve them in war."

During his term of office the Seminole war came on and the

difficulty with General Jackson in trespassing upon the Spanish territory and in hanging as spies two British subjects, which came near entangling us in a foreign war. Mr. Adams supported Jackson and made such convincing arguments in favor of his position as to soothe the British cabinet. He made arrangements with Spain to purchase the Floridas, and so get possession of all the territory on the Gulf east of the Mississippi. This was a great gratification to Mr. Adams, as it was an object he had labored for with great anxiety. While Spain owned the Floridas we were in danger of trouble. During nearly all of Mr. Adam's term of office under Monroe, he was the subject of bitter political persecution. The old hatred of the federalists was not all dead. Some of those who hated his father hated him for his father's sake. He was a mighty man, and had come from abroad to hurt somebody's prospects for the presidency. Henry Clay had wanted to be secretary of state under Monroe, so he was made an enemy of Adams and the administration. His prospects for the presidency were hurt. Crawford, of Georgia, was ambitious and sorry to see Adams called home to be in his way. Clinton, of New York, was an aspirant for the presidency also, and he and his friends were annoyed by the diplomat's occupancy of the first place in Monroe's government. The press, in the interest of these and other aspirants for position, failed not to serve them in roundly abusing Mr. Adams. It called him "a royalist," "a friend of oligarchy," "a misanthrope; educated in contempt of his fellowmen," as "unfit to be the minister of a free and virtuous people." Mr. Monroe was warned of him as "full of duplicity," as "an incubus on his prospects for the next presidency, and his popularity." In reply to all this and much more Mr. Adams went quietly on doing his duty. When asked by his friends to defend himself against these abuses, he replied that a faithful discharge of his duty to his country was his best defense.

The introduction of Missouri into the Union was an event which occasioned one of the most thorough discussions which the question of slavery had ever had. It was really the beginning of the great struggle, which never ended till that institution went down in a sea of blood. Missouri was the first state to be admitted which had grown up on the Louisiana purchase. Others were to follow. The south desired to carry slavery into all that territory and to carve it up into states devoted to its interests. The north wished to devote it to the freedom which the republic was founded to promote. The south had sent its best men to Congress, as was its custom in the days of slavery, when there was little to employ its best talent but politics. The north was busy in its multiplied business affairs. It was Mr. Adams' opinion that the southern side of Congress was the stronger and much more persistent. It was perfectly united, and had a great interest as it believed to contend for; while the north had many opinions and no interests in the question but those of patriotism and humanity. William Pinkney, James Barbour, Henry Clay, John C. Calhoun, were then leaders in the debate on the southern side, while Rufus King, perhaps, was the only northern man then in Congress, equal to them in debate. Mr. Adams, as secretary of state, was simply a looker on in the public debate, except as he conversed frequently with the speakers on both sides. He recorded his conversations and opinions and the essential facts in the whole case. He was himself intensely opposed to slavery, so much so, that he felt that the makers of the constitution had made a mistake in compromising with it. He saw that it was imperiling and must ultimately destroy the union or be itself destroyed. The subject went into cabinet meetings. Mr. Calhoun did not think the Union would be dissolved, but if it was, the south would join with England and make their states military communities. Mr. Adams assured him that if the matter was pressed to a dissolution of the Union, it would be followed by universal emancipation; and a more remote result might be the extermination of the colored race in this country. Mr. Adams would defend the colored people against slavery on account of their weakness, "and if the dissolution of the Union must come," he said, "let it come from no other cause but this. If slavery be the destined sword, in the hand of the destroying angel, which is to sever the ties of this Union, the same sword will cut assunder the bonds of slavery itself." It was his conviction that slavery could not long survive the dissolution of the union. He thought then was the time to settle the question of the extension of slavery, for he said: "Time will only show whether the contest may ever be renewed with equal advantage." And he wrote: "Oh, if but one man could arise with a genius capable of comprehending, a heart capable of supporting, and an utterance capable of communicating, those eternal truths which belong to the question,— to lay bare in all its nakedness that outrage upon the goodness of God, human slavery,—now is the time, and this is the occasion, upon which such a man would perform the duties of an angel upon earth."

Again he wrote: "Slavery is the great and foul stain on the American Union, and it is a contemplation worthy of the most exalted soul, whether its total abolition is not practicable. This object is vast in its compass, awful in its prospects, sublime and beautiful in its issue. A life devoted to it would be nobly spent and sacrificed." His soul revolted at human slavery as containing every foul principle against which the American revolution was waged, and opposed to every good principle of the American republic. It violated the rights of human nature and the political freedom our government was established to guarantee to its people. This discussion intensified his abhorrence of slavery and the bitter fruits it bore in the slaveholders themselves, and did much to give a strong anti-slavery tone to the rest of his life.

The debate resulted in a compromise, known ever since as the "Missouri Compromise," which admitted Missouri as a slave state, but prohibited slavery in the remaining portion of the Louisiana purchase north of latitude thirty-six degrees and thirty minutes.

Mr. Monroe's administration was so wisely conducted that it resulted in great prosperity to the country. The war was over and brought its good results to our commerce and the increased confidence of foreign nations; agriculture developed rapidly; manufactures increased and were protected and fostered by the government; political animosities and jealousies subsided, and the people began to feel that their government was founded to be permanent. Internal improvements were begun and the people began to accept the lessons of experience and the wisdom of righteousness as worth more than ideal theories. In all these good attainments of Mr. Monroe's administration, Mr. Adams is to be credited with no small share of honor. He was the diplomat; his the great philosophic mind which did much to shape and give tone to the measures and spirit of the government. Adams was the thinker, Monroe was the practical executive of the administration. They complemented each other and did more and better together than either could have done without the other. The "era of good feeling" which they secured was first realized by the president and secretary in the unity and harmony of their deliberations. During Mr. Adams' secretaryship, the affairs of our government were put upon a better footing than they ever had been before.

### THE PRESIDENT.

On the fourth of March, 1825, Mr. Adams was inaugurated sixth president of the United States. There was no election by the people on account of the many candidates. "Of two hundred and sixty-one electoral votes, General Jackson received ninety-nine, Mr. Adams eighty-four, Mr. Crawford forty-one, and Mr. Clay thirty-seven."

By the constitution the election was thrown into the House of Representatives, in which Mr. Adams received a majority of all the votes and was elected. John C. Calhoun was nearly unanimously elected vice-president.

Mr. Monroe's administration, by various causes, had nearly silenced the federal party, so that the several candidates for the presidency were essentially of the same party. The differences were chiefly local and sectional. They inaugurated a season of stormy strife in which personal qualities more than political principles, carried on bitter controversies.

Andrew Jackson, one of the defeated candidates, claimed at once that he was defeated by a bargain between Adams and Clay, the outward evidence of which was that Clay was made secretary of state. Jackson took his state, Tennessee, with him in his denunciation of Adams and Clay, and opposition to their administration. That state took "time by the forelock," and at once nominated Jackson for the next president. He resigned his seat in the United States Senate to conduct his campaign for the next election. This raised at once personal animosities, ambitions and partisans, which easily disturbed the peaceful administration of the government. Jackson was not a man to soften any personal prejudice, or yield any personal ambitions; Adams was not a man to yield any conscientious conviction or swerve from any duty. Two strong men could not well be more unlike in character, education and purpose in life. One was educated, broad, generous, high-minded; the other was natural, concentrated, passionate, generous to his friends and vindictive to his supposed enemies. They agreed in party affiliation, but Jackson's defeat put him upon his military spirit, and he marshalled his forces for a battle.

Mr. Adams was the first man made president, who had no personal part in the revolution. Yet he was born of its spirit and true to its principles. No man ever understood better its fundamental principles, or gave them a heartier devotion, or a grander illustration in his life. No man ever threw upon them a clearer light from a great intellect and a noble heart.

Mr. Adams was the second president from the northern states, his father being the first. The four others were from Virginia. Three southern candidates ran against him and no northern one.

The removing and appointing power of the president is very great; yet Mr. Adams "made but two removals, both from unquestionable causes; and in his new appointments, he was scrupulous in selecting candidates whose talents were adapted to the public service." He appointed some federalists to office, but was severely censured by his southern democratic friends for it. It was his intention invariably to make ability and integrity the qualifications for office.

In his first message, Mr. Adams made several important recommendations: "The maturing into a permanent and regular system the application of all the superfluous revenues of the Union to internal improvement;" "the establishment of a uniform standard of weights and measures;" "the establishment of a naval school of instruction for the formation of scientific and accomplished officers;" "the establishment of a national university," which had been recommended by Washington.

In all these recommendations, he was looking to the permanence, progress and character of the nation. He was not simply playing president for the glory of it, he was nation building. He was a national man; had studied national affairs in this country and Europe, in history and in the nature of men, all his life, and now ripened, conscientious and large-hearted, he was applying his knowledge, patriotism and humanity, to the conduct and development of the national character and resources. He was too clear-seeing, downright and genuine to be understood by the average politicians and people of his day, unless they were those who came into daily intercourse with him. He would not truckle; he would not conciliate to the loss of self-respect; he would not yield to partisan wrong; so he was misunderstood, maligned, abused, by multitudes in high places and low, incapable of appreciating his disinterested, manly and dignified character. In that early day he wanted to protect and encourage American manufactures; wanted a system of internal improvements; wanted a civil service based on merit; a uniform system of weights and measures, a subject which he had deeply studied, a written report of which had gained him great credit in Europe; wanted a naval academy and a national university, all of which are level with the best thought of our time. On these things, and many more, he was simply fifty years in advance of his age. Indeed, his was the colossal mind of his time, enriched beyond any of his countrymen in political learning, and fired with a noble patriotism.

During Mr. Adams' administration, the Marquis de Lafayette visited the United States for the last time. Congress desired to send a ship for him, but he preferred to come in a less formal way. He arrived in New York on the fifteenth of August, 1824. His reception in New York was sublime and brilliant in the extreme. He proceeded from New York on a tour through the United States, which was everywhere a pageant and an ovation. The people gathered *en masse* from hamlet, village and city to welcome and honor him. Every possible form of demonstration was made to assure him of the love of the American people for their nation's benefactor and guest.

On the seventeenth of June, 1825, the anniversary of the battle of Bunker Hill, he assisted in laying the corner stone of the Bunker Hill monument, which now stands a grand granite story-teller of that great event.

On the seventh of September, 1825, he took his leave of a grateful people, in the president's house at Washington, in the midst of the officers of the government, civil and military. President Adams addressed him in golden words which will never die, and he responded in a tender, felicitous and impressive farewell, which unborn generations will read with tearful eyes. He then threw himself into the arms of the president and gave free vent to sobs and tears, the whole assembly joining with him. As he left the president he said, in broken accents, "God bless you," and then reached out his hands for the embraces of the assembly, and for a little while the "hero was lost in the father and friend."

In a little while the boat was ready that was to convey him down the river to the Brandywine, which frigate Congress had provided to take him home.

When the boat reached Mount Vernon, Lafayette went in silence to the tomb of Washington. "All hearts beat in unison with the veteran's bosom as he looked *for the last time* on the sepulcher which contained the ashes of the first of men. He spoke not, but appeared absorbed in the mighty recollections which the place and the occasion inspired."

After this he returned to the boat, which proceeded to the Brandywine, where the secretaries and escorts took leave of him, and he went on board and departed from the country he had loved and had offered his life to found and make free.

While Mr. Adams was president, July 4, 1826, his father, John Adams, and Thomas Jefferson, gave up this life, in the midst of the festivities of the nation's jubilee.

His mother had died in 1818. Mr. Adams was deeply moved

by these events. He had a profound regard for his great and honored parents.

Mr. Adams' administration closed as it began and was carried through, with the utmost purity, dignity and political wisdom. It was devoted to a pure public service and a zealous and patriotic development of the national resources and character. From the beginning it was opposed by unscrupulous, vindictive and partisan men and measures, which, in the light of after developments, only set forth his worth in a richer light. By falsity, malice and unscrupulous personal ambition, the people were deceived in relation to him and the purity and wisdom of his administration, and so he was remanded to the quiet of Quincy at the close of his one term of service as president. Now it is known to all unbiased students of history that our country has had no wiser or purer administration than that of John Quincy Adams.

### REPRESENTATIVE IN CONGRESS.

Mr. Adams remained in retirement only about a year. In the autumn of 1830, it began to be talked that the people of Plymouth county would like to have the ex-president represent them in Congress. Impossible, thought some men, who stood more on dignity than patriotic service. Would he accept an election to the House of Representatives? asked a great many. Some thought it would be improper; some thought it would be degrading; some thought it would be a noble thing to do. So was the public mind divided. But in due time he received the nomination, and said in a letter of response: "I am not aware of any sound principle which would justify me in withholding my services from my fellow citizens." So he was elected, and in December, 1831, took his seat in the lower House of Congress. And his reputation did not suffer by this patriotic acceptance of a post of heavy labor, but was immeasurably advanced by it. He exhibited a fund of knowledge, so vast and profound; a familiarity so perfect with nearly every topic which claimed the attention of Congress; he could bring forth from his well-replenished store of memory so vast an array of facts, shedding light upon subjects deeply obscured to others; displayed such readiness and power in debate, pouring out streams of purest eloquence, or launching forth the most scathing denunciations, when he deemed them called-for—that his most bitter opposers, while trembling before his sarcasm, and dreading his assaults, could not but grant him the meed of their highest admiration. Well did he deserve the title conferred upon him, by general consent, of "The Old Man Eloquent."

He was at once made chairman of the committee of manufactures; then a most important committee, as it involved the question of tariff, which separated the north and south. The northern manufacturers wanted their goods protected against a ruinous competition, while the southern planters wanted free trade. The difference was so great, and the discussion of it so violent, that some feared it would break up the Union. Mr. Adams on this committee urged moderation upon both sides; and with his profound knowledge of the whole subject, and all the interests involved, he was able to keep a living harmony between them, by adjusting the tariff to the diverse conditions of the whole country.

He was able to be the great pacificator on this vexed subject.

In 1835, the people of Texas, then a province of Mexico, took up arms against the Mexican government. In essence, it was a rebellion. The inhabitants of Texas were, for the most part, emigrants from the south and southwestern states of our Union, and some of them emigrants for their country's good. Mexico had abolished slavery, so that Texas was free territory. These emigrants from the southern part of the Union, desired to reëstablish slavery in Texas. It was easy to find an occasion for war against their adopted country, for this purpose. The plan was to get up a war, declare independence, get help from the United States to maintain it; annex to the United States, and so become a slave country again. And the plan carried in every particular.

General Jackson, president at that time, sent troops to the border, ostensibly to see that the Indians did not assist the Mexicans. A call was made on Congress for a million of dollars to carry on the military operations for keeping the Indians from aiding the Mexicans.

Mr. Adams, in a speech made in Congress, on this call for money, in May, 1836, unriddled this whole plan; and in another speech pointed out the course of the administration toward Mexico, and its desire to get a large slice of her territory, enough for several new slave states.

Charge was made against Mr. Adams, that in negotiating for the Floridas he had ceded the whole of Texas to Mexico, and General Jackson, the president, was referred to as authority for the statement. Mr. Adams assured Congress, that when that negotiation was made, he laid it before General Jackson and it received his approval. Jackson denied this; but Mr. Adams produced his diary, where the facts and dates were recorded as he had stated.

This movement to enlarge the slave territory, aroused the people of the north to the aggressive and multiplying and overbearing character of slavery; and they at once began to discuss it, and consider the subject of its restraint. Petitions began to be sent to Congress for the abolition of slavery and the slave trade in the District of Columbia and the territories. These petitions were usually sent to Mr. Adams and he presented them. They multiplied, and he still presented them. He respected the people's right of petition, and felt it his duty to give their respectful petitions a respectful presentation. Whatever the subject petitioned for, he presented the petition. He did it chiefly to maintain the right of petition to a free people. It often caused fearful and disgraceful scenes in the House of Representatives, brought upon him storms of abuse; yet, with unflinching moral purpose and courage, he continued, through several terms to present the petitions, sometimes two hundred a day, and the House continued to lay them on the table. By resolutions, votes, intimidations, threats of assassination and expulsion, and the most insulting abuse, he was resisted. The House was often in anarchy, but with unwavering firmness, adroitly watching his opportunity to speak for the right of petition, he presented petitions, till at last he won a triumphant victory. Long is the history of that memorable contest, but there is room here for only this reference to it.

In December, 1835, President Jackson sent to Congress a message relative to a bequest of four hundred thousand dollars, from James Smithson, of London, to the United States, for the purpose of establishing at Washington an institution "for the increase and diffusion of knowledge among men," and referred the subject to Congress for its consideration. The message was referred to a committee of which Mr. Adams was made chairman. He entered into the acceptance and use of this gift with great spirit. He gave the whole strength of his mind and heart to carrying the designs of Mr. Smithson into effect. Mr. Adams made a report to Congress on the subject in which he set forth the nobleness of the purpose of the donor, the breadth and grandeur of the results to mankind of that purpose faithfully and wisely carried out; the honor thus conferred upon our country, and something of the history of the Smithson family as among the most honored in the British kingdom. He concluded his report by offering a bill authorizing the president to receive and take measures to found The Smithsonian Institute. Few public acts of Mr. Adams gave him more pleasure. When the fund was received he was more instrumental than any other man in founding the great institution which is such an honor and aid to our country and mankind. In his addresses on this subject he displayed a great amount of scientific and historical learning. Probably no other public man in the country so valued solid learning or so signally illustrated its effects in his own life.

In the latter part of his life, when he was ripe in years as he was in learning and virtue, he gave in many parts of the country and on many important occasions, addresses, orations, speeches, which abound in wisdom, learning, patriotism and high moral sentiment. There was hardly any subject of great importance that he did not speak upon in and out of Congress. The subjects of slavery, internal improvements, the advancement of the country, dueling, intemperance, corruption in office and in politics, were constantly receiving his most vigorous attention. He often arraigned his country for its injustice and cruelty to the Negro and the Indian. On every possible occasion he pleaded for justice in their behalf, and righteous dealing as the law for a nation as for an individual.

His discussion in Congress of the subject of dueling in the presence of duelers, illustrates the courage and character of the grand old man who never cowered in human presence or was turned from duty by human insolence or power.

He was often pained and mortified by the sectionalism, venality and brutality of members of Congress and higher officers of government, and never hesitated in his place to censure those whose conduct disgraced his country. He was such a living encyclopædia of learning, history, law, moral principle and religious devotion, that he was a standing rebuke to the selfish, sectional and party spirit that controlled many of the officials and politicians about him. He was profoundly anxious lest these evil spirits should degenerate and destroy his country which to him was the hope of the world. He had lived through its whole existence, been honored by all its presidents, held high offices under them all, been president himself; had a history of every important transaction and of the attitude and conduct of every leading individual connected with the government from the beginning; had a record also of the action and politics of all foreign governments and our relations to them; of the progress of our legislation, of the tariff, internal improvements, the development of our manufactures, the extension of our territory; of the extension of slavery and the artifices by which it had been accomplished; in a word he had a record of our national life in his and his father's diary and his accurate and capacious memory supplied all the details; so that he was authority—the nation in himself, all the later years of his life; the patriarch of America, having been instrumental in developing and preserving this grand national estate.

He had great interest in the temperance cause, which in his later years was commanding the attention of his countrymen. He understood its necessity and usefulness, and gave it the powerful support of his voice and example.

Through his whole life Mr. Adams was an intense worker; he studied everything he took hold of to the bottom; always made sure that he was right before speaking; always knew his authority; took infinite pains to know the whole of every subject that was important to the well being of his country. He was usually the first man in his seat every morning in the House, and the last man to leave at night. He gave an absorbing interest to the business in hand; and was very much of the time in resolute opposition to the legislation of Congress, as it was through his whole congressional career, in the interest of slavery and its extension. That interest removed him from the presidential chair and controlled the administrations of Jackson, Van Buren, and Tyler — controlled the government from his removal from the presidency to the day of his death.

Mr. Adams was a man of great physical vigor, which sustained him in active health through the intense labors of his long life. He was an early riser, an absteminous liver, temperate, prudent, regular in all his habits; an excellent walker, often walking a number of miles before breakfast; a good swimmer; fond of good company; an excellent talker; a lover of home; simple and republican in dress and manners; plain, honest, genuine; too fair and square, and positive to be popular; yet so thorough, and manly and grand as to command almost universal respect. He was a genuine Puritan, deeply and consistently religious; a great student of the bible, a Unitarian in theology, yet in hearty sympathy with all christian people. He was a reformer — a maker anew of life's ways, so vigorous and persistent as to seem to be an iconoclast. In his opposition to wrong he used solid shot — words that wounded, that smelt of passion and power. He was no milk-and-water man, was mighty in fire and storm — a granite tower in the whirlwind defying its assaults. All in all, he was one of America's grandest products, honored at last in all the world as one of its greatest and best men. On the twentieth of November, 1846, he was stricken with paralysis at his son's house in Boston. This confined him for several weeks. But at the opening of Congress he returned to his post, and was prompt and active as he had always been.

until the twenty-first of February, 1848, at half-past one o'clock in the afternoon, he was stricken again. He was caught and held from falling by members near him. He was unconscious, till three o'clock, when consciousness returned and he said, faintly: "*This is the end of earth,* I AM CONTENT." These were his last words. He lived until seven o'clock in the evening of the twenty-third, when the spirit of John Quincy Adams left the scenes of earth for those in the immortal realm of its father, in the eighty-first year of its age. Thus closed a life which will ever be worthy of the profoundest study and emulation of mankind.

# The Grave of John Quincy Adams.

In the crypt in that portion of Braintree, Massachusetts, now known as Quincy, with the immortal remains of John Adams, his father, rest the forms of John Quincy Adams and his wife, Louisa Catharine. The tomb is surmounted by a bust, beneath which are the words, "*Alteri Sæculo*," divided by an acorn and two oak leaves. Over the tablet is "Thy Kingdom Come." As on the tablet of John Adams, the first column is devoted to the president and the other to his wife. The inscription reads as follows:

Near this place reposes all that could die of
### John Quincy Adams.
SON OF JOHN AND ABIGAIL (SMITH) ADAMS,
Sixth President of the United States.

Born 11 of July, 1767, Amidst the Storms of Civil Commotion,
He Nursed the Vigor which Inspires a Christian
For more than half a Century.

Whenever His Country Called for His Labors,
In either Hemisphere or in any Capacity,
He Never Spared them in Her Cause.

On the Twenty-fourth of December, 1814,
He signed the Second Treaty with Great Britain, which Restored
Peace within her Borders.

On the Twenty-third of February, 1848, he closed sixteen years of eloquent defense of the lessons of his youth by dying at his post in her great National Council.

A Son Worthy of His Father,
A Citizen shedding Glory on His Country,
A Scholar Ambitious to Advance Mankind,
This Christian sought to Walk Humbly in the Sight of God.

The second column on this tablet records the important facts in the life of his "Partner for fifty years":

### Louisa Catharine.
Living through Many Vicissitudes
And under Many Responsibilities as a
Daughter, Wife and Mother, she Proved Equal to All.

Dying,
She Left to Her Family and Her Sex the Blessed Remembrance of
"A Woman that Feareth the Lord."

Under the parallel column is this verse:

"One soweth and another reapeth. I sent you to reap that whereon ye bestowed no labor. Other men labored, and ye are entered into their labor."

The church in which the remains were deposited in 1848 is a massive structure, the front being supported by heavy columns, with a graceful cupola and dome above it. It is embowered in immense elm and chestnut trees, near the old Adams homestead, and is now owned and used by the Unitarian congregation of Quincy, with which the Adamses were associated.

## CHAPTER VIII.

### ANDREW JACKSON.

#### Seventh President of the United States.

IN turning from the great men who have thus far occupied the executive chair of the United States, to those who immediately follow, one feels that he has been among the gods, and is now going down to dwell among perverse and passion-scarred men. The descent is so sudden, and the change is so marked with violence and paltriness that it is like going into another climate or civilization. The first six presidents were men of strength, breadth, nobility of character, and life—great products of a great era. They differed much from each other, but each was great and noble in his way, a tower of strength to the republic, a royal illustration of its principles, a magnificent specimen of manhood. Americans have never had to apologize for their weaknesses, while the world has been quick to do them honor, and the greatest of every country and age since their time have accepted them as peers in the highest realm of thought and action. As the ages move away, their renown will grow, and the study of their exalted characters and lives will quicken the generations of men in what is most manly and meritorious. It was theirs to act conspicuous parts in founding the republic, and conducting its affairs in the first forty years of its existence. It is largely the product of their wisdom and energy, and will forever stand the monument of their greatness of mind and worth of character.

## ANDREW JACKSON, SENIOR.

Andrew Jackson, Sr., and his wife, were of Scotch-Irish descent. Their ancestors had gone from Scotland to the north of Ireland, many years before their time. They were poor, and had suffered much from the British misgovernment of always oppressed and unhappy Ireland. They had little love for England, she had so dealt with their adopted country with an iron hand. To get away from her immediate oppression, into an American colony where land was plenty and cheap; where fish and game could be had for the taking; where sunshine and fuel were abundant, and frost and snow troubled not, became an object of their desire. Gathering up their scanty store of goods and money, they set sail for Charleston, South Carolina. This was in 1765, just about the time that the colonies began to feel the heavy hand of British oppression, hindering their natural development.

A seaport town was not the place for a farmer to settle, so Mr. Jackson's face was soon set toward the country. He fixed on the Waxhaw settlement, on the creek of that name—a branch of the Catawba river—one hundred and sixty-five miles northwest from Charleston, near the line of the two Carolinas. The creek and settlement took their name from a tribe of Indians which had formerly occupied that vicinity. Here the Jackson's planted their hearthstone. They had two young sons, Hugh and Robert. Here they erected their cabin and began life in the American wilderness. The next year, after one crop had been raised, Mr. Jackson died. The desolate widow, in this wild waste of woods, soon became the mother of a third son, which she named for his father, Andrew. He was born March 15, 1767. When the mother had laid the form of her husband in the grave, she went immediately to her sister and husband, Mr. McKinney, a few miles away in North Carolina. There was born the seventh president of the United States. To all human appearance nothing was more improbable than that this babe of sorrow, poverty and extreme humility, would ever rise to greatness and honor among men. All that could be said of his parents was, that they were good, well-meaning people. They had come to America to better their humble condition. They were of the Presbyterian faith, and the sorrowful but trusting mother conceived the idea that, if possible, this babe of her sorrow and her faith should be educated for the ministry. Even this would have seemed impossible to everybody but a mother. With this thought actuating her, she trained his young mind to duty, and religious faith and life. And although she did not see her desire accomplished in him, she made good the saying that widow's sons often rise to distinction. Events were soon to transpire to give his career a different course.

The improbable thing that this child of most unpropitious birth should become distinguished among great men, would hardly have been possible any where but in America, and in this free republic. Such is the fruitage of republican institutions.

### JACKSON'S BOYHOOD.

Three weeks after Andrew's birth, Mrs. Jackson went to the home of another sister and her husband, Mr. and Mrs. Crawford, where she did the work of the family for ten years, her sister being an invalid. The eldest boy was left at Mr. McKinney's. Andrew gained here in a rude school the elements of an education. It was with great difficulty that he learned to spell; he never became accomplished in that art so difficult to some. He did better at reading and writing. But he did not take kindly to his books. He was frolicsome, fond of athletic sports, and grew up to be rough and coarse, and after his mother's death, very profane. "He was a rude, turbulent boy;" imperious, headstrong, brave, but yet generous. In person and character he presented little that was attractive or hopeful. He was tall and ungainly; coarse in features, lank in form; his hair coarse, face freckled and hard, manners rough and independent, "very irascible to his equals and superiors," but generous to the younger and weaker.

One biographer says ne went to an academy kept in the old Waxhaw meeting-house, by a Mr. Humphreys, where he studied the classics and mathematics and made considerable progress in that education which his mother wished him to have.

When seven years old the Continental Congress had met; when eight, the battles of Lexington and Bunker Hill were fought; when nine, the Declaration of Independence was signed. Of course these great events were talked over in the Waxhaw settlement and in the school where Andrew was studying. These distant communities were stirred by these things. South Carolina and Virginia caught the fire of the times very early. The boys grew warlike as well as the men.

When Andrew was thirteen years old, the war came to his wilderness home.

On the twenty-ninth of May, 1780, Colonel Buford, who had a small American force at Waxhaw, was attacked by Colonel Tarleton, and had one hundred and fifteen of his men killed and one hundred and fifty wounded. It was a fearful loss. The meeting-house was converted into a hospital. Andrew saw this battle and its terrible works in the dead and suffering men about him. This was his first sight of war. He and his brother Robert and his mother, ministered to the suffering militia. His brother Hugh, now eighteen, had gone with a detachment of men to meet and head off Tarleton, and died of heat and exhaustion at the battle of Stono.

In the following August, a portion of Cornwallis' army rushed upon Waxhaw, and the inhabitants fled, and among them Mrs. Jackson and her two boys.

The next year the family returned to desolated Waxhaw. Andrew was now fourteen, tall, slender and weak from his rapid growth. His passionate nature was aroused to avenge his brother's death and the slaughter of his neighbors.

The strife between the whigs and tories was a state of war. A band of tories made a midnight attack upon the house of a whig. Andrew Jackson was there as one of the guards. A little battle ensued in which the tories were repulsed. Two of Jackson's associates were killed by his side. He showed the warrior in him at that early age.

Not far from this time he was in the battle of Hanging

Rock. It was probably before he and his brother Robert had both enlisted. Soon after, when a company of some forty of the Waxhaw patriots were making their headquarters in the meeting-house, they were deceived by a band of tories who led behind them a company of British soldiers. The tories came as friends, and by this stratagem the patriots were taken by surprise. The two Jackson boys were in the company surprised, but with several others escaped to the woods. The next day, however, while in at a neighbor's house eating a hasty meal, they were broken in upon by a party of British dragoons, and taken prisoners.

After being put under guard, Andrew was imperiously ordered by a British officer to clean his boots. "I am a prisoner of war, and not your servant," replied the dauntless boy. The brutal officer drew his sword and aimed a desperate blow at the head of the young soldier. He threw up his hand and parried the blow in part, yet he received two fearful cuts, one in his hand and one on his head. The mark of the wound in the hand he carried through life. The officer then made the same request of Robert, and met with a similar refusal, and gave him a like blow which so wounded him as to cause his death not long after.

The wounded boys, with the rest of the prisoners, were marched off to Camden, South Carolina. They were hurried through without food or drink, a distance of forty miles; thrown into a contracted enclosure without beds, medical attendance, or any means of dressing their wounds. They were shortly fed and badly treated. In a few days the virulent small-pox broke out. The dying and the dead were all together. Mrs. Jackson, hearing of the suffering of her boys, hastened to their relief. She succeeded in obtaining the release of her sons by an exchange of prisoners. Obtaining two horses, she put Robert, who could scarcely stand, upon one; she rode the other, and Andrew, half-famished, bare-headed, bare-footed, and in rags, walked in pain and toil the weary forty miles, suffering the first stages of the small-pox all the way. A heavy rain, which they could not avoid, impeded and endangered them all the more.

At length the home was reached, and the boys, raging sick of small-pox, under the weary mother's care. Robert died in two days, and Andrew was soon wild in delirium. After a long struggle with the loathsome disease, he recovered.

As soon as she could leave him, she hastened to Charleston to care for the sick prisoners there, among whom were her sister's sons, but in her mission of mercy was attacked with a severe sickness, died, and was buried so obscurely that her grave has never been found.

Thus in the fifteenth year of his age Andrew was left alone in the world, with his mother and two brothers taken from him by the brutal barbarity of the British soldiery. Is it any wonder that a nature like his became ferocious and furious when aroused? Is it any wonder that such a schooling carried its hard lessons deep into his strong and passionate nature? Barbarous war, thy cruelties belong to demons rather than men!

### JACKSON THE YOUTH.

Andrew Jackson was now a mere youth, overgrown, not firm in health, coarse, wild, reckless. About this time he attempted to learn the saddler's trade, and worked at it for six months, but he was better at his games, sports and reckless ways than at his work, and gave it up.

While the British occupied Charleston, many of the inhabitants found homes in country places, and some of them in the Waxhaw settlement. Among these were some youth that became the associates of young Jackson, and of whom he learned city ways of dissipation and gambling. When they returned to their homes he went with them, riding his fine horse, which he had got of the little property left him. He soon ran up a bill at the tavern; the city attractions used up all his money. Strolling, one evening, into a gambling place, he was challenged to stake his horse against two hundred dollars. He accepted the challenge and won in the game. Putting his money in his pocket and resisting further invitations to play, with the iron will which always constituted such a strong element of his character, he bade his companions good evening and went to his room and bed. He saw his way out of the poverty and disgrace which would soon be upon him if he staid in the city, and so, early in the morning, he paid his bill, mounted his horse and rode toward Waxhaw.

On his return he set up for a schoolmaster. In a log schoolhouse, with a few children, he tried the art of imparting knowledge to the young mind. But his tastes were more with his wild companions than with his scholars, and this was given up for the study of law. Like many another, he made teaching the stepping stone to a profession; but in his case it was a thin stone. He gathered up what means he had, mounted his horse, and went to Salisbury, North Carolina, a distance of seventy-five miles, and entered the law office of a Mr. McCay.

At eighteen years old he was better skilled in the ways of his hard, rough companions than in anything else. He remained two years in this office, studying some, but frolicking more. One biographer says of him: "He was the most roaring, rollicking, game-cocking, horse-racing, card-playing, mischievous fellow that ever lived in Salisbury."

At twenty years old, six feet and one inch in his stockings, slender, graceful in his movements and manners, when he chose to be, fond of horses, riding, rough adventures, developing some manly and dignified qualities in the midst of, generally, profane and coarse ways.

He was now a lawyer, but without books, office or clients. There seemed to be no business for him where he had studied; so he rode to Martinsville, North Carolina, where he spent a year as a clerk in a store, waiting for some opening in the line of his profession.

North Carolina, at that time, extended west to the Mississippi river. It was a long, wild tract of country west of the mountains, ravaged by Indians, who had become hostile and bitter toward the whites. It is now the State of Tennessee. North Carolina afterward ceded it to Congress, and Congress at length made it into a state.

At the time Jackson was at Martinsville, there was a settlement a little west of the mountains, called Jonesborough; and five hundred miles west of the summit of the mountains was another, called Nashville. All else was wilderness and the home of Indians and wild beasts.

Andrew Jackson, when twenty-one years old, was appointed public prosecutor for the district of Nashville. It was an office without honor, with but little pay, and hazardous in the extreme. Few men that had anything else to do would accept it. It was Jackson's only opportunity.

At that time there was gathering at Morgantown, the frontier settlement of North Carolina, a company of emigrants for the wild country of the west. Jackson joined this company. They were mounted on horseback, and carried all their goods and luggage on pack horses. They followed an Indian trail in a long cavalcade, camping at night in the open air, stationing pickets about to give warning of the approach of Indians. A few days' journey took them to Jonesborough, a village of about sixty log huts. Beyond this all was wilderness for two hundred miles, to Nashville, the western limit of settlement. At Jonesborough they waited for several days the arrival of other parties of emigrants, and for a guard from Nashville to escort them. Something like one hundred men, women and children were in the company.

The second night out, after the women and children were all asleep in their tents, and the men wrapped in their blankets by the side of the fire, Andrew Jackson sat up, quietly musing, when he heard now and then unusual noises. He listened, and soon became convinced that there were Indians about them. He crept to the nearest men and awakened them. Soon the whole company was awake, and moved on toward Nashville as fast as possible. An hour afterward a party of hunters came in sight of the fires, and gathered about them and went to sleep. Before daylight the Indians sprang upon them and killed all but one.

The emigrants reached Nashville the last of October, 1788. These emigrants carried the news of the adoption of the new constitution, and that Washington would probably be chosen the first executive of the new government. This outpost of civilization felt the joy of an organized government under the paternal administration of Washington, and anticipated the time when the long reaches of the great wilderness between them and their friends in the East would be settled with thriving communities. It was estimated that there were in and about Nashville some five thousand people, clearing up the wilderness and planting homes. The dangers from the Indians were great and constant. Men carried their rifles wherever they went. Stockades were made for all the people to flee to in case of an attack.

### JACKSON THE LAWYER.

Jackson soon determined to make Nashville his home. There was but one lawyer there before him, and he had fallen into the hands of the roughs and the delinquents to the merchants and land owners, and defended them. He set up an office, and at once had an immense amount of collections put into his hands. He made out some seventy writs the first day. The merchants and land owners had been unable to force their claims, and they welcomed a new lawyer. The roughs sought to intimidate and drive him out of the place, but his imperious will and fiery temper soon taught them that such a course only endangered them. He never shunned a fight; often had personal encounters; was fierce and fearless, wiry and powerful, and withal, so much of a man that he was not long in conquering a victory, and forcing the respect of the delinquents and bellicose men of that hitherto lawless community.

With his energy and push, and the monied portion of the community as his clients, his business flourished. His official business as prosecutor took him frequently to Jonesborough and other settlements far apart, which journeys he made on horseback, and with constant danger from the Indians, and exposure to storms and floods.

When he first went to Nashville, he found a boarding place with a Mrs. Donelson. She was the widow of Colonel John Donelson, and was much respected. She lived in a cabin of hewn logs, which was then the aristocratic style of a house. She had a married daughter, Mrs. Robards, the wife of Lewis Robards, of Kentucky, and her husband living with her. Their marriage relation was not happy. He is said to have been a man of whom not much good could be said. His wife was beautiful, sprightly, a lover of mirth ; and a woman of excellent natural ability. He was jealous of her, and greatly annoyed her by it; and once left her for a time, before Jackson knew them. Now that Jackson had come into the family as a boarder, who had agreeable manners with women, and a fund of anecdotes and entertaining conversation, Robards became jealous of him, and made it exceedingly disagreeable for him. He sought to talk with him about it; but got only abuse.

The matter grew into a scandal, and Jackson concluded to leave the house; but so uncomfortable had Mrs. Robards become, that she determined to leave the place, and go to Natches, into the family of Colonel Stark ; an elderly gentleman and friend of the family.

The way was dangerous on account of Indians, and Colonel Stark invited Jackson to go along as a protector, who had become known and feared among the Indians as "Sharp Knife." This did not mend the scandal.

This was in the spring of 1791. Robards left, and applied to the legislature of Virginia for a divorce. This was granted, provided the supreme court should see cause for a divorce. It was reported, and became the universal belief in Nashville that Robards had obtained a divorce. Mrs. Robards came back in the fall, and was married to Jackson. The marriage was a happy one, and gave them both great joy through their whole lives.

After they had been married two years, Robards obtained a divorce in a court in Kentucky; then Jackson saw that he had been married two years to a woman who was legally another man's wife. To make their union legal, they were married again.

But happy as was their marriage, the unfortunate circumstances, the suspicion and the scandal always greatly marred their peace. Jackson's enemies always used it against him; and many of them, no doubt, believed that he broke up a family to get another man's wife. His past manner of life; his lawlessness and imperiousness, and passionate nature, did not do much to prove his innocence. But his friends believed him every way pure and worthy in the whole transaction. It is worthy of note that no reproach was ever cast upon him for any misconduct toward women, save this; which goes far to prove him what he always seemed to be—magnanimous, just and true to her.

While practicing law in Nashville, he soon began to get hold of land; and in a few years became an extensive land owner. This he sold to settlers at advanced prices, and became wealthy for that region of country. Loving agriculture, he practiced it more or less. He was always a careful business man, thrifty, efficient, successful. With his law business, his much journeying, his extensive land and agricultural business, he became a man of affairs.

### THE LEGISLATOR.

In January, 1796, the territory of Tennessee, then containing nearly eighty thousand inhabitants, had ripened for admission into the Union. A convention was called at Knoxville to frame a constitution. Five delegates were sent from each of the eleven counties. Andrew Jackson was one of the delegates from Davidson county. They met in a shabby building outside of the city, which was prepared for the convention at an expense of twelve dollars and sixty-two cents. Each member was entitled to two dollars and a half a day; but they voted to give one dollar of it to pay the secretary, printer and doorkeeper, reserving only a dollar and a half a day to themselves. A constitution was formed, and in June, 1796, Tennessee became the sixteenth state in the Union.

The new state could have but one member in the United States House of Representatives. Jackson was elected to that position, and took his seat in December, 1796. He rode on horseback from Nashville to Philadelphia, a distance of eight hundred miles. Albert Gallatin thus describes him as he appeared in the house: "A tall, lank, uncouth-looking personage, with locks of hair hanging over his face, and a cue down his back, tied with an eel-skin, his dress singular, his manners and deportment those of a rough backwoodsman."

Mr. Jackson took his seat near the close of General Washington's administration. He heard the farewell address of "The Father of his Country" to his people. A committee drew up a complimentary address in reply. Jackson was one of twelve to vote against that reply. He would not say that Washington's administration was "wise, firm and patriotic."

Jackson was an intense democrat—a disciple of Jefferson, an admirer of Bonaparte, a lover of France, a hater of England, a slaveholder who saw no wrong in slavery—nothing undemocratic in buying and selling men and women and working them for their pretended owner's profit; yet he could vote in censure of Washington's administration.

Tennessee had gone into warlike operations against the Indians without authority, and contrary to the policy of the government. A proposition had been made in the House to refund to Tennessee the expenses she had incurred in this unordered Indian expedition. Jackson advocated it with great zeal, and the proposition was supported. This made Jackson still more popular in his state; and a vacancy occurring the next season, he was elected United States Senator. But he remained in the position but a little while, resigning in 1798.

### JUDGE JACKSON.

Soon after his return from the United States Senate, he was chosen judge of the supreme court of Tennessee, at a salary of six hundred dollars a year, which office he held for six years.

At the time Jackson was a judge, John Sevier was governor of the state. They had had a personal difficulty, and Jackson had challenged him for a duel, which Sevier had declined. At an accidental meeting in the streets of Knoxville, unfriendly words soon began to be bandied between them, in which Jackson spoke of his services to the state. "Services!" rejoined the governor, "I know of none but a trip to Natchez with another man's wife." "Great God!" shouted Jackson, "do you mention her sacred name?" and in an instant drew a pistol and fired at the governor, and the governor returned the shot; but in their frenzy, both shot at random, and neither hurt each other or anybody else, or at all wounded their reputations as wise and dignified and law-honoring judge and governor. Meeting soon after on a highway, when Doctor Vandyke was with Jackson, he drew a pistol and called to the governor to defend himself. The governor leaped from his horse, and the animal, in self defense. took to his heels. His son, who was with him, drew his pistol; Vandyke drew his. In this war-like attitude, some travelers came up and put a stop to the fray.

This standing quarrel between judge and governor, broke out anew whenever they met, and involved many of their friends in it. Neither of them seemed to see that it reflected on the dignity of their official standing. In 1804, he resigned his judgeship.

### BUSINESS EMBARRASSMENTS.

In his land speculations, and mercantile and produce business, he became financially involved. He had sold land to a Philadelphian who had failed and could not pay him. His partners had made mistakes and involved the firm. He sold property, paid all, and began again, in a smaller and safer way. His business difficulties came through others' mistakes, not his own.

### PERSONAL COMPLICATIONS.

Early in 1806, Jackson got into a difficulty with Mr. Charles Dickinson, a young lawyer, who was also engaged in trade. It grew out of something that Dickinson had said disparaging of Mrs. Jackson. He had explained the words, and the offense was smothered.

Soon after, at a horse-race, where his favorite horse was to run on a stake of two thousand dollars, he got into an altercation with a young man by the name of Swann. Swann challenged him for a duel, but he refused to accept it, on the ground that Swann was not a gentleman; but he beat him with a bludgeon, a disgraceful affair in the dueling code. This led the way to a revival of the Dickinson trouble, as he had been referred to by Swann, and a duel was brought on with Dickinson. Dickinson was regarded as the best shot in the world,—could, at the distance they were to stand apart, hit a dollar every shot. He was a brilliant young man, and very popular. The distance was eight paces. Dickinson fired at the word, and struck a rib near the breast bone, breaking it, but turning the ball so it only inflicted a fearful wound, but did not enter his vitals. Jackson gave no sign of being hit, and Dickinson exclaimed, "Good God! have I missed him?" Jackson then fired with deliberate aim, and shot his antagonist through, who died that night, without knowing that he had hit Jackson.

This duel, so needless, cutting down a young husband, and man of many friends, hurt Jackson's popularity, till he retrieved it with his mititary successes.

In 1805 Aaron Burr visited Jackson in the interest of his contemplated expedition in the southwest. Jackson fell readily into his blandishments, and entered into his project arranging to furnish men and boats. He proposed to conquer the Spanish dominions, and it is believed he secretly intended to establish a separate government making the seat of it on the Red river where he purchased four hundred thousand acres of land. But Jackson's suspicions of his integrity were soon aroused and he withdrew from all connection with him. Burr was afterward tried for high treason, but the charge was not sustained. At Burr's tial in Richmond, Virginia, Jackson was summoned as a witness. He championed Burr's cause. Mr. Parton, one of his biographers, says: "'There he harangued the crowd in the capitol square, defending Burr and denouncing Jefferson as a persecutor. There are those living (in 1859) who heard him do this. He made himself so conspicuous as Burr's champion at Richmond, that Mr. Madison, secretary of state, took deep offense at it, and remembered it to Jackson's disadvantage five years later, when he was president of the United States, with a war on his hands. For the same reason, I presume, it was that Jackson was not called upon to give testimony upon the trial."

After this time he lived for some years in private life at the Hermitage, the name of his home. But, as was so common with him; he had his troubles with various parties, among them "an animated quarrel with Mr. Dinsmore, agent of the Choctaw Indians."

### GENERAL JACKSON.

Jackson had now been general of the militia for some years. In 1812 when the war with England broke out he offered his services to the government with two thousand five hundred men of his division of the Tennessee militia. His offer was accepted. In October Governor Blount of Tennessee was asked to send one thousand five hundred men to New Orleans. Jackson called for a meeting of troops at Nashville, December 10. A force of infantry and cavalry met and was organized amounting to two thousand and seventy men. On January 7, 1813, the infantry embarked in boats for Natchez, and the cavalry marched across the country.

No use was made of this force, and in the spring it returned to Nashville. The General offered it for an invasion of Canada, but no answer was received from Washington and it was disbanded.

While on the march from Natchez to Nashville the soldiers called their general "Hickory" on account of his toughness. In later years he was called Old Hickory, and hickory poles and trees abounded in his campaigns for the presidency, and at the celebrations of his victory at New Orleans. So identified did he become with this symbol of his toughness, that an old man who was a democratic boy in his time, cannot see a hickory tree without being reminded of Jackson. The hickory was one of the means of his popularity. The woodsmen over the whole country took to him on this account.

In 1813, Jackson's friend, who afterward became General Carroll, got involved in a quarrel with Jesse Benton, a brother of Thomas H. Benton, and was challenged for a duel. Carroll asked Jackson to be his second. Jackson prevented the duel for awhile, but Benton was bound to have it out according to the code of honor's barbarity. Benton sent an account of it to his brother at Washington. This led to an angry correspondence between Colonel Benton and Jackson. Jackson threatened to horsewhip him at their first meeting. They met in a street in Nashville, September 4. Jackson advanced upon him. Benton retreated backward till he stumbled down the stairway of a hotel. Just at this moment Jesse Benton fired at Jackson a pistol loaded with two balls and a slug, shattering his shoulder and bringing him to the ground. A general melee among the friends of both followed in which several were hurt, but none killed. All the doctors but one recommended the amputation of the shattered arm. But Jackson would not consent to it, and in due time it become a useful arm.

On the thirtieth of August, 1813, the massacre of Fort Mimms, by the Creek Indians, created a great excitement throughout the southwest. Jackson, from his bed, addressed circulars to all who would arm themselves to punish the Indians, to meet at Fort Stephens. On the twenty-fifth of September the legislature of Tennessee called for three thousand five hundred volunteers, besides the one thousand five hundred that were in the national service. Still suffering from his wound, Jackson met and took command of this force October 7. On the eleventh he moved rapidly toward the Indian's center of operation. After two or three severe battles with the Indians which severely punished them, the half-fed army became mutinous, and many went home. Some new recruits came in, some friendly Indians joined him, and with such an army as he had, he plunged into the midst of the Indian territory. After two or three successful battles in January, troops began to come to him. In February he had five thousand men. He followed and attacked the Indians in their own strongholds in such rapid succession that by midsummer they were completely conquered, their chief surrendered, and he made a treaty with them by which the most of them left the country and went north. A few fled to Florida. So thorough was his work, that it is said to have broken the power of the Indians in North America.

This gave General Jackson a national reputation. Occurring at the time the country was at war with England, and perhaps an Indian outbreak which the English had incited, it made him a hero, even more than it would to have gained a victory over so many English soldiers.

In May, 1814, General Jackson was major-general of the United States army in the southwest over six other generals who had claims to the position.

The English were preparing for a grand attack on the southwest in July. General Jackson pushed forward to Mobile to hinder as much as possible their operations in that quarter. They had possession of Pensacola in Spanish territory, which they used as though it were their own. Jackson wrote for orders, but getting no answer moved against it with three thousand men and cleaned it of British war force and materials. He sent a force against the Florida Indians with equal success. He was soon back to Mobile in force; but finding he had swept that region clear of the enemy, he sent the mass of his army to New Orleans, and reached that place himself December 2, 1814.

On December 14, a powerful British naval force came up the river and captured several gunboats and a schooner. The next day Jackson proclaimed martial law in New Orleans. On the morning of the twenty-third the advance of the British army came within nine miles of New Orleans. At two o'clock that afternoon, with a little over two thousand men, Jackson attacked the enemy. A severe battle ensued, aided by Lieutenant Henly in the schooner Carolina. This battle gave the British warning of the welcome they might expect when they went nearer the city.

That night the British were heavily reinforced, and had an army of trained soldiers and marines of fourteen thousand effective men armed and supplied according to the best art of war at that time. This is the highest estimate. Their own writers have put their force as low as eight thousand. To oppose this force Jackson had a force of less than four thousand, composed of Kentucky, Tennessee and Louisiana militia, with a few regulars. He had two sloops of war in the river and one colored battalion.

After the battle of the twenty-third of December, Jackson fell back to within four miles of the city, and began to throw up an embankment from the river back to the swamps, a distance of more than a mile. He employed every available force of men and boys, to complete his line of defense as soon as possible. He could dig only about three feet before coming to water. He filled his poorly equipped and raw soldiers, who were there for the defense of their homes and country, with the spirit and power of heroes. They were there a wall of defense to save the city and the country behind it. The caution of General Packenham, the British commander, kept him bringing up reinforcements and making preparations till the twenty-eighth. On that day he came on, confident and strong, with his battalions that believed themselves invincible. Steadily, solidly, with bands playing, banners flying, swords and bayonets glistening, they marched upon the line of the American defense. The artillery led, and opened the attack. The Americans waited till the British column was within easy gun shot, and then opened on it to give it no quarter till it was swept away as though it were of gossamer. Two hours of steady cannonade and musketry work sent the shattered British columns back in confusion, leaving the field strewn with the dead and dying.

They retreated two miles and encamped. They began at once to repair their losses. From their ships they brought more cannon and marines. On the night of the thirty-first, which was very dark, they moved forward to within three hundred yards of the American line and under cover of a heavy cannonade, began to dig for protection against the American fire in the morning. The next morning was Sunday. A dense fog shut everything from sight, till about ten o'clock it lifted, revealing the pageantry of grim war covering all the plains. The batteries at once opened; the British columns moved forward and opened fire. The air was perfectly still, and soon dense with smoke; but Jackson's men knew the range and fired continuously into the fast falling ranks of their enemy. It was a short work. The British fled to their entrenchments and ceased firing. For this battle cotton bales had been brought for better protection, but they did not serve the purpose, and were abandoned.

Three times now the enemy had been beaten back. What

would he do next? He had immense resources, and England's best military talent and skill to use them. The people of the city and our army were in intense anxiety. That thin wall of human flesh and blood, with the mighty will of Andrew Jackson, was all that stood in the way of destruction. Every preparation to receive the next shock, which could be made, was adopted.

Sunday morning, January 8, about half an hour before sunrise, the hostile line began to move again. Intrepid and firm stood Jackson and his men in their places. The battle array had now stretched across the river, and Jackson had to provide an additional force for that side.

The enemy came on steady and resolute; now for the fourth time, only to fall in almost whole regiments before the deadly fire of Jackson's men. Two hours of such work sent them flying back, with Packenham, their leader, dead on the field, General Gibbs mortally wounded, and General Keane severely wounded. They rallied again; but it was only the effort of an exhausted and beaten army. So was fought and won the great battle of New Orleans. Nothing more courageous and decisive had been done on this continent. With everything against him, and double the number of his own men at least, and trained soldiers against raw recruits, he held England's pride and power at bay for two weeks and then sent them away shattered and beaten.

They remained ten days in their encampments, then stole away to their ships and departed.

General Jackson now became the hero of the American people; he had settled with the Indians; had saved New Orleans; had won imperishable honors for American arms; had sent England's last army back in disgrace from our shores. His faults, vices and crimes were now forgotten. His savage temper, foul speech and barbaric will all grew virtuous in the white glory of this great victory. For the time being the common people were mad with delight, and were ready to canonize Jackson and hold him the paragon of all virtues. They have at last come to see him as a craggy mountain, rough, stormy, bold, with great defiles, dark recesses and jutting points, yet solid and grand in strength.

General Jackson had his troubles at New Orleans with citizens. His enemies were severe on him for establishing martial law. He had one man arrested and imprisoned. The judge set him at liberty on a writ of *habeas corpus;* then Jackson banished the judge from the city. The news of the treaty of Ghent and peace came right on; then the judge returned and fined Jackson a thousand dollars. The people wanted to pay it, but he would not permit it. Years after, it, with interest, was refunded to him by Congress.

But not to Jackson alone was due the victory over the Indians and British. The people of Tennessee, Kentucky, Louisiana, and the whole southwest, were joined with him, and are to be accorded their full share in the struggle, patriotism and glory of the great consummation.

General Jackson retired to the Hermitage, near Nashville, but to remain but a little while. Near the close of the next year (1817) the Seminole Indians in Florida were on the war path. General Jackson was ordered to take the field against them. He gathered a large force of regulars, Creek Indians and militia of Tennessee and Georgia. He went into Florida while it was yet a Spanish territory, took Fort St. Marks, where he captured a Scotchman named Arbuthnot, and at Suwanee captured one Ambrister. Both these were British subjects. He tried them by court martial, found them guilty of inciting the Indians against the United States, and had them executed. Two Indian chiefs were hanged by his order. He continued his march, and took Pensacola. The Spanish authorities complained. The country was divided on the subject of his invasion of Spanish territory; some condemning, some approving, his course. The secretary of state, John Quincy Adams, approved it.

In 1821, when Spain ceded Florida to the United States, Jackson was appointed governor of the territory, but he held the office but a little while. President Monroe offered him the post of minister to Mexico, which he did not accept.

In 1823 the Tennessee legislature elected him to the United States Senate, and nominated him for the presidency. This nomination was treated as a joke by many, so unfit did they regard him for that place. But in the ensuing presidential election, in 1824, he received ninety-nine electoral votes; but, as there was no choice by the electors, the House of Representatives elected John Quincy Adams. He retired again to the Hermitage; but at the next presidential election the entire opposition to Adams united on Jackson, and he was elected.

## PRESIDENT JACKSON.

The political and sectional contest which elected Jackson was a severe one. The opposition to Adams was chiefly a sectional one. He was a northern man; was personally opposed to slavery; his father was a federalist, and he was elected by a federalist district. Though non-partisan and a most just and wise president, he did not suit partisans or sectionalists. Both wanted more influence in the government than they could get under him. Jackson was a democrat of the radical type. The slave states were democratic in theory, though autocratic in practice toward Africans; Jackson was a democrat and a slave holder; so, as a democrat and a slave holder, he suited the southern section of the country.

He was very bitterly opposed. All his strong peculiarities; his hot temper; his irresistible will; his quarrels and duels; his marrying another man's wife; his lack of an education; his ignorance as a civilian — all were used against him to make the contest personal, sharp and severe. There were no principles involved that it did the people good to consider and discuss. There were no measures before the people which related to good government and the improvement of the country. The whole contest was personal, partisan and sectional, educating the people only in things harmful and belittling.

Before General Jackson was inaugurated president, his wife sickened and died. It was said at the time that the public recital of all her marriage troubles, hastened her death. It was a heavy blow to her most loyal and devoted husband. Few men were ever more genuinely married to a woman than was Jackson to her. Her happiness was his pleasure. His imperious nature was lamb-like in her presence. To her he was gentle, patient, self-forgetful. This manly devotion to his wife through all their years together, was the most redeeming and honorable trait in his character. It opens into green fields and blooming gardens in his soul which the world knew but little of. It indicated a greatness far surpassing any other he ever exhibited.

March 4, 1829, Andrew Jackson began a Jacksonian administration. It was like everything else he did, peculiar, positive, imperious. In two years he made an entire new cabinet; said to have been brought about by a scandal relating to Mrs. Eaton, the wife of his secretary of war. The other ladies of his court did not fancy Mrs. Eaton. She was the wife of his friend and he was bound to sustain her. But probably the dislike of Calhoun and his friends had something to do with it also.

In 1832 Congress rechartered the national bank, through which the national finances had been conducted and in which the national deposits were made. The president vetoed the bill. This created great alarm among monied men and an immense excitement. It struck at the center of business and portended commercial disaster. He made many removals from office on partisan grounds and filled their places with his friends. And this made the more comment as he had approved Mr. Monroe's non-partisan appointments. Up to this time all presidents had respected the rights of the minority and been presidents of the whole people. He instituted the new order of "to the victor belong the spoils." He made partisanship venal.

He continued the war on the national bank; removed two or three secretaries from the cabinet to get one to do his bidding in making the national deposits in state banks; was opposed by the Senate, which refused to confirm some of his appointments. The Senate passed a resolution of censure on him.

He opposed the extension of the national road and internal improvements generally. His administration was narrow, bellicose and imperious. It produced a great panic in business; was a hindrance to the growth of the country, which advanced only in spite of it. The country bore the evils of state bank currency till the Jackson faction in politics was overcome and the present national currency established.

Mr. Calhoun was his vice-president and opposed him. Jackson was a moderate tariff man. Calhoun was opposed to any tariff, and led a faction in South Carolina, who wished to nullify the tariff laws by refusing to pay duties on imported goods at the port of Charleston. It was the state rights doctrine put in practice — the seed of rebellion — was rebellion on a small scale. Jackson opposed it fiercely, and was widely sustained in his opposition.

The foreign affairs of his government were better conducted.

Just before the close of his administration, the Senate expunged its resolution of censure of the president.

Yet imperious, factional, and ill-judged as Jackson's administration was in most particulars, and opposed as it was to the established principles of the government in many particulars, it continued to be popular with the masses. The "Old Hickory" furor did not die. The battle of New Orleans could not be forgotten. His absolutism gratified the democratic love of a powerful leader — a king in the people's name.

Jefferson's fears were realized. Before Jackson's election Mr. Jefferson said to Daniel Webster : "I feel much alarmed at the prospect of seeing General Jackson president. He is one of the most unfit men I know of for such a place. He has very little respect for law or constitutions; and is in fact an able military chief. His passions are terrible. When I was president of the Senate he was senator; and he could never speak on account of the rashness of his feelings. I have seen him attempt it repeatedly, and as often choke with rage. His passions are no doubt cooler now. He has been much tried since I knew him; but he is a dangerous man." But it turned out that his passions had not much cooled. He was Jefferson's disciple in political doctrines, but he was a man so different that there could be but little affinity between them.

Mr. Parton, his appreciative biographer, says of him : "His ignorance of law, history, politics, science, — of everything which he who governs a country ought to know, — was extreme. Mr. Trist remembers hearing a member of the general's family say that General Jackson did not believe the world was round. His ignorance was a wall round about him, high and impenetrable. He was imprisoned in his ignorance, and sometimes raged around his little dim enclosure like a tiger in his den." Yet he had many grand qualities which will never be forgotten to be set down to his credit.

March 4, 1837, he retired from public life to the Hermitage, where he lived in rural peace, growing calmer, sweeter, gentler, till the close of his earthly life. In his later days he became a devout christian. He had always believed in christianity as taught by the Presbyterian church. The evening of his life was a benediction. Every day he gathered his family servants about him, and led them in family worship. His spirit became Christ-like. He loved to read the scriptures and meditate upon their teachings. Heaven was near and dear to him, especially so as his wife waited his coming there. His was a great soul, which had a rough voyage on this turbulent sea; yet it went calmly and grandly into port at last. It was one of the great products of the republic—tropical and vigorous; yet it is a beacon of warning to the generations, against the neglect of education, the spirit of faction and the narrowness of partisanship, as well as against elevating to national leadership men undisciplined in self-control and untrained in civic affairs.

# The Grave of Andrew Jackson.

Jackson and the Hermitage are associated terms, like Washington and Mount Vernon. Man and his home ought to be associated terms.

Eleven miles from Nashville, Tennessee, on the Lebanon turnpike, that affords a beautiful drive between rows of shade-trees, is the Hermitage, where Andrew Jackson dwelt and died, and where many great men used to go to see him. It is a two-storied brick house with porticos, supported by corinthian columns. It is neglected, and slowly going to decay. Some fifty or sixty rods away is the old wooden house he lived in before this was built. Other old time buildings are not far away.

At a little distance from the house, perhaps two hundred feet or more, in the corner of the garden, are the graves of President Jackson and his wife, beneath a massive monument of Tennessee limestone. There is a circular area of earth, eighteen feet across, and elevated some two feet. On a base covering the graves, are erected eight fluted columns, which support a plain, but well-conceived entablature, surmounted by an urn. Within, the ceiling and cornice are ornamented with white stucco work. In the center of this column-enclosed platform, resting on a square base is a pyramid. On the left, just over the body of the president, is a stone with this inscription:

> General Andrew Jackson.
> BORN MARCH 15, 1767;
> DIED JUNE 8, 1845.

On the right of the pyramid is a similar stone, the inscription on which records his profound estimation of his wife: "Rachael, who died December 22, 1828, at the age of sixty-one. Her face was fair; her person pleasing; her temper amiable, and her heart kind; she delighted in relieving the wants of her fellow creatures, and cultivated the Divine pleasure by the most liberal and unpretending methods; to the poor she was a benefactor, to the wretched a comforter, to the rich an example, to the prosperous an ornament; her piety went hand in hand with her benevolence, and she thanked her Creator for being able to do good. A being so gentle and yet so virtuous, slander might wound, but could not dishonor; even death, when he tore her from the arms of her husband, could but transport her to the bosom of her God."

# CHAPTER IX.

## MARTIN VAN BUREN.

### Eighth President of the United States.

TURNING from General Jackson's to Martin Van Buren's life is like leaving the turbulent ocean and gliding into a peaceful, land-locked harbor. Between the two men there could not be sharper contrasts; yet they were ardent personal friends. Jackson was nearly sixteen years the senior, and had the combined feelings of a father and elder brother, after their acquaintance, toward his young friend and political co-worker.

It is instructive to trace the history of men so different, reared in the same country, accepting the same political principles and trained in the same school of partisan life. It shows the power of original endowment and social surroundings.

#### ANCESTRY, BIRTH AND BOYHOOD.

As the name indicates, the ancestors of Martin Van Buren were Germans. They belonged to that thrifty and solid-sensed class which settled in the valley of the Hudson and put so much good blood, muscle and character into the society of the New World.

The emigrants from Holland and Germany have had a strong life in America. Holland was quite abreast of England in advanced ideas in the seventeenth century. The men of the Mayflower went first to Holland, and then came to the new continent. Emigrants from Holland followed right on. Their life and work are mingled in the people and institutions of this country.

Martin Van Buren's father, Abraham Van Buren, was a farmer in the old town of Kinderhook, a few miles east of the Hudson. When Martin was once asked how far he could trace his lineage, he replied, "To Kinderhook." Up from the common people the great minds of the republic have come. Mr. Van Buren was also a tavern-keeper, turning thrifty pennies from a double calling.

Martin was the eldest son, born December 5, 1782, just as the revolutionary war was closing. The valley of the Hudson had been swept over and over by the tides of that war, and its inhabitants were charged with its public and patriotic spirit. The generation to which Martin belonged was born of that spirit. That great "time that tried men's souls" projected itself into the next generation.

As the boy-of-all-work on a farm and the general helper about a country hotel Martin was taught a variety of useful lessons—the use of his hands and muscles in work and of his mind and manners in mingling with men. He had an early contact with material nature and human nature, both of which he studied to profit.

To most boys the old country tavern was an unprofitable place. The waste of time and money in the bar-room, the profanity and ribaldry too common there, the company that drags down and the lessons that corrupt, all tend to make it the last place to look for the boys that make presidents. While a hundred boys would have been weighted down by the depressing influences of such a place, Martin Van Buren set his face upward, treated everybody with respect, learned to be courteous, a gentleman to everybody, and at the same time how to serve, please, keep his own counsels and what are the mainsprings of human action. It was not the highest practical education which he got in this place, but it was one, no doubt, which did much to shape his character and career. It made him observant, studious to please, bland, genial and shrewd without the appearance of effort. It is interesting to connect his later life and character with this practical school of his boyhood.

His early education was got in the schools of his village, which he attended until he was fourteen. It is said that he finished his academic studies in his native village when fourteen.

He then began the study of law in an office in Kinderhook, and perseveringly pursued it six years. Then he went to New York city and studied under the tuition of William P. Van Ness, who afterward became much known, and especially for his connection with the Burr and Hamilton duel, in which the latter lost his life. Martin became acquainted with Burr, who was intimate with Van Ness. Burr was at this time a brilliant and seductive man in the midst of a very popular career. Martin Van Buren was a handsome, polite, precocious and talented young man of twenty. There was much that was congenial between them. They were both men of fine manners and forceful and brilliant minds. Burr was unprincipled and came to a great fall, but at this time was suspected by none. His brilliance was froth on a foul pool.

At the end of a year in New York city, in seeking a knowledge of law, he returned to Kinderhook and set up the practice of his profession. At that time such a long study was demanded to get admission to the bar, because he had not a college education. The defect was not remedied by the long study; for beyond a doubt, his whole career was narrowed, weakened, less dignified and high-minded than it would have been had he had the bracing and broadening of a full course of academic study. He became noted as a politician rather than a statesman—just the result that such a defective beginning might have been expected to produce. He was narrow, local, time-serving, studious of expedients, managing for men and votes, artful in management, shrewd in partisanship, rather than broad, general, long-seeing, comprehensive, national. His popularity was temporary and not permanent. He built no great monuments for the ages to remember him by. And not because he had not ability, but because he did not educate himself broadly.

17

He sought only a boy's education, the rudiments, not the principles of learning. The education obtained before sixteen is such as a boy comprehends; that got afterward lays the foundation of the man. The boy Van Buren was educated; the man Van Buren was not. The man was put to the law, and made a technical, close, formal lawyer, rather than a broad, great-thinking, fresh and expansive man. A born gentleman, with a rich and vigorous mind, active, studious, eager for knowledge, ambitious for honorable distinction, patriotic and humane, he yet only began to study, and then hurried on to the technology of the law—to the often belittling drudgery of detail. Always will the readers of his externally successful life deplore its too narrow and stinted beginning.

### VAN BUREN THE LAWYER.

In 1803, in the twenty-first year of his age, young Van Buren was admitted to the bar as an attorney at law. He immediately entered into partnership with his half brother, James I. Van Allen, and entered into the practice of law in Kinderhook. While a student he often tried cases before justices of the peace, and showed a cleverness and penetration which augured the successful lawyer. Four years later he was admitted to the supreme court. In 1808 he was appointed surrogate of Columbia county; and soon after that he removed to Hudson, the county seat of his county—a thriving town on the Hudson river. His practice increased and became extensive in a few years. His devotion to his profession, his readiness as a speaker, his bland ways and manly and courteous bearing won him friends and success. For some twenty-five years he continued his successful and lucrative practice. In 1806 he married Miss Hannah Hoes, to whom he had been sincerely attached for a number of years. It was an agreeable marriage and brought to both its mutual pleasures and profits. Four sons were born to them when his wife began to decline with consumption, and died in 1818. He remained a widower through his life.

## A POLITICIAN.

Mr. Van Buren embraced the political views of his father who was an enthusiastic admirer of Jefferson. Many of the young man's relatives were federalists. The federalists were in the majority in his state. They endeavored to persuade him to the majority as a matter of good business policy. But he was a sincere democrat and gave no heed to such persuasions. As early as his eighteenth year he was appointed a delegate from his native town to a political convention, to nominate a candidate to the legislature. He prepared an address to the electors of his dristrict, young as he was.

When he was twenty years old Mr. Jefferson was elected to the presidency. He was young Van Buren's ideal statesman. By this event his enthusiasm for his ideal teacher of political truth was all that an ardent young soul could give. Jefferson's messages, addresses, statements of policy, were his study. He gave his ardent support to all the president's men and measures. The eight years of Jefferson's administration fixed Mr. Van Buren deeply in the grooves of the democratic party. He was too ardent a follower of his great master to raise any doubts or queries about any of his teachings, and too little breadth of intellectual culture to be an original thinker concerning them. He was educated to the level of partisanship, and not to that of leadership in political thought. He took his doctrines ready formed from his teacher. He was a second and reduced edition of Jefferson. And it was the misfortune of his education, or lack of it, that he was so.

In 1812, when thirty years of age, he was elected in a closely contested election, a member of the State Senate. Mr. Madison was now president, and the second war with England was just opening. Mr. Van Buren gave the force of his influence to the support of the administration and the war. He was a true patriot, a genuine American in a Dutch setting.

In 1815, at the age of thirty-three, he was elected attorney-general of the state of New York—a mark of respect for a young man which indicates an early ripeness in his profession.

He was also elected a regent of the university. The next spring he was re-elected state senator for four years. This was about the time De Witt Clinton was projecting and urging his internal improvements, especially the canal through the state of New York, that has ever since been called "Clinton's Ditch." It received great opposition and was hotly denounced by many of the tax payers. It was the introduction to canal building in the country and did great service in its day in helping to develop the settlement and resources of the country.

Mr. Van Buren took the side of Mr. Clinton on the internal improvements of the state. Afterward De Witt Clinton was elected governor of the state by the democratic party. Mr. Van Buren, in 1818, set up an opposition to the governor's administration, and organized what was called "The Albany Regency," a sort of tammany club, or self-appointed clique, which in a few years got the politics of the state in its hand and held it for many years. It was a break in the party, occasioned by its two leaders, which was fierce for a considerable time. Van Buren won in the end and gathered pretty much the whole party around him.

In February, 1821, the legislature of New York elected Mr. Van Buren to the Senate of the United States, when he was thirty-nine years of age. Mr. Van Buren's opposition to Governor Clinton, division of the democratic party, formation of the Albany Regency, and managing it for fifteen years, got him the name of a politician. His enemies called him a wire-worker, a fox, an oily, deceptive managing man. Many regarded him as the impersonation of cunning. His good looks, his nice taste, which always dressed him like a fine gentleman, as he really was, his polished manners, his absolute self control, his suavity and courtesy, were all interpreted as evidence of his sly cunning and innate duplicity. Because he would not be a boor, many believed him to be an autocrat under the polished garb of a democratic gentleman. The same year that he was elected to the Senate, a convention was held in the state of New York to revise the constitution. Mr. Van Buren was a delegate to this convention, and was of such practical service as won the approval of all parties. He was opposed to universal suffrage; was in favor of a property qualification; was in favor of colored men having the right of suffrage on the same terms as white men. His course in this convention was so judicious and conservative, that even the federalists had no fault to find with him. In his work here, he showed the real quality of his mind, because he was not acting as a politician, but as a statesman. He was a man of quick and strong power, but that power, for the most part, was put to the service of a party, rather than to the broader and nobler service of the country.

In the Senate of the United States, Mr. Van Buren was active and influential, advocating the abolition of imprisonment for debt, in actions in the United States courts, amendments to the judiciary system, a general bankrupt law, a just investment of the money for the sales of public lands in the states where they were made.

Mr. Monroe was now president. It was the "era of good feeling." The federal party was dead. The democratic party was in full power. The whig party was not yet organized. The old federalists were a scattered host of strong, good men, feeling about for some way to act together. But no great question had come up, around which they could rally in opposition to the triumphant democracy. John Quincy Adams was secretary of state, and conducting the duties of that office with great ability, and to the satisfaction of the federalists. Mr. Monroe respected the rights of the minority, and appointed many moderate federalists to office, as had been the costom thus far by the presidents.

In 1825, John Quincy Adams took his seat as president. Mr. Van Buren opposed his election, advocating the claims of Andrew Jackson. Mr. Adams was a scholar, a non-partisan, a statesman of the largest type, outranking in ability and in knowledge of the world's affairs and history, any statesman in Europe—honest, patriotic, non-sectional, a gentleman and christian. Andrew Jackson was his opposite in almost everything but integrity and patriotism. And yet, Mr. Van Buren threw his great influence and skill in manipulating elections, in favor of Andrew Jackson. Party considerations in the main actuated him. Socially, intellectually and morally, his sympathies were with Mr. Adams. He did not comprehend Mr. Adams on account of the narrowness of his studies, and the meagreness of his knowledge of nations, their laws, histories and developments. In knowledge he was nearer the level of Jackson than Adams. Yet in the main, party moved him in this choice.

After Mr. Adams became president Mr. Van Buren opposed his administration and began at once to shape the next campaign for Jackson. In this work he was skillful. He was schooled in it. In the Senate of New York he had planned and secured the manipulation of the party in that state, and held it for fifteen years. Now in the Senate of the United States he was doing the same work for the party of the country. He became chief manipulator. He was not too scholarly, nor too moral, nor too great-minded to enjoy this work; nor was he so broad a lover of his country as to feel the degradation of this intense partisanship. The way was making for a great change in the partisanship of national politics, and Mr. Van Buren was perhaps as influential in that direction as any other man. The change to come was expressed in the phrase: "To the victors belong the spoils." One meaning of it was, "the minority have no rights which the majority are bound to respect."

In February, 1827, Mr. Van Buren was re-elected to the Senate of the United States. In 1828 Governor Clinton died and Mr. Van Buren was chosen to fill his place, as Governor of New York. In this position he sought to improve the finances of the state by recommending and urging to adoption, the famous funding system. But it was a scheme of his fertile brain, and proved a failure. He had not studied finance, or political economy—was not a scholar in any of the great matters of political science, and of course could not recommend anything out of any large knowledge of the subject. His meagre mental furnishing was constantly showing itself.

## SECRETARY OF STATE.

March 4, 1829, Andrew Jackson became president. He appointed Martin Van Buren to the first place in his cabinet — secretary of state. Jackson began at once the great partisan measure which had been foreshadowed, "to the victors belong the spoils." Federalists and opponents of all kinds were removed from office without cause only that they had voted against Jackson. He made his adminstration partisan from center to circumference, and Jacksonian in its destructive vigor. Mr. Van Buren was one with his chief, and it may, perhaps, have been as much due to him as to Jackson, that these strong partisan measures were put into force. When Mr. Monroe was president and selected Mr. Adams for secretary of state, and retained the most of the officers of his predecessor, and appointed many moderate federalists, Andrew Jackson commended him for it. But now he was in a different mood. How much Van Buren's partisanship did to produce this different mood, of course is not known; but that Van Buren approved of Jackson's slaughter of his opponents in office, seems now clear. Two men of absolutely different mould had now met and worked in fraternal partisanship to defeat their partisan adversaries and reward their friends. Mr. Van Buren was a state rights advocate, and was professedly jealous of national power. When elected Senator, in his letter of acceptance, he said: "It shall be my constant and zealous endeavor to protect the remaining rights reserved to the states by the federal constitution, to restore those of which they have been divested by construction, and to promote the interest and honor of our common country." His main thought seemed to be to guard the rights of the states.

The national bank, which Jackson fought and destroyed, and by doing so brought financial ruin to the whole country, was opposed chiefly because it was a national and not a state institution, and was in danger of becoming an overshadowing monopoly; it was also a federalist institution, established by them, who believed in a strong and stable central government. It must, therefore, be destroyed and the funds of the government be deposited in state banks. The state banks were Jackson's pets and must handle the funds of the national government; that was democracy, he fancied. He and Mr. Van Buren were one in opposition to the national bank and in favor of the state banks, and doubtless were agreed in the veto of the renewal of the charter of the national bank and the removal of the deposits to the state banks, and were together the cause of the immense mischief that followed, when every state bank failed or suspended, business stopped, a wreck, and the government had to go into the markets of Europe a bankrupt, to borrow money to keep its machinery moving. What was national was suspicious to minds like theirs, fevered with the partisanship doctrines of states rights.

While Mr. Van Buren was secretary of state there occurred one of those strange episodes in high life that once in a while shake a nation. There was a tavern-keeper in Washington by the name of O'Neal. When Jackson was United States senator he boarded at this tavern. Peggy O'Neal was a lively daughter who made herself so social with her father's guests as to throw suspicions upon the propriety of her conduct. Miss O'Neal at length married a Mr. Timberlake, a purser in the United States navy. Major John H. Eaton, of Tennessee, Jackson's secretary of war, boarded at O'Neal's and was much captivated with the society of Mrs. Timberlake. The tongue of scandal was not still. Timberlake committed suicide in the Mediterranean sea; Eaton married his widow. Now Peggy O'Neal was the wife of a cabinet officer. The wives of the other members of the cabinet were shocked, and would not receive her into their society. Jackson impetuously defended Mrs. Eaton as an abused and innocent woman. Van Buren, without wife or daughter, was one of the most pliant and polite of men, and as politic as he was courteous. He called upon Mrs. Eaton; treated her with marked attention, and made parties for her and her husband; all of which was very grateful to his chief and in keeping with Mr. Van Buren's politic character. But the Eaton controversy raged for two years. The wives of foreign ministers were drawn into it. Washington society was shocked and shaken by it.

The president and his cabinet and vice-president were eight; four were for Mrs. Eaton, four against her. At length the president determined to secure harmony in his cabinet by the Jacksonian method of dismissing them all and appointing a new cabinet. This was accomplished by having those in sympathy with him resign and he would appoint them to other places. Van Buren was immediately appointed to the court of St. James. The others took the hint and resigned. All this redounded to the popularity of Van Buren. He was now regarded as a sort of political magician whose will moved cabinets and senates.

But this was not all. This Eaton embroglio, intensified likes and dislikes that before existed. Van Buren had secured Jackson's friendship in his work for his election. He had pleased him in everything as a cabinet officer; now this kindness for the traduced and charming Mrs. Eaton had won his heart. Henceforth he loved Van Buren; and Jackson's love was a great volcanic fire that ceased not to flow from its deep sources. On the other hand, Calhoun had labored for Crawford in the campaign; had not given him great pleasure in the cabinet; and had taken bitter ground against Mrs. Eaton, and greatly embittered the president against him. This bitterness followed Calhoun as much as the president's love followed and rewarded Van Buren. Jackson's opposition to Calhoun for his nullification of the tariff laws, in his next term, had in it not a little of the spite of the Eaton controversy. He probably never ceased to regret that he did not get the chance to "hang Calhoun high as Haman."

Mr. Van Buren met a triumphant reception in New York, and sailed very soon for England. He was cordially received in England. His courtly manners, great personal beauty, and distinguished position in his own country, were at once recognized, and he was received with honor.

But when Congress met in the winter, it refused to approve his appointment. Calhoun, Clay and Webster opposed him bitterly, "accusing him of such a spirit of narrow partisanship as to unfit him to be the representative of the whole country." He was acused of being "the originator of the system of removing from office every incumbent, however able and faithful, who did not advocate the principles of the party in power."

Mr. Van Buren's rejection by the Senate, it was supposed by some, would operate against his popularity. Mr. Calhoun, who most bitterly hated him, said triumphantly: "It will kill him, sir,—kill him dead. He will never kick, sir,—never kick." But Jackson's mighty energy was roused in his behalf, and he determined to do everything in his power to elevate him.

### VICE-PRESIDENT VAN BUREN.

March 4, 1833, Jackson was re-elected president and Martin Van Buren vice-president. This made him president of the Senate. It was a stormy administration, with a strong and determined opposition from the Senate.

The president's destruction of the United States bank, and removal of the funds of the government to the state banks, so paralyzed the monetary affairs of the country as to alarm business, awaken distrust, and put a stop to all development of resources.

This made the opposition fiercer and the party contests more bitter. This was the condition of the country when Jackson retired to the Hermitage, and Van Buren came to be inaugurated in his place.

### PRESIDENT VAN BUREN.

On the fourth of March, 1837, Mr. Van Buren was inaugurated President of the United States. This was a result greatly desired by his great predecessor. Jackson had set his heart on this; partly because he loved him, partly because Calhoun hated him, whom he would like to have hanged for his nullification.

"Leaving New York out of the canvass," says Mr. Parton, "the election of Mr. Van Buren to the presidency was as much the act of General Jackson as though the constitution had conferred upon him the power to appoint a successor."

Mr. Van Buren selected John Forsyth, of Georgia, secretary of state; Levi Woodbury, of New Hampshire, secretary of the treasury; Joel R. Poinsett, of South Carolina, secretary of war;

Mahlon Dickerson, of New Jersey, secretary of the navy; Amos Kendall, of Kentucky, pastmaster-general, and Benjaman F. Butler, of New York, attorney-general. They were all, but Mr. Poinsett, in the cabinet under Jackson. Mr. Van Buren started out with the announcement that he should "follow in the footsteps of his illustrious predecessor." The country, therefore, had no right to expect any change in the policy of the goverment. The fruits of Jackson's administration must be reaped in Van Buren's also, and in greater abundance. The stagnation of business which had already become general and alarming, would be sure to become greater on the announcement of no change in the policy of the government. And so it proved. Early in May the pressure on the banks became so great that they were obliged to suspend specie payments. On the sixteenth of May the legislature of New York authorized the suspension of specie payments for one year. There had then been two months of unparalleled financial embarrassment in the whole country. It followed right on after Mr. Van Buren's inauguration. Failure followed failure in rapid succession. Two hundred and fifty houses failed in New York city in three weeks. Business was at a stand still in all the cities. Property fell rapidly in value; men were idle; suffering was extensive; complaints were bitter against Jackson and his successor. Petitions poured in upon the president, praying that the circulars issued by Jackson requiring that the payments for public lands should be made in gold or silver, should be rescinded. They asked also that he would not commence suits on unpaid bonds; and also that he would call an extra session of Congress. He hesitated for some time, but the pressure became so great that he at length called a meeting of Congress for the first Monday in September.

The session lasted forty days. The democrats held the majority of both Houses, but not all of them agreed with the president's policy. Some voted with the whigs, and defeated the independent treasury scheme of the president. The payment of a fourth installment to the states was postponed. Ten millions of dollars of treasury notes were authorized. The independent treasury scheme was defeated again in the regular session of Congress the next winter; but near the close of his term of office it became a law. Its object was to divorce the government from all connection with banks, and to do all government business with gold and silver. The financial policy of Jackson and Van Buren grew out of a prejudice against the United States bank as a federal and national institution as against state institutions. That prejudice at length extended to all banks, and resulted in the independent treasury scheme. It was one of the heaviest blows on the prosperity of the country that it has ever had. Business floundered for years in a stagnant sea. The hard-money craze captured the yeomanry of the country, whose small trading could be readily done with gold and silver; but it was a heavy burden on large transactions, and crippled the country for a generation. The two administrations that were so much alike in policy as to be one, Jackson's and Van Buren's, were narrow and hindering to the prosperity of the country, for lack of breadth of understanding and thorough knowledge of the subject of finance, on which they assumed to be wise.

The state currency, upon which they threw the country, was always weak and fickle, and their course made us a nation without a national currency.

To add to the discontent of Van Buren's term, the Seminole war in Florida continued to draw great sums from the treasury; the northeastern boundary question threatened a war with England, and the slavery question took on a more threatening aspect in the House and all over the country. A resolution was passed laying all petitions on the subject on the table without reading, which led to John Quincy Adams' stout and long defense of the right of petition. Threats of a dissolution of the Union became common, especially where nullification had sown its seeds of discontent.

An act was passed in Van Buren's term giving settlers on public lands the first right of purchase, which was just and encouraging to western settlement.

Mr. Van Buren's last message gloried in the independent treasury, and in a country "without a national debt or a national bank." In this message he recommended the enactment of more stringent laws for the breaking up of the African slave trade.

But a new election was coming. The opposition had become intense, and was early in the field. The old federalists, with large numbers of disaffected from the banks and business, and intelligence of the country, had grown into the organized whig party. In every part of the country the strong opposition was alert. It charged the administration with every extravagance and corruption, with indifference to the laboring masses, with neglect of the country's good. Van Buren was called an autocrat eating with gold spoons, a fox, a monster of selfishness. Even his virtues were perverted into vices. The canvass was fierce and universal. On the fourth of December, 1839, the whig party nominated William Henry Harrison for president and John Tyler for vice-president. The democratic party, on the fifth of May, 1840, nominated Van Buren. The whigs had five months the start which they improved in thorough organization and in rousing the whole opposition force into intense activity. The canvass was made a memorable one by the "log cabins" that were everywhere paraded as symbols of Harrison's humble origin, and the songs of "Tippecanoe and Tyler too," which recited the story of his famous Indian battle and victory. Monster meetings were addressed by inflamed orators; banners, badges, bonfires, songs, processions, torchlights, were everywhere in vogue to stir the masses and intensify the opposition. It was a desperate canvass, as though a monster had got the country by the throat and he must be struck off by a tremendous blow at the ballot box. And the blow came. Van Buren received only sixty electoral votes and Harrison two hundred and thirty-four. It was the rising of an ill-governed country to shake off the incompetent governors.

In 1844 Mr. Van Buren was again urged upon the democratic convention as its candidate; but he was rejected because he was opposed to the annexation of Texas to extend the realm of slavery, which had been an object arranged for for many years by the supporters of that institution.

In 1848, when the leaders of the party avowed themselves ready to tolerate slavery in New Mexico, not satisfied with the area of Texas for that institution, Mr. Van Buren and a portion of the party set up as the free democracy, and held a convention at Utica, at which he was nominated for president. Another convention was held at Buffalo, August 9, and Charles Francis Adams was nominated for vice-president. This convention declared that "Congress had no more power to make a slave than it had to make a king," and that "it is the duty of the federal government to relieve itself from all responsibility for the existence, or continuance of slavery wherever the government possesses constitutional authority to legislate on that subject, and is thus responsible for its existence." Mr. Van Buren gave full assent to these anti-slavery principles. But General Taylor, the regular candidate, was elected.

After this election, Mr. Van Buren lived quietly and elegantly at Kinderhook, in the enjoyment of a refined and placid old age. He traveled two years in Europe, enjoyed much society of the wise and good. On the outbreak of the civil war he was strongly for the government. He wrote a work entitled, "An Inquiry into the Origin and Course of Political Parties in the United States," which was edited by his son in 1867. He died July 24, 1862, at the age of eighty.

Few public men have been more misunderstood, than Martin Van Buren. He lived in a critical period of his country's history, just as it was passing out of the revolutionary era when its fortunes were managed by the great men who were the glory of that era, and into the era of popular conceit when a rough frontiersman was counted a magician of political wisdom, and when learning, civil experience and large knowledge of law, government and history, were held of secondary importance. He himself fell into this error when a boy, and had the misfortune to have no friend to counsel him, to educate himself before he entered upon the large affairs of public life. In this state of mind he early followed the erratic leadings of erratic minds, and drifted helpless into a sea he found it hard to navigate. He was accused of art, deceit, the wily legerdemain, of the heartless and ambitious politician, and yet was honest in intention, and sought to serve his country well. He had a just pride of character and conduct; was singularly self-possessed, and was a gentleman everywhere and always, but did not see the high moralities of thought and statesmanship which alone give glory to a public career.

Mr. Forsyth, his secretary of state, made this estimate of him: "I have never witnessed aught in Mr. Van Buren which requires concealment, palliation or coloring; never anything to lessen his character as a patriot or a man; nothing that he might not desire to expose to the scrutiny of every member of this body, with a calm confidence of unsullied integrity. He is called an artful man, a giant of artifice, a wily magician. Those ignorant of his unrivaled knowledge of human character, his power of penetrating into the designs and defeating the purposes of his adversaries, seeing his rapid advance to power and public confidence, impute to art what is the natural result of those simple causes. Extraordinary talent; untiring industry; incessant vigilance; the happiest temper, which success cannot corrupt, nor disappointment sour,—these are the sources of his unexampled success, the magic arts, the artifices of intrigue, to which he has resorted in his eventful life. Those who envy his success may learn wisdom from his example."

# The Grave of Martin Van Buren.

Martin Van Buren was born, lived and died at Kinderhook, Columbia county, New York. And there reposes what was mortal of him. The graveyard at the northern end of the village is filled with tenants. The Van Buren lot is at the northeast corner of the yard. It is crowded with graves; is unfenced; is even without boundary marks; is flowerless and shrubless. The president's grave is in the center of the lot. Over it is a plain granite monument fifteen feet high. Half way up on one side is this inscription:

> **Martin Van Buren,**
> Eighth President of the United States.
> Born December 5, 1782,
> Died July 24, 1862.

Immediately under this is that of his wife:

> **Hannah Van Buren,**
> his wife.
> Born March 3, 1783,
> Died at Albany, New York,
> February 3, 1819.

Mr. Van Buren had three sons, the remains of one rest with him; the rest elsewhere. His parents and brother Lawrence were buried here.

Two nieces, daughters of Lawrence, were all of the family that lived there some few years ago.

ENGRAVED EXPRESSLY FOR WEAVERS' "LIVES AND GRAVES OF OUR PRESIDENTS."

# CHAPTER X.

## WILLIAM HENRY HARRISON.
### NINTH PRESIDENT OF THE UNITED STATES.

#### ANCESTRY.

IN the opening life of William Henry Harrison, we are carried back to Virginia, mother of presidents, nursery of freedom and the revolution, home of great men and great deeds; we mingle again with the Washingtons, the Randolphs, the Lees, the Masons, Marshalls, Henrys, Wythes, Jeffersons, Madisons and Monroes, and their great compatriots; we see again that rich and picturesque land, rivered with the Potomac, the James, the Shenandoah and the Rapidan, washed by Atlantic tides and overlooked by the peaks of the Blue Ridge—land of sunshine and fruitfulness, which will ever hold a great place in American history because of its production of so many great men.

The father of William Henry was Benjamin Harrison, of Virginia, associate of the great patriots of the revolution. He was in comparatively opulent circumstances; was an intimate friend of Washington; was among the first in Virginia to resist the oppressions of England; was a member of the Continental Congress, and was three times governor of Virginia. When in Congress he was chosen to preside over that body, but in deference to Massachusetts and John Hancock, from that state, he declined; and seeing that Mr. Hancock, who was a small man, while Harrison was very large, strong, and full of fun, modestly hesitated, he caught him in his arms, carried him to the speaker's chair and placed him in it, amid roars of laughter from the members; then turning round, his honest, ruddy face beaming with merriment, he said: "Gentlemen, we will show Mother Britain how little we care for her by making a Massachusetts man our president, whom she has excluded from pardon by a public proclamation."

Mr. Harrison always saw the ludicrous side of things, and often had his joke over serious matters. He was a signer of the Declaration of Independence. It was solemn work, in the face of British power, for the colonists to put their names to their own death-warrant, if they failed to maintain their independence. They realized it all, and opened that solemn work with prayer. While the signing was going on, Mr. Harrison turned to Elbridge Gerry, who was a small, fragile man, and said: "Gerry, when the *hanging comes* I shall have the advantage. You'll kick in the air half an hour after it is all over with me."

This was the father of the ninth president, a brave, hearty, magnificent man, loyal, loving, and overflowing with good-humor.

### BIRTH AND YOUTH.

William Henry was the third and youngest son of this brave Virginia patriot. He was born at Berkeley, on the banks of the James river, February 9, 1773. His early education was got in the schools of Virginia, but no small part of it came to him unconsciously from his family associations—from the men of the revolution whom he knew and heard talk of the times and men that gave being to the nation. The air of Virginia was alive with patriotism. He was born three years before the Declaration of Independence. He was ten years old when Cornwallis surrendered to Washington near his home, and remembered well the rejoicings when peace was declared. He was fourteen when the convention met to form the constitution; was sixteen when Washington was inaugurated president, and twenty when he entered upon his second term. He was the child of that great era. His mind fed on its great deeds, and his soul drank in its spirit. He was educated on patriotism, liberty and martial valor. The speeches, messages, constitutions and laws of his time were his youthful studies. His youth was the constitution era of the young country. The principles of civil liberty and law were the talk of the men and youth about him. It was the organizing era of nationality. To live then was to be in a great school. It was especially so to active and aspiring minds like young Harrison's. They were taken out of themselves and made public-spirited. Selfishness was made subservient to the great interests of society. To live for the general good was the great and manly ambition. Boys that otherwise would grovel, were made aspiring. It was a magnificent age to live in, and blessed were the youth who were born to an education in those principle-discussing and state-making times. Mean and sordid living was not in fashion. Effeminacy had no place. Courage, stalwartness, generosity, large-mindedness, were the qualities of manly virtue. A son of the times was William Henry Harrison.

His father died in 1791, when he was eighteen. He was left under the guardianship of Robert Morris, the distinguished financier. He entered and graduated from Hampden Sidney college. So, to the educating and enlarging influences of the times, he added a course of liberal study. He did not cheat his mind to serve his pocket; did not give to youthful frivolity the time that manly culture demands. The youthful years were ripened in the college classes. His good endowments were quickened by the added strength of the athletic discipline of academic study. He carried no boy's mind into a man's place; but with furnished powers, ripened and energized by the training of the schools, he entered upon a man's course a man indeed, with a man's breadth of mind and strength of action.

### OPENING MANHOOD.

During his course of study young Harrison had concluded to study medicine and make its practice his profession. He went to Philadelphia to study with Doctor Rush, who was a friend of his father and a signer with him of the Declaration of Independence. It does not appear how long he remained with Doctor Rush, but it could not have been long, for before he was twenty-one he was westward bound, as a soldier to defend the frontier against the murderous Indians. His guardian and his friends generally tried to dissuade him from it. He consulted with Washington, who approved it, who secured for him a commission of ensign. Washington was greatly interested in the settlement of the west and knew how needful it was to have an army to defend the settlements against the savages; and also what opportunities were open to the youth of the country in that great field of enterprise. With Washington's approval he turned his young face, not yet twenty-one, toward the setting sun.

Many considerations doubtless entered into his resolution to go as a soldier into the new west.

When he was eighteen years old he became a member of an abolition society at Richmond, Virginia, the object of which was to ameliorate the condition of the slaves and secure their freedom by all legal means. In speaking of this later in life, he said: "From my earliest youth and to the present moment, I have been an ardent friend of human liberty. The obligations which I then came under I have faithfully performed. I have been the means of liberating many slaves, but never placed one in bondage. I was the first person to introduce into Congress the proposition that all the country above Missouri should never have slavery admitted into it." He could see that slavery was entrenched in Virginia, and it might be long before it would be abolished. It troubled his conscience and his heart. It would be better to go away from it at once into a free territory and there help build up a free community.

Again his young blood was patriotic; he lived in stirring times; he was ambitious to serve a country the birth of which he had seen; why settle down to the humdrum practice of medicine when the great west was calling for soldiers and settlers? Washington began as a soldier, why should not he? There was great suffering in the west, there was need of soldiers to defend the settlements. So he went — went a soldier boy.

At this time he was tall, slender, fragile. His friends feared he would not be equal to the hardships of campaign life in an Indian war. Some had anxiety lest he would not be able to get there. It was autumn; but nothing daunted, he started and crossed the country and mountains on foot to what is now Pittsburgh, and thence down the Ohio river to Fort Washington, located where Cincinnati is now situated.

General St. Clair had a considerable military force at Fort Washington, and had charge of the army on the frontier.

A little while before Harrison started on his mission into the wilderness, General St. Clair had made a western movement with fourteen hundred men to rout the Indians from along the Wabash river. Near the headwaters of that river, he was attacked by a large body of Indians, who gave a desperate battle and utterly routed him, killing five hundred and thirty and wounding three hundred and sixty of his men. Almost two thirds of his men were killed or wounded.

Very soon after reaching the fort, Harrison was assigned to the duty of leading a pack-horse train of supplies to Fort Hamilton, twenty-five or thirty miles north, on the Miami river. It was a perilous undertaking, for the skulking foe was nearly omnipresent, and if met, the pack-horses would be at his mercy, as well as the few men with them. The young officer performed so well his duty as to get the special approval of General St. Clair.

The delicate and boy-like face and appearance of the new soldier who had come from Virginia with a commission from Washington, attracted attention from all who met him. After his return from Fort Hamilton, an old frontiersman said of him: "I would as soon have thought of putting my wife into the service as this boy; but I have been out with him, and find those smooth cheeks are on a wise head and that slight frame is almost as tough as my own weather-beaten carcass."

It was not long before the young ensign was promoted to the rank of lieutenant. Very soon after he joined the army of General Wayne, who had been sent to prosecute more vigorously this war with the Indians. General Wayne had a brilliant revolutionary record, and had won the title of "Mad Anthony" by his impetuous and fearless assaults on the enemy.

It is to be remembered that this was not long after the revolutionary war, and that during that war the British had armed the Indians as far as they could, and sought to incite them against the American settlers; and that this Indian war was a kind of lingering result of the revolutionary war. At this time the Indians had become very widely aroused, and had determined to beat back the tide of settlement and retain the territory which is now Ohio, as hunting ground for their children.

Lieutenant Harrison soon saw the evil results of intemperance in the army — that it was even worse than in civil society, as the soldiers were without the restraints of home, regular employment and religious influence. He believed in temperance as a personal virtue and a cardinal principle of morality; but in the army he saw it was important as an example, and especially in an officer, so he adopted high temperance principles, and sought in all legitimate ways to inculcate temperance habits among the soldiers. He was not yet twenty-one, and he was principled against slavery and intemperance, and an ardent patriot and a friend of humanity, having cast himself into the great army of settlement that was moving on for human advancement. He had also given his adherence to the cause of education by a thorough collegiate course of study. This was an equipment for the soldiership of life, that made a fine promise for young Harrison's future. Here was a foundation for a noble manhood.

On the twenty-eighth of November, 1792, with an army of about three thousand men, General Wayne went down the Ohio river from Pittsburgh, about twenty-two miles, and encamped for the winter. The next spring he transported his army in boats down to Fort Washington. Here Lieutenant Harrison joined "The Legion," as General Wayne's army was called.

Several months passed in waiting for supplies, so that the army was not ready to move till autumn. In October a movement was made north about eighty miles, to a place which the army called Greenville. Here an encampment was made for the winter. About twenty miles north of this was the disastrous battle ground of General St. Clair with the Indians. A strong detachment was sent to possess that ground, bury the remains, and build there a fort, which they called Fort Recovery. In this enterprise Lieutenant Harrison rendered such conspicuous service as to secure the especial notice of his general.

In the spring the Indians attacked the fort with great resolution, and were beaten back time after time. General Wayne's army had now been in the territory some fifteen months, and had advanced into the heart of their country. They knew him as a warrior who fought every time for victory. They had had time to gather their best forces, and they attacked with a view to demolish his army as they had that of St. Clair on the same spot, and drive him from their hunting grounds. But he was prepared for them, terribly punished their temerity and drove them far into the wilderness. He then advanced with his whole army some sixty miles north to the junction of the Auglaize and Maumee rivers, where he constructed a fort. Having thus a base of operations on the Maumee, he moved down the river to meet his wily foe somewhere in ambush. Moving cautiously as they went, not to be ensnared, on the twentieth of August he met some two thousand chosen Indian warriors ambushed for his reception at a place of their own choosing. A desperate battle followed; but the fierce men of the woods were worsted with great losses and driven still farther to the northwest by the more enlightened invaders of their territory. It was the old result over again—intelligence winning the victory over ignorance—civilization bearing down triumphantly upon barbarism—the old and effete passing away before the new and vigorous. General Wayne was hundreds of miles in the wilderness, away from reinforcements and supplies; still pushing on from these essentials of support, in a country he had never seen and of which he had no knowledge. His savage adversary was at home and in the midst of his supplies, and could muster more men, and yet he could only fly before the more intelligent invaders.

In these frontier battles Lieutenant Harrison was one of

General Wayne's most active and efficient officers. Quick, active, brave and discreet, he could serve equally well in any place—he could lead an assault, strengthen a weak place, draw in an exposed regiment, or follow into the wilderness the routed foe. His educated mind and intense spirit fitted him to serve such a leader as Anthony Wayne. For his excellent military conduct in this campaign, Lieutenant Harrison was promoted to a captaincy, and given the command of Fort Washington. About this time the British military posts of the northwest fell into the hands of our government, and it became Captain Harrison's duty to receive, occupy and supply them. While engaged in this duty, he married the daughter of John Cleaves Symmes, the founder of the Miami settlements, whose land covered a portion of the present site of Cincinnati.

In April, 1798, Captain Harrison resigned his place in the army to receive the appointment of secretary of the northwestern territory, made vacant by the removal of Winthrop Sargent to the office of governor of the southwestern country. The next year Secretary Harrison was chosen the one delegate to represent the northwestern territory in Congress.

Up to this time the land in this great territory was subject to a law which allowed of its disposal only in tracts of four thousand acres. Mr. Harrison exerted himself, against much opposition, to get this law changed so as to bring the public lands within the purchasing power of small farmers.

There was, from the beginning, two ideas of agricultural life in this country—the Virginia idea of great landed estates, brought from England and applied to this country with a view to build up great and influential families, like those in aristocratic society in England, which were supposed to constitute the strength and stability of a nation, and the New England idea of small farms, which grew out of the necessities of a poorer people. Mr. Harrison had learned that the latter idea applied more generally to those who desired to be actual settlers on the new lands of the northwest, and secured the passage of a law which authorized the sale of the public lands in alternate sections of six hundred and forty and three hundred and twenty acres. This was not all he desired, but it was the most he could get, and was the beginning of that true idea, as applied to the public lands, for a great and free country, of having the people own and cultivate their own lands.

### GOVERNOR HARRISON.

In the year 1800 the northwestern territory was divided, the territory of the present state of Ohio being made one, and the western portion, which now constitutes Indiana, Illinois and Wisconsin, being the other, which was called "The Indian Territory," and Secretary Harrison was made governor of this latter territory. As governor, he was made superintendent of Indian affairs. His area of authority was soon enlarged by his being appointed governor of upper Louisiana. In these great territories he had almost absolute authority. He was first appointed to these important trusts when he was twenty-seven years old by President John Adams. He was afterward reappointed twice by Thomas Jefferson, and again by James Madison; so that he held those offices through three administrations. Those were the times when "rotation in office" had not been learned, and merit held its well-earned place in public affairs.

When Governor Harrison began his administration there were but three white settlements in the Indian territory. But they soon began to increase, and now the wilderness over which he presided is an empire of civilization. His subjects were chiefly Indians, who claimed ownership in their tribal relations of the most of the land. During his official career as governor, he made thirteen treaties with the Indians, and secured to the United States sixty millions of acres of land. He thus became the pioneer of possession and civilization.

In the revolutionary war the early settlements along the Atlantic coast became free, and afterward organized into the United States. Then began the process of acquisition and extension, which has made them the mighty nation they now are, and which is to go on, it may be, till North America shall be the area of their territory. In this process, no man has acted a more conspicuous and important part than William

Henry Harrison, or left a whiter or more manly and patriotic record. Though governor over sixty millions of acres of public lands, making purchases and disposals at will, he appropriated no lands to himself, made his office in no way lucrative to himself, but only serviceable to the enrichment and honor of his country and its people. In all his treaties with the Indians, he was sole commissioner, as absolute as any king or autocrat, and yet so deep was the confidence imposed in him, that the thought of anything wrong in his transactions seems not to have entered any mind connected with the government. No pages of our national history are whiter than those which record the life and deeds of Governor Harrison.

One man, and he a foreigner, a man of wealth, by the name of McIntosh, accused the governor of having defrauded the Indians in the treaty of Fort Wayne. The governor demanded an investigation in a court of justice; and the court not only did not find against the governor, but fined the complainant four thousand dollars. The four thousand dollars the governor divided, giving one third of it to the orphan children whose fathers had died in battle, and two thirds he returned to McIntosh himself to teach him how to be both just and magnanimous.

Through the whole of his career as governor, opportunities for improvement of his personal fortune occurred, but he always rejected them, because he would not have the semblance of using his official opportunity to enrich himself appear to the discredit of himself or his country. He had a fine sense of honor and patriotic integrity. In his official capacity he lived for his country and was his country. His acts and character were his country's, and so he guarded his conduct as the apple of his eye.

### THE TECUMSEH WAR.

A singular and tragic episode in Governor Harrison's career occurred, beginning about the year 1806.

The Indians had become comparatively peaceful, and many of them were adopting many of the ideas and practices of civilized life, when there arose two brothers among them of unusual ability and devotion to the ancient Indian customs. One of them was a chief and warrior of great sagacity and enterprise, who conceived the idea of not only putting a stop to the civilizing of his race which had so clearly begun, but of restoring them to their original estate. He hated the whites; he deplored their influence over his people; and saw the inevitable loss of all their hunting grounds to the Indians, and their style of life. He was a savage, and wanted to continue to be, and have all his tribes with him continue as they had been. His name was Tecumseh, or "The Crouching Panther."

He had a brother of equal ability and of equal devotedness to Indian life and history, who was a man of fervid imagination, a religious man, a great orator who held a powerful sway over his people by his great gifts; and being their medicine man, which in their idea was equivalent to being a magician, he had still greater influence over them. His name was Olliwacheea, which being interpreted, is "The Prophet." The brothers were in as thorough sympathy as were Moses and Aaron and bore a similar relation to each other. They conceived the idea of being the deliverers of their people from their subjection to the whites.

They began their career by preaching to the tribes immediately about them, their doctrines of fidelity to ancient Indian customs and resistance of the customs of the whites — especially the custom of drinking whisky. Olliwacheea was a fierce teetotaler, and harangued his people eloquently in its favor, so much so that all who came under his influence became teetotalers and rejected whisky as the fire-water of the Evil Spirit. But they did not stop with this, but secretly aroused them to prepare for desperate resistance. It was Tecumseh's plan to arouse and unite all the Indian tribes far and near, to form a great army of resistance, and to use all the methods of Indian warfare to beat back the encroachments of their white enemies. To this end the two brothers visited and preached and planned that they might inaugurate their great movement with such force as should strike alarm to all the white frontier settlements, for some years.

In the summer of 1808, Olliwacheca gathered an encampment on the banks of the Tippecanoe river, a tributary of the Wabash. To deceive the government as to their plans, the prophet proposed to visit the governor and make a speech to him, and hold some of his religious meetings in his presence. He came, with a large number of his devoted followers. He delivered his speech, and made frequent addresses to his associates on the evils of war and whisky drinking. He had so thoroughly indoctrinated them against whisky, that no persuasion could induce them to drink. Rumors increased among the whites, that the Indians were preparing for war. Anxious to know the exact facts about their movement, Governor Harrison sent for both Tecumseh and the prophet to visit him. Tecumseh visited Vincennes, at length, to pay his respects to the governor. He went with four hundred plumed and painted warriors, and held a council on the twelfth of August, 1809. The governor had not invited such an army, and was not prepared to make an equal demonstration. He gathered the judges of the court, a few army officers, a number of citizens, and a small body guard, consisting of a sergeant and twelve men, and cheerfully met the savage chief and his warriors, as though they had come on the most peaceful of missions. When the high ceremonies brought the time, Tecumseh affirmed, in a dignified speech, his peaceful intentions; but declared that he proposed to combine all the tribes, to stop the further encroachments of the whites; that no more land should be sold to them without the consent of all the tribes; and that the chiefs who had lately sold land to the United States, should be put to death.

The governor, in his reply, remonstrated strongly against the murder of the chiefs. Tecumseh interrupting him in angry tones and threatening gestures, accused him of having cheated the Indians. The warriors, who had been squatted on the ground, caught the spirit, rose up and brandished their clubs. The governor drew his sword. The army officers drew around him; the guard presented their arms ready to fire. The governor calmly ordered all to be quiet. Then, turning to Tecumseh, told him he should hold no further intercourse with him, but to go in peace from their council-fire. The chief and his warriors retired; but from this time the governor knew that there was fire in the forests and danger ahead.

That night, the militia of Vincennes was under arms, expecting every moment the bullet in the dark, and the howl of the savage. But the night passed in quiet.

The next morning Tecumseh called upon the governor, apologized for his hasty conduct the day before, and repeated his statement of no hostile intentions; yet he was firm in his purpose to oppose any further transfer of land without the consent of all the tribes; and he now affirmed that he and his fellow chiefs would hold as null and void the treaty which the governor had lately made at Fort Wayne with a few chiefs.

A short time after this Governor Harrison resolved to visit Tecumseh at his encampment on the Tippecanoe. He was politely received, and was informed in courteous language that the Indians were very unwilling to go to war with the United States; but were resolved that the recently ceded land should not be given up; and that no further treaties should be made without the consent of all the tribes.

No further intercourse was held over the matter. The chief and the prophet were out among the tribes holding meetings and consulting. In the meantime the awakened Indians of the baser sort were committing depredations on the settlers, in the way of stealing horses and stock, breaking into houses and lawlessly plundering the farms, and annoying the white people in many ways. Affairs were growing worse, indicating the approach of a border war. The people were everywhere anxious and alarmed.

In this state of things the governor resolved to visit again the prophet at his encampment on the Tippecanoe. Tecumseh had gone south to visit and consult with the tribes in that part of the country. It was decided that the governor should go with force enough to secure his own safety, and at the same time overawe the savages somewhat, with a view to preventing hostilities. Nearly a thousand troops were gathered and put in marching order for this visit. This little army, as the governor's escort, moved out from Vincennes on the twenty-eighth of October, 1812. It was accidental, apparently, but this was the year war was declared with England. This Indian disturbance had been fermenting about as long as that with England. And this seemed to be independent of that.

The movement of the army was cautious, being always ready to form instantly into a line of attack or a solid body of defense. It moved along an Indian trail, in two lines of march, near enough to come quickly together if attacked. Early in November the governor and his escort reached the valley of the Tippecanoe. Very soon after they began to observe bands of Indians prowling about at a distance. When the army had reached within three miles of the town, three Indians of rank made their appearance and inquired why the governor was approaching their town in such hostile array? After a short conference, arrangements were made for a council-fire on the next day to agree on terms of amity and peace.

The governor was too well acquainted with the Indian character to take this as any indication of what they intended to do; so he made every provision for a night attack. His little army was formed into a solid body, the dragoons in the center. Every man was ordered to sleep on his arms if he slept at all; and every direction was given, as to their action in case of an attack.

The wakeful governor rose between three and four o'clock in the morning, and was sitting by the embers of the last night's fire, talking low with his aides. It was a dark, cold, cloudy, almost rainy morning. Just then the Indians in force had crept close to them, and with a yell and war-whoop fierce enough to rend the forest with dismay, poured into them a volley of bullets, and kept up their work of death and alarm. But the camp-fires, which had served to light the savages to their prey, were at once put out, and then Harrison's men rose and stood in their tracks and poured an incessant fire into the places where flashed the Indian guns. As soon as it was light enough to see to move, they made a simultaneous charge into the woods and among the Indians and made fearful slaughter in their midst.

The poor savages soon learned that the prophet's predictions that the white men's bullets would not hurt them, were not true. They soon took alarm and many of them fled to a swamp, where the governor's soldiers followed them and made fearful havoc among them. They lost sixty-one dead upon the field and one hundred and twenty bleeding and helpless. The prophet was present to see the rout and defeat of his select warriors. Harrison lost nearly as many, but his little army was intact and as intrepid as when it began the bloody work.

After burying the dead, the army destroyed the town and everything that could aid the Indians in their further hostilities and then returned to Vincennes.

This battle afforded the chorus for the campaign song that did not a little in the election of Mr. Harrison to the presidency, later in life. He little dreamed then of the use that would be made of it.

This battle would have nipped in the bud this great revolt of all the tribes which Tecumseh had so long worked hard to bring about, had it not been for the English using their influence to fan its dying flame. The tribes began at once to sue for peace and a good understanding, but Tecumseh returned from his southern tour and, joining with the English, kept up the war spirit toward the United States.

The war with England had now taken on a fierce aspect. Our whole northern frontier was exposed to incursions from Canada. The St. Lawrence river and the lakes afforded a highway for the enemies' ships, and through that highway he could come into the heart of the Indian territory. He at once availed himself of that opportunity. In the revolutionary war, England allied herself with the savages of the forest, to lay waste the settlements of the frontier. So now, she revived her old policy, and Tecumseh's revolt favored her wishes. She made an ally of him.

The battle of Tippecanoe was on the seventh of November 1811.

### COMMANDER-IN-CHIEF.

In September, 1812, Governor Harrison was made commander of all the forces of the northwest. He at once turned his attention toward the recapture of the fort at Detroit, which General Hull had ignominiously surrendered. That fort was the British key to the northwest. Between him and that point was a body of Indians on the Maumee. He ordered the scattered forces, in southern and central Ohio, to move toward Detroit. His plan was to overcome the Indians, gather at and retake the fort at Detroit, and so get repossession of the peninsula of Michigan. In this way he would make it difficult for the British to coöperate with the Indians. The lateness of the season and the early autumn rains filling the swamps and streams, made it impossible to carry his plans immediately into effect. A portion of his forces met the Indians on the Maumee and were almost destroyed. This disaster helped to retard the movement upon Detroit. In the meantime, the Indians all along the frontier let loose their dogs of savage warfare upon the scattered settlements. Robbing, plundering, killing, scalping, burning, were everywhere going on. The men from the settlements had for the most part gathered into Harrison's army, which had to wait for winter to freeze up the swamps, so it might make its way to Detroit. It was a terrible winter to the exposed settlements

In the spring the British had come to the assistance of the Indians on the Maumee, and the way of Harrison was hedged by this union under Proctor and Tecumseh. Severe fighting ensued with varied results, from time to time for some months. Reinforcements continued to come from Kentucky, under Governor Shelby, and from Ohio, to Harrison's army. Affairs grew more and more favorable to Harrison, and the prospect looked encouraging for sweeping the valley of the Maumee to the lake.

Just at this juncture of affairs Commodore Perry gained his great battle on Lake Erie, September tenth, 1813, which secured to the United States the command of the lake as the gateway to the northwest.

On the twenty-seventh of September, Harrison and his army

embarked on Perry's ships, to cross the lake to the Canada shore in pursuit of Proctor and Tecumseh, who had gone to the valley of the Thames. "On the twenty-ninth Harrison was at Sandwich, and McArthur took possession of Detroit and the territory of Michigan."

"On the second of October the Americans began their march in pursuit of Proctor, whom they overtook on the fifth" in the valley of the Thames river. Here was a concentration of the most of the land forces on both sides. Commodore Perry acting as one of General Harrison's aides. The forces on both sides were arranged with deliberation. The battle was brief but decisive, on account of a wedge of dragoons which Harrison formed in the beginning, of men accustomed from their youth up to ride through the woods musket in hand. They broke the British line and put it into confusion in their first charge, and it could not recover. It soon became a rout. The Indians made a more stubborn resistance and held out longer; but Tecumseh falling dead, they took alarm and became a rout also. The victory to the Americans was complete. General Harrison had urged upon Congress from the beginning of the war, the construction of a fleet of gunboats to command Lake Erie. Their importance was demonstrated in Perry's battle, which was a part of General Harrison's campaign. That, followed so closely by the battle of the Thames, brought Harrison's part of the war to a close.

Congress recognized the great value of General Harrison's services, in the following resolution:

"*Resolved*, by the Senate and House of Representatives of the United States of America in Congress assembled, that the thanks of Congress be and they are hereby presented to Major-General William Henry Harrison and Isaac Shelby, late governor of Kentucky, and through them to the officers and men of their command, for their gallant and good conduct in defeating the combined British and Indian forces under Major-General Proctor, on the Thames in Upper Canada, on the fifth day of October, 1813, capturing the British army, with their baggage, camp equipage and artillery; and, that the president of the United States be requested to cause two gold medals to be struck, emblematical of this triumph, and presented to General Harrison and Isaac Shelby, late governor of Kentucky."

From the beginning of his career as a soldier, his services were of great practical value to his country, increasing constantly, till now they brought peace to the great northwest.

His work so nobly done, he repaired to Washington and resigned his office as major general of the armies, on account of some want of harmony of views with the secretary of war, greatly to the regret of President Madison. He repaired to his home on the Ohio, for the domestic repose which of all things he most enjoyed. But the following summer, the president appointed him at the head of a commission on Indian affairs, with Governor Shelby and General Cass as his associates.

In 1816, he was elected to the House of Representatives in Congress, from Ohio. He had but just taken his seat when his conduct in the war was called in question. No more than Washington did he escape traducers. But he triumphantly vindicated his conduct.

While in Congress, he labored for a reform in the militia, which he did not accomplish; and for pensions for the soldiers of the revolution and the late war, which he did secure, which has carried comfort and joy to multitudes of soldiers' homes, and established the custom which makes the United States the best country in the world to its defenders. Let all pensioned soldiers remember General Harrison with gratitude.

When General Harrison was in Congress, the celebrated resolutions of censure of General Jackson, for his taking possession of Spanish territory, and hanging two British subjects, in the Seminole war, were offered. Harrison supported the resolutions in an elaborate and powerful speech, yet paid a high tribute to the patriotism and noble intentions of the impetuous and resolute general. The following extract from that speech, which is a choice specimen of the delicate and dextrous use of elegant English, will show the spirit and refined talent of the great patriot.

"I am sure, sir, that it is not the intention of any gentleman upon this floor, to rob General Jackson of a single ray of glory;

much less, to wound his feelings or injure his reputation. If the resolutions pass, I would address him thus: 'In the performance of a sacred duty, imposed by their construction of the constitution, the representatives of the people have found it necessary to disapprove of a single act of your brilliant career. They have done it in the full conviction that the hero who has guarded her rights in the field, will bow with reverence to the civil institutions of his country; that he has admitted as his creed, that the character of the soldier can never be complete without eternal reverence to the character of the citizen. Go, gallant chief, and bear with you the gratitude of your country; go under the full conviction, that as her glory is identified with yours, she has nothing more dear to her than her laws, nothing more sacred than her constitution. Even an unintentional error shall be sanctified to her service. It will teach posterity that the government which could disapprove the conduct of a Marcellus, will have the fortitude to crush the vices of a Marius.'" Noble words, classic in finish, christian in morality!

But Jackson was not equal to their comprehension. He never forgave Harrison for their utterance.

In 1819 Mr. Harrison was elected to the Senate of Ohio; in 1824 one of the presidential electors of that state; in 1829 was appointed minister to the republic of Columbia; in 1836 was named as a candidate for the presidency, and in 1840 was elected in opposition to Van Buren, who ran for a second term.

The Harrison campaign was one of the most exciting ever known in this country. The bad effects of Jackson's and Van Buren's financial policy had paralyzed the business of the country, and little hope of any prosperity or security for business was to be seen by the wisest financiers. This produced the union of all the conservative and opposition elements in the formation of the whig party. The combination was so strong, and the determination to rout the Jackson dynasty so resolute, that the campaign became a blaze of popular enthusiasm. Mass meetings, processions, songs, badges, and every form of powerful popular demonstration, became the order of the day. Log cabins were drawn at the head of immense processions through all the cities and villages of the country. It was remembered for years as the log-cabin campaign. It was really the revolt of the country against the financial mistakes of the two previous administrations. Harrison was elected, and on the fourth of March, 1841, was inaugurated. John Tyler, of Virginia, was his vice-president. He selected a strong cabinet, with Daniel Webster, of Massachusetts, secretary of state. On the seventeenth of March he issued a proclamation for an extra session of Congress, chiefly to consider and try to remedy the deplorable condition of the finances of the country. It was called for the last Monday in May.

A few days after President Harrison began to suffer from a severe cold. It grew worse, and he was attacked with a severe chill, followed by a fever. This again was followed by a bilious pleurisy, which, on the fourth of April, terminated his life. His death shocked the nation. Hardly since the days of Washington had any man so held the hearts and hopes of the people. His excellent character, his devoted patriotism, his admirable self-poise, his great talents and uniform success through a long life of varied public services, had created great expectations at a time when all these qualities were greatly needed to improve the ill conditions under which the country was suffering.

His funeral was held on the seventh of April, 1841, at Washington; but public funereal honors were awarded him in churches, halls and public buildings in every part of the country. He lived just one month after his inauguration.

## The Grave of William Henry Harrison.

Fifteen miles west of Cincinnati, on the summit of a hillock at North Bend, in a brick vault, rest the remains of William Henry Harrison. Those of his wife and children repose with them. A large flat stone, two or three feet above the surface of the earth, covers the vault. No monument or slab is erected. No inscription telling who sleeps there, or indicating a surviving friend to keep the place in memory, has been made. A thick undergrowth covers the elevation, and evergreens cluster about the spot.

Reflections at the graves of the great and honored can hardly be crowded out from the minds of the living as they stand by honored dust. Here is the dust of Harrison, whose eyes, in his youth, saw all the valleys of the Ohio and the Miamis covered with the "forest primeval." These rounded hills and hollowed valleys were the homes of the red men and the wild animals. Nature ran riot in all her wild ways through this continent of forest. Here came this youth where few had come before him, educated, refined, aspiring, to begin his manhood in the midst of every possible obstacle to the attainment of what he most coveted — educated society, elevated pursuits, a peaceful home and an honored age. How could he expect to find these here? And yet he came with a great hope and a courage that braved everything. He foresaw the possibilities of this rich country. He believed in the free institutions which his father and Washington and their compeers had founded. He believed in humanity and righteous principles and honorable conduct; and so he came and lived nobly, and opened a highway for the coming generations. And how they have come! Here is the queen city of the west where was only a hamlet when he came. Here are the great states of Ohio and Indiana, where he hunted Indians, and, later in life, surveyed state, county and township lines. Here are beautiful farms where were swamps and morasses when he first searched for dry ways in these woods. Here are fifty millions of people in this young republic which had only three then. He came and opened the way for this change. Did he live in vain? No. He was a John the Baptist in this wilderness, a pioneer whom a host followed. It is given to but few to have a part in such great changes. His labors and struggles all told grandly for the future. His plantings have produced a rich harvest. To-day we can give him honor and speak his name by the side of his grave with profound respect. He went early into the forest, and because he there lived nobly his country called him to its highest position of honor.

Is there less for us to live for? By no means. The country is yet new. Opportunity still is open for grand life. We may not fight Indians, but we may fight evils. We may not clear away the forests, but we may clear away the ignorance and vices of society. There is as much for us to do as there was for him. There are more to copy our example, more to improve upon our doings, more to take up our work where we leave it. This silent grave may be an eloquent preacher of life and duty and destiny, if we will but hear its still, small voice of the spirit. Let us go away to live more nobly.

ENGRAVED EXPRESSLY FOR WEAVERS' LIVES AND GRAVES OF OUR PRESIDENTS.

# CHAPTER XI.

## JOHN TYLER.

#### TENTH PRESIDENT OF THE UNITED STATES.

##### ANCESTRY.

LIKE the other presidents from Virginia, John Tyler had a noble ancestry. He came into the world with an impetus of good blood and brain power, and came into good social surroundings. He was rocked in the cradle of intelligence; breathed the atmosphere of culture; and warmed in his infancy at the fire of patriotism.

His ancestors were among the early English settlers in Virginia and were of the same social standing as the Washingtons. Lees, Wythes, Madisons and Harrisons. It is understood that they were decendants of the celebrated Walter or Wat Tyler, of the fourteenth century, who led an insurrection in England, in defense of the rights of the people.

The grandfather of the president, John Tyler, was marshal of the colony under the British crown for many years, until his death, which did not occur till after the troubles occasioned by the Stamp act. He died possessed of a large estate of land in and about Williamsburg, which put his family into good financial circumstances.

The father of the president, John Tyler, again took an active part in laying before the king and parliament the grievances of the colonies, and in seeking relief therefrom. He became a distinguished patriot; was speaker of the house of delegates, governor of the state, and judge of one of the highest courts.

At the opening of the war of 1812, President Madison made him judge of the court of admiralty. In February, 1813, he died, full of years and honors, leaving three sons; Wat, John and William, to bear on his name and continue his work for home and country.

### BIRTH AND BOYHOOD.

John Tyler, the president, was born in Charles City county, Virginia, March 20, 1790, just after the adoption of the constitution, in the second year of Washington's administration. He was among the early children of the young nation and had wrought into his nature something of the spirit of which it was born. His parents and the people of their community were flaming patriots. His early life, at home, at school, and among his playfellows, was a growth among patriotic influences. The great names of his state were the great names of his country, and they became familiar to his youthful ears. The history of those great times was the conversation of the older people among whom he was reared. He was a precocious child, grew quick and ripened early—too precocious for great permanent strength, breadth, and stability of mind. His quick nature absorbed the opinions and the character of the life about him; before he had time or knowlege to know why he had accepted the political biases of his associates. His plastic mind filled quickly the mould which others made for it.

His early education was in the schools of his neighborhood. He moved on rapidly, and at twelve years of age entered William and Mary college. Of course the preparation was but a boy's preparation, and indicates both his extreme brightness, and that the requirements of the college for entrance were not such as are now made by all colleges. He graduated at seventeen, at about the age at which bright, well-fitted boys ought to enter. The subject of his address at his graduation was "Female Education." It would be interesting to read it now and compare it with the advanced ideas and practices of our time on that subject, yet from the nature of his mind, we may infer that he had advanced views, though no chronicler has preserved them.

Young Tyler studied law two years, from seventeen to nineteen, under the instruction of his father and Edmund Randolph, when he was admitted to the bar. He at once began practice, and in three months there was scarcely a disputable case on the docket in which he was not retained. He became a youthful legal prodigy. Everybody who went to court must have the boy lawyer to lead him through the intricacies of law. John Quincy Adams was four years in getting any practice, while John Tyler was overrun with practice in four months. Later in life the difference was the other way.

### POLITICAL CAREER.

At twenty, our brilliant, youthful lawyer was proposed as a candidate for the legislature, but declined. The next year, when twenty-one, he was elected. He at once entered actively into the business and political interests of the state and the times. By absorption he was a Jeffersonian. The great interests of the South, as they were understood about him, were held sacred by those of that line of politics.

The second war with England came right on, and he supported it with enthusiasm. He was a zealous advocate of Mr. Madison's conduct of the war. While the British forces were in the Chesapeake bay, Mr. Tyler raised a volunteer company and strove to organize the militia of his neighborhood and enlist them against the invaders, but they were driven out before his plans were consummated, and his military genius failed of development.

He was re-elected to the legislature for a number of years, and stoutly maintained the principles of the party. Among its teachings was the doctrine of the "Right of Instruction," which was that when a state instructed its members how to act on a given subject, they were under obligation to obey the instruction, even against their personal convictions. This matter came up anew while he was in the state legislature. Messrs. Giles and Brent were senators in Congress from Virginia, and had been instructed by their state legislature to vote against a renewal of the charter of the United States bank, when it should come up. Mr. Brent disobeyed. Mr. Tyler then introduced a resolution of censure against the self-acting senator, making a strong speech in favor of the resolution, and laying it down as a principle that any person accepting the office of senator from the state of Virginia obligated himself to conform to this rule. It afterward came in his way.

In 1815 Mr. Tyler was elected as a member of the executive council, and served until the autumn of 1816, when, after an excited election, he was chosen to fill a vacancy in Congress. His opponent in this contest was Andrew Stevenson, a politician of the same school. When he took his seat, in December, he was twenty-six and a half years old. The next year he was re-elected by a strong majority. In 1819 he was elected again.

In Congress he was a strict partisan of the southern democratic style; maintained the high states rights doctrines; the federative notion of the union; the pro-slavery doctrines of the South, which sought to extend the slave territory and power. He took an active part in the debate on the Missouri question, maintaining with great zeal the southern side, as though it had been the side of patriotism, of right and humanity. He voted to censure General Jackson for his abuse of his authority in the Seminole war; opposed a protective tariff, internal improvements by the general government, and a national bank. He was over-zealous in his promulgation of the doctrines of his party and section of the country, and broke down his health; so he was obliged to resign and retire to his country estate to recruit.

In the fall of 1823 he went again to the Virginia legislature. In his state legislature he urged internal improvements by the state, and introduced bills to this end. He lost no opportunity to magnify the state; appealed to state pride and cupidity to introduce improvements of every kind into the state by state authority and at state expense. He was chagrined that other states were surpassing Virginia in population, wealth and enterprise, and he sought to remedy the evil by state improvements.

He sought in his legislative speeches to arouse Virginians to a sense of their lethargy and the need of action that their state should not be left behind in the race for prosperity and power. His appeals were not without success, for many of the finest public works in the state were the result of his labors. Had his political philosophy for the whole country been as comprehensive and sound as was his zeal for Virginia, he would have won imperishable laurels. In his state he showed the qualities of a statesman, and the people appreciated them. Here his politics did not fetter him.

In December, 1825, Mr. Tyler was elected governor of Virginia, and the next year was re-elected. His success as a state legislator had won him great popularity.

John Randolph was then one of Virginia's United States Senators. His eccentric genius, singularity and general uncertainty, did not make him popular. He often hurt his friends and his cause. Many Virginia democrats regretted his eccentricities and mistakes. And yet a certain wild genius for public speech made him a hard man to displace. The most considerate men opposed to him, believed that Governor Tyler could be elected in opposition to him. The movement was made and the governor was elected to the Senate of the United States. A public dinner was given him; speeches were made; he made one himself in which he glorified his political principles, and announced himself as opposed to the president, John Quincy Adams. Adams' message he said, "Had in it an almost total disregard of the federative principle." His whole political career had stood for the "federative principle," that is, that the Union is a confederacy of the several separate states to remain while they are satisfied, and to fall apart one by one as they came in, when they are dissatisfied. This view magnified the states above the nation, made every citizen's supreme loyalty that to the state. In the beginning the democratic party favored this "federative principle," and it was always especially strong in the South. The federalists regarded the confederation as made by the "people of the United States," and hence the Union as indissoluble — the nation to be self-existent and self-defensive till some power strong enough should bring it to an end. This was the original and essential difference between the parties. There were other differences, but this was the vital one.

Yet it is worthy of note that though this difference was much discussed from the beginning, the federalists put their principles into the constitution, at the start, and though the government has much of the time been administered by democrats there has been no permanent law or amendment enacted since, contrary to the original federalist constitution. The essential principles which the federalists put into the government at the beginning, have stood as a wall against which the Jeffersonian opposition has beat in vain since. The true democracy which stands for the interests of the whole people, is in a strong government — an indissoluble union of the whole people — a bulwark against anarchy and misrule from within, and enemies from without. Adams stood for this idea of the government; Tyler went into the Senate to oppose it. It was this "federative principle," as Mr. Tyler called it, which from near the beginning, and especially after his time, dwarfed and misled the statesmanship of the South and of the party which maintained it. The Jeffersonian party, though it has always had great numbers and much of the time been in power, has never moved a foundation or turret stone of the government. The statesmanship which laid deep and built strong, has been in other parties; and this chiefly because of the political heresies that entered early into the doctrines of this party.

As soon as in Congress Mr. Tyler allied himself with the opposition. Mr. Adams was non-partisan, and was beyond question the broadest statesman of his age. But his very breadth spoiled him for the Virginia senator. Mr. Tyler lost no occasion to magnify his views so popular in his own state, especially those concerning the powers of the general government and the commercial policy of the country.

When General Jackson came in after Mr. Adams, Mr. Tyler gave a cheerful and sympathetic support to his administration in the main. He opposed the recharter of the national bank.

That was a national institution, gave circulation to a national currency, supported a national credit and tended to make the nation a monopoly over the states. His doctrine was that the states should authorize banking and the emission of paper money, and give the country what currency it had, save gold and silver, which should be the only national money. The heart of the objection to the national bank was the fact that it fostered a nationality which overshadowed state power. It was opposed to the "federative principle." The opposition was consistent with the "federative principle," which contained the seeds of nullification, rebellion, disunion and destruction. Nationality would not be long possible under the "federative principle" which Senator Tyler so magnified.

Senator Tyler opposed a protective tariff with great vehemence and show of political learning, and made a three days' speech against it, which of itself was enough to show the fallacy of his argument; and yet he contended for a tariff for revenue. In his opposition he complained that the tariff operated against the South and kept it poor and hindered it from keeping pace with the North in advancing in wealth and power. He failed to see that the South was her own hinderance in her slave labor which made white labor dishonorable, the whites idlers and cumberers of the ground, prevented immigration, invention, enterprise, education and civilization. He failed to see that slavery prevented all skilled labor, and, therefore, prevented manufactures, commerce and business enterprise, and reduced society to the dead level of slow producers of raw material from the soil with hand labor.

Could the rest of the world afford to wait for that slow process? Could the rest of the world afford to keep itself poor and weak in enterprise because the South was bound to so continue? If he would have looked as a statesman, instead of as a Southern politician, he would have seen all the white people of the North busy in the production of wealth, enterprise and character,— would have seen immigration pouring in from all Europe, with money, muscle, and energy, to settle up states, broaden and quicken society, a great variety of interests occupying the hands and brains of enterprising millions,—would have seen a nation-building North developing every kind of talent and power, while the South was busy hugging the Delilah of slavery and arguing against the tariff and nationality. The truth was that a tariff was the upbuilding agency of the country, and it was the business of the South to adjust itself to it, instead of trying to force its own paralysis of business enterprise upon the rest of the country.

Senator Tyler also opposed internal improvements by the general government. He did this on the same principle that he opposed a national bank, and a national tariff, that it encouraged nationality and reduced state supremacy. In this he was narrowed by his sectional and partisan ideas of the dignity of a state and the subserviency of the national government. He did not seem to see that business, travel, society, education, know no state lines, that commerce, agriculture, and the wide interests of the nation know no North or South, East or West, much less state boundaries; nor did he seem to see that these great interests that concerned the good of the whole, needed the fostering hand of the general government, and that good policy and sound principles demanded that they should have it.

It was during Jackson's presidency that John C. Calhoun's nullification scheme came to the front, which was to repudiate, or nullify the tariff laws so far as the port of Charleston and the state of South Carolina was concerned, so as to let foreign goods come in duty free. It was simply rebellion against the laws of the United States,—one state resisting all the rest. Senator Tyler supported Mr. Calhoun and South Carolina in this nullification of the laws of his country. In this he was consistent with his political theory of the subserviency of the nation to the state, and so were Calhoun and South Carolina.

Jackson entertained the same general views that Tyler did, and if Calhoun had been his friend instead of his enemy, might have taken a very different view of his nullification; for the law stood very little in the way of his supreme desires.

Senator Tyler agreed with Jackson in his opposition to a national bank, but opposed Jackson's removal of the deposits from the bank, on the ground that it was unlawful, or a nullification of the law.

In March, 1835, Senator Tyler was elected president of the Senate *pro tempore*, by the joint votes of the whigs and state-rights senators. In February, 1836, the legislature of Virginia passed a resolution instructing its senators "to vote for a resolution directing the resolution of March 28, 1834, censuring the conduct of General Jackson, to be expunged from the journal of the Senate." Mr. Leigh, colleague of Mr. Tyler, refused to obey, and gave his reasons. Mr. Tyler would not obey, because he did not believe in the expunging doctrine, and yet would not vote against the instructions of his state, because he believed in the "right of instruction," so he resigned and gave his reasons therefor. Both senators were feasted by their constituents for their integrity.

In 1835 Mr. Tyler was nominated for vice-president on the ticket with Harrison, but both failed of an election. In the spring of 1836 he was elected to the Virginia Legislature. At this time he acted with the whig party in opposition to Van Buren. In 1839 he was made a delegate to the whig National Convention at Harrisburg, Pennsylvania, to nominate candidates for president and vice-president. He labored for the nomination of Clay, but General Harrison secured the nomination. To conciliate the irritated friends of Mr. Clay, Mr. Tyler was put upon the ticket for vice-president. His whole life had been against the principles of the whig party. It was its especial object to establish a national bank and remedy the bad condition of the finances of the country. But he was put upon the ticket as a compromise with the South and Mr. Clay's friends. It was a dear compromise to whig principles and the party. But Mr. Tyler made his speeches, letters and labors in the canvass satisfactory to the party, and the ticket was elected.

## VICE-PRESIDENT AND PRESIDENT TYLER.

On the fourth of March, 1841, Mr. Tyler was inaugurated vice-president of the United States. In one month after being inaugurated, President Harrison died. Mr. Tyler was inaugurated president on the seventh of April. An extra session of Congress had been called by Mr. Harrison for the thirty-first of May, to try to benefit the ill condition of the country occasioned by the former administrations. When Congress assembled, the first question that came before it was as to how the acting president should be addressed. Was he president, or was he vice-president? It was decided that he was president. President Tyler's message was well received; his appointments were satisfactory.

On the twelfth of June, Mr. Ewing, secretary of the treasury, reported the condition of the national finances, and also a bill for the "Fiscal Bank of the United States." The plan for this fiscal bank was designed to be free from all features that would be objectionable to the president. A bill, such as the secretary recommended, was offered in Congress, and passed August 6. It went to the president. In ten days he returned it with a veto message. The party leaders were troubled. The president outlined a bank for national transactions, which he had wished to see established. A bill was prepared exactly to suit his ideal fiscal agent. It passed Congress, and went to the president on the third of September. On the ninth, he returned it with his objections. This was trifling; and astounding to his associates. Two days after, all the members of his cabinet resigned but Mr. Webster, the secretary of state, who had in hand an important transaction with England: the settlement of the north-eastern boundary. Soon after that was settled, in 1842, Mr. Webster resigned.

The whig party was shocked and shattered by the action of its president. The great Harrison campaign was lost; the will of the people was defeated by one man. The anticipated helps to the finances of the country were put off. Maledictions were freely showered upon the president.

At the extra session of Congress a protective tariff bill was passed and signed by the president. Also a bill for the use of the money accruing from the sales of the public lands; and a bill for a uniform bankrupt law.

At the next Congress, the twenty-eighth, which met in 1843,

the president found himself without a party. He had swung more and more over to the democrats, with whom he really belonged; had appointed many democrats to office, and some to his cabinet; and had shaped his official conduct more after democratic than other models; and yet the democrats did not accept him as their president. The Twenty-eighth Congress had a democratic House and a whig Senate. In a party sense, his hands were tied. Through Caleb Cushing, of Massachusetts, a treaty with China was formed, which was the opening of that greatest empire of the world to intercourse with the United States.

In 1844, a treaty of annexation was arranged with Texas, through Mr. John C. Calhoun, of South Carolina. Joint resolutions passed Congress March 1, 1845, formally annexing Texas with the United States. This was a consummation devoutly desired by the south, and long coveted and planned for, to open an empire of virgin soil to the extension of slavery, and the order of society it promoted. The growth of the north was a constant menace to the politicians of the south. They dreaded the time when they should be outvoted in Congress by the north. The south had little in business, manufacture, commerce, railroading, telegraphing, inventing, mining, navigation, engineering, science, education, to employ its men of talent. The north had much of its best talent employed in these great and civilizing affairs; and was widening their domains of enterprise all the time. The south had but one inviting field, which was politics. That field it kept full of first-class talent all the time. And its politicians made it a study, gave time, zeal, and their whole power to it. It was usual for Congress, and all the offices in its gifts, to be largely filled with the best talent of the south, devoted to politics as a profession. It was usual for the south to have its best debating talent in Congress; and there generally went with it the tyranny of will and purpose, born of the institution of slavery.

With southern politicians, therefore, it was always an object to extend slave territory, even though the territory they had was not half settled, nor half filled with enterprise. And when Texas was annexed, which had been fought for at the expense of the United States for a long time, it could be settled only at a snail's pace.

Mr. Tyler's last act as president was to pocket a river and harbor bill and go out of office without signing it, thus defeating it by what is called the "pocket veto."

On the fourth of March, 1845, he retired from office without the regrets of either party, and with little honor for his great vexation and trouble.

He retired to Sherwood Forest, Charles City county, Virginia, and lived in comfort and peace in a home he prized. He was a gentleman in manners and bearing, well furnished with information, of a refined taste and delicate sensibilities. It was his misfortune to have been born to the patrimony of that "irrepressible conflict" between slavery and freedom, which toned the society about him, and gave the politics he inherited from his state and section.

He was twice married; first to Miss Letitia Christian, of Kent county, Virginia, in 1813, who died in Washington, in 1842, leaving three sons and three daughters; second, to Miss Julia Gardiner, of New York.

In 1861, when the great rebellion against the Union, to establish an empire of slavery under the name of the "Confederate States," was inaugurated, Mr. Tyler, by sympathy and political doctrine, belonged to it and was a part of it. He was a friend and coadjutor of John C. Calhoun in his nullification doctrines and practice, which was rebellion on a small scale, and was the first planting of the seed of rebellion. He had always maintained the doctrine of state rights which exalted the state above the nation, and made the citizen's supreme loyalty that which was due to his state; had always believed in the "federative principle" which united the states during mutual pleasure and bearable conduct; and now that rebellion on a large scale had come by the legitimate effect of those doctrines, it was to be expected that he would be logical enough to rebel if his state did. He joined the confederates; was made a member of their congress; and while doing all he could to destroy the country that had honored him in her councils and with her chief-magistracy, was taken sick and in a few days died. Sad for the memory of President Tyler, that his name must forever stand associated with the misery and desolation brought upon the country, north and south, by the most ill-judged rebellion that ever crushed a fair land and an indulgent government. Pity is stronger than blame in all generous minds toward our only president who has lifted a hand against the government that had honored him. Still let his name be kept in the everlasting roll of honor which makes the presidents of the United States an honored and immortal few that "were not born to die."

## The Grave of John Tyler.

In Hollywood cemetery, near Richmond, Virginia, without obelisk, slab, or bust—ten yards from President Monroe's peculiar monument, sleeps obscurely the mortal body of John Tyler.

It is to be hoped that in the near future, the presidents' graves, which have now no fitting recognition, shall either by private patriotism or public justice, be monumented and honored by appropriate expressions of national gratitude and respect. It is due to the nation itself.

Hollywood cemetery is indeed an interesting city of the dead, not only on account of its beautiful situation in that noted part of the country where have originated and lived so many great men, but on account of the distinguished men whose mortal bodies repose in its sacred enclosure. All cemeteries are sacred to thoughtful and humane men, but those which hold the dust of great worth and honored characters are especially so.

About thirty feet from the grave of President Monroe, with its singular monument, in isolation and loneliness is the grave of President John Tyler. At its head has grown a small magnolia tree, which is its only monument; whether set there by human hand or by nature is not told in books. Other trees and shrubbery are about it.

At the time of his death, January 17, 1862, President Tyler was a member of the Confederate Congress. Virginia had attempted to secede from the United States, notwithstanding her history, her sacred relics of presidents and great men, and Mr. Tyler, deluded by the doctrine of state rights, which he accepted when a young man, thought he must be disloyal because a majority of his state legislature were at that particular time, and so he repudiated his country and joined the confederates in their attempt to form a new country in the old national home.

The disloyal state assembly, then in session at Richmond,

passed resolutions of respect and sorrow on account of the death of "the great and good man," and instructed the governor to have erected "a suitable monument to his memory." The Confederate Congress passed resolutions of respect, and three days after his death joined with the state officials and the dignitaries of the confederate government, military and civil societies, and a great body of citizens, in a great procession, which bore at its head the mortal remains of President Tyler to their rest in the peaceful grave, where rebellion and its bloody war would not disturb them. Bishop Johns conducted the funeral services. The great men among the confederates were his pall-bearers. The vast multitude stood in respectful silence while the grave was filled, and then departed, leaving the grave to the growth of nature's adornments, but returning not with slab or shaft to note the place where they had laid him. But it was for no want of respect or affection; for, as the multitude departed from his grave, so passed away the multitude of the confederates from state and national power.

All around him are the tombs of the great men of his section; and but a little way from it the dust of sixteen thousand confederate soldiers, whose tall, pyramidal monument tells forever of the heresy of "state rights" and the folly and wickedness of the rebellion. Singularly interesting are the names all about him that figure in the history of the rebellion, such as Governor Wise, James M. Mason, A. P. Hill, and many more equally noted. Few cemeteries in the whole country have more names to call up great memories and to stir reflection on great events, and principles, and awaken sad regrets of terrible misjudgments and mistakes. It is a good place to come and weave broadly the mantle of christian charity, so as to hold them all in the sweet heart of forgiving love.

Mrs. Tyler always believed that Virginia would erect a suitable monument over her husband's grave; but it is more properly the work of the United States, which can well afford to do it in token of its free forgiveness of its honored dead, for President Tyler is ours forever. This centennial decade should not pass without the erection by Congress of a suitable monument.

Mr. Tyler's bust, by Volk, taken from a mask made after his death, is in the state library. There is also in the library a large portrait, by Hart, presented to Virginia by his daughter, Letitia Tyler Sempte, of Baltimore.

## CHAPTER XII.

### JAMES KNOX POLK.
#### ELEVENTH PRESIDENT OF THE UNITED STATES.

FOR several reasons which will appear in the record, the biography of the eleventh president, is of interest aside from the distinguished position he attained.

On the banks of the Catawba, in the county of Mecklenburg, in the southwestern part of North Carolina, Andrew Jackson and his mother found protection and comfort among the ancestors of James K. Polk, and their neighbors, when they fled from their home at the Waxhaw settlement, as it was invaded by the British soldiery under Cornwallis.

Early in the spring of 1775 the people of Mecklenburg county heard of the atrocities the British soldiers were committing in and around Boston, Massachusetts. Public meetings were at once called to discuss these invasions of the public peace. By one of these meetings, Colonel Thomas Polk, was authorized to call a convention of the representatives of the people, to see what should be done about the troubles at Boston. He called the convention for the nineteenth of May, 1775, at Charlotte, the county seat. At this meeting, the announcement of the battles of Lexington and Concord was made. Great excitement was occasioned. The spirit of resistance and independence was awakened. Resolutions were adopted and read by Colonel Polk, from the court-house steps, "That we, the citizens of Mecklenburg county, do hereby dissolve the political bands which have connected us to the mother country, and hereby absolve ourselves from all allegiance to the British crown; and that we do hereby declare ourselves a free and independent people."

This first and heroic declaration of independence, is a testimony to the spirit of the people of that isolated county and to the ancestors of the eleventh president of the United States. It seems but a providential reward that from such a people and that place, should spring a president of the country, which was to grow from the seed there planted. From the spirit of the Mechlenburg declaration came the eleventh president.

## ANCESTRY.

Colonel Thomas Polk and his brothers Ezekiel and Charles, were decendants of Robert Polk, who came from the north of Ireland between 1735 and 1740, and settled in this vicinity. The name is a corruption of Pollock. The family were Scotch and were of those who early settled in the north of Ireland and constituted the people known as Scotch-Irish, Scotch in blood, but Irish in locality.

Samuel Polk was the son of Ezekiel Polk, and the father of the president. The Polks were all staunch patriots in the times of the revolution.

James K. Polk was born in Mechlenburg county, North Carolina, November 2, 1795, in the last term of Washington's administration. His mother was Jane Knox, daughter of James Knox, evidently of Scotch descent. He was the eldest son of a family of six sons and four daughters, and was named for his grandfather Knox, who was a captain in the revolutionary war.

The Polks were a substantial, industrious, self-reliant people. Samuel was a plain, frugal, enterprising farmer, who tilled his own farm and taught his sons his independent way of living.

With the close of the revolution there set in a strong desire to people the solitudes west of the Alleghanies. Washington favored it and did much to promote it. From Mechlenburg county and that vicinity many went. The Polks pretty generally were among them. But Samuel did not get away till 1806, when he went with his family to the valley of the Duck river, a tributary of the Tennessee. Here he secured land, erected his cabin, made his home, and with hardy enterprise set about developing a farm. The next year the vicinity about him was formed into Maury county. He was a practical surveyor, and was much employed in surveying the new lands of the county. His son James often went with him on his surveying expeditions, assisting in such ways as he could; and it was not long before he could make the mathematical calculations for his father. These studies of the woods availed him much, as they promoted his scholarship and quickened his mind for further study.

### HIS BOYHOOD.

The boyhood of James was that of a farmer's boy of all work. Being the oldest, he was the chore boy, the errand boy, the call-boy for all little jobs; the big boy to care for the little ones, help his mother and be generally useful. It is a rare thing if the oldest child does not find out many ways to be useful in the family. This was the favored opportunity for James. As his father was a surveyor, he added to the ordinary accomplishments of the oldest farmer boy, that of a surveyor's waiter, cook and teamster. In these many ways of usefulness, James was well trained in the helpful industries of everyday life and secured unconsciously the moral and courteous results of such training. There were business, duty, morality and manners in this training.

In study, he had such advantages as the schools of his time afforded — enough to give him studious habits, a love of reading, and a covetousness of knowledge.

His constitution not appearing to be strong, perhaps having been over-worked, his father thought it best to take him from the farm and put him into a store. This did not suit his taste, and he was allowed to leave and gratify his love of study, under the direction of Reverend Doctor Henderson. Afterward he want to the Murfreesburg academy, where he had excellent advantages. In about two years and a half, he prepared himself to enter the sophomore class in the University of North Carolina.

The farmer's boy, reared as he was, who out of his unconquerable desire to study, against his parents' wishes, and without encouragement from others, pushes on, and works his way into an advanced place in college, as he did, has already given assurance of a manhood that is likely to be marked.

His course in college was the counterpart of what it had been at home, faithful, industrious, pushing. He was happy, because he was gratifying a hunger for knowledge. He made rapid progress, honored the college with a loyal submission to its laws, made friends and took the honors of his class, graduating in June, 1818, in his twenty-third year.

His college life strongly impressed him; he became a college man, a lover of scholarship and scholars; often revisited his college; received from it, in 1847, the honorary degree of Doctor of Laws; and was its constant friend through the whole of his life.

### MR. POLK AS A LAWYER.

Leaving college with somewhat impaired health, he rested for a few months, and early the next year, entered the law office of Mr. Felix Grundy, at Nashville. Mr. Grundy, at this time, was a prominent national man, and for many years held a conspicuous place among the strong men of the nation. Mr. Polk had, for a considerable time, anticipated the study of law. He went to it with a zest, as fulfilling a long-cherished desire. While studying with Mr. Grundy, he made the acquaintance of Andrew Jackson, who occasionally called at the office, and who was then living at the Hermitage, a few miles from Nashville. A friendship grew up from this acquaintance, which was life-lasting. Jackson had lived in Mechlenburg, where Polk was born; had known his ancestors; was himself born and reared near the same place; they were both Scotch-Irish; their ancestors had come from the north of Ireland to this country about the same time; they were both born of humble parents, and in straitened circumstances; Mr. Jackson was quick and ardent in his likes, as well as dislikes, and Mr. Polk was cordial, frank, manly; so between them there was soon established the best of feelings. It was good fortune for Mr. Polk that he found two such friends in the office where he studied for his profession.

Near the close of 1820, Mr. Polk was admitted to the bar.

He was now twenty-five years old; with a very practical business education as a boy; a solid college education, and the acquaintance of scholarly men and class-mates, that comes with it as a youth; a good professional education, and the friendship of Jackson and Grundy, and their associates. This was laying a broad foundation for a strong manhood. It was wisdom in the beginning. It was the initiatory investment for a great and sure fortune. Added to all this, as more and better, were an excellent moral character, good habits, the manners of a gentleman, and the spirit of a generous and high-minded man. Under such a beginning, Mr. Polk's fortune was almost assured.

Mr. Polk entered at once upon the practice of law, and continued for several years, growing more and more efficient and eminent. Sometimes he was alone, sometimes in company with other eminent lawyers, among whom were Anson V. Brown and Gideon J. Pillow, major-general in the Mexican war. In his profession he won a place in the world, a competence, and the mastery of his powers and learning.

### MR. POLK A LEGISLATOR.

In 1823 he was elected to the legislature of his state, after an animated canvass, in which he took the leading part. Previous to this he had served as chief clerk in the House of Representatives. He remained two years a member of the legislature. This was during the presidency of Mr. Monroe, with whom Mr. Polk was in full political sympathy. He approved the action of the Tennessee legislature of 1822, in nominating Andrew Jackson for the presidency, and in 1824 assisted in nominating and electing him to the Senate of the United States.

While a member of his state legislature, Mr. Polk procured the passage of a law against dueling, for which he had a great aversion, as an unmanly and cruel "code of honor," which had come as a relic of barbarism from a brutal past. To take this high moral ground touching an immoral practice, in a community which had approved it, and among leading men like Andrew Jackson, his personal friend, who thought they were honored by its practice, was a fine demonstration of the moral courage and character of the man. Hardly anything in his whole life speaks better for his head and heart, or reveals more clearly the richness of his moral nature.

On the first day of January, 1824, Mr. Polk was married to Miss Sarah Childress, daughter of Joel Childress, a successful merchant of Rutherford county, Tennessee. He was now twenty-nine years old, well established in business, in reputation and in character. Mrs. Polk was a woman for her place, able to adorn and honor exalted station, a helpmeet, indeed, to him in the important public career that was opening to him.

### MR. POLK THE CONGRESSMAN.

In 1825 Mr. Polk was elected to the Lower House of Congress, and continued in this position for fourteen years. Into his duties as a national legislator he carried his studious habits, methodical ways and honest sense of duty. He was a working man, and he made a working member of Congress. He was elected to Congress the same year John Quincy Adams was inaugurated president. He served through his term, not in direct opposition to the president, but holding in the main quite different views on partisan subjects.

Mr. Adams' election by the House, defeating Jackson, who had the most electoral votes on the first ballot, caused a warm discussion of the constitutional plan of electing the president. Much was said of amending the constitution. Mr. Polk made his first speech in Congress on this subject, advocating an amendment which should give the choice of the president and vice-president directly to the people, without the intervention of an electoral college.

Mr. Polk was put on important committees, and more and

more, as his talents and fidelity became known, were the working oars of Congress put into his hands.

After General Jackson became president, the question of internal improvements by the general government came up for re-discussion. Mr. Adams, as secretary of state under Mr. Monroe, and Mr. Monroe himself, under the strong teaching of Mr. Adams, had favored judicious and important internal improvements, which single states could not make. For twelve years these ideas and practices had prevailed in the government, and prosperity had attended it and the country. The revenues of the government were strong and increasing. The public debt occasioned by the war of 1812 and the Indian wars, was all paid. There was money in the treasury to be distributed among the states. Business was good, commerce prosperous, immigration active. The policy of the government for the twelve years of the Adams-Monroe direction gave great prosperity to the country.

But internal improvement by the general government was contrary to General Jackson's theory. There was danger of national monopoly in too great national prosperity. The power of the general government was to be dreaded and guarded against by the states. And so he with a strong hand instituted a new order of things. The public works, like the Cumberland national road and the Maysville road, he stopped by vetoing the bills for appropriations to continue them. There was money in the treasury and no way to use it; and these roads were vastly important improvements, running through several states and benefiting the whole country; yet they must stop.

Mr. Polk, the warm personal friend, almost the *protege* of Jackson, took his view, and became the ardent and strong defender of the Jacksonian theory and policy. He had held different views, like most of the rising young men of that time. In Mr. Monroe's time, he saw the need of public improvements—roads, river and harbor improvements, and gave his adherence to the policy that prevailed. A pity he had not held on to his patriotic and statesmanlike views, so honorable to his young mind and consonant with his noble nature. But powerful forces were in the executive, and he yielded to them, after the Van Buren style. The veto of the national improvements, the veto of the national bank and the removal of the national deposits from that bank to the state banks were all a part of President Jackson's general theory that the states are in danger from the monopolies and oppressions of the general government. Mr. Polk fell so much under the influence of Jackson and his party as to go completely over to their views.

In 1835 Mr. Polk was made speaker of the Twenty-fourth Congress. At the next Congress he was re-elected speaker. He filled this responsible position with great credit to himself and satisfaction to Congress and the country.

At the close of the session, March 4, 1839, Mr. Polk gave a farewell address to the house, in which he had served with signal ability through fourteen years. His deliberative mind, enriched with learning, reading and experience, his considerate respect for men, and courteous manners fitted him well for this trying place.

### MR. POLK THE GOVERNOR.

The next August Mr. Polk was made the democratic candidate for governor of Tennessee, and after an unusually warm contest, in which he was the leading speaker in his own behalf, he was elected. He entered upon the discharge of the governor's duties on the fourteenth of October, 1839. He gave an address on this occasion, which was regarded as one of the ablest and best of his life.

Though opposed to internal improvements by the United States, Mr. Polk was in favor of improvements by the states; so in his opening address to the legislature, he advised the "vigorous prosecution of a judicious system of internal improvements." He also advised "a board of public works, to be composed of two or more competent and scientific men, who should be authorized and their duties established by law." He was a man of progress, had much state pride, and would commit his state to all improvements it could prosecute with vigor. He did not seem to see that every argument for improvement by the state was equally good for improvement by the United States, and that state pride in the true patriot is but the root of a more vigorous pride of country. His political theory fanned the flame of a state pride to the injury of national sentiments—made the state an object of more personal interest and affection than the country. This was an evil he did not see, though thousands of his countrymen fully apprehended it.

In the same message he recommended the passage of a law "prohibiting betting on elections," and gave many reasons for it which were alike creditable to his head and heart. His moral nature was quick and strong, and he believed legislation had moral interests to subserve. He would put law to the service of conscience as well as property.

Mr. Polk's administration as governor through his term of two years, was so satisfactory as to make him the acknowledged head of his party in his state. Mr. Grundy, his old law teacher and life-long friend had died.. He was now forty-six years old, in the full day of early manhood; had lived a discreet and well-preserved life; had a national experience in public life, as well as a wide knowledge in state affairs. He was a candidate for another term; but the Harrison canvass for the presidency had swept Tennessee with a heavy majority of the states, into the ranks of the whigs. The strong anti-bank, anti-tariff, anti-internal improvement, and pro-state doctrines and practices of the democratic party had produced a heavy reaction against it. The practical affairs of the country were disastrously deranged, and a new administration of public affairs was demanded by the people. Mr. Polk, therefore, was defeated, on purely political grounds, and his opponent James C. Jones, was elected.

Mr. Polk was again candidate for governor in 1843, but was again defeated. He had now a brief respite from public affairs, which he spent in home enjoyments and hospitalities.

But the political life and issues of the rapidly growing nation were rapidly changing. The death of President Harrison and the defection of President Tyler to the democratic party from which he had come, had lost to the whigs the fruits of their victory. The new question of the annexation of Texas to the Union, which had long been an object of southern enterprise and ambition, had now come to the front. President Tyler and his Congress were committed to it. It was at bottom a pro-slavery movement, but it had a national glamour in adding an empire of rich virgin soil to the national domain, which captivated many people who did not stop to inquire into the bad faith and immoral policy at the bottom of annexation. The partisan aspect of the subject was pretty well defined. The whigs, for the most part, were opposed to annexation; the democrats in the main were in favor of it.

The sectional aspect was about as well defined. A strong majority in the north were opposed to annexation; an equally strong majority in the south were in favor of it. It was at bottom a sectional matter, the child of the south.

The democratic party had always had its heaviest majorities in the south. Its state-rights doctrine was a favorite southern doctrine. This question of annexation tended strongly to promote the growing sectionalism which slavery had already caused.

The coming democratic national convention to meet at Baltimore, in 1844, was to be shaped to this new issue. Every prominent democrat who had presidential aspirations must avow himself. The prominent names likely to come before that convention, were Martin Van Buren, of New York; Lewis Cass, of Michigan; Richard M. Johnson, of Kentucky; James Buchanan, of Pennsylvania, and Levi Woodbury, of New Hampshire. Mr. Van Buren was opposed to annexation, and were it not for this, stood the best chance of the nomination. The rest were in favor of annexation.

Mr. Polk's friends, who for some years had presidential aspirations for him, were quick to see the possible prospect for him, and had him called out in a letter on the political issues. In that letter he took his stand for annexation. He was thus made ready for an emergency. The convention came. The rule of former conventions requiring a two-thirds majority to nominate was adopted. For several ballots Mr. Van Buren had a strong majority, but not two thirds. It was soon found that Mr. Van Buren's friends would not vote for any of the named candidates. Here was a chance for Mr. Polk's friend. On the eighth ballot several of them voted for him. This brought his name before the convention. On the ninth ballot he received nearly all the votes of the convention, and then was nominated by acclamation.

Henry Clay, of Kentucky, was the whig candidate. The election returns showed Mr. Polk elected by a strong majority.

When his name was announced as a candidate, many of the other party cried out in wonder, "Who is James K. Polk?" as though he was an unheard-of man. Now his friends could reply, "President elect of the United States."

## MR. POLK AS PRESIDENT.

Taking leave of his venerable friend, Andrew Jackson, and receiving the congratulations of his Nashville friends at a public dinner, Mr. Polk, with his family and a suite of friends, repaired to Washington, and was inaugurated as eleventh president of the United States, March 4th, 1845.

President Polk's first public business related to the great issue on which he was elected—the annexation of Texas. President Tylers' last public acts were preparatory to the final act of annexation. President Polk instructed the United States minister in Texas to bear to the Texan government the action of the United States' government. The people of Texas accepted the offer of annexation, held a convention, formed a constitution and came to the door of Congress with documents in hand, ready to be admitted. In his first annual message to Congress, President Polk informed Congress and the country of the attitude of Texas, and suggested the importance of speedily passing a recognizing act, and of receiving Texas with her senators, representatives, governor and people into the United States.

Now Texas added another to the pro-slavery states, and increased the pro-slavery strength in Congress by its senators and representatives. It had cost a war to get it, many lives, and much money; but the worst of the war was not over. Simply because the United States were strong enough to do it, and the

South was greedy enough for slave territory, they robbed Mexico of it.

To hold the new state against its old owner, General Taylor had been ordered, with the United States army, to occupy the territory between the Neuces river and the Rio Grande. It was called "The Army of Occupation." Commodore Conner, of the United States navy, was ordered to be with the naval forces of the government, in the waters of the Gulf of Mexico, adjacent to the territory occupied by the army. Mexico had not only been despoiled of Texas, but she must now be whipped for objecting to it. The "Army of Occupation" moved forward to the east bank of the Rio Grande and planted its batteries before a Mexican town. A collision was brought on and war was declared which cost some twenty thousand lives and a vast amount of money. Mexico was terribly punished; her territory laid waste; her capital occupied; and then the demand made upon her to pay for the war, which she could only do by surrendering to the United States, New Mexico and Upper and Lower California,— an empire of territory of vast dimensions. The people of the north were shocked at this immense increase of territory open to slavery, and at the way in which it was obtained. Sharp discussion followed; fierce altercation; plans for compromise, for provisos, all of which ended as they began. This great movement for southern territory which was so successful, really awakened the north to the real evil of slavery as it had never been awakened before. It was the beginning of the end of that institution. By the annexation of Texas and what followed it, the seeds of the republican party in the north were planted and the spirit of resistance to the aggressions of slavery was aroused.

By laws which politicians do not control, the results of this great acquisition of slave territory, were absolutely reversed from those intended by its promulgators. The southern party was over greedy. Pro-slavery society was slow-growing and unenterprising. It could hardly fill up the old states; it did not need new. Its greed of territory and power aroused the north to opposition. Its increase of territory augmented immigration to the north and enterprise in the north. Anti-slavery settlers pushed westward; took Nebraska; took Kansas; got possession of Upper California; pushed down into Lower California; urged their way into St. Louis, and held northern Missouri; got a foothold in Western Virginia; and then backed the whole line of their invasion upon slave territory, with tiers of new and enterprising free states. Then they filled the territory they settled with productive farms, machinery, shops, schools, villages, cities, wealth, and all the power these have in them. They over-grew the slower society of the south by the more productive forces of free society. This was a development the annexationists had not provided for; it came by the laws of social growth; by business enterprize; by immigration, which free society welcomes and absorbs; by education and the free play of human energies. The very institution which the south nursed with such passionate fondness, burdened and crippled her, and prevented her from going forward and occupying the territories she so eagerly acquired. If men had been philosophers, they would have foreseen the results that have come, as the inevitable work of social laws. A great world of blame, passion, prejudice, abuse, and misjudgments, could have been saved, if men would have seen that in the development of the social forces, freedom will always outdo slavery. This Mr. Polk and his administration did not see. In all his state papers, he labored to show that Mexico was the leading offender, and made it necessary, in honor and justice for the United States, to punish her and take her territory. It was the greatest misuse of his excellent talents, that he had ever put them to. But it was a part of the partisan and sectional politics to which he had committed his fortunes.

President Polk's administration was popular with his party and section. He had carried out the programme with which he started, and could congratulate the country that by the annexation of Texas, and the Mexican war, he had greatly increased its domain. What untold wealth was in the mines of the mountains he had secured, he did not know or dream. What busy populations would in forty years dwell on the soil he had brought to the nation, he did not conjecture. He was one of those who "builded better than he knew." He planned for the extension of slavery; the forces in the growth of civilization extended the area of freedom. He, and those who sustained him in his work, anticipated a great growth of southern power on the broad plantations of Texas; the march of events has put the northern and southern man side by side on the prolific soil of the "Lone Star State," to promote, not the glory of a section, but of the nation. He sought to magnify the state, and develop state loyalty, but a wise Providence has turned his work to the glory of the common country, north and south.

He loved his country, no doubt, but that love was distempered by theories which set in his mind a section before the whole.

The lessons of time have taught us all, north and south, east and west, to be broader than we used to be; and to join hands in making a country whose great heart shall beat for the whole of humanity. By and by it shall turn out that we all, like President Polk, are building better than we know; for the country in which we shall glory will be the world free and happy, in the spirit of the American republic.

On the third of March, 1849, Mr. Polk retired from office. The next day was Sunday. On the fifth he assisted in inaugurating his successor, General Taylor, and the same evening, in company with his family, started on his journey homeward.

They took a round-about course to visit the leading southern cities, in all of which they were received with demonstrations of pleasure by the people. In due time they reached their home, supplied with the comforts of taste and wealth. Though in youth his health was not the firmest, Mr. Polk had been so temperate and judicious in the care of himself, that he had long enjoyed excellent health. He returned to his home at fifty-four years of age. It was a year of cholera at New Orleans. On his way up the river, he felt the symptoms of that disease. Not many days after he reached there, the cholera took fast hold of him, and after a short sickness, he died peacefully on the fifteenth of June, 1849.

## The Grave of James K. Polk.

Nashville, which was the adopted home of Mr. Polk, is now the resting place of the honored remains of President Polk. It is, so to speak, his cemetery, his permanent home. Not in "the city of the dead," but in the city of the living, his form reposes. The sights and sounds of life with which he was familiar are still about his lowly bed of rest. Beautiful for situation is this thriving city of the living, which rises gracefully above the bluffs of the river to be crowned in its height with its elegant capitol. It is enriched with many elegant homes and many institutions of learning, both for white and colored youth. It is the Athens of the south. The Cumberland river, with its bluffs and promontories and variegated banks, sweeps by it; while far and wide from its capitol stretches, every way, delightful scenery. Almost in sight, twelve miles from the city, is the Hermitage and grave of President Jackson. These two presidents, adopted sons of Tennessee, warm personal friends in life, sleep almost together in death. The generations rising up around them who look upon their tombs and read their histories may be quickened by them to add new honors to the country they served and which honored them with its highest confidence. Over the grave is a limestone monument, designed by William Strickland, the architect of the capitol. It is about twelve feet square and of a similar height. It is in Grecian-Doric style, a cover or roof supported with columns. On the architrave of the eastern front is the inscription:

> James Knox Polk,
> ELEVENTH PRESIDENT OF THE UNITED STATES.
> Born November 2, 1795,
> Died June 15, 1849.

On the eastern and southern faces of the monument is the following record:

THE MORTAL REMAINS OF<br/>
JAMES K. POLK<br/>
Are resting in the vault beneath.<br/>
He was born in Mecklenburg county, North Carolina,<br/>
And emigrated with his father,<br/>
SAMUEL POLK,<br/>
To Tennessee, in 1806.<br/>
The beauty of virtue was illustrated in his life; the excellence of<br/>
Christianity was exemplified in his death.<br/>
By his public policy he defined, established and extended<br/>
the boundaries of his country.<br/>
He planted the laws of the American Union on the shores of the Pacific.<br/>
His influence and his counsels tended to organize<br/>
the National Treasury on the principles of the Constitution,<br/>
and to apply the rule of Freedom to Navigation, Trade and Industry.<br/>
His life was devoted to the public service.<br/>
He was elevated successively to the first places of the State<br/>
and Federal Governments;<br/>
A member of the General Assembly;<br/>
A member of Congress;<br/>
Chairman of the most important Congressional Committees;<br/>
Speaker of the House of Representatives;<br/>
Governor of Tennessee, and President of the United States.

*Zachary Taylor*

ENGRAVED EXPRESSLY FOR WEAVER'S "LIVES AND GRAVES OF OUR PRESIDENTS"

## CHAPTER XIII.

### ZACHARY TAYLOR.

#### Twelfth President of the United States.

F the thirteen presidents in the first sixty years of the United States government, seven were born in Virginia; so it became common to call Virginia the "Mother of Presidents." No state was more forward in the revolution and for independence; no state furnished more soldiers, officers, and statesmen; no state gave more patriotic or brilliant talents to the councils of the colonies; no state had more weight in the whole movement that inaugurated the republic, than Virginia. Massachusetts and Virginia stood together at the front. Different in the manner of settlement, class of people and style of life, they were yet one in political sentiment and national aspiration. Massachusetts was the first to suffer; yet Virginia, in a noble sympathy, made the suffering her own. Massachusetts nominated the great son of Virginia as commander-in-chief of the American forces. Though far away, her quick judgment saw his great worth, and begged to trust her all to his wise leadership. When appointed, Washington hastened to Massachusetts, as though it were his home, and left it not till he had delivered it from the oppressor. Henry, in Virginia, sounded one of the first notes of the war of independence, which rang through all the colonies like the clarion of deliverance; and Jefferson's quick pen wrote the immortal Declaration of Independence. Massachusetts, with a wisdom and fortitude half divine, worked out the patterns of nationality, while she fought off the oppressor. These two great colonies must ever be held the two elder sisters that led all the rest to the achievements of state and national existence.

The seven Virginia presidents, in their order, were: Washington, Jefferson, Madison, Monroe, Harrison, Tyler and Taylor.

Virginia has long been called, the "Old Dominion." In her old estate she was grandly productive of great talent, particularly talent for statesmanship.

It is to be hoped that in her new estate, she may be nourishing the scions of the old stock, which shall give the country more and still more, through all the generations, such men as honored her and the nation in the past.

### BIRTH AND BOYHOOD.

Zachary Taylor was born November 24, 1784, in Orange county, Virginia. He was the third child of Colonel Richard Taylor, who was an active patriot and soldier of the revolution. Little is given of his father's history, only that he became colonel in the army under Washington. This indicates something of his ability and standing.

Like many other Virginians, Colonel Taylor turned his face westward, soon after the revolution, to help settle up the rich lands occupied only by the wild animals and savage Indians. Washington did much to promote this westward movement. In his early life he had become familiar with much of the territory on the Ohio and Lake Erie, and saw the possibilities for civilization there opened to the human tides that would soon flow that way. While Zachary was an infant, Colonel Taylor, in 1785, moved with his family to Kentucky, a few miles out from what is now the city of Louisville, and there built his cabin and founded his home. This year, 1884, is the hundredth anniversary of Zachary's birth; next year, the hundredth of his removal to the western wilds. Did his father, did Washington, did any of the men of that time, foresee, or even dream of, what a hundred years would bring to these lands of the forest, the wild animals and the Indian? Did they conceive of Louisville, Cincinnati, Pittsburgh, Cleveland, Detroit, Chicago, St. Louis and New Orleans, and all between and beyond them in the brief period of one century? Were any so fanatical on American development, as to anticipate what has really come to pass? The American revolution and American respect for humanity, gave such an impetus to men's desire for improvement, that the eyes of millions of Europe's cramped and oppressed people were turned to the room and freedom and comfort offered to them in America. How much greater was the work of Washington and his compatriots, than they conceived! May it not be as true that the good work of this generation may be as much greater than we conceive? Who can fathom the efficiency that Providence gives to the good works of men?

Zachary Taylor grew up in the wilderness. He was educated to the use of the axe, the hoe and the plow; to the use of the rifle, the capture of the wild beast and the defense against the Indians. This education of the forest is far greater than many suppose. It develops strength, resolution, fortitude, shrewdness, sagacity, courage, foresight, independence of judgment, promptness of action, anticipation of danger; in a word, all the qualities of mind necessary to a frontiersman, to a remarkable degree.

To a quick, bold, hardy, clear-headed boy like Zachary Taylor this education of the woods was not without its grand results. If it did not give polish, it gave strength; if it did not acquaint him with the world, it gave him a knowledge of the forces of nature and of himself, and of that part of mankind that he came in contact with. It was an education that made him a man mighty in his field of action. When about six years old he had a private teacher by the name of Ayers, who instructed him in the rudiments of English learning. Something, no doubt, was gained from the rude schools of his neighborhood, while a youth. The help of his parents added something, and the books brought from Virginia contributed something; but, in the main, his was the education of face to face contact with things. The work and business of his father's large plantation and the contact with the wild world around him were his principal schools.

### ZACHARY TAYLOR THE SOLDIER.

His elder brother, Hancock, a lieutenant in the United States army, died in 1808, when Zachary was twenty-four years of age. His father secured the commission for him.

His father's military career, his reminiscences of the revolutionary war, Hancock's interest in the army, followed by Zachary's desire to take his place after his death, indicate a military tendency in the family.

He soon joined the army at New Orleans as lieutenant in the seventh regiment of United States infantry.

In 1810 he was married to Miss Margaret Smith, of Maryland. The next November he was promoted to the rank of captain. In 1811 he was given the command of Fort Knox, on the Wabash, in the vicinity of Vincennes. This was at the time Tecumseh and his brother, the Prophet, were seeking to arouse and ally all the Indian tribes in opposition to the further advance of the whites upon Indian territory. The Prophet had established his headquarters on the Tippecanoe, a branch of the Wabash, and formed there an Indian town, where the chiefs and leading warriors gathered for consultation and action. The threatening danger from this Indian gathering and hostility made it important that all the outposts which had been planted should be firmly held. Captain Taylor was sent out on this mission against the Prophet, to watch him and hold him in check.

In 1812 the war with England broke out, and the Indians were made all the more bold and determined. There was still a more advanced post which General Harrison had established the year before, and was called by his name, seventy-five miles from Vincennes and fifty beyond any white settlement. It was hastily made, and consisted of a row of log huts as one side of a square, the other three sides being defended by rows of high pickets. At each end of the row of huts was a block-house. To this fort Captain Taylor was ordered with a company of infantry of some fifty men, illy provided both for comfort and defense.

On the third of September, two of his men were murdered not far from the fort. Late in the afternoon of the fourth, thirty or forty Indians came from the Prophet's town, bearing a white flag. They were chiefs of different tribes. They told Captain Taylor that the principal chief would make him a speech the next morning, and that they had come for something to eat.

Captain Taylor was too shrewd to be deceived by their craft. As soon as they were out of sight, he had everything put in order for an attack. Many of his men were sick, yet they were all provided with arms and commanded to sleep on them. About eleven o'clock at night the garrison was aroused by the firing of a sentinel. The Indians were there in force, and rushed to the attack with their deafening yells and war-whoops. The firing on both sides became general. The fierce yells of the savages who filled the woods and crowded about the fort, firing rapidly, made night hideous. Soon it was learned that the savages had set fire to one of the block-houses. The flames spread rapidly, and the Indians redoubled their yells and work of death. The women inside, for there were a few women in the camp, added their screams to the horrid tumult of the scene. The captain ordered buckets of water to be put on the fire, but many of his men were too much excited to execute orders. He had to personally superintend the putting out of the fire and repairing the breach. There were quantities of whisky stored in the block-house which got on fire and increased the fierceness of the flames. Altogether it was a scene of horror. Yet Captain Taylor so controlled his men as to keep them at their posts and their work, keep the fire under control, and hold the desperate savages so at bay that they made no inroad, till the morning light sent them flying from the sure aim of his men.

There were but two men wounded and one killed, while the Indian loss was heavy. The failure of the fire to open a way into the fort, made the defeat of the Indians inevitable with so cool a leader in the fort as Captain Taylor.

For this heroic defense of this exposed fort, Captain Taylor was promoted to the rank of major, by brevet.

Major Taylor continued in the service in the vicinity till 1814, when he was put at the head of troops in Missouri.

The next December he was ordered to return to Vincennes, to have charge of the forces in Indiana, where he continued till the close of the war.

After peace was declared, he resigned his commission and retired to his farm near Louisville.

In 1816, he was reinstated in the army with his original rank of major, and placed in command of Fort Crawford, at the mouth of Fox river, which empties into Green bay.

His command was changed from place to place in the west till the breaking out of the Black Hawk war in 1832, when he was again called to active service in the field.

In 1832, he was promoted to the rank of Colonel, and served under General Atkinson in his various campaigns against the Indians. He commanded the regulars in the battle of Wisconsin, which resulted in the capture of Black Hawk and the Prophet, and the termination of the war.

The Seminole war in Florida still dragged along. For years and years it had been a vexation and an expense. The deep everglades of Florida afforded retreats for the Indians, where they lived in safety and from which they came out at their pleasure, to annoy and destroy. Different generals had been given command, and much blood and treasure had been apparently wasted. Even General Jackson had tried his skillful hand at it, and gave it up.

Now Colonel Taylor was ordered to this disheartening command. He concluded at once not to let the Indians conduct the war any longer in their own way. That way had been to avoid a battle, and skirmish, creep up in ambush to sentinels, outposts, foraging parties, stragglers, and kill, destroy and steal. They destroyed our forces in detail, and were not long in decimating an army and sending it back for recruits. Colonel Taylor resolved to force them to fight his way, which was in open battle. His plan was to penetrate their jungles and find their headquarters and to force them to defend them. He made the needful preparation, and went in where white foot had never trod before. Following their trails, he crossed rivers, bayous, bogs, swamps; cut his way through tangles; bridged, waded, made roads; taking his army in force, and bringing along provisions and hospital stores, bound to sweep the dismal regions clear of savages. He was shrewder than any Indian, and knew his game.

After something like a hundred and fifty miles of this boring into the wilds, he came to the vicinity of his enemy. His lair was on a gentle elevation of dry land, in the midst of a vast swamp. It was an island in a morass. Here were the Indian stores, cattle, horses, everything they had stolen for years. In this retreat they had believed themselves safe. It was called the Okeechobee.

On the twenty-third of December, 1837, Colonel Taylor led his army through the swamp into the face of the foe he had so long hunted for. A general engagement was brought on, which lasted about three hours, when the Indians gave way and scattered into the swamp. Both sides suffered about equally. Colonel Taylor lost thirty men and had one hundred and twelve wounded. The wounded were carried back on rude litters made from dried hides found at the Indian camp, fastened to poles. In Colonel Taylor's report he says: "This column in six weeks penetrated one hundred and fifty miles into the enemy's country; opened roads and constructed bridges and causeways, when ecessary, on the greater portion of the route; established two depots and the necessary defenses for the same, and finally overtook and beat the enemy in his strongest position. The results of which movements and battle have been the capture of thirty of the hostiles, the coming in and surrendering of more than a hundred and fifty Indians and negroes, mostly the former, including the chiefs Oulatoochee, Tustanuggee, and other principal men; the capturing and driving out of the country six hundred head of cattle, upward of one hundred head of horses, besides obtaining a thorough knowledge of the country through which we operated, a great proportion of which was entirely unknown, except to the enemy."

Colonel Taylor was employed some two years in this service in the everglades, swamps and wilds of Florida. He brought to an end the long Seminole war. The Indians never recovered from the blow given them at the Okeechobee. A few of them did private mischief for awhile, but gradually disappeared west of the Mississippi and coalesced with other tribes.

For this signal service Colonel Taylor was breveted with the rank of brigadier-general.

General Taylor, at his own request, was relieved from further service in Florida and given command of the department of the southwest, which embraced Louisiana, Mississippi, Alabama and Georgia. He made his headquarters at Fort Jessup, in Louisiana, and purchased a plantation near Baton Rouge, to which he removed his family. Here, in this department, he remained for five years in the faithful discharge of the duties of his position, almost buried from a knowledge of the world.

General Taylor had now fought through three Indian wars— the Tecumseh war, the Black-Hawk war and the Seminole war—had done much hard service, and seen much privation and suffering. The good of life had almost entirely been sacrificed to his country, on these out-posts, as life's good is usually understood. Now a new experience is about to open to him.

In the spring of 1845 Congress passed a joint resolution annexing Texas to the Union. Texas had been a scene of conflict for many years. It had declared itself independent of Mexico, and fought to maintain its position. It became an indepent republic and was called the "Lone Star," because it was a single state. Then it asked for annexation to the United States, and Congress heard the request with more than willing ear, expecting it would bring on a war with Mexico. General Taylor, being the nearest commanding general to Texas, was asked to have his troops in readiness for service on the western Texan border. He was not commanded to go, yet it was made clear to him that the government wanted him on the frontier. It was, morever, made clear to him that the government would be pleased if he would so annoy the Mexicans on the border as to bring on a conflict. Mexico was weak and treacherous, and would never be submissive to the loss of Texas till she was whipped into submission. Knowing what was desired of him by his government, yet receiving no direct command, he could only wait. But after awhile Secretary Marcy ordered him to repair to the Neuces river and take up a position of observation at Corpus Christi, on the *western* bank. In August he took his position at the designated place with fifteen hundred men; in November his army was increased to four thousand men. Hints came frequently from Washington that he ought to move forward to the Rio Grande, two hundred miles further west. But he was a soldier and obeyed *orders* from authority, not *hints* from anywhere.

The situation was about this. Mexico held that the Neuces river was the western boundary of Texas. By her claim General Taylor was already on her territory with an armed force, which was a cause of war. But as yet she did nothing about it, and he had peaceable possession. The southern people of the Union, in the main, coveted the territory to the Rio Grande. The United States as a whole was covetous. The people generally wanted all the territory they could get. They were not particularly scrupulous about how they got it. A few people, especially at the North, and more especially those opposed to slavery, objected to any extension of territory southwestward. In due time it became apparent to the government that the people would sustain its movement to the Rio Grande, and General Taylor was ordered forward, and Commodore Conner to the mouth of the river with his naval force.

On his march across the prairies of the region between the Neuces and the Rio Grande, General Taylor found a Mexican force drawn up on the western bank of the Colorado river, but too weak to offer any resistance. The Mexican commander simply protested against an invasion of Mexican territory. But Taylor pushed on and was soon on the east bank of the Rio Grande opposite the Mexican city of Matamoras. Here General Taylor built Fort Brown, the guns of which pointed into the public square of Matamoras, within easy range. Twelve miles south was Point Isabel on the gulf, selected as the supply station from the ships of the navy.

General Taylor blockaded Brazos Santiago, the port of Matamoras, and ordered off two supply ships of the Mexicans. He acted as though on his own territory.

A deputy quarter-master was killed not far from the camp. A band of United States soldiers in pursuit of those who had killed him, were met by a band of Mexicans and several shots exchanged. Before they reached the camp another band of Mexicans fired upon them. A few of the United States cavalry on an excursion, were attacked and several killed. So, little by little, a general conflict was brought on.

Point Isabel was threatened with a force of fifteen hundred Mexicans. General Taylor, in force, went to its relief. Fort Brown, left in charge of Major Brown and a small force, was fired upon from the Mexican ranks in Matamoras. The Mexicans kept up the bombardment for several days. They sent a force of six thousand across the river to surround it and attack it in the rear. Major Brown was killed.

General Taylor, hearing of the attack, started back with twenty-two hundred men. On reaching the vicinity of the fort he found the Mexican army drawn up on the open prairie to dispute his further progress. He at once arranged his army of about one third the number, in battle order. The armies stood for twenty minutes, facing each other in silence. At length a Mexican battery fired a single shot, which opened the conflict. It was chiefly a battle of artillery and lasted till night closed it. The tall prairie grass took fire and added to the fierceness of the scene.

The Mexicans retired and took up a well-selected position a few miles distant. This was the battle of Palo Alto, about which great things were said. Four Americans were killed and thirty-two wounded. The Mexican loss was two hundred and sixty-two.

The next morning General Taylor pushed on in pursuit of his departed enemy, which he found some three or four miles away, posted in a ravine called Rasaca de la Palma. The position was in the midst of a thicket of dwarf oaks. Here Arista, the Mexican general, thought to make a firm stand. The battle began with artillery, and soon engaged the infantry and cavalry. It was hotly contested. But the superior intelligence of General Taylor's men made their work more efficient, and the Mexican line broke and gave way, pursued by Taylor's troops for some distance. General Taylor's loss was about one hundred and fifty, while the Mexicans are said to have lost a thousand in killed, wounded and missing.

The news of these two victories was trumpeted round the land, rousing the martial valor of the people to a high enthusiasm. "On to the halls of the Montezumas," was the war cry now. The opposition to the war was overwhelmed in the tumult of the war excitement. Congress authorized the president to accept fifty thousand volunteers. Brigadier-General Taylor was promoted to the rank of major-general by brevet. He became a hero at once. Congress and several state legislatures passed resolutions of compliment. The papers lauded him. The people talked about him. The title his soldiers sometimes called him by, "Old Rough and Ready," sounded euphonious to the people who were hungering for a military hero. The parties interested in the war and the extension of territory it was meant to secure, had an easy time in kindling a flame of patriotic enthusiasm over the glory of American arms.

On the eighteenth of May, a few days after the two battles, having obtained pontoon bridges, General Taylor crossed the Rio Grande, unopposed, and took possession of the city. He was now on Mexican territory, and in possession of a Mexican city, by common consent. War was declared by his action. The thing so long desired and planned for—war with Mexico—was now a reality. That part of the country which favored it was ablaze, and the light of that blaze was pretty much all there was to be seen.

President Polk hastened to write to him, in transmitting his title of major-general:

"It gives me sincere pleasure, immediately upon the receipt of official intelligence from the scene of your achievements, to confer upon you, by and with the advice and consent of the senate, this testimonial of the estimate which your government places upon your skill and gallantry.

"To yourself, and the brave officers and soldiers under your command, the gratitude of the country is justly due. Our army have fully sustained their deservedly high reputation, and added another bright page to the history of American valor and patriotism. They have won new laurels for themselves and their country."

But while the government and people were in this frenzy of delight, General Taylor was anxious and restless. He had now Fort Brown, Point Isabel and Matamoras, all in his possession, and must hold them. General Arista had proposed a cessation of hostilities, till the two governments could settle the question of boundary, and he had refused it. He was in the enemy's country, with hardly men enough to hold his position, while the country expected him to go on to the capital. And yet he must wait here for reinforcements. And he did wait three months.

Late in July the reinforcements, supplies, and sixteen hundred mules, to carry the luggage, came and made it possible to move forward. His plan was to go to Monterey and take that. Of course the long delay had given the Mexicans ample time to prepare to meet him.

It was generally supposed that the Mexicans would not attempt a strong opposition at Monterey, but would tempt the Americans farther into the heart of the country, and General Taylor was of this opinion. But as they neared the city the people told them of the opposition they would meet. As they approached the city they found it a military garrison. The houses were of stone and flat roofed, and the soldiers were posted on the roofs. Every street was barricaded, and every preparation which Mexican ingenuity could invent was used to defend the city. After viewing the situation, so as to understand it, General Worth was sent with a strong force around to the opposite side of the city to begin the attack. The city was defended by ten thousand men, about two thirds of them regular troops. General Taylor had six thousand two hundred and twenty men.

The attack was begun by General Worth on the twenty-first of September. General Taylor opened upon the city from his side. By evening both parts of the army had gained a foothold in the city. The next day the Mexicans had withdrawn from before Taylor, and not much was done by his division. Worth pressed forward and attacked and carried the Bishop's Palace, which was one of the most strongly fortified positions. On the twenty-third both divisions pressed the attack with great force. The next morning, the twenty-fourth, preparations for capitulation were made, and before night Monterey, with its munitions of war, was in the hands of General Taylor. General Ampudia, with his Mexican force, was allowed to retire. The loss of the Americans was one hundred and twenty killed and three hundred and sixty-eight wounded. The Mexican loss is not known. Here was another victory for General Taylor, which was sounded through the country with the greatest enthusiasm. Those who had instigated the war did not fail to make the most of their new opportunity to carry the popular thought from the cause and purpose of the war to the glory of the national arms. The battle no doubt was a fierce one, and was conducted with great skill and courage.

After this battle, General Taylor took possession of the smaller places about Monterey, and the country in the vicinity.

Santa Anna had by this time been recalled to the presidency of Mexico, and Parades deposed. Santa Anna was made commander-in-chief of the Mexican forces, with the power of dictator. He at once set about raising all the forces and using all the power of Mexico to resist the invader. Before December, he had gathered an army of twenty thousand men, at San Luis Potosi, which he fortified according to his best skill, and provided with ample military stores.

In the meantime, General Taylor had been superseded in the general command, by General Winfield Scott.

General Scott fixed his attention on Vera Cruz as the point of chief importance, and withdrew some of General Taylor's experienced soldiers. As early as February, recruits were obtained to fill the places of those taken away, and General Taylor resolved to move toward Santa Anna. On the twentieth he reached Agua Nueva, some thirty miles from Monterey. Here he learned that Santa Anna was approaching with a force of twenty thousand men, some thirty miles away. He at once resolved to choose his battle-ground and wait for his adversary. On the twenty-first, he moved to his chosen position, a little in front of the hacienda of Buena Vista, seven miles south of Saltillo. Before arrangements could be completed on the morning of the twenty-second, the advance line of Santa Anna was in sight. At eleven o'clock Santa Anna sent a summons to surrender at discretion. He received for answer that General Taylor did not surrender. Very soon after, skirmishing began, but no general fighting. The next morning, the twenty-third, the battle became general, which lasted with varying fortunes for more than two days. On the twenty-sixth, Santa Anna withdrew; and on the twenty-seventh General Taylor returned to his former camp at Agua Nueva.

The strength of the Mexican army was stated by Santa Anna, in his summons, to be twenty thousand men. The American army engaged was three hundred and thirty-four officers and four thousand four hundred and twenty-five men. The American loss was two hundred and sixty-seven killed, four hundred and fifty-six wounded, and twenty-three missing. The Mexican loss in killed, wounded and missing was supposed to be over one thousand five hundred. In its results, the victory was more decided than any gained before, and gave greater enthusiasm to the country. As a consequence, the glory of conquest filled many minds, and General Taylor grew into a military genius.

This closed General Taylor's military career. It had been one of uniform success. Whatever foe he had met, he had conquered. He had mastered every position he had occupied. He had not left Mexico, before he began to be talked of for president.

### PRESIDENT TAYLOR.

As soon as General Taylor could close up the affairs of his command he returned to his plantation in Mississippi, receiving the congratulations of the people on the way. It became evident very soon that he would not be allowed to rest. The papers and the talk of the people were full of the exploits of the hero of four Mexican fields.

In June, 1848, the national convention of whigs met in Philadelphia. The name of General Taylor was presented as a candidate and urged with great zeal. The success of a military candidate in General Harrison had not been forgotten. The need of a hero to carry the masses, and the certainty that General Taylor was the hero of a vast multitude of voters, were too important matters to be overlooked. No matter if he knew nothing about politics; no matter if he were not a statesman; no matter if he had not voted for forty years, he could get the votes to elect; and that was the principal thing, the party managers would see to the rest. So on the third vote he was made the nominee of the convention, with Millard Fillmore, of New York, as the candidate for vice-president.

General Taylor did not seek, but rather dreaded the promotion which the majority of the party desired to give him. He knew little of statesmanship and was satisfied to serve his country as a soldier. "The canvass was an exciting one," and resulted in making General Zachary Taylor twelfth president of the United States. On the fourth of March, 1849, he was inaugurated, with Millard Fillmore as vice-president.

In Congress the democrats had a majority. The question of slavery was the principal one that disturbed the country. California applied for admission into the Union. The southern democracy opposed it. Texas claimed a portion of New Mexico, and threatened to take forcible possession, but the question of the prohibition of slavery was in the way. Neither the north or the south could do as it desired, because of this slavery question. The whole question was discussed under Clay's compromise measures.

An attempt was made from some southern ports to revolutionize the island of Cuba. President Taylor issued a vigorous proclamation against it, which was generally approved. On the fourth of July, 1850, President Taylor attended the laying of the corner-stone of the national monument to Washington. The heat of the day, it is believed, brought on a sickness of which he died on the ninth. His last words were: "I am not afraid to die; I am ready; I have endeavored to do my duty."

General Scott thus sketched his character: "With a good store of common sense, General Taylor's mind had not been enlarged by reading or much converse with the world. Rigidity of ideas was the consequence. The frontier and small military posts had been his home. Hence he was quite ignorant for his rank, and quite bigoted in his ignorance. His simplicity was childlike, and with innumerable prejudices, amusing and incorrigible, well suited to the tender age. Thus, if a man, however respectable, chanced to wear a coat of an unusual color, or his hat a little on one side of his head, or an officer to have a corner of his handkerchief dangling from an outside coat pocket—in any such case this critic held the offender to be a coxcomb (perhaps something worse), whom he would not, to use his oft-repeated phrase, 'touch with a pair of tongs.' * * * Yet this old soldier and neophite statesman had the true basis of a great character—pure, uncorrupted morals, combined with indomitable courage. Kind, sincere and hospitable in a plain way, he had no vice but prejudice, many friends, and left behind him not an enemy in the world."

## The Grave of Zachary Taylor.

In the old cemetery on the ancestral farm of the Taylors rest the remains of President Taylor. It is five miles from the city of Louisville, Kentucky, on the Brownsboro turnpike. The cemetery is about a hundred yards from the family mansion, and holds the dust of three generations of this family. A few years after President Taylor's death, Congress made an appropriation for the construction of an appropriate vault in which the honored remains should repose. Within a few years, the State of Kentucky appropriated five thousand dollars for the erection of a suitable monument over the vault. The caskets containing the dust of President Taylor and his wife are separated by a marble bust of the president.

Many stories have been written and widely circulated to the effect that President Taylor's remains have had many burials and removals, and many have not known where to locate their permanent resting place. But all such stories are mistakes, according to the following note received from General Richard Taylor, nephew of President Taylor, December 31, 1883:

> General Zachary Taylor has never been buried, notwithstanding the many stories to the contrary. He died in 1850, and his remains were immediately brought to Kentucky by his brother, Commissary-General Joseph P. Taylor, and placed in a vault in the Taylor cemetery, on his father's old farm, five miles from Louisville, on the Jefferson and Brownsboro turnpike. A few months later, his wife died at Washington City and was brought and placed in the vault, and I have had the key of the vault and cemetery ever since. It is a very pretty place; an acre in size and inclosed by a nice, substantial stone wall. It belongs exclusively to our family. General Taylor's father and mother, brothers and sisters, nieces and nephews, and grand-nieces and nephews, are there. The monument is gray granite, surmounted by a marble statue from Italy, life-size and a fine likeness, the whole being about forty feet from the base. The inscriptions were all suggested by me, and are very appropriate. The monument was virtually completed July 4, 1883, but was not unveiled until September.

The granite was quarried and worked in the State of Maine. The lower base is seven feet six inches square; upon the third or upper base rests the die block, on the front of which is this inscription:

---

**Maj. Gen. Zachary Taylor.**

TWELFTH PRESIDENT OF THE UNITED STATES.

Born November 24, 1784.

Died July 9, 1850.

---

On the opposite side, in base relief, are the coat of arms of the United States with the implements of war.

On the other two sides of the monument are inscribed the names of his principal battles in the Mexican war:

> PALO ALTO.
>
> Resaca de la Palma.
>
> MONTEREY.
>
> Buena Vista.

On the other side:

> Fort Harrison.
> BLACK HAWK.
> Okeechobee.

On the front of the cap is the monogram

Z. T.

Just above this are inscribed the dying words of the old hero:

> *I have endeavored to do my duty;*
>
> *I am ready to die;*
>
> *My only regret is for the friends*
>
> *I leave behind me.*

On the front of the shaft is a medallion of the general, cast in antique bronze. It is encircled by a wreath of olive, carved from the granite. Upon the shaft rests the capital, surmounted by a colossal statue of the finest Italian marble, representing General Taylor in full military dress, standing at rest with sword and cap in hand.

So, though late, President Taylor's grave is monumented, and the country is honored by it.

# CHAPTER XIV.

## MILLARD FILLMORE.

### THIRTEENTH PRESIDENT OF THE UNITED STATES.

NOTHING in American biography, is more thoroughly American than the story of Millard Fillmore's life. It compasses the distance from the least to the greatest in human condition—from the farm to the presidency. And it is so full of what is genuine and common in the life of the American people, that it illustrates the meaning of this government and the providential power of this American development of humanity. Here is a great life which shoots up from a humble home in the forest, because it grows from a strong root of human worth and is nourished by freedom and the fostering aids of wholesome christian society.

### BIRTH AND EARLY LIFE.

Milliard's father was Nathaniel Fillmore, of Bennington, Vermont, who fought as a lieutenant in the battle of Bennington, under General Stark. His grandfather had the same name and was a soldier in the French war. Millard's mother was the daughter of Doctor Abiathar Millard, of Pittsfield, Massachusetts. She is said to have been a woman of great ability, personal worth and accomplishments. Mr. Fillmore, early in life, went into the wilderness of Cayuga county, New York, where Millard was born January 7, 1800. The place he purchased in the wilderness was four miles from any neighbor. He soon found that the title to his land was defective, and in 1802 he left it and went to Sempronius, now Niles, where he lived till 1819, when he moved to Erie county.

Millard was trained to the work of the farm, having only the simplest advantages for the rudiments of an education. At fifteen he had read almost nothing but his primary school books and the bible. At this time he was sent into Livingston county to learn the clothier's trade. After a few months an arrangement was made for him to pursue the same business, near his father's. Here he found a small village library, from which he read all his odd time for four years. He was now nineteen, well grown, manly, intelligent. The village library had quite transformed him. Judge Walter Wood had watched him with interest, and suggested to him that he ought to study law. Millard indicated his lack of education and money. The judge told him that hard study would supply the want of education, and he would himself furnish the needed money. So he left his trade for the law office of Judge Wood, where in study and business and winter school teaching, he spent two profitable years. Such a friend as Judge Wood had changed the course of his life, and put him into that ascending way which was so important to him, and for which his benefactor was amply repaid in due time.

In the fall of 1821 he went to his father's new home in Erie county; and the next spring into a law office in Buffalo. While studying here he supported himself by teaching school, assisting the post master and doing such little tasks as he could get.

### MR. FILLMORE THE LAWYER AND PUBLIC MAN.

In the spring of 1823, Mr. Fillmore was admitted to the bar and began practice in the village of Aurora. He remained here seven years, and while here, married Miss Abigail Powers, daughter of Reverend Lemuel Powers.

His success as a lawyer gained him an invitation to a partnership with an experienced lawyer in Buffalo. But before going, he took his seat in the lower house in the legislature to which he had been elected. In 1830, he went to Buffalo; was re-elected the two succeeding years to the legislature; made such a record and reputation that he was elected to Congress in 1832; and served so satisfactorily that he was re-elected in 1836. On his second term in Congress Mr. Fillmore was made chairman of the committee of ways and means, which made him the leader in the House. The country was in need of wise legislation, to restore the finances, quicken business, pay off the public debt and regain confidence. The committee of ways and means were to lead in all this. One of the most difficult works this committee had to do was to revise the tariff. Mr. Fillmore was an ardent friend of a protective tariff; but he must so arrange the tariff that all parts of the country would accept it. He gave a long and arduous labor to this subject and with eminent success.

In 1844, Mr. Fillmore was nominated by the whig party of New York as its candidate for governor; but he was beaten by Silas Wright, the popular candidate of the other party.

In 1847, the whigs, still confident of his popularity, nominated him for comptroller, and elected him by a heavy majority.

In June, 1848, the national whig convention nominated Mr. Fillmore for vice-president on the ticket with Zachary Taylor for president. The popularity of the old soldier who had fought the Indians through half his life on the frontier, and who had just gained new laurels in four battles in Mexico, was measurably enhanced by the dignity, solidity and statesmanship of Millard Fillmore. The campaign was one of great enthusiasm, and the whig nominees elected with a strong majority.

## VICE-PRESIDENT FILLMORE.

On the fourth of March, 1849, Mr. Fillmore was inaugurated vice-president of the United States. His chief duty was to preside over the Senate. Mr. Calhoun, his predecessor, had made it a rule not to call a senator to order, but to give full liberty of debate, as each one chose to conduct it. On taking his official place, Mr. Fillmore addressed the Senate on the importance of dignity, decorum and directness in the debates of the Senate, and declared it his sense of duty to hold each member to the order of debate and to be himself the judge of that order, subject always to an appeal. His statement of his idea of his duty gave great satisfaction; and although he presided through stormy debates, no one ever questioned his impartiality, fairness, or correctness.

### MR. FILLMORE THE PRESIDENT.

On the ninth of July, 1850, President Taylor died, and it devolved upon vice-president Fillmore now to become president in his stead. He appointed an able cabinet, with Daniel Webster as his secretary of state. Mr. Fillmore came into the presidency at a time when the whole country was in one of its sharpest debates on the question of slavery. The war with Mexico, preceded by the annexation of Texas, had opened immense territories for the extension of southern institutions, and this had awakened the north to a new zeal against the extension of slavery and the abolitionists to new fervors in their opposition to slavery itself. Mr. Clay's compromise measures had failed in Congress. So Congress was open to do what it could. Both north and south were intent on doing something. Texas, the "lone star," warlike, pro-slavery, newly-made sister state, was threatening to invade New Mexico, and the president sent troops there at once to keep the peace, and laid the matter before Congress.

Various acts were soon passed by Congress instead of Mr. Clay's compromise bill, all carrying out the compromise features of that bill, among them, one for the return of fugitive slaves. Mr. Fillmore asked the attorney general's opinion as to its constitutionality. That officer gave a written opinion in favor of the bill's constitutionality. Mr. Fillmore was opposed to slavery in policy and principle. Yet he was a whig with Henry Clay. Mr. Clay was the great compromiser. Whenever slavery, or north and south difficulties, came up, Mr. Clay was ready with a compromise bill as a remedy. He was a great leader in the whig party, and led it into the compromise theory of legislation and morality. The great majority of the whig party of the north was anti-slavery, as was Mr. Fillmore himself. Yet the compromise spirit that possessed it did not give it difference enough from the democratic party to maintain its life. Mr. Fillmore signed the fugitive slave bill, and thus destroyed the possibility of his re-election and closed up the life of the party. The north demanded a more pronounced opposition to the extension of slavery.

The fugitive slave law created intense excitement in the north. Slaves could scarcely be captured anywhere without a mob. It was a law which many people felt themselves under no moral obligation to obey. The law was resisted in Boston, Syracuse, and Christiana, Pennsylvania, and would have been almost anywhere had the occasion occurred. The president announced his purpose to enforce the law, and issued a proclamation calling all officers to faithfulness of duty in executing it. All measures were taken that well could be to carry the law into practical effect, yet it was so unpopular, and made the president so unpopular, that all his merits as an executive officer were forgotten, and the many popular things of his administration were lost sight of. The truth was, that all other questions were eclipsed by the great one of slavery. It was felt that humanity, justice and honor were outraged by the law that made every man an abettor of slavery in compelling him to catch the runaway. The people of the south felt that all this was demanded by their constitutional right to property in slaves. But it was simply morally impossible for the people of the north to see that they were under any constitutional obligation to catch such departing property. No matter how many popular measures a president had approved, to attempt to force such a measure upon them was to make himself unpopular.

President Fillmore, in his messages, proposed many important matters to Congress which were not acted upon, because the majority of Congress were democratic.

On the fourth of July, 1851, the president laid the cornerstone of the extension of the capitol. An immense concourse of people were present, who were addressed by Daniel Webster.

The slavery excitement quickened in the minds of some southern fanatics a desire to possess Cuba as a slave island, and they started an expedition under a man by the name of Loper, in the steamer Pampero. It left the port of New Orleans on the fourth of August, by the connivance of the collector of the port, and landed in Cuba. The president had issued a proclamation of warning against the expedition before it left, putting the Cubans on the lookout for it. It came to grief.

In the autumn of 1852 an expedition under the command of Commodore Perry was sent to Japan, which resulted in forming a treaty with that island country, which has been of mutual benefit to both countries. The changes and improvements which have been made in that country, resulting from that treaty, are among the wonderful and beneficent works of the century. Nothing more signalized Mr. Fillmore's administration than this. It is one of the most marked cases of the good which our republic is doing abroad. Our system of education, laws, and to a large degree our civilization, are being adopted by the Japanese.

During Mr. Fillmore's administration treaties were formed also with the South American States, Peru, Costa Rica, and Brazil. A steamer was sent by the government to explore the Plata and its tributaries. An expedition was sent by the president to explore the Amazon and its tributaries, to get instructive reports in the interests of science and general knowledge.

Mr. Fillmore conducted the intercourse of our government with foreign nations with ability and success. His messages were wise, strong and replete with the practical counsels of a statesman. His cabinet were in perfect harmony with himself and each other, and, upon his retiring from office, they did the unusual thing of addressing to him a congratulatory letter, expressing their "united appreciation of his abilities, his integrity, and his devotion to the public service."

Mr. Fillmore retired from office March 4, 1853, with the country at peace and in a state of great prosperity.

His first secretary of state, Daniel Webster, died October 24, 1852, and Edward Everett was appointed in his place; both men renowned for their great ability and learning. Daniel Webster will ever be held as one of the intellectual giants of the republic. But, like Mr. Fillmore, he was drawn into sympathy with the compromise measures on the subject of slavery, and lost favor with the northern public. This was a whirlpool that took in many great and ambitious men in those days. It was a time that tried the metal of the moral character of our statesmen.

### THE EVENING REPOSE.

Mr. Fillmore was a candidate for nomination to the next presidency in the whig convention of 1852; but though as president he had given great satisfaction to the party and country, his signing the fugitive slave bill had put him in such ill odor in the north that he could command but twenty votes in the free states.

In the spring of 1855 Mr. Fillmore traveled through New England, then went to Europe, and while in Rome, 1856, he received intelligence of his nomination as a candidate for the presidency by the American party. He accepted the nomination, but before the election it became evident that the real struggle was between the democratic and the new republican party. The intense ambition in the south to extend slavery had produced a strong party in the north against its further extension; and the struggle was now between extension and non-extension of slavery.

Mr. Fillmore lived in peace in the evening of his days at his palatial home in Buffalo, New York, enjoying the honors and rewards of a nobly spent and successful life. He died March 8, 1874, aged seventy-four years and two months.

During the war of the rebellion he remained so quiet as to throw suspicion upon his loyalty in some minds; but his life of faithful public service; his long-avowed espousal of high principles of national rectitude and honor; his personal character, so above all suspicion, stand as the perpetual testimonials of his patriotism. He was a true representative of American character, and honored his country in both his private and public life.

## The Grave of Millard Fillmore.

Some three miles north of the city of Buffalo, and a little east of the Niagara river, is Forest Lawn cemetery, one of those beautiful cities of the dead which the affection and taste of the people of our time make in memory of the departed. The living city is already coming near to it, and the sounds and sights of the generation of to-day already mingle with the silence and sacredness of this home of mortal dust.

The Fillmore lot is thirty by forty feet, enclosed with an iron railing set in a stone curb. It contains five graves. The monument is of highly-polished Scotch granite, twenty-two feet high. The word "FILLMORE" is on the northern side of the base, in raised letters.

At the eastern side of the lot is Mr. Fillmore's grave. Near its head is the monument, on the northern side of which is this inscription:

> Millard Fillmore.
>
> BORN
> JANUARY 7, 1800.
>
> DIED
> MARCH 8, 1874.

In the lower and western side of the lot are four graves, that of his first wife, Mary Abigail Fillmore; that of her mother, Mrs. Abigail Powers Strong; that of their daughter, Mary Abigail Fillmore; and that of his last wife.

Near by are the graves of Mr. Fillmore's law partners, Hall and Havens, and a splendid centennial monument, erected by Mr. E. G. Spaulding to the memory of his ancestors who fought at Bunker Hill, making it possible for us to have a country, and presidents to rule over it.

# CHAPTER XV.

## FRANKLIN PIERCE.

#### FOURTEENTH PRESIDENT OF THE UNITED STATES.

GENERAL BENJAMIN PIERCE was a soldier in the revolutionary war, was afterward a radical Jeffersonian democrat, who hated England and loved France; was an independent, large-hearted farmer; was for many years a representative of his town in the New Hampshire legislature; was a general in the state militia; was for a time a member of the governor's council, and two years governor of the state. He was an ardent politician, and with political weapons fiercely fought the federalists.

#### BIRTH AND EARLY LIFE.

Franklin Pierce was the son of Governor Benjamin Pierce—the sixth of eight children.

Franklin was a bright, handsome, active boy, who took his father's politics by inheritance and repeated the ancestral arguments till they became his own. He was a generous boy, who won favor at home, at school, and wherever he was known. His father had suffered much for want of an education, and as Franklin inclined to it, he resolved that he should be educated. The district school gave him a good start; the farm gave him practical industry; the academies at Hancock and Francestown fitted him for college; Bowdoin college gave him a classical course of study; Judge Levi Woodbury and the law school at

Northampton, Massachusetts, trained him in law; so that at a little past twenty-three, Franklin Pierce the boy, had become Mr. Franklin Pierce, the man and the lawyer.

Among his classmates in college, were Professor Calvin E. Stowe, a theological teacher and writer of note, and the husband of Harriet Beecher Stowe; Nathaniel Hawthorne, a very distinguished writer of romance, and who has written a biography of Mr. Pierce up to his nomination for the presidency; and John P. Hale, a statesman, orator and foreign minister, much distinguished in his day. Other noted men were in college with him, among whom was John S. C. Abbott, much known as an author, who wrote a sketch of Mr. Pierce's life in "The Lives of the Presidents."

### MR. PIERCE THE LAWYER AND THE POLITICIAN.

Mr. Pierce entered upon the practice of law in Hillsboro, his native town; succeeded poorly in the beginning, but persevered and attained reasonable success. His bent of mind was to politics. His father was a radical partisan politician. The son was a chip of the old block. His politics was partisanship. Judge Woodbury, his law preceptor, was a strong politician of the same school. New Hampshire politics was the kind he was trained in. He was cradled, bred, educated in radical, partisan democracy. The air was too full of it, it was too one-sided, it had too little opposition, to rise to philosophical, or statesman-like democracy. He was honest and hearty in it. His cast of mind, under his training, made that kind of politics his meat and drink. His cheerful, confident, frank and winning manners, made him a favorite with intensely clanish politicians of his school. Between thoughtful, broad, humane democracy, which is founded in the rights of human nature, expressed in the Declaration of Independence, and which was meant by the originators of the party that bears that name, and that to which Mr. Pierce lent his life service, there is but little affiliation.

The town of Hillsboro elected Mr. Pierce, when twenty-five, its representative in the legislature, and re-elected him for four successive years; the legislature made him its speaker the last two years; his congressional district elected him to Congress when twenty-nine, the youngest member in the House, and re-elected him in two years; his legislature elected him to the Senate of the United States in 1837, when he was thirty-three years old — the youngest member of that body. He thus went rapidly up the stairway of political promotion, till, while yet a youth, he sat in the most dignified and honorable body of men in the nation, with such men as John C. Calhoun, Thomas H. Benton and James Buchanan around him.

While a member of the House, Mr. Pierce opposed all forms of internal improvement by the general government, the bill authorizing a military academy at West Point, and all anti-slavery measures. Young as he was, he was fast in the partisan ruts. His political career had thus far been in President Jackson's time, to whose policy and fortunes he adhered with filial devotion.

As a senator, he was in Mr. Van Buren's administration, which was but a prolongation of Jackson's, with the bitter results keenly felt in the prostration of all business and fearful hopelessness and want of courage among the people. Under Mr. Van Buren, his old law preceptor, Judge Levi Woodbury, was secretary of the treasury.

In 1842, the year after General Harrison's election, Mr. Pierce resigned and returned to the practice of law in Concord, New Hampshire, whither he had moved in 1838.

In 1846, President Polk offered him the attorney-generalship of the United States, but he declined it, though in full sympathy with him, his administration, and the measures he was expected to carry out. About the same time the democratic party of New Hampshire proposed to put him in nomination for governor, which was equivalent to an election; but he declined this also.

Mr. Pierce was in hearty sympathy with the annexation of Texas and the course pursued to bring it about, and when the war opened with Mexico, which it caused, volunteered to fight for the state we had severed from our neighbor to become slave territory, with as much zeal as though a great benefit was to be bestowed upon an oppressed race. He enlisted in the ninth regiment and was made its colonel. Soon after he was promoted to the rank of brigadier-general. He embarked with a portion of his troops at Newport, Rhode Island, May 27, 1847.

In a month he landed on a sand-beach at Virgara, Mexico; collected, by great efforts, wild mules and mustangs enough to transport his luggage; broke his prairie animals to the harness; in the tropical heat of the middle of July started on the Jalappa road over sand-hills, and stream-beds and prairie stretches for Puebla, to reinforce General Scott. By labor, fatigue, skill and devotion worthy of the best of causes, he made bridges, fought off guerillas, captured villages, took possession of *haciendas* or Mexican estates; cared well for his four hundred sick men, and transported his twenty-four hundred men to a union with the main army at Puebla, without the loss of a wagon.

At Contreras, by order of General Scott, General Pierce, with four thousand men, fought twice that number and gained a complete victory. Though he was severely hurt by a fall of his horse, he kept his post of duty against the advice of officers and surgeons. He followed the enemy and fought him again desperately at Cherubusco, though faint and haggard with pain and loss of sleep; and still again at Molino del Rey. But so badly injured was the intrepid and ardent young soldier, that he had to be carried to the hospital, and the city of Mexico was taken without his further help. He remained in the captured city till December, and then returned to his home in New Hampshire.

At Concord General Pierce took up again the practice of his profession, and also the advocacy of his party politics, defending stoutly the pro-slavery wing of his party, the compromise measures of Congress, the fugitive slave law and its enforcement, as though there were no defiance of democratic principles in all this, and no violation of enlightened conscience.

In 1850 General Pierce presided over the constitutional convention in his state.

In 1852 the democratic national convention, at Baltimore, after thirty-five ballotings for a candidate for the presidency, brought in the name of Franklin Pierce, and on the forty-ninth ballot he was nominated, receiving two hundred and eighty-two votes to eleven for all others. His name was proposed by the Virginia delegation. The election was an active one. The compromise measures and the fugitive slave law had secured possession of the country. Quiet had settled down upon the opposition, and with it had come apathy to many. General Scott was the whig candidate. He received the votes of Vermont, Massachusetts, Tennessee and Kentucky; all the rest went for General Pierce.

### PRESIDENT PIERCE.

March 4, 1853, Mr. Pierce was inaugurated fourteenth president of the United States. In his inaugural address he maintained the then dominant doctrines of his party on the subject of slavery, and reprobated the discussion of that subject.

Very soon came a further dispute with Mexico about the boundary, which was settled by the acquisition of Arizona. It was Mexico's misfortune to lose by all her disputes. Under this administration routes to the Pacific were explored; a settlement with Great Britain of the fishery question was made; the Missouri compromise was repealed; the territories of Kansas and Nebraska were organized, by a special act, under which came the desperate efforts of the south to organize a pro-slavery government in Kansas. The recital of the events of what was called the "Kansas War" would be too long for this place. It intensified the differences of the time between north and south, and was participated in chiefly by those of extreme views and excitable dispositions. Few cool heads went to Kansas at that time from either section of the Union. If any went there cool they soon became heated. Missouri desperadoes played a strong part in that Kansas trouble that so shook the country in the administration of President Pierce, who was so warm in his espousal of extreme southern views that he got the name of "the northern man with southern principles."

Mr. Pierce vetoed bills for the completion and improvement of certain public works; for appropriating public lands for the indigent insane; for the payment of the French spoliation claims, and for increasing the subsidy of the Collins line of steamships. On the twenty-fourth of January, 1856, he sent a message to Congress, in which he regarded the formation of a free-state government in Kansas as an act of rebellion, and justified the principles of the Kansas-Nebraska act.

Many southern men took a more just view of the subject than he did. In his over-zeal for the extreme southern principles and measures he did much to hasten the formation of the republican party, the leading doctrine of which was the non-extension of slavery.

The Congressional complications were such over the Kansas embroilment that the Congress of 1856 adjourned without providing for the payment of the army. President Pierce immediately called an extra session, to meet on the twenty-first of August. His message to that body was chiefly devoted to the Kansas trouble, concerning which he took strong ground against the free-state party. He closed his administration as he began, a radical northern man with southern principles.

Mr. Pierce was a candidate for re-election, but his extreme officiousness in behalf of slavery had disgusted many of his northern friends, and led his southern friends to see that he could not longer serve them with success. So James Buchanan was put in nomination as his successor.

After President Pierce left Washington, he took an extended tour through Europe, from which he returned in 1860. He continued to reside at Concord, where, during the Rebellion, he made a speech, which was called the "Mausoleum-of-heart's Speech" on account of its sympathy with the confederates.

In 1834, Mr. Pierce was married to Miss Jane Means Appleton, daughter of Reverend Doctor Appleton, president of Bowdoin college. Three sons were born to them, but all died before their mother. She died in 1863, and Mr. Pierce in 1869. He was for many years a communicant of the Episcopal church.

## The Grave of Franklin Pierce.

After three months sickness Franklin Pierce closed his eyes on terrestrial scenes and passed within the vail to the realm hid from mortal sight. His body was laid in state for two days, in Doric hall, in the capitol. It was borne in funeral procession to Minot cemetery, where was sung over it his favorite hymn:

> While thee, I seek, protecting Power,
> Be my vain wishes stilled,
> And may this consecrated hour
> With better hopes be filled.

The Minot enclosure adjoins the old town cemetery and is fenced with a neat iron paling six feet high; is traversed with concrete paths and smoothly sodded. The Pierce lot is in the northwestern corner. The monument over the grave of the president is of Italian marble, elaborately wrought. The base is of granite, three feet and three inches square. The plinth, die and cap are in artistic proportions. The word PIERCE, is on the plinth in large raised letters; and on the panel of the die is the inscription:

> Francis Pierce,
> Born November 23, 1804.
> Died October 8, 1869.

Why Francis, instead of Franklin, does not appear in any public record, but it is presumed that Francis was the name originally given him. Everything is neat and in order about the grave and lot.

On the south side of the president's grave is that of Mrs. Pierce. It is marked with a neat marble spire, with a heaven-pointing hand, indicating the faith in the home above, in which she lived and died. Over the hand, in an arc of a circle, are inscribed the words:

"OTHER REFUGE I HAVE NONE."

On the north side of the president's grave are the graves of their two sons, Robert and Franklin. The whole family are gone together; only their history left. So pass away the families of earth. And so are being monumented the graves of our republican presidents in the cemeteries of the people all over the land. State after state holds the grave of a president. Some of the states already have several. The people, in this people's country, make the rulers from among themselves, and then reverently and tenderly lay their bodies away among the bodies of those over whom they ruled; ruler and ruled, alike in the feebleness of their beginning, and in the impotency of death. There is a dignity and consistency in this form of government which reflects honor upon our nature and our kind. When the people honor the rulers of their choice, chosen from among themselves, on account of their ability and worth, and then bury them in their own family burying grounds, monument their graves, and keep them green with hallowed memories, it indicates the true meaning and use of government. This is as it should be. "Honor to whom honor is due." In honoring their noble dead, the people honor themselves.

By the side of President Pierce sleep many of the most honored of New Hampshire's citizens, those with whom he lived and labored, who bore with him the cares of government and the burdens of our popular institutions. Death is republican.

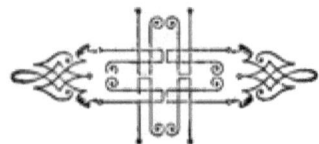

## CHAPTER XVI.

### JAMES BUCHANAN.

#### Fifteenth President of the United States.

HE value of a government or an order of society is tested by its results in human ability and character. The fact that American society has been very productive of great men, and that even from its primitive plantings its products have been large and generous, indicates that it is founded upon principles promotive of human well being. A tree is known by its fruits; men by their deeds, and society by the people it produces.

#### ANCESTRY AND EDUCATION.

We have, in James Buchanan, another instance of a distinguished man rising from the humblest origin. His father was a poor Irish immigrant, who came to the New World to better his fortune, in 1783, just as the revolutionary war was closing. He settled in Pennsylvania, and five years after did the right thing to mend his fortune by marrying Elizabeth Spear, the daughter of a good farmer.

The next good thing he did was to go a little way into the "forest primeval," stake out a tract of land for a farm, build a cabin, and establish a home. Now he was an American citizen, a freeholder, a husband, a farmer. The independent, thinking, self-directing American man was enthroned in this new home in the woods. Soon came the little boy, whom they named James, to cheer the solitude and add for a time to the work and responsibility. In this sylvan retreat this child of the woods had the freedom of his obscure home in which to get a good start in muscle and mind. The place was called Stony Batter, Franklin county, Pennsylvania, where, April 22, 1791, James Buchanan was born.

When he was eight years old the family moved to Mercersburg, and the boy went into school to go rapidly through the rudiments of an education, and be fitted for college at fourteen. He entered Dickinson college, and graduated at eighteen. This quick transit through a course of collegiate study told the character and force of his mind. He was now tall, athletic, vigorous, graceful, and exuberant of spirit.

### BUCHANAN THE LAWYER.

He began at once the study of law in the city of Lancaster. When twenty-one he was admitted to the bar. He entered immediately upon his profession, and soon attained a lucrative practice.

### BUCHANAN THE LEGISLATOR.

In 1820 Mr. Buchanan was elected to the Lower House of Congress, where he continued ten years.

He was a federalist in his early life—believed in the constitution, in a secure and strong government, capable of self-perpetuation; he believed in the nation having power over all its parts.

But as the Jeffersonian party, in opposition to the federalists, went over more and more to the state-rights doctrines, and became more and more assured in its majorities and power in the country, Mr. Buchanan went with it, so that he said, a little after middle life: "The older I grow the more I am inclined to be what is called a state-rights man."

When the second war with England, in 1811, broke out, Mr. Buchanan vigorously supported the government, and enlisted himself as a private soldier to repel the British, who had sacked Washington and were threatening Baltimore.

In Congress, and as a politician, Mr. Buchanan was opposed to internal improvements by the national government; opposed to a protective tariff; opposed to a national bank; was afraid the national government had in it some root of tyrannical power which would grow to be a dangerous oppression upon the states, if not held vigilantly in check. He became a zealous Jackson man in his time, and supported him in his erratic and dictatorial administration. In the succeeding administration he supported Van Buren with equal zeal; so that when the slavery question came to the front he was so committed to all the doctrines and measures of the democratic party of that time, that the defense of slavery seemed to him to be the support of the country. Jackson sent him to Russia to arrange a treaty of commerce with that country. Under Van Buren, he supported the president's independent treasury scheme. Under Polk, none was more active and pressing in support of the annexation of Texas, as he said, "to afford that security to the southern and southwestern slave states which they have a right to demand."

In 1833, he was elected to the Senate of the United States, and in his position as an influential and untiring advocate of the doctrines of his party and its presidents, he was able to wield a great influence in shaping its course in its sectional measures which were all the while tending to make slavery paramount to country or humanity, in the minds of its advocates. And yet all the time he seemed to himself to be a national politician, broad and fair-minded to all sections. He said: "If I know myself, I am a politician neither of the east nor of the west, of the north nor of the south. I therefore shall forever avoid any expressions, the direct tendency of which shall be to create sectional jealousies, and at length disunion — that worst and last of all political calamities." In his argument for the annexation of Texas, he seemed to make himself believe that the benefit would accrue more to the north than the south, for he said: "But to the middle and western, and more especially to the New England, states it would be a source of unmixed prosperity. It would extend their commerce, promote their manufactures, and increase their wealth." So do great men, perhaps meaning well, misunderstand themselves.

He stoutly approved of Jackson's doctrine, that "to the victors belong the spoils," and his practice of removing from office all not of his party.

### SECRETARY OF STATE.

Upon Mr. Polk's ascendency to the presidential office, he appointed Mr. Buchanan to the cabinet office of secretary of state.

He had the settlement of the northwestern boundary question, with England, which had remained open until now.

In all the sectional questions of Mr. Polk's administration, Mr. Buchanan was loyal to the pro-slavery views which he had so strongly advocated. He sustained the Mexican war in its beginning, progress and close, and counted it a national glory.

At the close of Mr. Polk's administration, Mr. Buchanan retired to private life, having served his party to its great satisfaction, and especially the southern portion of it. Yet he was too deeply interested in the great questions of the time to keep quiet concerning them, and in letters and public addresses sought to allay the northern agitation of slavery by advocating the southern view of it, in all the differing phases in which from time to time it came up.

### MINISTER TO ENGLAND.

Soon after Mr. Pierce became president he appointed Mr. Buchanan minister to England. The principal object of his mission related to the settlement of questions left open in relation to the Central American States and Spain. Cuba was Spanish territory and near the southern states. Spain might resolve to free the slaves, or the slaves might do as they did in St. Domingo, free themselves. In either case it would be dangerous to slavery in our country, and must be looked after. Mr. Buchanan was a self-constituted servant of the institution, and willingly took up this mission. After awhile Mr. Mason and

Mr. Soulé were appointed to meet him at Ostend, where the celebrated "Ostend Manifesto" was agreed upon. It was written by Mr. Buchanan, and set forth the importance of Cuba to the United States, by purchase, if it could be so secured, or by conquest, if slavery in it should be interfered with. In his own country or abroad, north or south, in Congress or out, Mr. Buchanan found slavery demanding his service, and he always responded with alacrity.

### PRESIDENT BUCHANAN.

In June, 1856, Mr. Buchanan was nominated for the presidency by the democratic convention, and the next autumn elected, receiving one hundred and seventy-four electoral votes from nineteen states, while his opposing republican candidate, John C. Fremont, received one hundred and fourteen, and Millard Fillmore eight. The anti-slavery agitation had increased more and more for many years. All that had been said and done to make slavery secure and to extend it, had only served to endanger it. The federal party had gone down in its care not to oppose it; the whig party had died in its efforts to treat it respectfully; the democratic party had grown mighty and arrogant in defending it. Now there had come into the field a new party which did not believe in slavery, many of the members of which were in judgment and conscience opposed to it; and yet as a party its one doctrine was non-extension of slavery. It had grown steadily for a number of years and had now cast one hundred and fourteen electoral votes, and had gained a clear majority of about one hundred and ten thousand in the popular vote of the whole country. This looked ominous for the extension of slavery, to prepare for which the whole machinery of the government had been used through several administrations, and to accecomplish which Mr. Buchanan had been elected. It put Mr. Buchanan in a difficult place. He had taken and continued to take the southern side of the Kansas embroglio. In every case he did what he could for slavery, not seeming to see any questions of morality or humanity connected with it, or feeling any pang of pity for the suffering slaves or the unfortunate whites who held them in bondage to their own harm.

A rebellion in Utah broke out, which Mr. Buchanan quelled by sending a wise commissioner to the disaffected. A homestead bill for settlers on the public lands was passed, which he vetoed. It was something for the extension of freedom and the help of freemen.

As Mr. Buchanan's troubled administration drew near its close, the great discussion of slavery and the national situation called out the mighty men of the whole country, and the intellectual battle of the giants was brought on. The rostrum, the lyceum, the press, the pulpit, were all at their best. Over the whole country there was profound study and deep and thorough dicussion. The best was said for both sides. The most notable discussion was that between Stephen A. Douglas and Abraham Lincoln—perhaps the greatest political oral discussion ever held in the world. The country read it with breathless interest. This, together with Mr. Lincoln's great speech in the Cooper Institute, New York, resulted in his nomination for the presidency by the republican party, in 1860, and his election.

The pro-slavery leaders of the south had threatened disunion if Mr. Lincoln was elected. The people of the north had but little confidence in or fear of this threat. They believed the *people* of the south were loyal, and prized the Union more than the extension of slavery. They understood the threat to be that of the political leaders, and not of the considerate people. Indeed, the north has always had far more confidence in the southern people than in their leaders, because political leadership has been almost the only way to notoriety in the south.

The last Congress under Mr. Buchanan met early in December. His message was full of weakness. He said the constitution had given him no power to coerce a withdrawing or a withdrawn state; that he could not call out the army except upon the requisition of judicial authority, and that authority did not exist in a rebellious state. The way was full of lions to the president who was in friendly sympathy with the seceding leaders. South Carolina formally seceded on the twentieth of

December, and set up as a separate commonwealth, and sent commissioners to treat with the president. He met them, "but only as private gentlemen of the highest character."

The simple fact was, as the French writer, De Tocqueville, had foretold some years before, the doctrine of "State Sovereignty" had sapped the life blood of the loyalty of those who had espoused it as a political truth, and he, like those who went out, had no patriotic soundness in him. Since the days of Calhoun the immoral and dangerous heresy had been growing, and now had brought forth its first bitter fruit.

Not Mr Buchanan alone, but all who had joined with him in the great heresy, were in the fault and jointly responsible for the great disaster. His patriotism was dead, and the moral stamina and the manly courage of the man had died with it. He was a body of political rottenness in the chair of state—a pitiable shame to American manhood.

As soon as Mr. Lincoln was inaugurated Mr. Buchanan retired to his home in Lancaster, Pennsylvania, where he lived in quiet obscurity till June 1, 1868, when he passed away, aged seventy-seven years.

This wreck of patriotism and loyal manhood seems all the worse as Mr. Buchanan was really a great man, and had risen rapidly from obscurity to the highest place in the gift of the nation. He had many virtues, and some marked excellencies; had a fine physique, a noble face and a manly bearing, and ought to have been among the grand American men.

## THE GRAVE OF JAMES BUCHANAN.

At Lancaster, Pennsylvania, Mr. Buchanan lived from the time he began to study law till the close of his life. His residence was about a mile west of the town on the Marietta road. He called it Wheatland. It is an old-fashioned brick mansion in the midst of a pleasant lawn well supplied with shade and ornamental trees. Not far from the entrance is a fine spring, overshadowed with willows, which was always an object of interest to its owner, and where he often sat on summer days and read, and greeted his neighbors as they passed. It is now owned by his niece, Mrs. Henry E. Johnston (Miss Harriet Lane), of Baltimore, who was reared from childhood by him, and who now makes this her summer residence.

Mr. Buchanan's grave is in Woodward Hill cemetery, in the southeastern part of the city, on a somewhat bluffy and fine outlook over the valley of the Conestoga. The cemetery contains twenty-seven acres, tastefully arranged and ornamented for the resting-place of human mortality. A chapel crowns the highest point, not far from the center. Near the chapel and a little down toward the river is the grave of the fifteenth president. The plat of ground enclosed with an iron fence is thirty feet by twelve. The fence is interlaced with thrifty and well-cared-for rose bushes; while the well-kept lawn is dotted over with clumps of rare roses. The one grave is in the center of the lot. The remains rest in a vault of strong masonry, covered with heavy slabs of rock. A base of New Hampshire granite, some seven feet by three and a half, rests on these slabs, and on the base a single block of Italian marble six feet four inches long, two feet ten inches wide, and three feet six inches high, wrought with a heavy moulded cap and base. A branch of oak with leaves and acorns is cut in the cap. On the end of the block next to the chapel is this inscription:

> HERE REST THE REMAINS OF
> **James Buchanan,**
> FIFTEENTH PRESIDENT OF THE UNITED STATES.
> Born in Franklin County, Pa., April 22, 1791.
> Died at Wheatland, June 1, 1868.

ENGRAVED EXPRESSLY FOR WEAVERS LIVES AND GRAVES OF OUR PRESIDENTS

# CHAPTER XVII.

## ABRAHAM LINCOLN.

### Sixteenth President of the United States.

WITH an inexpressible sense of tenderness and respect for the unique and providential character of Abraham Lincoln, we come to the task of setting in order a sketch of his life. He stands in our history by the side of Washington in excellence of character and the greatness of his life work for human well-being. Yet he is so near us who now live, and had such a tenderness for humanity, such a sensibility to human suffering and sorrow, and such a commanding respect for personal rights, that he seems to us a great brother of mankind, for whom we have a personal affection. He is not to us like other great men, afar off and grand, but near and dear in his greatness.

Washington wrought out his greatness by a long life of conspicuous toil and self-sacrifice in high places of trust and honor. Lincoln came suddenly before the world, a genius in philanthropic wisdom and power; and yet in sterling worth and commanding ability they were much alike. One was a child of fortune, the other of poverty; one the associate of the educated and the great, and the other of the illiterate and humble; and yet they were equals in all that most commands the affection and gratitude of humanity. They will always have the worshipful affection of the great and good of all the world.

### ANCESTRY AND EARLY LIFE.

Abraham Lincoln was born February 12, 1809, in Larue county, Kentucky. It is a picturesque and attractive region of country, at that time two-thirds timbered and fertile and the other third in rounded knolls and hills — "barrens" — covered with scattered oaks and other trees. About a mile and a half from Hodgenville, the county seat, near Nolin creek, in a rude log cabin, our child of the woods came into the hands of his humble parents. After two years they moved to a cabin on Knob creek, six miles from Hodgenville.

Abraham's father's name was Thomas. He had two brothers, Mordecai and Josiah, and two sisters, Mary and Nancy. Their father's name was Abraham, who was shot while at work in his field by an Indian who had crept stealthily upon him. This Abraham had come from Virginia. The Virginia Lincolns came from Berks county, Pennsylvania. The Pennsylvania Lincolns were Quakers, and may have come from England, or, more probably, from the Lincolns of Massachusetts, among whom the family names Abraham, Mordecai and Thomas abounded.

Abraham Lincoln went from Rockingham county, in the Shenandoah valley, Virginia, to Kentucky about the year 1780. His children were all born in Virginia. Thomas Lincoln, by the early death of his father, was thrown out among the early settlers, to live as he could by wandering from cabin to cabin and working as he could get opportunity. Until he was twenty-eight years old he worked around for others, without money, without object, without education. At that age he married Nancy Hanks, who was also born in Virginia. He took her to the little cabin which he had built, where were born three children, Sarah, Abraham and Thomas. Thomas died in infancy; and Sarah after her marriage. She had no child. Abraham's mother was a slender, delicate woman, pale, sad, heroic and yet shrinking. He always held her memory in the profoundest respect, and said once to an intimate friend, with his eyes suffused with tears: "All that I am or hope to be I owe to my angel mother — blessings on her memory."

While at Knob Creek, Abraham went to school a few months, to two different teachers. His parents were both religious persons—Baptist communicants. Their pastor, Parson Elkins, came once in a few months and preached in the neighborhood. His coming was a great event in the Lincoln family, and deeply impressed the sensitive minds of Sarah and Abraham. From Parson Elkin's fervent and eloquent sermons came Abraham's first ideas of public speaking, as well as his first impressions of religion.

In Abraham's eighth year, his father concluded to go west and north of the Ohio river. He sold his rude home for three hundred dollars and took his pay in ten barrels of whisky and twenty dollars in money. He made a flat-boat and launched it upon Rolling creek, loaded it with his whisky and heavy household goods, and pushed off. Soon after he reached the Ohio he wrecked his boat and lost two thirds of his whisky and some of his goods and farming utensils. Getting help, he gathered up what he could, repaired his boat and floated on till he reached Thomson's ferry, Spencer county, Indiana, where he landed, and fixed on a place to live, eighteen miles from the ferry. Leaving his goods in the care of a settler, and crossing the river at the ferry, he took a bee line through the woods for his home. This was in the autumn of 1816. The family soon started with their bedding and light goods packed on three horses, for their new home.

In their new place in the heavy forest of Indiana, they built a cabin; cleared up land as fast as they could, and tride to find rude comfort in close proximity to the wild beasts. They had been here but two years when Mrs. Lincoln died. This was an inconsolable sorrow to the sensitive, deep-thinking children. Her worn out body was buried under a tree near the cabin. But it was a great pain that they could have no religious burial service. Abraham had had some further attendance upon a school, and had learned to write a little, so, after consultation, it was agreed that Abraham should try his skill in writing a letter to Parson Elkins to ask him to come and preach a funeral sermon on his mother's death. This was no doubt the first letter he ever attempted to write. If Parson Elkins could have known that it was from a future president of the United States, it would doubtless have been preserved. Great was their comfort in getting a letter, in a few weeks, from Parson Elkins, setting a Sunday some months ahead, when he would be there, and preach as desired. The mystery of writing now seemed to have a sacred meaning, and the marvels of an education to grow sublime in the thought of these afflicted children of the woods. They thought and longed, talked and waited the time out, sending word everywhere for twenty miles around to their forest neighbors, when lo, at the appointed time, the good man came, an angel of comfort and blessing indeed. It was the coming of the Lord to their poor hearts. The day was pleasant; the people came to the number of some two hundred; and sitting on the stumps, logs and ground around the grave of the mother of our great president, they listened to the gospel of immortality and divine love as preached by this Saint John of the wilderness, crying unto men, "Prepare ye the way of the Lord." That day was one of the Lord's precious days in making the character of Abraham Lincoln. The tender reverence of that holy day never left his spirit.

Abraham's mother had some education, and a few books which she read often to her two children. She read to them from the bible such parts as was best for them. The influence of these lessons was very great on the receptive heart of her son. The poor father sat by and listened, only to value an education all the more because he had it not. On this account he embraced every opportunity to give Abraham as much as he could.

The mother died in 1818, so that Abraham could not have been quite ten years old.

He had three different teachers while living in Indiana, but studied only a few weeks with each. All his school opportunities, both in Kentucky and in Indiana, did not amount to more than one year. But he read much—not many books, but the few he had. He read the bible so much that he could repeat many parts of it. Æsop's Fables he read till he knew them by heart. Pilgrim's Progress, Weems' Life of Washington, and a Life of

Henry Clay, he read over and over. These books were food for his hungry mind.

The great life of Washington impressed him deeply, and in it he got the story of our national life, and the principles on which the republic started. Henry Clay, as a living man, won his interest.

In a little more than a year after his mother's death his father married a Mrs. Sally Johnston, of Kentucky, who brought with her three children by a former marriage. She was a good step-mother, and the united families lived in peace.

At this early age Abraham began to show the elements of character for which he was afterward noted—great good-nature, fondness for sport, and story-telling. This last quality was marked in his father. When about eighteen years of age he built a flat-boat and took the products of the farm to Louisiana. The next year he was applied to, by a trading neighbor, to take a boat-load to New Orleans for him, in company with his son. These voyages gave him a glimpse of the world and some knowledge of business. At this time he had become a vigorous youth, six feet and four inches high, athletic, muscular and enduring. His reading, his two journeys to New Orleans, his quick wit, his story-telling and great sociability, his honesty and freedom from every vice, his powerful and athletic frame, and the odd and attractive peculiarities of his ways and conversation, already made him the center of attention among his neighbors. Everybody liked him, and confided in him. In his circle he already had the first place.

### EARLY MANHOOD.

But the family got tired of heavy-timbered Indiana, and when Abraham was a month past twenty-one, started for the prairie state of Illinois, and settled on the Sangamon river, about ten miles from Decatur. After Abraham had helped his father build a cabin, fence in, break up and plant to corn ten acres of prairie, he announced his intention of striking out for himself. He at once sought work among the neighboring farmers, breaking up prairie, splitting rails, putting up fences and chopping wood, or doing any work that offered. From this work he got the name of "rail-splitter." There was no money then, and he split rails for the cloth to make his clothes, for his board and the things he needed. One who used to work with him at this time says that he was the roughest looking person he ever saw; was tall, angular, ungainly, dressed in flax and tow garments, out at the knees; was very poor, and often walked six or seven miles to his work, yet was welcome at every house and made friends as fast as he made acquaintances.

About this time he was applied to to take a flat-boat to New Orleans, for one Denton Offutt, a trader. But as Offutt could not find a boat, he arranged with Lincoln to build one on the Sangamon river, seven miles from Springfield. Two other men were joined with him. They had twelve dollars a month each. They completed the boat, loaded it with hogs, and young Lincoln and one of the men took it to New Orleans and sold the load and boat, with such good results that Mr. Offutt put Abraham in charge of a mill and store at New Salem. Store-keeping was a new business to him, but he soon became such an object of interest that the people came from far and near to trade with him. Several incidents are related of him while here that gave him the name of "Honest Abe." By a mistake he had taken six and a quarter cents too much of a woman on a bill of goods. He did not sleep till he had carried it to her, on foot, some miles away. By another mistake, he put too small a weight on his scales for a pound of tea, and, after closing his store late in the evening, carried the rest of the tea to the woman, who had got less than she paid for.

There was a bullying set of young roughs about New Salem who tried the mettle and strength of every young man who came into the neighborhood. One of them came into the store in a profane and abusive way when some ladies were in. Abraham begged him to desist from such language till the ladies had gone. He finally said: "If you are aching for a whipping, just go outside till I am done with these ladies, and I will come out and attend to you." As good as his word, he went out and laid the fellow on his back, and, in the utmost good nature, rubbed his face with smartweed till he begged lustily for quarter. Then he let him up, got water and washed his face, and made the bully and his associates his friends by the operation. A few other such experiences with the rough elements of that community won them all to him. They could always get fun but never a fight out of him; and he soon became their ideal good fellow. His imperturbable good nature made him the master of every situation and won him the victory in every coarse onslaught upon him.

While engaged in Offutt's store, Abraham began the study of English grammar, borrowing a copy of Kirkham's grammar of L. M. Green, a lawyer of Petersburg, and walking eight miles to get it. He used to talk with Mr. Green of his aspirations and ambitions; said his family seemed to have good common sense, but none of them had become distinguished; that possibly he might. He had talked with some men who had the reputation of being great, and he could not see as they differed much from other men. It is evident, from all we get of him at this period, that he had begun to feel the ground-swell of the grand impulses that were in him and to think of the greatness possible to all true souls and the service they may render their country and kind. He read much while at New Salem. He devoured newspapers, particularly the Louisville "Journal," so long edited by the witty and brilliant Prentice.

### LINCOLN A SOLDIER.

While Mr. Lincoln was at New Salem the Black Hawk war broke out. Mr. Lincoln enlisted himself, and enough in his vicinity to make a company. When the company was ready to organize, two men were named for the captaincy, Lincoln and a Mr. Kirkpatrick, who had been such an oppressive employer of young Lincoln, at one time, that he had left him. When the company was collected the two candidates stood at a little distance, and each man in the company went to the man he wanted for captain. When the word was given nearly all went to Lincoln, and those that did not immediately left the other man and went over to him. Lincoln said of it: "I felt badly to see him cut so." Here was an opportunity to be avenged for his old employer's abuse of him; but he seemed to have no such feelings, but rather pitied him.

In the army Captain Lincoln was a great favorite. His wonderful fund of good humor; his kindness to his men; his patient industry and tireless energy; his readiness to join in all their sports and outdo them all in their athletic feats, made him captain indeed.

Mr. Lincoln often spoke of his early war-experience in a jocose spirit, but it had lessons and opportunities for him, as everything he touched seemed to have. Zachary Taylor was in the Black Hawk war also, so that two embryo presidents had a part in conquering the fierce savage.

When the soldiers from Sangamon county reached home, an election was just coming on. They at once proposed Captain Lincoln as a candidate for the legislature. He was now twenty-three years old, just emerging from obscurity. He was a whig, an admirer of Henry Clay, the story of whose life had captivated him when a boy. Andrew Jackson then led the democratic hosts. Sangamon was a democratic county, and Illinois was a democratic state. There was apparently no hope for the promotion of a whig. Yet Abraham Lincoln had adopted the politics of the minority, and accepted the nomination as a minority candidate. In New Salem he got almost the entire vote, but in other parts of the county he lost the election.

Mr. Offutt had failed in business. Mr. Lincoln was mustered out of the military service, was not elected to the civil service, and therefore was without employment. What should he do? He thought of learning the blacksmith trade. He was handy with tools; something of a general mechanic; he must do something. While meditating upon this matter, a friend bought the goods in the store in New Salem, at a venture, and asked Mr. Lincoln to take an account of his stock of goods. The result of it was that Mr. Lincoln and another man bought the goods. The other man proved a trifler and Mr. Lincoln's speculation brought him considerable in debt to his friend of whom he had bought. He afterward spoke jocosely of this indebtedness as "the national debt." While in this store he was appointed postmaster, by President Jackson. This he liked, for he could read all the newspapers; but when the store "winked out" as he said, he put the postoffice in his hat and carried it wherever he went.

### LINCOLN A SURVEYOR.

But now again came the question, what should he do? Just as he was considering this, the county surveyor proposed to him to do the surveying about New Salem. He knew nothing of surveying, but arranged to do the job, went right at the study, and soon was running lines and staking out lots. It is said that his surveying has stood the test of time. This surveying led him to a wide acquaintance in the county. He was much among the farmers, in their homes, at their gatherings. He was in the villages professionally, and came close to all the people. And everywhere he was a marked man. Everybody liked him. His quaint ways, his fascinating stories, his knowledge and common sense, his freedom from selfishness, his warm friendship and readiness to lend everywhere a helping hand, and his transparent simplicity and good nature, with his long, gaunt, peculiar figure, made him the most popular man in the county.

### LINCOLN A LEGISLATOR.

In 1834, two years after his first candidacy, he was again a candidate for the legislature. Now his friends persuaded him to make speeches, which he said he would do if they "wouldn't laugh at him." His quaint speeches told. They were like himself, somehow, strangely influential. He was elected. In the same legislature was Major John T. Stuart, who had conceived a strong personal interest in him in the Black Hawk war. Mr. Lincoln said and did but little in this legislature, but observed and thought much. It was a school to him.

Mr. Stuart suggested to him to study law, and offered to lend him books. He walked to Springfield for the books and studied and surveyed by turns. He was often buried in his studies, lost to everything else. Some said he was crazy. He was simply absorbed in his life's work, now open to him after a singular succession of experiences, that seemed to have no relation to this study, yet led him in a roundabout way to it.

In 1836 he was renominated to the legislature. The canvass was a very warm and able one. Many strong men were in the field. Mr. Lincoln had now had two years of thorough study. His mind had been stirred to action. The political field was alive with agitation. He had recast his thoughts in his late studies, and now with a man's grasp of mind he used them in his speeches. There was a meeting of candidates at Springfield for discussion, and a great gathering of the people. Ninian W. Edwards opened the discussion for the whigs. Doctor Early followed him for the democrats. He was then the great debater in Illinois on that side. He had the faculty of merciless severity which he used against his antagonist, who desired an immediate reply; but Mr. Lincoln got the floor and proved himself master of the situation. He took up Early's speech and riddled its weak places, shook it to pieces and ridiculed it, all the time weaving in his own views with such masterly adroitness that he aroused a great enthusiasm in the audience. Cheer on cheer followed his strong points. He kindled into a flame of impassioned speech. His countenance was transformed. His eyes were fire; his stature majestic; his voice powerful and persuasive. The effect of his speech was so electrical and triumphant, that from that hour he was held as one of the great orators of the state. And yet he was but twenty-seven years old. He went to the legislature that year with a strong body of men, himself recognized as their peer. Among them were several who afterward held high national positions; one of them was Stephen A. Douglas.

The great work of that legislature was to institute a system of internal improvements and remove the capitol to Springfield, both of which objects were included in one bill. Mr. Lincoln was put forward to do the leading work for the bill. The bill was carried and it made him a very popular man in his county, and especially in Springfield.

But this session of the legislature was more remarkable for what seemed to be an insignificant matter. Abraham Lincoln and Stephen A. Douglas met here for the first time. Mr. Douglas was but twenty-three years old, the youngest and smallest man in the house—"the least man I ever saw," Lincoln said. The state was overwhelmingly democratic. The slavery agitation was getting strong all over the country. The democratic party was pro-slavery; the whig party not anti-slavery, but complacent and conciliatory toward "the institution." To show its loyalty, the democratic party in the Illinois legislature, took pains to pass some pro-slavery resolutions. Stephen A. Douglas was zealous for these resolutions, and then and there took his public position on the side of slavery and its bad policy and inhumanity, to be carried on to an untimely grave and a disappointed and unfruitful life. Abraham Lincoln had seen slaves sold in New Orleans, and had felt a pang of sorrow for the poor victims of human cupidity and power. His judgment, his conscience, his heart, were against slavery. Politically he held it as bad policy to hold slaves even where the constitution allowed it. Into the territories the constitution could not carry slavery, he said. Only the people of the territories could establish it there. So on this mild anti-slavery ground he took his stand in this legislature, against the democratic policy, in advance of the whig policy, in what seemed a hopeless minority, to rise in power and influence and win a victory for his principles throughout the world and an immortality of glory and renown for himself.

When the resolutions were passed, Mr. Lincoln and Dan Stone, whig members from Sangamon, entered their protest upon the Journal of the House, with their reasons, which were, that "While the Congress of the United States has no power to interfere with the institution of slavery in the different states, and while the promulgation of abolition doctrines tends rather to increase than abate its evils, still the institution of slavery is founded on both injustice and bad policy, and Congress has power, under the constitution, to abolish slavery in the District of Columbia, though this power ought not to be exercised unless at the request of the people of said district."

This was Mr. Lincoln's mild position, then taken, and there he stood until military necessity compelled him, as the commander-in-chief of the Union army, to grant freedom to all the slaves.

The positions then taken by Douglas and Lincoln were argued by them through many years, and on many platforms, and their arguments had more to do in bringing the subject in a political form before the people than any other. They must be pronounced the foremost men in this battle of the giants.

It must be kept in mind that Mr. Lincoln had not yet entered his profession; was very poor; practicing, surveying, to earn his bread while studying law; that he walked to and from the legislature, a hundred miles each way, and yet had already become a central figure around which was soon to gather the moral and political forces of one of the greatest movements of the world. His strong common sense, becoming bright with the light of genius, won him favor wherever he was known, and fixed upon him the eyes of some as one who might develop great power.

He had long been in the habit of putting his thoughts into writing. He wrote much. This gave him the power of clear statement. His knowledge was limited, but what he knew, he knew well; and he thought and wrote about it, till it became a part of himself.

With all his joviality, he was a serious man, and studied profoundly the problems of life. "Oh! how hard it is to die and not be able to leave the world any better for one's little life in it," he said to a friend in his early manhood. In his seriousness, he was sometimes oppressed to melancholy. He often meditated upon the sad side of life, and groaned in spirit over the corruptions of the world. His own life was a profound study to him. Opening so obscurely and humbly, and coming on by such unpromising ways, hindered and oppressed, and set back and defeated so often, where was it leading to? He felt an inexpressible yearning for knowledge, usefulness and recognition;

but would he ever attain these? He was childlike in his simplicity and honesty. He assumed nothing, but was always just himself and nothing else.

Mr. Lincoln, from his early youth, was religious in spirit. He had no professional or dogmatic religion, but was tenderly reverent toward the great Father of his spirit, and the souls of his children. His early bible study, his "angel mother's" reverent lessons, and Parson Elkin's influence, made impressions that he never lost. He adopted no creed, joined no church, yet respected all.

In his later readings he had fallen in with some works of science. He was much interested in geology. It brought him close to nature and nature's God. He studied human nature everywhere. Even when jovial he was studious, and through the apparently trifling side of his life, found avenues into serious reflections and reverent communings.

### MR. LINCOLN A LAWYER.

In the autumn of 1836, Mr. Lincoln was admitted to the bar, having done nearly all his studying by himself, and having been a surveyor, and a legislator, and a general reader of politics and the news in the meantime. While studying, he had attended some courts, and familiarized himself a little with their proceedings. He received at once an invitation from Major Stuart to become his law partner in Springfield. Mr. Lincoln was already well known in Springfield, and honored for what he had done to make it the capital of the state. In April, 1837, he took up his abode there.

Mr. Lincoln was now well established in the principles in life to which he always adhered; was a genuine temperance man, openly and actively on the side of that great reform; was a politician of moderately reformatory tendencies; was a humane man, and profoundly sincere and honest.

He had had a curious and marked experience at New Salem. This rude country village had served him well as a place in which to get a start in life; and he now left it with many misgivings and questionings as to his future career.

The next July he was summoned to an extra session of the legislature, and very soon after Mr. Stuart was elected to Congress; so that their legal practice was somewhat interrupted. The next year he was re-elected to the legislature. At once he was recognized as the leading whig member, and he came within one vote of being made the speaker. The partisan aspects of the state had changed much. The result of Jackson's financial policy had, as the whigs said, brought the cruelly hard times of 1837, under which the country was yet suffering terribly; the gag-law in Congress, under Van Buren, which refused to consider all petitions and papers relating to slavery, was unpopular with all free-speech men, and the two together being democratic measures, had weakened the democratic and strengthened the whig party. No business of great importance came before this legislature.

Mr. Lincoln's notoriety soon brought him legal business, which he attended to with the utmost fidelity. It was not long before he secured a great reputation as a case and jury lawyer. His good humor, fairness, his knowledge of jurors and persuasive power over them, and skill in managing cases, gave him an extensive business, so that in all the circuit of counties through which he practiced he was often on nearly all of the important cases.

In 1840 Mr. Lincoln was again elected to the legislature, and served because it was at home, but he refused longer to accept this office.

About this time a strange episode in Mr. Lincoln's life occurred, not at all creditable to his judgment or moral courage, according to our notions of these things. A poem appeared in the Sangamon "Journal" sharply reflecting on James Shields, a young lawyer of Springfield, afterward General Shields and United States senator. It was anonymous, but written by a young lady. Shields was fiercely angry about it, and must know the author or fight the editor, Simeon Francis. The young lady was a personal friend of Mr. Lincoln. Francis went to Lincoln for counsel. It was understood that somebody must fight a duel with the hot-blooded young Shields or be branded as a coward. Lincoln told the editor that if the young man should again demand the author's name to tell him that he, Lincoln, held himself responsible for the poem. When Shields was told this he at once sent a challenge to Lincoln. It was accepted, and Lincoln chose broadswords as weapons, and put himself under training. The duel was to be on Bloody Island, in the Mississippi river; but friends interfered and prevented it, but its contemplation was a stain on both their reputations.

It has been charged upon Mr. Lincoln that he indulged in smutty stories unfit to be heard by chaste ears, and his biographers accept the charge as true, but explain it on two grounds: First, that it is common in the members of the legal profession, who in their business become familiar with the filth and smut of humanity; and second, that he told these stories because of their wit, and not because of their smut. They say he was intensely fond of wit, and had no sympathy with human filth. But no explanation atones for the blemish of such a practice. It is no part of a true man, and no matter who indulges in it, nor under what circumstances, it is not only a fault but a vicious practice. We can well understand how Mr. Lincoln had been familiar with such jokes and stories from his boyhood, by the society in which he had mingled, but that when he became a man he did not revolt against their use and discontinue them is against his taste and moral sensibility.

In 1840 Mr. Lincoln dissolved his partnership with Mr. Stuart, and formed one with Judge S. T. Logan, of Springfield. He now resolved to devote himself more to his profession, but each new political canvass called for his strong services.

In 1842 he married Miss Mary Todd, a daughter of Hon. Robert S. Todd, of Lexington, Kentucky. Miss Todd had resided for some time at Springfield. They did not set up a new home at once, but boarded at the Globe Tavern. His private letters at this time indicate much pleasure in his new relation.

The next year he began to have Congressional aspirings, but his friend Baker got the nomination, and he helped elect him.

Mr. Lincoln was a party man, and trained himself to keep step with his party. His ideal statesman was Henry Clay, and he was a close party man and went himself no farther in any direction than he could carry his party.

In 1844 Henry Clay was the whig candidate for the presidency. Mr. Lincoln supported him with his whole heart and power, speaking in many parts of Illinois and Indiana, and everywhere putting all his energy and enthusiasm into the canvass. But he was defeated, and great was Mr. Lincoln's chagrin and sorrow. It weakened his respect for the popular judgment. He had built up great hopes for the country on his party and his political idol, hopes not so well founded as he thought. Neither his party nor his idol had the merit he attributed to it. The whigs of the country were woefully disappointed. Mr. Clay had captivated many as he had Mr. Lincoln. Everywhere there was grief and disheartenment among the defeated partisans of the great Kentuckian.

In 1846 Mr. Lincoln went to Lexington, Kentucky, to hear Mr. Clay's speech on the gradual emancipation of the slaves. The speech was written and read. It disappointed him. It was cool and commonplace. The fire and force he had expected were not in it. The great orator and statesman were not manifest in the performance. He was introduced to Mr. Clay, who was cool and condescending, though he knew what a friend and helper he had in Mr. Lincoln. He invited Lincoln to his home at Ashland. It was such a gracious expression of friendship as was infinitely pleasing to our humble Illinois devotee of the great sage of Ashland. He went and was graciously entertained and patronized by the honored whig leader. But he came away a sad though a wiser man than when he went. Mr. Clay, while polite, polished and hospitable, was so conscious of his superiority, so condescending, as to make his guest painfully sensible of his common littleness. Mr. Clay was proud, princely, dignified; Mr. Lincoln was humble, plain, childlike; how could they affiliate? He felt that Mr. Clay was overbearing and domineering, not only to him, but to everybody. And so he saw his idol broken. It was a good lesson to the partisanship and idolatry of Mr. Lincoln to a great leader. It taught him that principles rather than men are to be followed and have the devotion of true men.

## MR. LINCOLN A CONGRESSMAN.

December 6, 1847, Mr. Lincoln took his seat in the Thirtieth Congress, as a member of the Lower House. He was elected the autumn before, and made an active canvass of his district, which gave him the highest majority it ever gave to a whig. In his canvass he discussed the annexation of Texas, the war with Mexico and all the affiliated measures of the pro-slavery democracy, protesting against the whole; and also the importance of a protective tariff to the industries of the country which were then suffering, as he claimed, by a democratic reduction of the tariff.

Mr. Polk was then president, and it was his custom, in his messages, to set forth the raiding practices of Mexico upon the territory of the United States, as though against the laws of nations, and patiently borne by us till forbearance had ceased to be a virtue, and, that war had been declared against Mexico only when she had practiced war upon us, when the simple facts were that we had sent our army all the way from the Nueces to the Rio Grande, some two hundred miles into the Mexican territory, and provoked the Mexican soldiers to raid upon our outposts. Mr. Lincoln took up this matter in a series of resolutions, which he offered, asking of the president information as to the spots where our settlements had been invaded, the particular spot where our peaceful citizens had been murdered, by Mexican soldiery, and for detailed information as to particulars. They were so full of "the required spots" where Mexican outrages had been committed upon our quiet citizens that they got the name of the "spot resolutions." In view of the facts in the case, they made the president's messages ridiculous. Mr. Lincoln made a characteristic speech in behalf of the resolutions, but, as the whigs were in the minority, the resolutions were laid on the table. The whigs in Congress were in a dilemma. They did not believe in the war; knew it had been provoked and forced upon the Mexicans by our government to filch from them their territory, and yet, if they did not vote supplies to carry it on, and support our soldiers in their dangerous exposures, they were called unpatriotic and barbarous. In a speech in Congress, January 12, 1848, Mr. Lincoln, in a cool, clear and exact statement of the facts in the case, showed how the country stood in relation to the war, and how it placed the whig party.

On the first of June, 1848, the whig convention met at Philadelphia, to nominate a candidate for the presidency. Henry Clay was the idol of the party, but he had been defeated. Mr. Lincoln had seen him and lost his former confidence in him. Mr. Lincoln was in the convention, and did not approve of nominating Clay.

General Taylor, a nominal whig, though he had not voted for forty years, had come back from the Mexican war covered with the glory of a military chieftain. His career had been a succession of victories, which the democratic papers all over the country had magnified into most magnificent and brilliant exploits of military genius. His dispatches had been the simple, unpretending facts of what his army had done. Their modesty was praised as much as his military genius. He was the hero— the Cincinnatus of the hour. The democrats made his glory and fired the country with it, and the whigs in convention caught it upon their banner. They nominated General Zachary Taylor as their candidate. Of course it put them in an awkward position to glorify General Taylor and denounce the war that made him their candidate and was sure to elect him. But this was their good luck, and Lincoln urged his nomination and that they should make the most of the tide in his favor. He counseled saying as little as possible about the beginning of the war which the whigs were in no way responsible for.

Mr. Lincoln took up the canvass in behalf of General Taylor with great zeal, going first from Washington to New England and making several speeches there. He canvassed Illinois and in his own district gave Taylor almost as large a vote as he had got himself when elected to Congress.

Early in the winter Mr. Lincoln returned to Congress, and

went as a recognized anti-slavery man, who would do as much against slavery as the constitution would permit him to do. He was a constitutional man, loyal to that great charter of American liberty as to the rights of man and conscience. In his first session in Congress he had voted forty-two times for the Wilmot Proviso, had stood with John Quincy Adams stoutly for the right of petition, and was counted as an ally of Joshua R. Geddings and men of his convictions and conscience. During this session he prepared a bill for the abolition of slavery in the District of Columbia with the consent of the people of the District. But some of the people who agreed to his plan at first, withdrew from it, and time was not permitted him to begin anew, and so his bill fell through before coming to a vote. His service in Congress closed with honor and profit to himself.

As Mr. Lincoln became more acquainted with educated men and society, he felt more intensely his lack of early education; and he returned from Washington to his home resolved to make up for his deficiency as much as he could. So he took up the study of geometry and went through the first six books of Euclid. His success among educated men surprised him. He felt a constant gratitude to them for their appreciation of his motives and their kindness to him. He was always self-deprecating, and often wondered how others could think so well of him. This self-deprecation was greatly magnified by his conscious lack of an education.

### RETURN TO HIS PROFESSION.

On his return from Congress Mr. Lincoln took up again the practice of his profession; and now for a number of years had one of the most peaceful and enjoyable portions of his life. He had attained a conspicuous place among his countrymen; had formed a large acquaintance among the great and good; had put his original obscurity far behind him; had in his profession a way to obtain an honorable living and be useful; had a wife and little family; had books, friends, appreciative society; all of which he enjoyed in their full measure.

By the distinguished lawyers who knew him well and practiced with him, he was profoundly appreciated as a man and lawyer. Judge Caton, said of him: "He applied the principles of law to the transactions of men with great clearness and precision. He was a close reasoner. He reasoned by analogy and enforced his views by apt illustrations. His mode of speaking was generally of a plain and unimpassioned character, and yet he was the author of some of the most beautiful and eloquent passages in our language, which, if collected, would form a valuable contribution to American literature. The most punctilious honor ever marked his professional and private life."

Who will ever know what society, literature, learning, the country and humanity, have failed to have that is rich and grand, because his great soul was cheated of an education by the hard fortune of his early years?

Judge Breese, said of him: "For my single self, I have for a quarter of a century, regarded Mr. Lincoln as the finest lawyer I ever knew, and of a professional bearing so high toned and honorable as justly, and without derogating from the claims of others, entitling him to be presented to the claims of the profession, as a model well worthy the closest imitation."

Judge Drummond, said of him: "I have no hesitation in saying that he was one of the ablest lawyers I have ever known. No intelligent man who ever watched Mr. Lincoln through a hard-contested case at the bar ever questioned his great ability. With a probity of character known of all, with an intuitive insight into the human heart, with a clearness of statement which was itself an argument, with uncommon power and felicity of illustration — often it is true, of a plain and homely kind — and with that sincerity and earnestness of manner which carried conviction, he was, perhaps, one of the most successful jury lawyers we have ever had in the state. He always tried a case fairly and honestly. He never, intentionally, misrepresented the evidence of a witness, or the argument of an opponent. He met both squarely, and, if he could not explain the one, or answer the other, he admitted it. He never misstated the law according to his own intelligent view of it."

In 1852, on the death of Henry Clay, Mr. Lincoln delivered a eulogy on that famous statesman of his day. The eulogy was calm, and probably quite less enthusiastic than he would have given before his visit to Ashland. The closing words are worth repeating here. "Such a man the times have demanded, and such, in the providence of God, was given us. But he is gone. Let us strive to deserve, as far as mortals may, the continued care of Divine Providence, trusting that in future national emergencies, he will not fail to provide us the instruments of safety and security." No instrument, since the days of Washington, has seemed to the lovers of our republic, so providential as Mr. Lincoln himself. To no other have his words such a profound application. And it seems almost certain, that in the generations to come, he will be held as the preserver of the country of which Washington was the father.

But great national events were in progress. The northern section of the country was rapidly overgrowing the southern. The great northwest was inviting settlements. The western prairies were attracting the hardy and enterprising from the eastern states and Europe. It was becoming clear that the balance of power was soon to be in the north. The political leaders of the south who were devoted to slavery, were getting uneasy and absolute in their determination to rule or ruin. In 1850, the free state of California was admitted to the Union. There was no balancing slave-state to come in with it. California had grown to a free state on territory won from Mexico by the pro-slavery war. This was a result not in the original calculation.

In the whig canvass for General Scott, in 1852, Mr. Lincoln took but little interest, and General Pierce, who ran against him, was elected.

In 1854, the Missouri Compromise of 1820, which shut slavery out of the whole northwest, was abrogated, with a view to force slavery into Kansas and Nebraska. This was an act of bad faith, which stirred Mr. Lincoln deeply. Northern democrats, particularly Mr. Douglas, acted in complicity with the south in the matter, and this stirred northern blood far more than the action of southern men. It was understood that Mr. Douglas was the author of the Kansas-Nebraska bill, which opened those territories to slavery. It made him unpopular with many of his friends, and when he went home to Chicago and attempted to make a speech in defense of his work, he was prevented.

A few weeks after, at the autumnal fair at Springfield, he made, before a great audience of representative men from all parts of the state, his defense of the Kansas-Nebraska bill, which Mr. Lincoln heard, and the next day replied to in one of the most masterly efforts of his life. He spoke three hours, but no complete report of his speech was made. The press, which sympathized with him, gave enthusiastic accounts of it. It is certain that it inaugurated a new political era in Illinois. A few days after, Mr. Douglas spoke again in Peoria, and Mr. Lincoln followed him with much the same effect. This speech was reported. Mr. Douglas retired, and they held no more debates that season. But a mighty wave of thought and emotion was started among the people which would not stop.

On May 29, 1856, a convention was held at Bloomington, Illinois, of all men in the state opposed to the democratic party. Mr. Lincoln was present, and made a most powerful speech. One biographer says of it: "Never was an audience more completely electrified by human eloquence. Again and again during its delivery they sprang to their feet and upon the benches, and testified by long continued shouts and the waving of hats how deeply the speaker had wrought upon their minds and hearts. It fused the mass of hitherto incongruous elements into perfect homogeneity; and from that day to the present they have worked together in fraternal union." The republican party was there organized in Illinois. It sent delegates to the next national convention with Mr. Lincoln's name as a candidate for the vice-presidency. But Mr. Dayton was nominated with Mr. John C. Fremont, and Mr. Lincoln was only thus formally introduced to the nation.

The Kansas-Nebraska excitement grew rapidly. Mr. Lincoln, like all northern men of his opinions and character, grew more and more resolute in the republican doctrine to stop the spread of slavery, and lead it into its present constitutional localities. And with this resolution grew a stronger and stronger opposition to slavery itself.

## THE GREAT DEBATE.

In 1858 began the celebrated campaign for the United States senatorship between Mr. Douglas and Mr. Lincoln. Mr. Lincoln began his discussion of the great subject then before the country in June, at the state republican convention in Springfield, with the following almost prophetic opening:

"If we could first know where we are, and whither we are tending, we could better judge what to do and how to do it. We are now far into the fifth year since a policy was initiated with the avowed object and confident promise of putting an end to slavery agitation. Under the operation of that policy that agitation has not only not ceased, but has constantly augmented. In my opinion, it will not cease until a crisis shall have been reached and passed. 'A house divided against itself cannot stand.' I believe this government cannot endure permanently half slave and half free. I do not expect the Union to be dissolved. I do not expect the house to fall, but I do expect it will cease to be divided. It will become all one thing, or all the other. Either the opponents of slavery will arrest the further spread of it, and place it where the public mind shall rest in the belief that it is in the course of ultimate extinction, or its advocates will push it forward till it shall become alike lawful in all the states, old as well as new, north as well as south."

The speech went on to show what the advocates of slavery, then in charge of the government, had done to open the territories to slavery, to prevent them from rejecting slavery; to carry slaves into the free states, and what they were preparing to do, to open the way to force slavery, by a Supreme Court decision into the free states. But this result must be prevented, he contended, by putting the government into new hands which would put it back into its original condition in which it should move toward the ultimate extinction of slavery. He closed in these words: "We shall not fail—if we stand firm, we *shall not fail*. Wise counsels may accelerate or mistakes delay it, but sooner or later, the victory is sure to come."

He made two or three other speeches, and Mr. Douglas made some, to one or two of which he replied, when he made a proposition to Mr. Douglas to canvass the state together. But Mr. Douglas objected on the ground that his arrangements were too far made, but proposed to join with him in a discussion at seven places in different parts of the states. This arrangement was made and these discussions were held, awakening an immense interest among the people, not only of Illinois, but of the whole country. The great issue of that time was laid bare before the people. The discussion went over the whole country as a republican campaign document, and was read and talked of till the whole reading north became acquainted with the issue as there presented.

Mr. Lincoln lost the election to the Senate, but he gained the ear and confidence of the republican north. The discussion consolidated the republican party, intensified the northern opposition to slavery, and still more the opposition to the party in power which was using all its energy to carry out the grasping purposes of a few radical pro-slavery leaders. The ultimate result of the discussion was that Mr. Lincoln won the presidency, the destruction of slavery, a country all free, and a martyrdom that put his name where it stands among the "immortal few that were not born to die."

In 1859, at the republican state convention at Decatur, two rails from a lot of three thousand which Mr. Lincoln had made when he first came to the state, were brought into the convention where he was soon to speak, considerably ornamented, and bearing this inscription: "Abraham Lincoln, the 'rail-splitter,' candidate for the presidency in 1860."

During the latter part of 1859 and the early part of 1860, Mr. Lincoln traveled into Kansas, Ohio, New York and New England. His visit in Kansas was an ovation. The people knew they had a friend in this great-hearted man, and they came in immense throngs to see and hear him. They knew him, his principles and power, already, by reading his discussions, and they wanted to look at his person and hear his voice. In Ohio he found a hearty reception, and his speeches kindled the usual enthusiasm. He went on to New York, under an arrangement with Reverend Henry Ward Beecher, to speak in Plymouth church. He heard Mr. Beecher, which was a great pleasure to him; but found that arrangements had been made for him to speak in Cooper Institute. He was anxious about his speech. He knew his lack of polish; his crude appearance; his want of education; now to come before the educated, polished and strong men of this great city, was a trial to his courage. The great hall was packed with brains, culture, worth. The magnates covered the platform. William Cullen Bryant, whose poems he had read and admired, introduced him. As he rose and stood in his great height, six feet and four inches, in that dazzling throng, he was bewildered. What business had he, a poor, awkward, uneducated man of the wild west, to stand there and expect to be heard with patience? He was embarrassed and humiliated; but he had something to say, and he must say it. He began with a low voice and a slow utterance. He laid down his iniatory propositions with great deliberation. The great audience listened with breathless attention. It was something new, a new man, manner and statement; it was clear, convincing, brilliant. He had got but little way on in his terse and strong work, before a vigorous round of applause assured him that he was understood and appreciated. He now began to be at home; his manner became more free and confident; his voice filled and yielded readily to the sentiment. He became master of the situation, and went through to the close carrying his great audience with him in rapturous admiration of his argument, rhetoric and unique and wonderful illustration. The whole performance was so original, incisive, marrow-searching and powerful that it became the great political and literary feast of the season. The papers spread it and eulogized it; the people read it and talked about it. The writer of this sketch well remembers the enthusiasm he felt in reading the speech, and in the conviction that a great and brilliant star had risen in the political firmament.

Mr. Lincoln made many valuable acquaintances in New York, who served him and the country well in his time of sore need.

He had a son in Harvard college whom he went to see; and while there he made speeches in different places, always with similar results. It was a study to him to know why educated New York and New England so readily accepted and enjoyed his humble efforts at public speaking; why college presidents and professors came to hear him and set him before their students as an example in many particulars. Perhaps never in his life had he been more appreciated than in the speeches made on this eastern trip. They were the best he had ever made. He was really all the while improving. They told mightily for his future and for his country. His manner of treating the southern people in these speeches was very acceptable to the people of the north. He was fair, candid, kind — even affectionate toward them. He was southern born; his wife was southern born and reared. His heart was large, and he really loved everybody. This good nature so pervaded his speeches that they won upon the public. Then they were intensely logical and searching. They went to the roots of right and wrong; they magnified just principles; loved freedom and hated slavery; they were put in simple but choice language; they were full of nut-shell statements of important facts and principles; and, beyond all this, they were unique in their quaint and crystaline originality.

## THE COMING STORM.

During all this great discussion, which was getting more and more intense and thorough, there were constant threats of secession and disunion from the southern leaders. The northern people were but little moved by these threats. They counted them as the bravado of the fire-eating radicals in which the solid southern people took little part. They believed the *people* of the south loved the union and would stand by it. They could see nothing but disaster and wretchedness to the south in any attempt to be separate from the north, peaceably or otherwise. The north had numbers, wealth, mechanism, skill, productive ability, a laborious people, who had never been found wanting in patriotism far surpassing the south; and the people of the north could not believe the people of the south would be so unwise as to deliberately commit themselves to the folly of secession—to their own certain ruin. Moreover, they thought the people of the south wanted to maintain slavery, which they would be sure to lose if they attempted disunion.

In April of this year, 1860, the national democratic convention met in Charleston, South Carolina, only to fail to nominate Mr. Douglas, or any other man. It adjourned till June to meet in Baltimore. In the meantime the radical southern element nominated John C. Breckenridge, of Kentucky, and the constitutional union element nominated John Bell, of Tennessee. The regular convention at Baltimore nominated Mr. Douglas. This break-up forced by the southern radicals made sure the election of the republican nominee. The republican convention met in Chicago, June 16, a very large and enthusiastic convention. William H. Seward and Mr. Lincoln were the leading candidates. On the third ballot Mr. Lincoln was nominated. So it turned out that Mr. Douglas and Mr. Lincoln ran for the presidency at the same time, the one the leader of a broken and discordant party, the other of an enthusiastic and united host.

Mr. Lincoln soon began to realize both the pleasures and annoyances of his candidacy. Friends came from everywhere to see him. Nobody seemed to have so many friends as he. He had to abandon all attempts to see them at his house, and resort to the executive chamber of the state house. It seemed sure to his great party, now full of enthusiasm for its principles, that he would be elected, and office-seekers became abundant. That which began as a pleasure soon began to have its vexations. He accepted the nomination in humiliation. He had always distrusted his own capacities, and this feeling of incompetency often overwhelmed him. He was intensely honest and earnest in his republican principles. They had come to be his religion.

He felt that a crisis had come to his country when the spread of slavery must be stopped, or the foul leprosy would spread over the whole country and the republic would become a slavocracy more unendurable than any monarchy. In one of his anxious, desponding moods, he one evening asked Mr. Newton Bateman, superintendent of public instruction, whose office opened into the executive chamber, to come in. He locked the doors and they sat down and talked. Mr. Lincoln had done this to unbosom himself to his friend. He took a little book from his drawer containing the names of all the voters of Springfield and how they would vote. They ran them over together. He was particular to note the names of the ministers and leading churchmen. At length he said in great sadness: "Here are twenty-three ministers, of different denominations, and all of them are against me but three; and here are a great many prominent members of the churches, a very large majority of whom are against me. Mr. Bateman, I am not a Christian — God knows I would be one — but I have carefully read the bible and I do not understand this book," and he drew from his bosom a pocket New Testament. "These men well know," he continued, "that I am for freedom in the territories, freedom everywhere as far as the constitution and laws will permit, and that my opponents are for slavery. They know this, and yet with this book in their hands, in the light of which human bondage cannot live a moment, they are going to vote against me. I do not understand it at all."

Here he stopped, overcome with emotion. Then he walked the room, seeking to regain self-possession. At length, his cheeks wet with tears, he said, with a slow, tremulous voice: "I know there is a God, and that he hates injustice and slavery. I see the storm coming, and I know that his hand is in it. If he has a place and work for me, and I think he has, I believe I am ready. I am nothing, but truth is everything. I know I am right, for Christ teaches it, and Christ is God. I have told them that a house divided against itself cannot stand, and Christ and reason say the same; and they will find it so. Douglas don't care whether slavery is voted up or voted down, but God cares, and humanity cares, and I care; and with God's help I shall not fail. I may not see the end, but it will come, and I shall be vindicated, and these men will find that they have not read their bibles aright."

In saying this his manner was indescribably solemn. After a little silence he resumed: "Doesn't it appear strange that men can ignore the moral aspects of this contest? Revelation could not make it plainer to me that slavery or the government must be destroyed. The future would be something awful, as I look at it, but for this rock on which I stand [the New Testament, which he still held in his hand], especially with the knowledge of how these ministers are going to vote. It seems as if God had borne with this thing [slavery] until the very teachers of religion have come to defend it from the bible [quite common in the south], and to claim for it a divine character and sanction; and now the cup of iniquity is full, and the vials of wrath will be poured out."

It was not often that Mr. Lincoln so revealed his inner self; but Doctor Bateman was his intimate friend, whose excellent christian character he profoundly respected. This conversation reveals one of the secrets of Mr. Lincoln's power with the people. He was profoundly confident of being on God's side in these great matters of slavery and the existence of the republic. Mr. Lincoln lived two lives, one a profoundly thoughtful and religious one, the other an outward, jocose one. Few saw much of his inward life, though his great speeches gave enough of its flavor to win and carry all true souls who heard or read them.

But the great canvass moved on. The votes of the nation were cast and counted. Mr. Lincoln was elected. The friends of equality and liberty were jubilant. The friends of slavery were sullen and threatening.

At once secession began to be prepared for. South Carolina, the hot-bed of nullification under Calhoun, was now the breeding place of secession. On the tenth of November, 1860, four days after Mr. Lincoln's election, a bill was introduced in its legislature calling out ten thousand volunteers. On the tenth and eleventh of December, its senators in Congress resigned. A convention was called on the seventeenth, and on the twentieth South Carolina seceded, and arranged for a convention of seceding states at Montgomery.

On the tenth of December the United States secretary of the treasury, Howell Cobb, resigned. On the eighteenth, Floyd, the secretary of war, accepted a requisition from South Carolina for her share of United States arms for 1861. Meetings were held all over the south to prepare for secession. On the eighth of January, 1861, a caucus of southern senators at Washington counseled immediate secession. Soon Mississippi, Florida, Alabama, Georgia, Louisiana and Texas, accepted the counsel. Forts, and arsenals and arms were seized in all these states. In Mr. Buchanan's cabinet the southern secretaries boldly demanded the giving up to South Carolina the forts at Charleston. Edwin M. Stanton, attorney-general, told Mr. Buchanan he had no right to do it; that it would be treason to the United States. Buchanan's government was full of treason; Washington was a hot-bed of treason. All through the north were sympathizers with southern traitors who had done much to mislead them concerning the true public sentiment of the north. Madness and wickedness ruled the hour. Secession and the Southern Confederacy became accomplished facts under Mr. Buchanan, and by the aid of his partisans in the north. The whole south was seething with disloyalty and secession. Never were so many well-meaning people blindly led into ruin by fire-eating and selfish leaders. Virtue had set down in the lap of vice; the milk of human kindness had soured in christian bosoms; wisdom had lost its brains, and patriotism its heart, all over the volcanic secession realm.

On the eleventh of February Mr. Lincoln started for Washington. At the depot he made this farewell address to his neighbors: "My friends, no one not in my position can appreciate the sadness that I feel at this parting. To this people I owe all that I am. Here I have lived for more than a quarter of a century. Here my children were born, and here one of them lies buried. I know not how soon I shall see you again.

A duty devolves upon me which is greater, perhaps, than that which has devolved upon any other man since the days of Washington. He never would have succeeded except for the aid of divine providence, upon which he at all times relied. I feel that I cannot succeed without the same divine aid which sustained him, and on the same Almighty Being I place my reliance for support, and I hope you, my friends, will pray that I may receive that divine assistance without which I cannot succeed, but with which success is certain. I bid you all an affectionate farewell."

All the cities through which he passed, gave him great receptions. When he reached Philadelphia the plot against his life had become well understood, by the detective who for many days had been in search of it, and it was arranged that he should go to Washington in a sleeping car some two or three days before his family and traveling friends, which he did in quiet and safety. It was not true as reported, that he went concealed in a cloak and Scotch cap.

He went where he was not wanted; probably four out of every five persons in Washington, wishing he could not get there.

### MR. LINCOLN PRESIDENT.

On the fourth of March, 1861, Mr. Lincoln was inaugurated president. His inaugural address was conciliatory and assuring to the south. Had it been well read and considered in the south, there would have been no more trouble. It was rational, constitutional, humane, patriotic.

He appointed William H. Seward, his great republican competitor, as his secretary. Other great men were put into his cabinet. He acted with the greatest prudence and conciliation. Only seven states had declared for secession. It would be impossible for them to run a government unless more joined them. There were fifteen slave states. It was his policy to save the other eight slave states to the union if possible. All his earlier efforts were made to retain the border states. There was great wisdom in this. It kept the war, when it came, mainly in the slave states. It was his effort, also, to do nothing which the red-hot seceders could construe into an act of war. He repaired forts, furnished arms, and put defenses in order with the utmost quiet. In every way he dealt patiently and tenderly with the eratic sisters. But when the suppressed secession rage could be no longer restrained, it burst out, in the onslaught upon Fort Sumpter. Now, war was begun by the seceders; and the poor, misled people of the south shouted for joy. How little they knew what they were doing. They had followed their blind leaders to an awful precipice, and now were clamorous to jump off. That cannon boom which so elated the south, filled the north with inexpressible sorrow. In that sorrow was pity for the misled southern people, patriotism for their endangered country, and indignation for the traitor leaders.

At once the thinking and loyal people of the north felt sure, that the first ball that struck Fort Sumpter, struck with a greater force the chain of the slave. Many in the north welcomed it as the quickest way out of the slavery iniquity; yet with a great pain they turned away from their peaceful employments to go south and punish the traitors for their treason. In the north there were two great ruling ideas,— we will save the country and destroy slavery. Yet always there was a good feeling for the southern people. Mr. Lincoln soon found that the ears abroad had been tampered with; that Mr. Buchanan's foreign ministers had poisoned public sentiment abroad and secured southern sympathy almost everywhere. He found, too, that the northern forts and arsenals had been robbed of arms and ammunitions, which had been carried south; that President Buchanan's administration, had in many ways been an administration of secession and rebellion.

All these things taught Mr. Lincoln to move with prudence, and to move very slowly,— to wait till the people could learn all the facts and become thoroughly united and aroused in their opposition to rebellion. Many of his friends found fault with him for his good nature toward the south; and for his tardy and weak movements in resisting rebellion.

At half-past four o'clock A.M., April 12, 1861, the rebel batteries opened on Fort Sumpter. April 15, Mr. Lincoln issued his call for seventy-five thousand men. The writer of this sketch was then pastor of a church in Lawrence, Massachusetts. The sixth regiment of the Massachusetts militia had its headquarters there, though some of its companies were in towns twenty miles away. Colonel Watson, who commanded it, received the call for his regiment at five o'clock P.M. The next morning at 7:30 o'clock the whole regiment were at the depot at Lawrence, and took the cars for Washington. Its way to Washington was an ovation, except at Baltimore, where it was met by a rebel mob and four of its members killed. The first to fall was Sumner H. Needham, a member of the writer's congregation. His body was sent back, and early the next week the first funeral services occasioned by the war were held in his honor, his pastor preaching the sermon, and the other clergymen of the city taking part in the services. The text was from Heb. xi., 4, "He being dead yet speaketh." "He speaks," said his pastor, "from that scene of conflict with a silent yet terrible eloquence which is heard all over our great country, and which stirs the moral indignation of twenty millions of freemen at home and ten times that number abroad. That blow that broke in upon his brain struck upon the conscience of a nation. That wound has a tongue speaking with a trumpet of thunder among the northern hills and on the western prairies." And it did speak, and freemen answered in quick response to the full number of the call.

The others who fell in Baltimore were Charles A. Taylor, a stranger, who enlisted in Boston; Luther C. Ladd and Addison O. Whiting, of Lowell, Massachusetts.

The spirit of this regiment was the spirit of the north. The death of these men was the death of four brothers, which called the whole family to sorrow and self-defense.

The night before Mr. Lincoln made this call, Mr. Douglas, at the instance of Mr. Ashman, of Massachusetts, seconded by Mrs. Douglas, called upon Mr. Lincoln and assured him of his sympathy and coöperation. Mr. Lincoln read him the call, which he had just written. He approved it heartily, only he said it should be for two hundred thousand instead of seventy-five thousand. The next morning a dispatch went with the call assuring the country of Mr. Douglas' approval. Thence onward till Mr. Douglas' death he coöperated with Mr. Lincoln.

On the seventeenth of April Virginia seceded. North Carolina, Tennessee and Arkansas soon followed.

In July the battle of Bull Run was fought, which proved a rout of the Union army, and was misleading to the rebels in suggesting to them that they had not an equal foe in the soldiers of the north. This mistake led ultimately to a more complete destruction of the south, as it continued the war so long. Over confidence was the weakness of the rebel cause in the beginning. It held them to their evil work till the south was a wreck, while the north was steadily growing in numbers and wealth.

An extra session of Congress was called, and the president was authorized to call out half a million of soldiers and use five hundred millions of dollars. This meant the preservation of the Union.

The first thing the north had to do was to organize and drill its army. It was nearly two years before this was completely done. Many officers had to be tested. During this period many reverses came to the Union cause. But all the time Mr. Lincoln was growing in public estimation and endearing himself to the people as the preserver of that country of which Washington was the father. And all the time the patriotism of the loyal people was developing into a great and permanent passion, which was willing to make all sacrifices for the national honor and cause.

During this most trying time of the war, France and England, to their great disgrace, gave sympathy and aid to the rebellion and the war for slavery. It was a wicked and cruel support of barbarity and crime, done in the greed of gain and the desire to see the United States broken to pieces in the hope that they might gather up the fragments. Slow will the people of the north be to forget this cruel affiliation with rebellion and repudiation of all just principles of inter-national honor and fraternity.

Through all the earlier period of the war, Mr. Lincoln took

all possible pains to express his kindly feeling to the people of the south, and that he had no purpose of destroying slavery if it could be avoided. He had taken his oath to maintain the constitution. If it could be done, he was resolved on doing it. If the constitution could not be preserved, then he would let that go and save the nation.

Many of his friends were greatly tried that he would make no movement against slavery. It was quite a common feeling among them that it was impossible to preserve the Union and slavery. The old abolitionists did not think it desirable to preserve the Union with slavery in it. Many sympathized with them. But Mr. Lincoln had studied prayerfully his duty as a president sworn to obey the constitution. His conclusion was, that as a military necessity and a last resort, he could and must destroy slavery. So he said in a letter to a friend: "When early in the war General Fremont attempted military emancipation, I forbade it because I did not then think it an indispensable necessity. When, a little later, General Cameron, then secretary of war, suggested the arming of the blacks, I objected because I did not then think it an indispensable necessity. When, a little later, General Hunter attempted military emancipation, I again forbade it, because I did not yet think the indispensable necessity had come. When in March and May and July, 1862, I made earnest and successive appeals to the border states to favor compensated emancipation, I believed the indispensable necessity for military emancipation and arming the blacks would come unless averted by that measure. They declined the proposition; and I was, in my best judgment, driven to the alternative of either surrendering the Union, and with it the constitution, or of laying a strong hand upon the colored element. I chose the latter."

When urged to emancipate the slaves, by a body of clergymen, he said: "Whatever shall appear to be God's will I will do."

In the middle of the summer of 1862, when things appeared to be going badly enough, he concluded that he must "change his tactics or lose his game." So he set about preparing an emancipation proclamation. About the first of August, he called a cabinet meeting. None knew what they came for. He told them that he had called them to read to them a proclamation he had resolved to make, and ask them to criticise it. Mr. Chase "wished the language were stronger." Mr. Blair deprecated the policy. Mr. Seward approved, but did not think this the opportune time, and gave his reasons. So it waited yet longer. Before they separated, he said in a low, solemn voice. "I have promised my God that I will do it." Mr. Chase, who was near him, asked if he understood him. He replied, "I made a solemn vow before God, that if General Lee should be driven back from Pennsylvania, I would crown the result by a declaration of freedom to the slaves."

So September 22, 1862, the proclamation was issued, to take effect January 1, 1863. After it was done he said: "What I did, I did after a very full deliberation, and under a heavy and solemn sense of responsibility. I can only trust in God I have made no mistake." Two years later, he said: "As affairs have turned, it is the central act of my administration, and the great event of the nineteenth century."

After this proclamation, the cause of the Union began to mend. Within a year a hundred thousand colored men were openly allied with the army and the cause, and over half of them carrying muskets. Victory became assured; it was only a question of time. Money and men, and ability and loyalty in the leaders and commanders, were now abundant.

In due time Mr. Lincoln was re-elected, and from that time on the tide of sentiment and events was more and more assured in his behalf. The war became a succession of triumphant victories. At his recommendation, Congress passed an amendment to the constitution abolishing slavery in the United States. His great generals, Grant, Sherman and Sheridan, now had everything well in hand. The surrender of General Lee soon followed, which put an end to the great rebellion.

But in this giddy moment of glory, when the whole loyal north were praising him, he was stealthily approached by John Wilkes Booth, at a theatre, where he had gone with his family, to forget for an hour his burdening cares, and shot in the back and side of his head. It was a fatal wound. He lived in a state of unconsciousness till morning, and at twenty-two minutes past seven o'clock, April 15, 1865, breathed his last.

The nation which yesterday was jubilant with an abounding joy, was now in tears. Oh that terrible day! How our lips were struck dumb, and our hearts were palsied! Never such a day in America! So the rebellion ended in the martyrdom of the grandest soul of the nation he had saved. How he loved his country and kind! How he loved the people of the south who would not then accept his love, but have since learned that it was sincere, wise and noble. What blessings have come to his country and to humanity and especially to the redeemed south, by his great, honest, hearty life!

## The Grave of Abraham Lincoln.

What was mortal of the great and good martyr president rests in Oak Ridge cemetery, Springfield, Illinois, about two miles out from the city. The tomb in which his body reposes is in the base of the National Lincoln monument, which is one of the finest in this country. The base on which the obelisk rests is seventy-two feet six inches square, with a projection in front and rear for the catacomb and memorial hall, making a length of one hundred and nineteen feet, six inches. The height of the base from the terrace at the bottom, is fifteen feet and ten inches. Around the top of the base is a rich, strong railing. A finely wrought pedestal, twenty-eight feet four inches across, with four elegant pieces of bronze statuary at the corners, sustains the obelisk. The obelisk is square, eighty-two feet and six inches high from the base. The statue of Lincoln stands in front of the obelisk on a separate pedestal, and is eleven feet in height, and stands thirty-five feet and six inches above the terrace. The whole height from the terrace to the apex of the obelisk is ninety-eight feet and four and a half inches. The statue holds in its right hand an open scroll representing the

Proclamation of Emancipation. The whole cost of the monument, statuary, statue and coat of arms, was two hundred and six thousand five hundred and fifty dollars. It is a fitting monument to the great emancipator.

The tomb is in the catacomb which is in the front projection of the base. The body is enclosed in an air-tight lead case. This is in a sarcophagus; and this in a strong vault. An attempt was made some years ago to disturb, perhaps to steal, the body of the martyred president. When it was discovered, an end of the sarcophagus had been broken off and an opening made in to the lead coffin, but being discovered before any further damage was done, the broken place was repaired, further securities adopted, and greater precautions instituted, so that no further attempts have been made upon the security and sacredness of the place.

Under the pedestal on which the statue of the president stands, is the simple inscription:

### Lincoln.

Around the large pedestal that sustains the obelisk, on small shield-like projections, are the abreviations of the several states. The top of the base and the platform around the pedestal of the obelisk is reached by two flights of steps of twenty-four steps each, with heavy railings and pilasters. These are on either side of the catecomb. It must be seen to be appreciated.

ENGRAVED EXPRESSLY FOR WEAVERS "LIVES AND GRAVES OF OUR PRESIDENTS"

# CHAPTER XVIII.

## ANDREW JOHNSON.

### SEVENTEENTH PRESIDENT OF THE UNITED STATES.

#### ANCESTRY.

IN attempting to write of the ancestry of Andrew Johnson, we are met at once by that sadly expressive term, "poor whites," so common and so well understood in the old days of the south. Poor indeed was his father, Jacob Johnson, whose employments were city constable, sexton and porter of a bank. He lost his life in attempting to save a man from drowning in 1812. But this humble origin is no discredit to him in American society, while the fact that he was born at the bottom and rose by his own force to the top, is one of the common things that glorifies our political institutions. Such instances as Jackson, Johnson, Lincoln, Garfield, no American recurs to but with pride. In no other country in the world can they so often occur. Parents are often best known by their children, and we may reasonably infer from these men the qualities and powers which existed in their ancestry unseen. Beneath common soils there are often precious ores.

#### CHILDHOOD AND YOUTH.

Andrew Johnson was born in Raleigh, North Carolina, December 29, 1808. His father died when he was four years old. His childhood was subject to the hardships of the poor and fatherless in that section of the country. How he got up to ten years old his biographers do not say, but we must suppose that such a mother as Andrew Johnson must have had, found a way to care for him. At that age he was put to service with a tailor by the name of Shelby. While at work in this man's shop learning his trade, a neighbor who was fond of reading used to go in and read to the workmen from the "American Speaker." Andrew was an interested listener. That book became to him a wonder. He craved it for his own, but he knew it would reveal none of its secrets to him till he should learn to read. So he at once set about learning his letters, and then to spell and read. He became an industrious student in all his odd hours from work. He had an object to study for—to read that book for himself, and as soon as he could read, became an earnest reader of such books as he could get.

When he was about sixteen years old he got into trouble by throwing stones at an old woman's house, and started at once for unknown parts. He found his way to Laurens Court House, South Carolina, where he procured work at his trade. Two years after he returned to Raleigh, and learned that Mr. Shelby had moved twenty miles into the country. On foot he sought and found him. He made all due apologies for his unceremonious departure two years before, and desired to go to work again for Mr. Shelby. But he demanded security for his faithfulness, which Andrew could not give, and so, heavy-hearted, he had to look the world in the face, which had no home and but little encouragement for him.

In September, 1826, he went to Tennessee and took his mother with him. He found work at Greenville. During his first year there, with the courage of youth he took a wife to help him enjoy his poverty. Having married, he went west to find a place to make his fortune. After a fruitless search of several months, he returned to Greenville and went to work at his trade.

He was fortunate in his marriage in this, that he found a teacher in his wife of whom he was glad to learn. The difference between him and most men is that they accept with ill grace the good lessons of their wives, while he gladly and teachably learned of his really wiser and "better half." She was a fair scholar and taught him writing and arithmetic, and stimulated him to the acquisition of further knowledge.

### EARLY MANHOOD.

Mr. Johnson's studious habits soon gave him information and mental activity above his associates, and began to make him conspicuous as a leader of opinions and in conversation. He began to be a center around which clustered his class. He had a turn for politics in a local way, and organized a workingmen's party in opposition to the aristocratic element which, in the main, managed the politics in those parts. His new party elected him an alderman. He was re-elected for two successive years; and the next year was elected mayor. During these years he was active in a debating society composed of the young men of the place and college. One of the students of the college at that time later in life described his house as being in the outskirts of the village, about ten feet square, with a tailor's bench in one corner, and with but little furniture. The students often called to see him, because he welcomed them with heartiness and entertained them with his spirited conversation. Probably on account of his influence with the students he was appointed by the court a trustee of the Rhea academy. About this time he was active in behalf of a new constitution for the state.

In the summer of 1835 he offered himself a candidate for the lower house of the legislature, and took the field for his own election, claiming to be a democrat. At first he was coolly received by the leaders, but he made his canvass so intelligent and vigorous that he not only won his way to their confidence, but to an election. At ten he could not read; at twenty could read only; at twenty-one he married and began to learn writing and arithmetic; at twenty-seven he was a member of the state legislature, and yet earned his living all this time on the tailor's bench.

### JOHNSON A LEGISLATOR.

Mr. Johnson took his seat as a legislator, and very soon made himself conspicuous as a resolute opponent of the principal measure of the session, which was a plan to institute a system of internal improvement in the way of road making and macadamizing, which was to involve the state in a debt of four millions of dollars. He predicted disaster to the scheme if it was attempted. The plan was adopted and all the disasters came, with but little benefit. In 1839, he was re-elected to the legislature. In 1840, he took an active part in the canvass for Van Buren, making speeches in all parts of the state. He was made elector at large and voted for Van Buren. In 1841, he was elected to the State Senate, into which he introduced measures for a number of moderate improvements in the eastern part of the state.

In 1843, he was elected to the Lower House of Congress, and held his place by successive re-elections for ten years. He was elected as a democrat, and sustained in the main, the measures of the democrats during that time. He at length became a slave holder, though he thought slavery would ultimately be abolished. Though reared in poverty, he seemed to have no strong repugnance to slavery, or strong convictions against it. When the rebellion broke out and he took the Union side, the confederates confiscated his seven or eight slaves. He had but a superficial view of slavery, as he had of politics generally. He was essentially a southern man, with southern principles, till he declared for the Union. He had gratitude enough to realize what the Union had done for him, and to be faithful to it.

In 1848, he made an elaborate argument in favor of the veto power.

In 1853, he was elected governor of Tennessee; and at the next election re-elected. The excitement at these elections was great, and his life was threatened. He spoke sometimes with a revolver on the table and his hand on it. On one occasion he proposed that those who had threatened should do the shooting first. As nobody shot, he proceeded.

In December, 1857, he took his seat in the Senate of the United States, to which he had been elected by his state legislature. In the Senate his course was much as it had been in the House—democratic, southern. In the House he had made himself conspicuous by advocating a homestead bill giving one hundred and sixty acres of the public lands to actual settlers thereon. He took up this again in the Senate and carried it through, only to have it defeated by President Buchanan. In this he acted out of his better nature, and not in sympathy with the pro-slavery policy of his party.

He fought vigorously for economy in the management of the national finances, and opposed the Pacific railroad scheme. He opposed the compromise measures of 1850, yet voted for them in the end.

In the Charleston-Baltimore convention of 1860 he was proposed by the Tennessee delegation as a candidate for the presidency. In the contest which followed with four candidates he sustained Breckenridge, the extreme southern candidate. His associates had, in the main, been with the radical pro-slavery men. He was trained in their school; bought slaves to be one of them; desired to nationalize slavery, and hated black republicanism. Such moral notions as he had were based in the pro-slavery code; and when the question of secession came, he maintained the Union, largely on the ground that the battle for slavery could best be fought, as he said, "under the battlements of the constitution." He presented strongly the right of the Union to New Mexico, Texas, Louisiana and Florida and the great river courses of the west, by purchase and conquest. He said: "I am opposed to secession. I believe it no remedy for the evils complained of. Instead of acting with that division of my southern friends who take ground for secession, I shall take other grounds, *while I try to accomplish the same end.* I think that this battle ought to be fought, not outside, but inside, the Union." Being of them, and because he would not go out with them, the secessionists made war upon him, burned him in effigy, insulted him with mobs, threatened him with lynching, sacked his home, drove his sick wife and children into the streets, stole his slaves, which he called property, and turned his house into a receptacle for secession soldiery. But all this only made him more resolute for the Union, and he took the high ground that secession was treason. He said in the Senate, March 2, 1861: "Were I the president of the United States, I would do as Thomas Jefferson did in 1806 with Aaron Burr: I would have them arrested and try them for treason, and if convicted, by the eternal God, they should suffer the penalty of the law at the hands of the executioner! Sir, treason must be punished. Its enormity and the extent and depth of the offense must be made known." In a speech at Cincinnati he said: "I repeat, this odious doctrine of secession should be crushed out, destroyed and totally annihilated. No government can stand, no religious, or moral, or social organization can stand, where this doctrine is tolerated. It is disintegration; it is universal dissolution."

### MILITARY GOVERNOR.

In February, 1862, the Union forces got possession of the middle and western portion of Tennessee, and President Lincoln appointed Mr. Johnson military governor of the state. He had twice before been civil governor of the state, now he was governor by a northern appointment, the most offensive that could be, to the secession portion of the south. A great deal was said about a "solid south," but probably there never was a solid south. Many were always Union people, and were taken out against their wills. No doubt many loyal Tennesseeans welcomed their old governor, as a representative of the Union. He held a difficult post of duty with great resolution, often terribly tried by halting, and half Union men and fierce rebels. His headquarters were at Nashville, which was for a considerable time under seige and doubtful of the result. He had difficulties with the civil authorities, some of whom he had to displace and put in others; difficulties with Union generals, who seemed to him half-hearted in their work; difficulties with the rebel and half Union citizens: but they all tended to carry him in sympathy and opinion nearer to Mr. Lincoln, and separate him more and more from his old opinions and life. Slavery began to look like an abominable thing.

In the Autumn of 1863, Mr. Johnson visited Washington to consult with the president about re-establishing a civil government in Tennessee. The visit brought him nearer to Mr. Lincoln and his views. It soon became apparent to him that the active Union and the republican party were identical, and so far as the broken Union was to be restored it must be done by the party in power.

His prompt and decisive treatment of the difficulties in his state won him the admiration of the loyal north, and before Mr. Lincoln's first term closed he felt himself in close sympathy with the administration.

## MR. JOHNSON VICE-PRESIDENT.

The republican convention of 1864, met in Baltimore, June 6, to nominate a president and vice-president. Mr. Lincoln was renominated without a thought of another, with Andrew Johnson for his vice-president. The sympathy which the loyal north felt for southern Unionists had much to do with this. The brave stand Mr. Johnson took for the Union and for the return of his state was regarded with great favor. His speeches, electric with patriotism, and stalwart with solid argument, were read all over the north with enthusiasm. His orders as military governor, his reorganization of a government in Tennessee, had prepared the way for his nomination. His past democracy was forgotten. By this time the Union cause was nobly sustained by multitudes of northern democrats who welcomed this nomination.

Mr. Johnson welcomed at once the inevitable result of the war, the death of slavery. He foresaw it, and all the terrible consequences of the war to the south and tried to stay it, but could not. When he found that slavery was ended he was glad, though he sorrowed over the great cost of its death.

When the news of Mr. Johnson's nomination reached Nashville, a great mass meeting was called to ratify the nomination, and Mr. Johnson was invited to address it. The speech he then made was one of the great speeches of that great period. It was a powerful presentation of the underlying principles of our government, the history of the government, the history of the rebellion, beginning in the early days of the republic, and its failure, and the permanent prospect for our institutions with slavery, their great antagonistic principle, out of the way. The enthusiasm among the people, white and black, was unbounded. Probably nothing surpassed it anywhere in the country. It was much like Patrick Henry's great speeches in the early days of the republic, in its effects. The poor colored people, when he said, "I, Andrew Johnson, do hereby proclaim freedom, full, broad and unconditional, to every man in Tennessee," gathered around him in a wild frenzy of joy, and called him their Moses. The reports of this great speech went through the country like an electric shock, and thrilled the loyal people. It gave a great impetus to the election and great expectations of him. It was the transcendent moment of his life. He was governor of the state which he had just restored to the Union; had just been nominated to the vice-presidency; three thousand people had gathered to do him honor and were electrified by his magnificent utterances, and now the grateful slaves of the state looked up to him as their deliverer.

The canvass proceeded; he was triumphantly elected, with his great leader — the savior of his country, and was inaugurated the fourth of March, 1865. The rebellion was rapidly going to pieces. General Sherman had made his great march to the sea; the Mississippi valley had been redeemed; General Grant was soon in Richmond; Petersburg was in his hands; and his army was in hot pursuit of General Lee. April 3, there was a great meeting in Washington to rejoice over the fall of Richmond and Petersburg; April 9, General Lee surrendered to General Grant; April 14, President Lincoln was shot, and died the next morning.

### MR. JOHNSON PRESIDENT.

Immediately after the death of the president, the attorney-general, Honorable James Speed, addressed a note to Vice-

President Johnson, informing him of the president's death and that the presidency now devolved upon him, signed by the members of the cabinet, except Mr. Seward, whose life had been attempted. At ten o'clock, two hours and a half after the death of the president, Chief Justice Chase administered to Mr. Johnson the oath of office.

Soon after, he was publicly inaugurated in the Senate chamber under circumstances which cast a still deeper sorrow over the afflicted country. He was just recovering from a fit of sickness, and it was feared he would be unable to go through the ceremonies of inauguration. To brace himself for the occasion he took intoxicating stimulants, and was so visibly under their influence as to shock all who were present, and bring a deeper grief to the country.

On the seventeenth he made a speech so resolute against rebellion, so loyal and promising, as to lead the people to hope for a continuance of a sound administration. But in a few days his actions were so different from what the people had been led to expect as to awaken distrust of his judgment or his loyalty. Almost the entire party which elected him soon lost confidence in him.

On May 1, he appointed a military commission for the trial of those concerned in the assassination of the president, and offered a hundred thousand dollars for the arrest of Jefferson Davis, and smaller sums for the arrest of others on the ground of complicity with the crime. May 9, he promulgated a set of rules for trade with the south, and on the twenty-fourth he removed all restrictions. On the ninth of May an order was issued for the restoration of federal relations with Virginia. On the twenty-ninth of May two proclamations were made, one establishing a provisional government in South Carolina, and the other offering a general amnesty to all persons who had been in rebellion, on condition of taking an oath of allegiance, excepting fourteen specified classes who might obtain pardon on personal application to the president. The president appointed provisional governments for the other returning states in rapid succession.

When Congress assembled in December there was soon found to be a determined opposition in that body to the president's reconstruction measures. In the judgment of Congress the returning rebels should make some proper guarantees of good faith to the government and provisions for the rights of the colored people now made free. A joint committee of fifteen was appointed, to which were referred all questions concerning the recognition of returning states. Congress passed the "civil rights bill" and one for the extension of the freedman's bureau, both of which were vetoed by the president and passed over his head. Early in 1866 the president publicly denounced Congress as in another rebellion. In June, a call for a convention to meet in Philadelphia, was issued, as it turned out, to try to organize a president's party; but nothing came of it. The members of the president's cabinet, one by one, resigned, except Edwin M. Stanton, whom the president sought to remove, but failed. The president, with several friends, went to Chicago in August to assist in laying the foundation of a monument to Stephen A. Douglas. He made speeches on the way of a strange and almost maudlin character, which many regarded as coming from an intoxicated brain. This trip he called "swinging round the circle." It was a great humiliation to a country so sensitive to the honor of its president.

In June, Congress resolved that no state should return without ratifying the fourteenth amendment. In succeeding sessions it required the elective franchise to be granted to persons in the territories without respect to color, and in the District of Columbia. All these and similar measures met the resolute opposition of President Johnson. They were passed over his vetos. He sought steadily to defeat the plans of Congress, and Congress sought to repress the influence and action of the president, regarding them as in sympathy with the pro-slavery south. Congress had passed a "tenure of office act," which required the approval of the Senate to dismiss or appoint federal officers. The president dismissed Mr. Stanton and appointed General Grant in his place as secretary of war, in the face of this Congressional requirement. Congress refused to approve his action. The president again sought his removal and appointed another man. Congress passed a resolution declaring that "the president had no power to remove the secretary of war and appoint another person to perform the duties of that office." The next day the House of Representatives resolved that the president be impeached for high crimes and misdemeanors. The impeachment movement, though carried by a large majority, failed for lack of the requisite two thirds.

At the next democratic national convention, Mr. Johnson was one of the candidates and received sixty-five votes on the first ballot.

Untoward and unhappy was the closing part of Mr. Johnson's life. As soon as the rebellion was conquered, he seemed to go back to his old sympathy with the slaveholders and the south, and to try to use the power of his high office in their behalf. The evil habit of the use of intoxicating drinks disturbed the poise of his judgement, and degraded his moral sense. He brought disgrace, at last, upon his country, after having won its highest honors. As seen to-day, it is pretty clear that he was over-estimated and over-trusted by the generosity of the loyal people. Having fine, natural powers, his lack of early education and life-long affiliation with slavery, made him unequal to the trying ordeal of the position he was called to occupy.

He died in 1875, sixty-seven years of age.

## THE GRAVE OF ANDREW JOHNSON.

The grave of President Johnson, is on a beautiful cone-shaped eminence, one half mile southwest of Greenville, Tennessee, where he had so long lived and been so much honored by the people. He selected the place for its fine outlook over the town and surrounding country. "From piers on each side of the graves where lie, side by side, the president and his wife, who survived him less than six months, springs a granite arch of thirteen stones, beneath which are the graves, covered with white pebbles." Upon this arch rests the monument. On the marble plinth four feet and a half square, and three feet and a half high, is this inscription:

> **Andrew Johnson,**
> SEVENTEENTH PRESIDENT, U. S. A.
>
> Born December 29, 1808.
> Died July 31, 1875.
> "His faith in the people never wavered."

His wife's name, the dates of her birth and death, and "In memory of father and mother," are inscribed below. The monument was erected by their three surviving children. On the die which is three feet and a half square, and three feet and two inches high, are carved a scroll of the constitution, without the fourteenth and fifteenth amendments, and an open bible on which rests a hand as in the act of taking an oath. From this die rises a tapering shaft of marble, thirteen feet high and two feet ten inches square at the base. The top is hung with the American flag and surmounted by an eagle with its wings half spread.

The graves of their two sons, Charles, a surgeon, killed by the fall of his horse at Nashville, in 1863; and Robert, colonel of a Tennessee regiment, who died in 1869, are a few feet from the graves of their parents.

The scenery as witnessed from this place is singularly picturesque, and diversified. It is a fitting place to hold the ashes of a great nation's president.

ENGRAVED EXPRESSLY FOR WEAVER'S "LIVES AND GRAVES OF OUR PRESIDENTS"

## CHAPTER XIX.

### ULYSSES S. GRANT.

#### Eighteenth President of the United States.

It is not great talents alone, nor favoring circumstances, which make men distinguished, but usually a combination of both. Many great minds pass through life in obscurity; much inestimable worth is known only to a few.

"Full many a flower is born to blush unseen
And waste its sweetness on the desert air."

There are vast amounts of unknown talent and unappreciated worth in all human society. In the dull mediocrity of common life there is much human gold, and not a few jewels of rarest water. Most men are under-valued. Most men under-value themselves. If men everywhere knew what they could be and do, and would put forth their best efforts constantly, we should live in the society of the noble and great. Nothing is so much against us as our disheartening estimate of ourselves.

The common saying that circumstances make men is only half true. Men can be great, in truth, with circumstances against them; and men can be distinguished by the favor of fortunate circumstances when they are not great.

The subject of this sketch must be classed among those who have become distinguished above their real merits by the circumstances which made the ladder on which they went up to fame.

Had it not been for the war of the rebellion, there is no probability that he would have attained the rank of an average man. His past life for several years, his apparent business incompetency, and his habits, indicated less than an average success in life. He was wasting rather than augmenting his power.

But the opening of the war opened a career to him which put him where he waked up to honor, to duty and to a great life. All credit is due him for using nobly his opportunity. His country and kind have reaped the benefit of it.

### ANCESTRY, BIRTH AND BOYHOOD.

The biographers of President Grant have generally said he was of Scotch descent. But Richard A. Wheeler, of Connecticut, claims to have traced his lineage directly to the west of England through the company of immigrants who came to Plymouth colony in 1630. Among those who came that year were Matthew and Priscilla Grant, who were then twenty-nine years old. "The west country people," as they were called in England, who came in that company, settled four miles from Boston, at Matapan, which is now Dorchester. Four years later several of these settlers went to the Connecticut valley, and among them was Matthew Grant, who had lost his wife and been left with four children. They settled at Winsdor, and much is said in the early records of the place of Matthew Grant as one of the most pious, honest and active citizens. His second son was Noah; and he had a son Noah who was active in the French and English war, in which George Washington began his career. During the war his wife died, leaving him two sons, Solomon and Peter. After a little while, with others, he went west to Westmoreland county, Pennsylvania, on the Monongahela river. Two years after, he married Rachel Kelly, a widow, by whom he had seven children. The fourth child by this marriage was Jesse Root Grant, born January 23, 1794.

April, 1799, Noah Grant and his family moved down the river and settled in Columbiana county, Ohio. He made but a short stay, but went to the Western Reserve, where many Connecticut people were settling. Jesse was ten years old. Soon after, his mother died. They settled in Portage county, near Deerfield. When Jesse was fourteen he went to Youngstown, Trumbull county, and lived with Judge Todd. Two years after, he returned to Deerfield, where he remained two years to work with a tanner and learn the trade. At eighteen he was apprenticed to a half-brother in Maysville, Kentucky. In 1815 Jesse, now twenty-one, returned to Deerfield and set up tanning business for himself in a small way. Two years later he went to Ravenna and prospered in business; but the fever and ague drove him to Maysville. He regained his health; settled in Point Pleasant, in Ohio, on the river; married Hannah Simpson on the twenty-fourth of June, 1821, and on the twenty-seventh of April, 1822, their first baby, Ulysses, came into their hands. He was named Hiram Ulysses.

Ten months after Ulysses was born the family moved to Georgetown, ten miles back from the river. Ulysses was a quiet, but not a diffident boy; was fond of sport, hunting and horses. When twelve years old he began to work with horses as a teamster in hauling lumber, logs, stone, etc., and soon showed unusual skill, for one so young. Hand work he disliked, but give him a team and he never wearied. He often took loads to Cincinnati, fifty miles away. When asked, once, "why his horses never got stalled," he replied instantly, "Because I never get stalled myself." Teaming, driving, working with horses was his favorite employment. He was shy of the tannery, but always glad to be with the team.

He went to school after he was four years old, summer and winter, and learned and recited fluently little pieces; was always ready with: "You'd scarce expect one of my age to speak in public on the stage," when his father asked for it.

After eleven he was too useful with a team to be spared for school, except three months in the winter. So his love of horses spoiled his early education. He was a sober, thoughtful boy, peaceful, helpful, showing no special talent for anything but teaming.

In school he was a little dull and slow, except in arithmetic, for which he showed more fondness.

He had two brothers and three sisters. His mother is always spoken of as a thoughtful, modest, sensitive woman, of much quiet worth, from whom he inherited the best of his characteristics. His father was a brusque, talkative, self-willed man, opinionated, dogmatic, at home with the coarser side of the world, not over-scrupulous, but self-urgent, pushing his own claims, because they seemed to him the all-important matters.

The family were brought up in the Methodist church, the mother of Ulysses being a devout and conscientious member. Some say his father was a member also. The father was a heavy, broad-shouldered, thick-necked man, with head bent forward. The dominance of the material over the mental in his make-up was strong. Ulysses inherited from him bodily form and force, self-will and material supremacy. The quiet, retiring thoughtful element of his mother, gave him a cool, modest self-poise, which was always one of the sources of his strength and success. In Ulysses there was a combination of the father and mother, but the mother prevailed. He grew up to a plain, chubby, round-faced country youth of seventeen, giving to those who knew him not the slightest glimpse of any ability to be a great leader or in any way a marked man. His characteristics as then known to his neighbors would have led them to expect from him a fair livery-stable man, rather than a military hero, or a president of the republic.

There was a military vein in the Grant family. One of the ancestors had been in the French and English war. He had often fired the younger members with his war stories. Ulysses had always evinced great interest in soldiers, trainings and musters. He hated the tannery, and when his father talked of his going to work in it, he spoke out his repugnance. "Well, what do you want to do?" the father asked. "I should like to be a farmer, or a river trader, or have an education," the boy replied.

A young man of his acquaintance had, not long before, gone to West Point. Jesse Grant had much admired some of the army men that he had known something of as military men. He was a democrat of the real Jacksonian stripe. It occurred to him to ask Ulysses how he would like to go to West Point. "First rate," was his prompt reply. Jesse knew the congressman from his district, and he at once applied for an appointment for Ulysses. The member had no vacancy in his district, but a neighbor member had, and so it was soon arranged that Jesse Grant's son should have the appointment. It was a quick, new turn of affairs in the Grant family. This silent, calm, oldest boy, that looked so little like a soldier, or anything very promising, to other eyes than his family's, must now be got ready for his cadet appointment at West Point. There was a buzz in the neighborhood. Some wise ones shook their heads. Everybody wondered. Of all the youth in the county, this was the last one the Georgetown people would have thought of for an officer to lead our armies. "Nothing against him;" but, then, "nothing of him," they thought.

Here comes in the glory of our institutions. This is the country that believes in the plain common sense and common talent of the people. Ulysses S. Grant could not have been the great man he is in any other country. The republic makes common men great when greatness is needed.

### GRANT A CADET.

The member of Congress who made the application for Ulysses, got the impression that his name was Ulysses Simpson Grant, because he knew one of the boy's names was Simpson, and so the name went upon the books at West Point in that form, and he never succeeded in getting it changed.

Before going, he took a short course of special study, by the aid of which he passed a fair examination. He went through his course at West Point respectably; averaging fair in his recitations; having a good record in deportment; awakening no suspicion of greatness to come. He was noted for calmness, fairness, for speaking without exaggeration, for being just what he seemed. He could master any studies easily, yet studied no more than was necessary for fair standing. He was not an ambitious scholar; had no craving for knowledge; yet could easily do much more than he did. In the final result of his course, he stood twenty-first in a class of thirty-five. But in one thing he surpassed all the cadets of all the classes there during his stay. That was in horsemanship. He was a graceful and skillful rider, and a master of the horses he rode. One horse, by the name of York, a tall, coarsely-made, but powerful and spirited animal, which few could ride at all, was his favorite horse. At the final examination, before the board of examiners and the great company of visitors, he appeared on York and made the celebrated leap, which stands recorded, "Grant's leap on York," six feet and some two or three inches, over a pole, the highest leap that had ever been made at the academy.

He graduated June 31, 1843.

### LIEUTENANT GRANT.

Mr. Grant was breveted at once Second-lieutenant Grant in the fourth infantry, then located at Jefferson barracks, near St. Louis. After the ninety days furlough given the cadets after their graduation. during which he visited his friends in Ohio, he repaired to his regiment. With little to do, and without studious habits, he must find some way to employ his time. The near city afforded much opportunity; but the home of his classmate's father, Colonel Frederick Dent, at Gravois creek, ten miles southwest of the city, offered special attractions. Julia Dent, three years younger than himself, with a slave waiter just her own age, so that she had nothing to do but make herself agreeable, made it exceedingly pleasant at her home for the young lieutenant. It soon became an apparent necessity for him to spend much time with the Dents.

Early in May, 1844, Lieutenant Grant visited his home in Ohio. But he had hardly got away from his barracks when his regiment received orders to start for Red river, to render assistance in the war with Mexico, just coming on. An order for him to meet his regiment at its place of destination followed him, and cut his visit short. The regiment remained there a year. In June, 1845, it moved to a point four miles below New Orleans, near the old Jackson battle ground. There it remained till August, when it went forward to Corpus Christi, Texas. In October Grant was made regular second-lieutenant. In March, 1846, the force at Corpus Christi was ordered to move forward to the Rio Grande. On the second of May it was in the battle of Palo Alto (high timber), near the Rio Grande, under General Taylor. The next day the battle of Resaca de la Palma (grove of palms) was fought. In both of these battles Grant's regiment was in active work. Nine days after, General Taylor with his force crossed the Rio Grande and took possession of Matamoras.

Grant's regiment moved on with the army and fought in the battle of Monterey. It was here where Grant did the fierce riding through shot and shell for ammunition. He had been made quartermaster; and losing several officers, he was made adjutant. Grant's regiment was in the battles of Buena Vista and Puebla. It led in the skirmishes of Contreras and San Antonio and in the battle of Cherubusco. At Chepultepec he was so conspicuous that he was breveted, then promoted to a first-lieutenancy. The army moved upon the city of Mexico and the next morning it surrendered and the war was over. It cost us twenty-five thousand men. It was some months before the army returned, but as soon as possible our lieutenant visited Miss Dent and his parents in Ohio.

### GRANT'S MARRIAGE.

On the twenty-second of August, 1848, at the Dent residence on Fourth street, St. Louis, Lieutenant Ulysses S. Grant and Miss Julia B. Dent, were married. After the visitings and pleasurings of such occasions were over, they went to the head quarters of his regiment, at Detroit. He was soon ordered to Sackett's Harbor, New York, where he and his wife spent the winter, returning to Detroit in the spring, and setting up housekeeping in such a moderate way as he was able.

In 1850, they broke up housekeeping and Mrs. Grant went to

her father. The next season the regiment was ordered to Sackett's Harbor, and the next to California. Here he was promoted to a captaincy, giving up the quarter-master's duties, which he had performed for some years. At Fort Humboldt, two hundred and forty miles north of San Francisco, where he was stationed, he found little to occupy his mind. His family was in St. Louis. He was lonely, and little interested in anything about him, and in this low state of mind he took to drink to drown his melancholy moods. At Sackett's Harbor he was a member of the Sons of Temperance and the Odd Fellows. No fraternities of this kind were here; no help from wife and children, for he now had two children, cheered him; no society guarded him. This lonely, far-off fort, offered the only enemy he did not resist with force and success. On this battlefield he was beaten. It was the misfortune of his life. It was an evil habit sooner taken on than put off. It followed him wherever he went and for some years produced failure in whatever he attempted, and put him among a class of associates and into places that did not belong to him.

Rumor came to his ears that he was likely to be displaced, or reprimanded if he did not reform; and so he at once sent in his resignation, remarking to a friend: "Whoever hears of me in ten years will hear of a well-to-do old Missouri farmer." He started at once for New York, and reaching Governors Island, forlorn and penniless; some brother officers gave him money and sympathy, both of which were equally needed now in his ill-fortune. He went to Sackett's Harbor to find the former sutler of his regiment, to whom, in the days of better fortune, he had lent sixteen hundred dollars, whom he found, but without the disposition, or the money to pay him. He returned to New York again, penniless and crest-fallen. Evil days had come upon him. He was out of the army, without employment, in disgrace and destitution. Like other prodigals, he thought of his father, and wrote to him. In answer, his brother Simpson came to his relief with the old home love, and money to take him to his wife and children, at her father's in St. Louis. After a visit there he went with his family to his father's, now at Covington,

Kentucky, where he remained for several months. He was now thirty-two years old and in this sad plight — a dependent on his and his wife's parents in consequence of his drunken habits.

### CAPTAIN GRANT A FARMER.

There seemed nothing else to be done but to go to White-haven, at Gravois (gravel) creek, ten miles out the Gravois road at St. Louis, and take up farming on sixty acres of the old Dent farm, which her father had given to Mrs. Grant. So, to her old birthplace they went, and put up a log cabin, and set up for farmers. He named the place "Hardscrabble." The writer of this sketch lived five years three miles out on the Gravios road, and often heard of "Hardscrabble" farther out, but little thought of its owner as the future president of the republic. Mrs. Grant had three or four slaves, but her husband knew little how to work them to advantage. Hauling wood to St. Louis, was an important item in the business of the new farmer. This seemed like his boyhood's employment returned under new circumstances. He drove a good team; but his evil habit, if the reports of the neighbors are reliable, drove him sometimes on his return from the city. Though it seems that he fought against this evil habit, refusing to drink with army friends, as some of them report. It was the old story, a hard fight and often worsted.

### GRANT A REAL ESTATE AGENT.

January 1, 1859, Captain Grant entered into partnership with Harry Boggs, who had married a niece of the Dent family. He rented Hardscrabble the next spring and hired a house in the city. He then sold his farm and bought in the city, but he found the scrabble quite as hard in the city as on the farm. In less than a year the firm dissolved. He then obtained a temporary position in the custom house, but in a month the collector died, and he was out again. Nothing opening, and having four children to care for, he went again to his father. His father had set up Ulysses' two brothers, Simpson and Orvill, in the tanning business, in Galena, Illinois. He referred the case of

Ulysses to them, and they proposed to give him employment at six hundred dollars a year; so, in March, 1860, he and his family went to Galena.

### GRANT A CLERK IN GALENA.

He set up housekeeping in a prudent way. His clerkship was a general one. He had not yet developed the business faculty. He was better at telling stories than making bargains. His income did not meet his expenses. Hardscrabble had come with him. His brothers raised his salary to eight hundred dollars. With this he did better, and had begun to be more hopeful of a fair living. His father had got reasonably wealthy; the brothers had a good start; he hoped for a partnership soon.

### THE OPENING REBELLION.

The presidential campaign of 1860 came on. Grant had never voted but once; that was against Fremont, and for Buchanan. He was ashamed of Buchanan. He had been a democrat in a quiet way, though his father and brothers had become enthusiastic republicans. He heard Douglas, and was dissatisfied with him. He was not a voter in Illinois, though he had began to feel much sympathy for the republicans, and when Lincoln was elected joined with his brothers in a celebration at their store.

When the war broke out he presided at the first meeting to raise a company of soldiers, yet another man was made captain. A neighbor took Elihu B. Washburne, member of Congress from that district, in to see Captain Grant. He invited him to go to Springfield with him in a few days. After much delay and confusion Governor Yates took him into his office to do the military part of the business. He soon brought order out of confusion. He was self-distrusting, and asked for no position, yet he wanted one. One of the clerks from the Galena store was one day in the Governor's office, and he asked: "What kind of a man is this Captain Grant; he seems anxious to serve, though reluctant to take any high position." The clerk replied: "The way to deal with him is to ask no questions, but order him, and he will obey." Just then a regiment from Decatur was disorderly and out with its colonel. The governor appointed Grant its colonel and ordered him at once to the command. Out of the confusion he soon brought order. In a few days Grant and his regiment were ordered to Missouri. He marched his regiment across the country for discipline.

In July Congress met. A delegation met to arrange army matters. E. B. Washburne urged Grant for a brigadier. Among some forty candidates he was the only one who received every vote.

### BRIGADIER-GENERAL GRANT.

Colonel Grant at once accepted the new position, and soon was in southern Missouri, holding in check the armed and unarmed rebels. Learning of rebels centering at Paducah, Kentucky, he proceeded, without orders, to possess the town and capture a great amount of military stores. He was thus soon in the heart of the enemy's country and in possession of this strategic point on the Ohio, and at the mouth of the Tennessee river. He soon had a staff of intelligent and patriotic men.

He was restive for action, and after too much waiting he received orders from Fremont to head off the rebels at Columbus, below Cairo, from reinforcing Price in Missouri. At once, he started a division down the west side of the Mississippi to Belmont, opposite Columbus, one down the east side in the rear of Columbus, and went himself down the river with three thousand men. At Belmont he had a sharp and victorious fight with the rebel detachment there, and returned to Cairo.

Here much delay occurred. Fremont was removed and Halleck put in his place, and army movements rested for a time. Sixty-five miles up the Tennessee was the rebel Fort Henry, and a few miles southeast on the Cumberland, Fort Donelson. Grant was anxious to capture these forts. Halleck put him off, and even censured him for interference. On the first of February, 1862, Grant received permission to proceed against Fort Henry. Commodore Foote was nearly ready, and they were soon off. The land forces left the boats three miles below the fort, to attack in the rear. The gun-boats moved up to within good firing distance, and opened upon the fort, which surrendered in an hour and a quarter, before the land forces could get into position on account of the mud.

The next move was to be on Fort Donelson, twelve miles across the country. Foote went round with his boats. Heavy rains, flooding the country, kept Grant back a few days, but he moved as soon as possible and stretched his line around the fort from the river above to the river below. Foote's boats came up but could do but little, the batteries of the fort were so high. Grant opened all around upon the rear works of the fort. The fight was a severe one, but the rebels surrendered the second morning. There were about twenty thousand soldiers on each side, the rebels thoroughly entrenched, and yet they were fought out of their entrenchments and forced to surrender.

These were two great victories, early gained. They opened the way into the very heart of the rebel territory. These movements of Grant, the only ones that had hurt the rebels much, made him famous.

But General Grant pushed forward into the rebellious regions, up the Tennessee river into the south part of the state of Tennessee, and had different parts of his army at Savannah, Shiloh and Pittsburg Landing, places only a few miles apart. The rebel generals, thinking to dash unexpectedly upon one of his divisions at a time, and destroy them by piece meal, made a forced march and attacked him at Shiloh. It was a fierce attack and a desperate battle, lasting all day Sunday, the rebels slowly gaining ground all day. In the night Grant's expected reinforcements arrived, and he opened the battle early, to become master of the field. Hardly any one battle did the rebels more harm. The battle was fought on the sixth and seventh of April, Sunday and Monday. So great was the rejoicing over this victory, won by some forty thousand of our soldiers, that President Lincoln appointed a day of thanksgiving.

But it was not without trial to General Grant. He was winning victory after victory. Some of the less fortunate generals were envious. General Halleck, his division commander, censured him for fighting without orders, and came into the field and took the command himself. Some accused him of being drunk, and slaughtering his men. This accusation often came up against him during the war, not because there was any truth in it, but because he had for a time, before the war, been subject to the drinking habit.

Halleck was slow, timid, halting; and the army did little else than use the spade for many weeks; but slowly he came to see that Grant was a winning officer, and gave him the command of West Tennessee. During the autumn he took Memphis, Jackson, La Grange, Iuka, and the regions about them. No one can read the story of that campaign without seeing that Halleck's jealousy of Grant put a stop to the victorious movements of our army in Tennessee.

But now Grant had his mind on Vicksburg, as the key to the Mississippi and the southwest. Early in 1863, he had the command of fifty thousand men, and all needful supplies. This movement upon Vicksburg was a great campaign, which many pages cannot adequately describe. It was attended with immense difficulties, which cannot be comprehended without a full geographical knowledge of the country around it. After many attempts to get below Vicksburg, on the west and east, it was at last determined to run the batteries, with gunboats, steamers, and flatboats, and march the army down on the west side of the river, recross to the east side, and fight the way back in the rear of Vicksburg on the east. In twenty days he marched two hundred miles, fought five battles, took ninety guns, and captured six thousand of the enemy, killing and wounding many more. And all this was done to get into position to fight Pemberton and his army in Vicksburg. Many of his best officers, and even Sherman, had no confidence in the success of the movement; but, when accomplished, all could see that it not only destroyed the army in Vicksburg, and took that stronghold, but conquered the supporting armies behind it, and opened all that region of country to the Union cause. The whole southwest was taken by this grand movement. On the fourth day of July, 1863, General Pemberton marched out, and gave his arms and the place to General Grant.

No words can tell the joy it gave the country. Henceforth, the complete re-establishment of the Union was only a question of time. After this, there were none to question the great military ability of General Grant, and his generous and loyal spirit. His two years of successes, without a failure, against trained generals of great ability, and as brave soldiers as ever went forth to war, put his name among the great commanders of the world. Whatever criticism may be made of him as a civilian, as a soldier he must be given a high rank.

The president, through the secretary of war, now consolidated the three western divisions of the army under General Grant, with his headquarters in the field. Chattanooga was the point he fixed on at once as his center of operation, and telegraphed to General Thomas to hold it. He telegraphed to Sherman, to Burnside, to Hooker, to reach Chattanooga with their armies as soon as possible. The rebels believed their position on Lookout Mountain impregnable. Jefferson Davis himself had visited it, and made a speech to the rebel army, there made secure.

All things being ready, on the twenty-third of November the battle opened. It lasted three days, and brought another great victory. Nothing more brilliant and satisfactory had yet been done. Grant said of it: "I presume a battle never took place on so large a scale where so much of it could be seen, or where every move proved so successful." President Lincoln thanked the commanding general and the whole army, and appointed a national thanksgiving. Halleck pronounced it "the most remarkable battle of history." The force of Grant was about sixty thousand; that of the rebel General Bragg about forty-five thousand, on chosen ground and in entrenchments and rifle-pits.

### LIEUTENANT-GENERAL GRANT.

Before Washington's death, when a war with France was anticipated, a new office was created for Washington, which would give him the command of all the armies without going into the field unless he chose. In the last days of General Scott it was revived again. After General Grant's remarkable series of successes without a failure, and his wisdom and modesty in his victories, the question of reviving the office was introduced into Congress.

Doolittle said: "General Grant has won seventeen battles, captured one hundred thousand prisoners, taken five hundred pieces of artillery and innumerable thousands of small arms on all these fields. He has organized victory from the beginning, and I want him in a position where he can organize final victory and bring it to our armies, and put an end to this rebellion."

Wilson added that "he had taken more prisoners and more cannon than ever Washington or Scott saw on all their battlefields."

A bill was passed reviving the office, and President Lincoln, who all along had held fast to Grant as the kind of man to lead our armies, appointed him to the office. This was March 9, 1864.

He immediately visited the army of the Potomac, which had so long exhibited a masterly inactivity. He recommended to the government the new policy of conducting the movements of all our armies by one plan, that of striking heavy blows everywhere at once. At once he went about arranging for it, and as soon as ready he crossed the Rapidan, Sherman and Thomas moved south, Sherman being left free to go as far and do what he pleased. Butler moved up the James, Sigel up the Shenandoah, Averill forward in West Virginia, Banks up the Red river and into Texas, McPherson into Mississippi. There was a simultaneous "forward, march." It busied every department of the rebel army at once with the army in its front. No more helping one another. Then the work everywhere went steadily on. Every part of the great army was busy and kept busy till the final victory came.

The great battles of the Wilderness, Spotsylvania and Cold Harbor, which cost fifty-four thousand Union lives, followed right on in quick succession; Sheridan swept the valley of the

Shenandoah; Sherman spread consternation in his march to the sea, and others in their spheres were doing like decided work. From the Potomac to the Rio Grande, Grant's spirit was in the army. Every man, from the lieutenant-general to the private, was at his post and at work. In this fearful work of war the fall and winter wore away, all the country seeing that the confederacy must soon collapse. In due time Richmond fell, Petersburg was taken, the country in that part of Virginia which had been the seat of rebel operations was in Grant's possession. The army of General Robert E. Lee, which had so long supported the rebellion, was conquered. Seeing the hopelessness of further resistance, on the ninth of April, 1865, General Lee surrendered to General Grant.

Both armies were now disbanded to go to their homes. The poor misguided Confederates went to desolated homes, to an impoverished country, to a wrecked and shattered state of society. The Union soldiers went home to prosperity, to plenty, even luxury among the people. But each carried home the moral degeneracy, the idleness and vices peculiar to war, to be slowly overcome by christian endeavor.

Terrible past expression, are the calamities of war. The outward destruction of property, the cost in money, life and limb, the immeasurable waste to industry, are not the worst of the evil. The brutality, coarseness, hardness, profanity, drunkenness, moral degeneracy, that it brings to and leaves in vast numbers, is a tremendous weight to be cast upon society. It takes a generation to overcome the moral evils of such a war. Let men engage in devil's work and they will make themselves devils. War is a mighty corrupter of men and morals. It is time the civilized world was done with it. It is a burning disgrace to manhood and christian society that war is yet tolerated as a mode of settling difficulties among men and nations. It is to nations what the duel is to individuals—a relic of barbarism. But it has rid the United States of slavery, it may be said. Yes, so it has, but it was only using one evil to destroy another. It killed a million of white men, made a million widows and sorrowing mothers, desolated the southern states and immensely indebted the whole country, to give freedom to four millions of slaves.

Then, it may be replied, that the south would never have given up its slaves in any other way. Possibly not. Yet it was the dearest possible way for the south to get rid of an evil which was its worst enemy. But it is past now, slavery, war and all. Let it be past, and all the enmity and moral and social evil that came with it. We are one country, one people, have one history and one future now. If we did have a war among ourselves, it was the greatest one ever had among men, and produced the greatest generalship and soldiership, on both sides, yet known among men on so large a scale.

But what did the war do for Ulysses S. Grant? It made him. It took him from a low place, from a weak self-respect and self-control, from obscurity, from a possible, and perhaps probable, life-struggle with poverty and bad habits, and put him upon the pinnacle of a world-wide fame — gave him friends, confidence, even adulation, wealth, and the highest honor of the republic. But even this is not the best it did for him. It developed through all the years of the war a better and better manhood, an improving excellence of character. It is difficult for one to study the life of Grant and not see that from the time he entered the army of the Union at Springfield, he began to be a better man — more self-respecting, self-sacrificing — that he had more of the feeling that he was in the world for a purpose, which was to serve his country and his kind, to be a man genuine, large and useful.

Six days after General Lee surrendered, President Lincoln was assassinated. Grant had no better friend than the president. Through all the fault found with Grant, he always believed in him, and defended him.

Now came Andrew Johnson, as president, who objected to, and sought to hinder, the reconstruction measures of Congress, which proposed to give the ballot to the freedmen. A long contest between Congress and the executive followed, in which General Grant sought to stand on neutral ground. The president removed Mr. Stanton, secretary of war, and appointed

General Grant; but Congress objected to the removal, and so General Grant's cabinet position was short-lived. Slowly dragged along the weary length of President Johnson's time, which made the general's neutral position an uncomfortable one.

### PRESIDENT GRANT.

On the twentieth of May, 1868, the national republican convention of six hundred and fifty delegates, met in Chicago and voted for a candidate for the next president. Every vote was for General Grant. Every state was represented. The enthusiasm on the occasion was intense and tumultuously expressive. It told of a united country; of reconstructed states; of slavery abolished; of harmony between the coming president and Congress; of a new south in the years to come, and of a country to be, with all the sections prosperous, and at peace with each other. It was one of the greatest occasions in the history of this country, full of great epochs. The great leaders in thought, like Horace Greeley, Charles Sumner, Abraham Lincoln, had done their work in the minds and hearts of the nation. Discussion had been deep and strong for years, all the time winning men more and more to the doctrines of the declaration of independence. Now the time had come when these doctrines could be put into practice, when they were no longer an idle declaration, but a practical reality; and the man who had been one of the most practical and powerful instruments in bringing about this state of things, was nominated for the presidency. It was inevitable that General Grant should be president. The people would have it so. His great work in the war, growing greater with each succeeding year, culminating at last in the destruction of the slave-holder's rebellion; his simplicity of life, modesty, and plain honesty and common sense, had made him the one man whom the people would promote to the highest place of honor and trust. No matter if he had not been a civilian; no matter if he had not voted but once, and then for Buchanan; no matter if he had been a slave-holder, and failed in self-government over his appetite, before the war; nobody else could be thought of for president. It was cruelty to him, but the people did not mean it so. It was robbing him of his just dues, an unsullied and immortal reputation, to grow brighter through the ages, as one of the world's greatest captains; but this was not the intention. It was a moral impossibility that he should do in the presidency which he knew nothing of, as he had done in the army for which he had been trained, and in which he had seen much service under those great generals, Taylor and Scott. The country was never fuller of great civilians than at that time. The country never needed great civil talent, knowledge and experience, more than then. It was putting a landsman on board of a ship in a storm, to command it. Yes, it was cruelty to the general, who would have lived forever in the hearts of the people as the Wellington of America. So unwise is the love of a good people under such circumstances.

The election went forward as did the convention, to the inevitable result, which made our great and lovable general a commonplace president.

Commonplace he was obliged to be in a place as new to him as a new world.

The place was as difficult as it was new. The conquered but sullen south; the humiliated but not conquered democrats of the north, would both make him all the trouble they could. The republicans anxious to punish the south, and the republicans greedy for places in the north, were neither of them helpful to him. He, like the martyred Lincoln, had only kindness for the south, and kindness for everybody; but he could not have his way in such turbulent times.

He sought at the start to reform the civil service by appointing politically unambitious men to important posts of duty, but in these attempts the political managers soon worsted him and got their own way, so that before his administration was through, he was quite in their hands. By his good nature he was led to accept many presents from men who had personal interests to serve, listen to many counselors who were ambitious of their own promotion, appoint many relatives and intimates to places of trust and profit, to his own discredit, and give credence to schemes of plausible theorists, which did not gain wise confidence for him.

In the army he easily and naturally controlled all opposing wills; in the government he was as easily controlled by adroit politicians; so that beginning his administration as a reformer, he ended in close affiliation with the old line managers, or "machine" men as they were called. Seldom have more men in high places fallen into evil and brought disgrace to the government, than during the second term of his administration. He meant well, but was too closely invested by men and things which he could not manage, to gain much credit for his well meaning. Since the days of Washington, no military man has given the country a wise civil administration. And it must always be remembered that he was more a civilian than a soldier. The nation loved General Grant; the nation bore with President Grant; and yet by and by the great general will overgrow the less president, and he will live in the military honor he justly deserves.

### PRESIDENT GRANT THE TRAVELER.

President Grant closed his public service on the fourth day of March, 1877. He had had sixteen years of continuous public duty, for the most part, in heavily responsible places. He had long desired to see the world. Now was his time. He had good health, as he always had, good eyes, and a placid spirit, which could sleep always, when it was time to sleep, and now he was in mood to go. On the seventeenth of May, 1877, he and his wife, son, and a party of friends, left Philadelphia, and went down the Delaware thirty-five miles, and boarded the "Indiana," which was ready for the voyage. They sailed directly for England, where he was received, as Lord Beaconsfield had determined he should be, "as a sovereign." Perhaps no public man was ever more feted and feasted, and publicly honored, in England, from the humblest citizen to the queen, than was he. England loves great generals, and knows when she finds one. It may be that she was making up for her bad treatment of us, during the war, but yet she was magnaminous enough to treat our great general as he deserved.

From England, President Grant and party went to Belgium,

to be received in a similar way; and then to Germany and Switzerland, to be regaled by the mountain air and views; and then across the channel to Scotland. Having taken a hasty run through Scotland and England, he crossed to France.

After seeing the principal sights of this country, the "Indiana" took its way, through the straits of Gibraltar, into the Mediterranean sea to Italy and Greece, and their wonders; and then southward to Egypt, where carpets were spread on the ground to receive him, and old army comrades, then in the service of the king of Egypt, greeted him. Here, as elsewhere, king and people gave him a welcome. The Pyramids, the Nile and Upper Egypt, were in turn visited. The ruins of the ancient city of Abydos, claimed to be the cradle of civilization, greatly interested the party. Then up the river to the ruins of Thebes, once a city of three hundred thousand inhabitants, stretched for eight miles along either side of the river, the party went. Ruins on ruins everywhere! The statue of Memnon, the temple of Medinet Haboo, the avenue of the Sphinxes, and Karnac with its wilderness of ruins, were visited.

From Egypt to the Holy Land they go, and instead of our general being allowed to enter Jerusalem thoughtfully and in quiet, he was met with an army with banners giving him a great welcome. From Palestine to Damascus, still ancient and beautiful, on to Constantinople, Greece and Italy, and then to the Paris exhibition, the party went.

Two weeks in Holland, then to Germany, King William and Bismarck, to Norway and Sweden, and Russia, to be cordially received by the Czar, and then hurried to Spain, makes travel a campaign indeed.

A French ship carried the general and party to Egypt again, and a Red Sea steamer took them to India, that wonder-world of the east. Hindustan, Siam, and then China and Japan were taken in the trip, and the strange, ancient, curious things they hold. But Japan was delightful, fraternal, profoundly respectful, and held our party long in a charmed life. Then the "City of Tokio" took them across the Pacific to San Francisco.

Soon followed a presidential election, and a strong movement among General Grant's friends, which many supposed he was party to, and in relation to which this trip had been planned, to make him president for a third term. But the general suspicion that it was a "ring" movement defeated it. Not General Grant so much as the friends that clung to him, was feared.

The life of Grant, like that of Lincoln, is a wonder life. It burst suddenly upon the world and strangely captivated it. By and by, when its mistakes sink more out of sight, and its real work and worth to the country rise into full view, it will be a wonder-chapter in the history of the republic.

Sincerely
R. B. Hayes.

## CHAPTER XX.

### RUTHERFORD BIRCHARD HAYES.
#### Nineteenth President of the United States.

PERHAPS few presidents have been more truly representatives of the American people than Rutherford B. Hayes. He was not remarkable in any sense — not a remarkable scholar, or orator, or lawyer, or general, or governor, or president; but did everything he undertook so well, and filled every place to which he was elected with such signal good sense, that he disarmed criticism and gained approval. He was nothing astonishing or captivating, but was simply a strong, good-sensed, practical man — as was said of another, "he was every inch a man." He was rounded, full of the meat of manliness, genuine in every phase of his ability and character. He was *sure*, and applied to his methods the rules of practical common sense. His every day and everywhere practical qualities made him a representative man. The common sense and common heart of the people he answered to and illustrated. He was not the marvelous product of a great period, nor the apostle of a great cause, nor the outgrowth of a great revolution, but was a naturally produced man of American society, reared by the rules of good living, and educated in the common, orderly way.

Being reared by his mother, as his father died before his birth, he was from the beginning, under her wise and healthful influence, without any counter influence from paternal misjudgments or misleading habits or practices.

It is common for men to be less thoughtful about the thousand little things that go to influence a boy and to make up his character, than for women. Most men have opinions and practices of which it would be better for boys to know nothing.

Many fathers lead their boys in the way of things of which they ought to be kept clear. Most fathers are skeptical about the need of so much guarding, cautioning and training, as mothers are impelled by their motherly instincts to constantly use in rearing their boys. Fathers often counteract the influence of mothers over their boys. Mothers usually give to fathers too much the direction of their boys, and are less mothers to them than they would be if they had no fathers. In the case of Mr. Hayes, the mother had her full power over him from the beginning, without any counteracting influence; and the harmony and completeness of his character and life are due not a little to this fact. He is another instance of the widow's son rising to life's heights of usefulness and honor. His successor, Mr. Garfield, is another.

### BIRTH AND BOYHOOD.

Rutherford Birchard Hayes was born in Delaware, Ohio, October, 1822. His father was Rutherford Hayes, who came from Vermont in 1817. The hardiness and energy of the Vermont quality of men went into this Ohio Rutherford, at the beginning. He started into life with a good ancestral momentum behind him. Such a start is about half the making of a man. His mother was Sophia Birchard. Strictly speaking, Rutherford was an Ohio Vermonter. He had Vermont blood and qualities on Ohio soil. His father died before Rutherford was born; so that his whole early training was given him by his mother. This was essentially Vermont training. She was reared in Vermont, and had the notions that prevailed there in her day, which were strict, leaning strongly to the puritanic. The moral atmosphere into which Rutherford was born was strong with positive qualities, and especially vigorous in the high moral forces. All the first years of his life he breathed this atmosphere, which was oxygenated by his mother's inward life. Out of this he went into the common school, where he enjoyed its opportunities through the whole period of his boyhood. A public school is a school in several senses; it trains the mind; it sharpens the common sense in its close intercourse with all kinds of children; it gives a good education in the science of human nature practically applied; in its feats of agility and strength, it develops the physical; and tries the temper and disposition in many ways. Fortunate is the child trained early in a good common school. In a republic, the common school is one of the great sources of self-reliant character and efficient, practical judgment.

### THE YOUTH AND STUDENT.

From the common school our young Hayes went into Kenyon college, Ohio, where he went through the prescribed course and graduated in 1842, a little before he was twenty years old. Here was good fortune again; for a small college, where the classes are so small that each student comes directly under the influence of the professors; where acquaintance becomes general and much of the family feeling is engendered, and life-long friendships are formed, exerts a positive and powerful influence for good over a manly and aspiring young mind. The college is the efficient training school of the youthful and ambitions mind. Many grand and brilliant men do well without it, but they feel sorrow over its loss all the years of their manhood. The question of its vast importance is settled by a wide experience in all civilized countries.

All the way, thus far, young Hayes has been moving along the best lines of ascending life. In this good and almost sure foundation everything has been well done. He is well born, well bred, well educated.

He went from college into the law office of Thomas Sparrow, Esq., of Columbus, as a student at law. In 1843 he entered the law school of Harvard university, and studied two years under Judge Story and Professor Greenleaf, and was admitted to the bar in March, 1845. Here was a symmetrical and full education, like the man and life that followed it. There was no attempt to skip the hard places, or to set up his judgment against the experience of the enlightened ages as to what is best in an educational course, or to take a short cut to his profession. He took the old well-beaten way, and followed it steadily through to the end.

### MR. HAYES THE LAWYER.

He was now nearly twenty-three years old. He began the practice of law in Lower Sandusky, now Fremont, in Sandusky county, Ohio. Here he remained till 1850, doing such business and getting such experience as come to a young lawyer in such places, already overrun with lawyers. Not satisfied with the outlook here, and being ambitious of a larger field, he moved to Cincinnati. These first years in a profession are the trying ones, in many respects. They try the character, the judgment, the ability and preparation. They are not yet removed from youthful temptation and follies, nor free from the misjudgments of inexperience. Mr. Hayes had gone safely through this trying ordeal. His feet were planted on manhood's ground without harm to his heart, character or life. He soon grew into a reasonable practice in his new field, and in 1856 was an unsuccessful candidate for judge of the court of common pleas. In 1859 he was chosen city solicitor, to fill a vacancy, by the city council, a handsome recognition of his rising capacity and merit. The next spring the people elected him to the same office. In 1851 he lost a re-election by the failure of the republican ticket.

### MR. HAYES THE SOLDIER.

Mr. Hayes early identified himself with the republican party. He was a whig, with strong anti-slavery convictions and sentiments, and came naturally into the new party. He took an earnest part in the election of Mr. Lincoln; and when rebellion began to defy the government it defied him, and he at once offered himself to the governor of the state to defend the government against the rebel disunionists. June 7, 1861, Governor Dennison appointed him major of the twenty-third Ohio regiment of volunteer infantry, which soon after went into duty in West Virginia. In September General Rosecrans appointed him Judge Advocate of the department of Ohio, which position he held about two months, when he was promoted to the rank of lieutenant-colonel. In this capacity he commanded the twenty-third regiment during the early campaign in West Virginia in 1862, and in the latter part of the year under General McClellan. In the sharp battle of South Mountain he was wounded. During this year he was appointed colonel of the seventy-ninth Ohio regiment, but was prevented from taking the command on account of the wound. Before he was able to go to the seventy-ninth he was appointed colonel of the twenty-third, and so remained with his old regiment.

In the spring of 1864 Colonel Hayes was given the command of a brigade in General Crook's army, and went further south with a view to cut the communications between Richmond and the western part of the confederacy. At Cloyd mountain he stormed the enemy's position and gained an important victory. In September, 1864, his command was enlarged to the Kanawha division, which he commanded the rest of the year.

While leading his brigade at the battle of Winchester, his command came suddenly to a morass about one hundred and fifty feet wide. It seemed to be a hinderance to their passage; but the colonel rode in till his horse got mired, then he dismounted and went through on foot, with the water up nearly to his arms, his men following in resolute determination not to be outdone by their colonel. He was in the heat of this whole action, but escaped without a wound, though men fell thickly all about him. He led his brigade in the battles of Berryville and Opequan. He bore a conspicuous part under General Sheridan, and had command of a division in the battle of Cedar Creek, where his horse was shot under him. On account of his great services in this and the battles that went before it he was made brigadier-general, and still later was breveted major-general for "bravery and distinguished services."

The Ohio war record says: "He had three horses shot under him, and was four times wounded, once very severely." His whole war record was one of a brave and morally earnest soldier. He did not enlist for glory, but to put down the rebellion and save the country, in the hope that slavery would go down in the crash of the rebellion. He was among the first to enlist and the last to sheath his sword. He went through the whole war; did noble service all the time; went up and up by successive promotions; made no failures; gained many victories, and made it hard for rebellion and well for his country all the time. His war career was an even and complete one, like his own manhood. He was an example to his men, an honor to his country, and a terror to rebellion.

While yet in the field, his district in Cincinnati elected him to Congress, and he took his seat December 4, 1865. He was re-elected the next year. In Congress he was not a noisy but a working member, and served his country with the same fidelity that he had in the field.

### GOVERNOR HAYES.

In 1867 Mr. Hayes was elected governor of Ohio. He resigned his seat in Congress, and was inaugurated January 13, 1868. In 1869 he was re-elected. These elections were very hotly contested, and the forensic power of Governor Hayes was well attested. The great questions of reconstruction, negro suffrage, finance, etc., were before the country. It was a great period in our national history when our public men had to consider the most important matters of political economy, and when great moral questions were at issue. It was the epoch of national reconstruction. Since the revolution no other so important epoch had occurred. All that went into the constitution and construction and life of the nation in consequence of slavery was now to be eliminated. The evil that our fathers had not the moral courage to put away must now be cut out from the body politic which had grown a hundred years with the evil in it. It required dextrous surgery. All involved in the issues of the time came into discussion before the people of Ohio through the candidates for governor. Mr. Hayes proved himself master of the occasion. A fine speaker, he comprehended and presented the issues of the occasion with convincing force. His clearness, his fairness, his thorough knowledge of the subjects he treated, his force of argument, and, above all, his strong moral perceptions of the duties of the hour, made his canvasses very influential with the people. They were significant occasions in the history of Ohio. And they had somewhat the effect with him that Mr. Lincoln's canvass of Illinois had upon his fortunes. They were heard by the nation. They gave him a national reputation. They were discussions of the great interests of the nation, and bore so strongly upon humanity and the enduring principles of right, justice and honor, that they won for him national respect and confidence.

In 1875, for the third time, Mr. Hayes was candidate for governor, and in the meridian of his strength rehearsed before the people of Ohio the principles involved in our form of government and the possibilities before the American people. The leading issue in this last canvass was the financial one. He argued for the resumption of specie payment, for a sound currency, for trade and commerce based on just principles, for national prosperity built upon integrity and mutual fairness. The currency was so disordered, and men's minds so disordered with it, that almost a craze had set in in favor of cheap money—congressional promises not representing any value nor having any specie equivalent. For some years neither banks nor government had paid specie on their notes. Business had prospered, had even inflated. Some thought that this state of things could go on indefinitely, and specie might be remanded to perpetual imprisonment or be used for mechanical and ornamental purposes. It took great discussion to lead the people to see the need of the resumption of specie payment and a currency based on specie. Mr. Hayes took an active part in this discussion, and did much to secure the sound conclusion which the country finally reached.

Previous to this last election for governor, Mr. Hayes had run for Congress and been beaten, giving him a brief respite from public life.

But this canvass, in which Mr. Hayes secured an election as

governor for the third time, so touched national issues, and was so commended by the better judgment of the nation, that he became a national man, and was looked to as one likely to be called upon to serve in national capacities.

Mr. Hayes was inaugurated governor the third time, in January, 1876, and served through the centennial year of the Declaration of Independence.

The republican state convention of that year met in March, and recommended the name of Rutherford B. Hayes to the national convention as the candidate for the presidency. The national republican convention met in that year, June 14, at Cincinnati, and after the convention was organized, June 15, ex-Governor Noyes, of Ohio, presented the name of Governor Hayes as Ohio's choice for the next president. He received the nomination, and the national canvass in his behalf was a very spirited one. Mr. Tilden, of New York, was the democratic candidate.

President Grant had been the national executive eight years. He began as a civil service reformer, but he soon fell into the good graces, and then into the hands of the machine rings, that during his time, held the party domination, and, under their lead, which in his last term he did not seem to try to resist, the party rapidly lost the confidence of the people. Many democrats, which, during the war and after, had acted with the republicans, went back and voted for Tilden. Many republicans got lukewarm, and lost their zeal, fearing that corrupt men were getting too much favor from the leaders. In Grant's eight years, the party had lost moral tone. It may have been inevitable as a consequence of war's demoralization. Incompetent and often demoralized soldiers claimed leading places of trust. Incompetency and defalcation became too common. Hence, though the republicans had been overwhelmingly triumphant, since the election of Mr. Lincoln, they now had so lost ground that when the electoral votes came to be counted, there were honest doubts as to who should be counted in. There had been great fraud in some of the southern states in forcibly refusing negro votes and in maintaining a reign of terror against colored supremacy, or even participation in elections. In the uncertainty, confusion and indignation, an electoral commission was proposed and agreed upon to go to the states where fraud and force were charged as having been used at the election, and inquire into the facts and determine what electoral votes should be counted. This commission performed its duties, and by its decision Mr. Hayes was counted in.

## MR. HAYES AS PRESIDENT.

Mr. Hayes was inaugurated President on March 4, 1877. Not before, perhaps, had any American executive taken his seat under such unfavorable circumstances. The democrats generally felt that their candidate had received a majority of the popular votes, and were in no mood to be pliable subjects of an executive who had gone into office under such circumstances. To their credit, it must be said, that they laid nothing in President Hayes' way. Much as they scolded, they behaved well. Much as their leaders were disappointed, they acted the part of men. They had agreed to the electoral commission, and submitted with manly grace to its decision, though they generally thought it was not right.

Our republican institutions have received few severer shocks than on that occasion. There have been many revolutions on less occasions. We may all feel safer and more in the right in our devotion to popular government, because our citizens so considerately bore themselves in peace through that emergency.

In his letter of acceptance of the nomination, Mr. Hayes had said: "Believing that the restoration of the civil service to the system established by Washington, and followed by the early Presidents, can be best accomplished by an executive who is under no temptation to use the patronage of his office to promote his own re-election, I desire to perform what I regard as a duty, in stating now my inflexible purpose, if elected, not to be a candidate for election to a second term."

This explicit statement was believed by the country. His public service in the army and in Ohio had taught the people that what he said he meant. The defeated party knew that a fair chance to vote again would be open to them in four years, when a new candidate would oppose them. They knew also the honorable, generous and truthful man who was to be president, and doubtless many had no doubt of a good administration at his hands. All things considered, with such a man they had nothing to fear.

In his letter of acceptance, he had also announced his belief in civil service reform. He said: "The reform should be thorough, radical, complete. We should return to the principles and practice of the founders of the government, supplying by legislation when needed, that which was formerly the established custom. They neither expected nor desired from the public officer any partisan service. They meant that public officers should owe their whole service to the government and the people." He pledged himself to these principles. The whole country knew that he would stand by these statements. Then what had any party to fear? His letter of acceptance, which covered the whole ground, was an assurance to the whole country that his would be a sound and useful administration. He gave as truly a national administration as a man elected by a party well can, and his party secured a revival of its old strength therefrom, so that its next candidate was elected triumphantly. His administration closed with general good feeling.

### MR. HAYES' MARRIAGE AND FAMILY.

Mr. Hayes was married December 20, 1852, to Miss Lucy Webb, of Delaware, Ohio, whom he first met while a young lawyer of Cincinnati, at the Delaware Sulphur Springs. She was at that time a member of the Wesleyan Female College, of Cincinnati.

The marriage proved most happy; and to it is attributed by many the uniform success of Mr. Hayes in every position, and the harmony and efficiency of his life. She has been a helpmeet indeed, and has won world-wide praise for herself as well as for the help she has given him. She is of excellent parentage; finely reared and educated; a sincere member of the Methodist Episcopal church; healthy in body and mind;

cheerful, and a lover of the beautiful, but simple in her tastes and strong in her purposes and sense of duty.

They have had eight children, five of whom still live to make glad their home circle.

While Mr. Hayes was governor of Ohio his wife contributed not a little to the harmony and efficiency of his official success. She was the happy and salutary center of a social circle and influence which made the executive mansion the promoter of good-will and all good offices. She took an active interest in state and local charities, in her church and the community about her, which brought a harvest of confidence and good-will, not only to herself, but to him. In the army she was much with him — was called the mother of his regiment, and won to him much good influence.

Mrs. Hayes' administration in the White House was as symmetrical and harmonious as his in the executive chair. She carried her own simple and hearty tastes into her home life and receptions there, and ordered all her conduct by her clear christian judgment, not asking what had been or would be done, but only what she thought most fitting for a christian woman in the executive mansion of the nation to do. All falsity was banished, and the president's home was just what it had always been, only it was in Washington and the White House. She was happy here, as she was everywhere, and kept away from him many an annoyance, complaint and trouble.

When President Hayes got to Washington he began to see at once the evil effects of intoxicating drinks on many men in high places. It soon became so apparent to him that he resolved on an example of total abstinence at the executive house. In this he had the grateful support of Mrs. Hayes. From his own statement it is to be inferred that this was his movement, knowing, of course, that it would meet with her heartiest approval.

No occupants of the White House ever more graced it with personal agreeableness or ease and animation of manners. Of elegant forms, fine features, healthful and happy bodies and spirits, they were pronounced by a long resident of Washington "the finest looking type of man and woman that I have seen take up their abode in the White House."

It has often been said that there has been no purer administration of the American government than that of President Hayes. Its effect on the country was healing and happy. In no place in this country is real virtue, judgment and high sentiment so beneficial as in the executive mansion. They are a benediction on the whole country. They permeate society and give strength to every good cause. Our best men and women are needed for that highest place in our free society.

It is a cause of profound thankfulness that in the first hundred years of our national existence so many grand men and women have been elevated to this highest place. It has been greatly honored by many of those who have occupied it. They have, without exception, been men of ability and commanding personal power. Their deficiencies have been chiefly in the moral qualities. Not that any bad men have been so elevated, but that some have risen to this place as successful politicians, as men of strong minds and ambitions, without any correspondingly great moral purposes. A strong moral equipment is an absolute necessity for a great president or a greatly successful administration.

### THE HAYES HOME.

At the close of his very successful administration, ex-President Hayes retired to his family home in Fremont, Ohio. It is on Birchard avenue, named for Sardis Birchard, uncle and guardian of Mr. Hayes. The house was built by Mr. Birchard in 1860. It is in the center of some thirty acres of woodland. The house is brick, two stories high, with wide verandas. The estate of this uncle came to Mr. Hayes, placing him out of want's way. In quiet and intellectual retirement ex-President and Mrs. Hayes give themselves to the social, charitable and religious duties of the society about them, honored and happy in their domestic and neighborly comfort.

## CHAPTER XXI.

### JAMES ABRAM GARFIELD.
#### TWENTIETH PRESIDENT OF THE UNITED STATES.

##### ANCESTRY.

IN the life and character of James A. Garfield there is much to instruct and stir every reader. No one can help feeling that he is reading of greatness, worth and power. There is a fineness, a stalwartness, a rich nobility so winning and commanding that his common acts seem invested with a manly charm. With a history reaching back in his ancestry to England, Wales, Germany and France, covering nearly the whole colonial history of America, rising into prominence in the first century of the United States, and in his person to the highest place in the gift of the people, he becomes a character to attract and hold the interest of all who read of him. He seems to have been a sort of reservoir, into which several ancestral streams poured their choicest waters. In his own case we are reminded of what he said in one of his great public addresses: "Who shall estimate the effect of those latent forces enfolded in the spirit of a new born child—forces that may date back centuries and find their origin in the life, thought and deeds of remote ancestors—forces, the germs of which enveloped in the awful mystery of life, have been transmitted silently from generation to generation and never perish! All-cherishing nature, provident and unforgetting, gathers up all these fragments, that nothing be lost, but that all may ultimately reappear in new combinations. Each new life is thus the 'heir of all the ages,' the possessor of qualities which only the events of life can unfold." This fine recognition of the law of heredity is illustrated in him. And another has said: "Nine tenths of a man's genius is hereditary. The inherited portion may appear large, but it is to be remembered that only possibilities are inherited, and that not one man in a million reaches the limit of his possibilities."

Mr. Garfield was of English descent, with a vein of Welsh blood. One of the family ancestors married into a German family, bringing in a current of Teutonic blood.

Edward Garfield, from Cheshire, England, settled in Watertown, Massachusetts, in 1636. From him down through several generations of hardy and patriotic men came Solomon Garfield, the great-grand-father of James A. Garfield. In this line was one Abraham Garfield, who was in the battles of Lexington and Concord, in 1775. They were a strong, heroic, industrious class of men; resolute, vigorous and common-sensed. Solomon Garfield was in the revolutionary war, did faithful service to the end, and soon after removed to Otsego county, New York, where he opened a small farm in the forest and reared his family of five children. Thomas was the oldest of the family, and was the grand-father of James A. Garfield. He married Asenath Hill, and in December, 1799, their son Abram was born. Abram Garfield was a man of fine physique, tall, broad-shouldered, sinewy, and very active. Many traditions are in the family of his feats of strength and agility. Thomas died just at the opening of this century, leaving Abram to fight his own battle of life.

Abram followed the setting sun to the Western Reserve, Ohio, where he built him a cabin, cleared his patch, and began life in the wilderness.

The maternal ancestry of James A. Garfield was still more marked in strong characteristics; but they were mental. On the father's side there was great bodily power; on the mother's side, great power of mind. His mother was Eliza Ballou, born in Richmond, New Hampshire, and was a relative of Reverend

Hosea Ballou, born in the same town, the distinguished pioneer of Universalism. Several Universalist clergymen of the same family connection have been noted for learning, piety and christian zeal. Honorable Maturin Ballou, member of Congress from Rhode Island, is of the same family and the same devotion to moral and religious life. The father of Hosea Ballou was a Baptist clergyman. "The Ballous were a race of preachers," says one of the biographers of Garfield. Probably no family in America ever gave the world so many strong and eminent clergymen. "One of them, himself a preacher, had four sons who were ministers of the gospel, and one of these had three sons who were preachers, and one of these had a son and grandson who were preachers."

The family descended from Maturin Ballou, who was a Huguenot and fled from persecution in France in 1685, and settled in Cumberland, Rhode Island. Here a church was built, which still stands, called the "Elder Ballou Meeting House," in which great numbers of the Ballous have preached. Of this family was Eliza Ballou. From her side her gifted son inherited his bright intellectuality, his strong moral and religious sensibilities, his oratory, love of study, his taste, suavity, and resolution in the performance of duty. Such a union as that of Abram Garfield and Eliza Ballou is prophetic of great possibilities in some of their children.

## BIRTH, BOYHOOD AND YOUTH.

James Abram Garfield was born in Orange, Cuyahoga county, Ohio, November 19, 1831. He was the youngest of four children, Mehetabel, Thomas, Mary and James. His parents had been in Ohio only long enough to get well started in their forest home when he came to cheer it. The log house, a little cleared land, a few acres fenced in and a crop well grown prepared the way for his coming.

In May, 1833, when James was eighteen months old, a fire broke out in the woods near the Garfield settlement, which threatened to destroy all their improvements. The few neighbors fought it with desperation. Abram Garfield, after a long contest with the fire, rested, only to take a severe cold, which brought on a congestion of the lungs, of which, in a few days, he died.

This was a fearful blow to this now apparently helpless family. The little farm was only partly paid for; only a little of it was cleared; Thomas, the oldest boy, was but ten years old; the afflicted mother's hands seemed to be tied with strings of care to her little flock. How could she feed and clothe them and pay the debt on the farm, so as to hold it as a home. The neighbors saw no way but for her to break up and scatter her children among relatives and neighbors, who would take them rather than see them suffer. But she said "No." She believed in the good Heavenly Father's providence over her and her dependent charge. She believed in love and duty, trust and hope, and she resolutely determined to keep her children to grow up together and love and do for each other. With a wisdom and fortitude found only in a mother's love, she faced the hard task before her, and with a bereft and lonely heart, put her life's toil and care into the ever-prayerful work that had come to her hands.

Thomas was her stay and help and comfort. Boy as he was, he had to be the man of the house and barn and farm. The crops were to be tended and harvested that season; the stock cared for; the wood chopped; provisions made for winter; all the little chores done; the milling and the business of the family attended to, and all by a ten-year-old boy. But Thomas did not falter. He did it all, save what his sisters and his mother could help. They worked and lived and loved together, and the laughing, growing, fat and healthy baby was the joy of them all. Many stories are told of this baby as peculiarly bright and forward, but it is altogether probable that he was much like others of his kind, and gave as few premonitions of his coming greatness. Babies are not often great. But one thing is certain, that Thomas Garfield must have his full share of credit for what James came to be. He was father and brother in one to the orphan babe, and led him on to youth and manhood with a noble and self-sacrificing fidelity. Few sights in this world are more tenderly beautiful than such a saddened yet chastened family.

In due time there was built near the Garfield home, that marvelous institution, the country school-house, and James with the rest went to be initiated into its mysteries. It is said of him that he was an uneasy little scholar, pestering the teacher out of her wits, in the effort to keep him still, and compelling her at last to go to his mother with the distressing story that he was doing no good in school. What should she do? And yet she must do something; and so she did what all good mothers do in such cases— she talked to him out of her mother heart, and he went to school the next day resolved to "sit as still as he could."

As soon as able, he became Thomas' helper on the little farm and a producer of the necessaries of life. He was born to work, as he was to poverty.

The nearest neighbor was a family of Boyntons, near relatives, in which were six children, which, with the Garfields, made a merry group. Their work and play, studies and reading, were had together, as much as possible. Of books, they had few, but they were read till they were familiar. The older children in this group formed a "class of critics," to watch each other's use of words and to study the meaning of words and the construction of sentences. James always thought this "class of critics" was of great help to him in giving him the quality of critical observation of language.

When James was about ten years old, Thomas went to Michigan to earn some money in clearing land, and when he returned, brought seventy-five dollars. They were rich now, they thought, and Thomas proposed building a frame house for the family. On this, James worked and took his first lessons in carpentry. After the house was built, he worked among the neighbors on barns and out-buildings, and thus became quite an adept in this business. While at this work, he put up a building for a potash-maker, who was a man of considerable means and business for that vicinity, who, because he could read and write and keep accounts, proposed to give James fourteen dollars a month to become his clerk and general helper. This looked like wealth coming in upon him like an avalanche. One day while here, one of the women of the family spoke to him as a servant, which so incensed him that he left at once. He was no slave, and would not tolerate such insolence.

In his sixteenth summer, he engaged to cut for an uncle, a hundred cords of wood at twenty-five cents a cord, which job he completed in due time. In these muscular, self-denying, and self-sharpening pursuits, James spent his boyhood and youth. The winter school was his opportunity for an education.

During this time, the subject of religion was presented to his young mind, by the Disciple preachers, who were urging their views with great persistency in that region. They discussed the subject of baptism with great positiveness, and their peculiarly literal interpretations of scripture were incisive, dogmatic, zealous and disputatious. They were often at his mother's, and won the confidence of the family. James became a "Disciple," and was thus early led to view life in its religious aspects, and to shape his thoughts, character and daily life under the light of christian teachings.

But the time had come when he must strike out for something definite in life. He had read some of Captain Maryatt's sea stories, and had become enamored of sea life. He mused on it by day and dreamed of it at night. And now that he had become old enough and Lake Erie with its many vessels afforded him a chance, he saw an opportunity, he thought, to make his vision of sea-going life a reality. His mother could not dissuade him from it, and with a heavy heart and many prayers for his safety, she fixed him off. With his bundle on his back and a few dollars in his pocket, she saw him depart on foot for Cleveland, but besought him again as he left her to get employment on land if possible.

He tried many places but found no open door, and then went down among the vessels, to find as he fondly hoped the open way to a life on the rolling deep. But to his modest inquiries he received only coarse and profane rebuffs. Failing here, he concluded to go up to the canal and see if he could find his cousin, who was captain on a canal boat. He found him and soon made a bargain to drive a team for the "Evening Star." The next morning he was promptly on hand and began his new employment which had a hint of sea life in it. Before the end of the first day he, with his mules, was jerked into the canal. When the captain called out, "Jim, what are you doing there?" he jocosely replied, "Taking a bath." Many stories of his canal-boat life are told of him, all characteristic of his energy, courage, cheerfulness and fidelity.

But not long did this continue, for one rainy midnight he was thrown into the canal where the water was deep, in uncoiling a rope. As he sank in the water with none to help, he saw nothing but drowning before him. But soon the rope which he held fast to tightened in his hand and he began to draw himself toward the boat, hand over hand. In this way he drew himself into the boat, when he found that a kink in the rope had held it for him to draw himself up. He threw the rope out again and again, and many times, to see if it would kink again, but it would not. He began to meditate on his singular deliverance. Was it providential? He could not comprehend how the rope should so kink, or how it should hold him when so kinked; and he said to himself, that if it was providential and his life was worth such a deliverance, he would go home, educate himself and make the most he could of it.

This accident, and the meditation it caused, changed the tone and course of his life. The sea-vision vanished. The romance of story life departed; and the counsel of his mother to get an education, came to him with overwhelming force. That was his last trip on the "Evening Star." His next trip was on foot to his mother's door, which he reached late in the evening, to see her through the window, on her knees before the open bible, and to hear her say in prayer: "Oh, turn unto me, and have mercy upon me. Give thy strength to thy servant, and save the son of thy handmaid." He waited but a moment, and opened the door and went in, in answer to her prayer. The feeling with which they embraced each other can be better imagined than expressed. Could they doubt that a kind Providence had kept him and led him back? All the religious trust and enthusiasm of his nature, which had come to him through generations of his mother's ancestors, now crystalized into a purpose to devote his life to an education and such usefulness as should open to him. No plan was formed; no vision seen; only a "Thy will be done," was prayed in his heart. Thus far his life had been a sort of seeding time—nothing more. Nothing visible had come of it but a large, muscular, active, cheerful youth; nothing invisible had come of it but this one newly formed purpose, and the discipline which his rude, hard-working experience had given him.

And yet this purpose was often shaken for a time. The old desire for the sea would return; the old longing for roving would almost command him to be away. He had a season of struggle to get his feet well on the right road. But he was helped in this by a period of sickness—fever and ague—which he had contracted on the canal, and which came on soon after he got home. It lasted him three months. During this sickness, the old longing for the sea would come on, and he would think that in the spring he would find a place on the lake. Then his mother would tell him of his enfeebled health, and how, if he would go to school at the academy a term, he could teach school the next winter. That winter, a young man by the name of Samuel D. Bates, taught the school near his mother's. He was a student from Chester, and was zealous to take back with him several young men. He won James Garfield to his project.

### GARFIELD'S SCHOOL LIFE.

Once at school, young Garfield's feet were planted in the new way. Two young men went with him to the Geauga seminary at Chester, Geauga county, Ohio. It was a Free Will Baptist academy. He at once entered into his studies with zeal. He made it a point to get every lesson well, to be present at every recitation, at every morning session of the school, and at every literary exercise. In the literary society he at once took an active part. Here he wrote his first essays, made his first speeches, was first awakened to the glory of a scholar's life. He became an enthusiast in his studies, in academic associations. Books, teachers, students, school, all became objects of delight to him. It was a new world, and he became enrapt in its charmed life.

Here was, a student with him, the daughter of a farmer, Miss Lucretia Rudolph, who afterward became his wife, and stood by him, with his mother, when he was inaugurated president of the United States.

Near the academy was a carpenter's shop where he worked Saturdays, and some mornings and evenings, to earn money to pay his board and buy his books. In the summer vacations he worked for the farmers at haying and harvesting. In the winters he taught school. He was self-helping and self-educating all the time, learning how to get and use money, the value of time, economy, plain living, simple dressing and self-restraint. Hands, heart, conscience and intellect were all being educated together. Young Garfield was at this academy nearly three years.

At Hiram, in the same county, the Disciples had started an institution of a higher grade, called at first the "Eclectic Institute," afterward Hiram college. His family, his neighbors, himself, were "Disciples," and it was natural, right and best that he should go to his own church school. At that stage of his life it was best for him to be with his own. He was in sympathy with them, had a religious and personal interest in their institution, and was not only ambitious for himself, but for his church.

In 1851 he went to Hiram and at once entered with great zeal not only into his studies but into all the interests of that young institution. It developed in him a public spirit, a larger purpose in his study than his own improvement. It was the consecrated door out into the great world, for which he afterward felt such a broad and humane interest. His student life at Hiram had the best possible educational influence on his character. It united religious and moral training with his mental growth, and gave them all a large outlook into the world. It gave him an opportunity to become a free and earnest speaker in religious meetings and on religious topics, so that he grew faster, and warmer, and broader than he would anywhere else. Hiram was the Providential place for Garfield. He was self-helpful, jovial and full of animal spirits, and yet reverent, tender and thoroughly conscientious of the minor strains to which his own life had been keyed from the beginning.

He went to Hiram when nineteen, and at once applied for the place of sweeper and bell-ringer, to pay his way. After three years at Hiram he went to Williams college, Massachusetts. His reasons for going there instead of to Bethany, the Disciple college, were that the course at Williams was better; Bethany leaned too heavily toward slavery; he was a "Disciple," and his family were, and he had been thus far, educated among "Disciples;" now he thought it would "make him more liberal in both his religious and general views and sentiments to go into a new circle, where he should be under new influences."

He remained two years at Williams, and won golden opinions from professors and students. The religious students, especially, enjoyed his simple, childlike piety. The intellectual students enjoyed his scholarly attainments and quick and strong grasp of mind. The hard-working students gloried in his studious habits, his drudgery in search of facts and the bottom of all subjects which he investigated. All classes felt drawn to him by his frankness, cordiality, great-heartedness.

He graduated in 1856, with the honor of the metaphysical oration, and his topic was "Matter and Spirit." He left Williams with the profoundest regard for its honored president, Doctor Hopkins, and full of rich memories of students, professors, people and place.

### GARFIELD A TEACHER.

Mr. Garfield began his teaching in the common school and always had excellent success both in instruction and government. At Hiram, he was employed the second and third years as assistant teacher in several studies. After his graduation from Williams, he returned to Hiram with all his ambitions quickened to a life of instruction. To graduate from a good college, had been the height of his ambition ; so now he took up his work in a kind of ecstacy of fulfillment. His nature was expanded, his heart full, his soul at peace. The next year, 1857, he was made president of Hiram college. It was his view that a "teacher must be full of manhood, full of life, full of those qualities which he would impart to others," and this was Garfield. He was abounding and running over with the freshness and exuberance, of mental, moral and physical vitality. His lectures in the chapel "were full of fresh facts, new thoughts, striking illustrations, and were warm with the glow of his own life." His students often felt that there was something marvelous in his overflowing fullness of knowledge and enthusiasm. He won them to himself and held by hooks of steel. He magnetized them with his personality.

Mr. Garfield came back to Hiram, to find his school friend and affianced a teacher in the college. On November 11, 1858, they were married. All their students and friends enjoyed this consummation of their desires. It seemed the fitting thing for them both.

While president at Hiram, he entered his name as a law student in a legal firm at Cleveland, and studied so thoroughly that in due time he was admitted to the bar, so well prepared as to be able to practice in any of the courts.

In 1859 he was invited to deliver the master's oration, at the commencement at Williams. On his return, he found he had been nominated for the State Senate. In January, 1860, he took his seat, when only thirty years old — the youngest member. That year he gave a Fourth of July oration at Ravenna, animated with the most fervid patriotism and expressed in terms of stirring eloquence.

It must not be forgotten that from the time Mr. Garfield began to study, through his life as a student, a teacher, law-student and state senator, he was an active religious man. He was faithful to his church, to his personal religious duties, and to the great gatherings of the Disciples. Quite early he began to preach. After he was through college and while teaching, he preached often at the gatherings of the brethren, to great acceptance. He supplied vacant pulpits, led prayer meetings, gave Sunday-school addresses, instructed classes in Sunday-school, and did all things needful to be done to bear on the work of the church. In all this he showed the versatility of his talents, the exuberance of his heart, and the laboriousness of his constitution. He was a living working machine—almost perpetual motion in every good cause.

Through the whole life of his youth and manhood he was actively anti-slavery; so that his political views were shaped to that view of political relations and duties. To him the slave was a man and had his natural rights which no other man might abridge. On this subject he was out-spoken, positive and religiously earnest.

A teacher, a lawyer, a preacher, a student, an anti-slavery man, and intensely patriotic, he went into the State Senate in 1860, and was in it in 1861 when Fort Sumpter was fired upon by pro-slavery secessionists. Of course all Garfield's power would be aroused in opposition. He had sprung from revolutionary patriots. His whole life had been one of humanity and fair-dealing. A secession and a war to promote slavery was to him a pair of atrocious crimes.

When President Lincoln's call for seventy-five thousand men was read in the senate, Mr. Garfield sprang to his feet and moved that Ohio furnish twenty thousand men and three millions of dollars, as her quota. Mr. Garfield at once offered himself to Governor Dennison to serve in any capacity in the cause of the Union. The governor sent him to St. Louis for five thousand stands of arms that General Lyons had placed there.

Having secured the shipment of these, the governor ordered him to hasten to Cleveland to organize the seventh and eighth regiments of Ohio infantry. The governor then appointed Mr. Garfield lieutenant-colonel and authorized him to raise a regiment on the Western Reserve. The Hiram students dropped their books and hastened to follow their president. The regiment was made up mostly of his personal friends. It went to Columbus without a colonel, because Mr. Garfield thought he was too inexperienced in military affairs. After much persuasion he accepted the appointment and went about training himself for a military leader. About this time he wrote to a friend: "One by one my old plans and aims, modes of thought and feeling, are found to be inconsistent with present duty, and are set aside to give place to the new structure of military life. It is not without regret, almost tearful at times, that I look upon the ruins. But if, as the result of the broken plans and shattered individual lives of thousands of American citizens, we can see on the ruins of our national errors a new and enduring fabric arise, based on a larger freedom and a higher justice, it will be but a small sacrifice indeed. For myself I am contented with such a prospect, and regarding my life as given to my country, I am only anxious to make as much of it as possible before the mortgage upon it is foreclosed."

### COLONEL GARFIELD.

Now it was military drill instead of college drill. President and students entered with zeal into the preparation for war's dread desolations. The regiment did not get off south till the middle of September. The colonel was invited personally to visit General Buell at Louisville. After consultation, Buell ordered him and his regiment to east Kentucky; made a new army division for him, and united the troops in that section under him to operate against the rebel Marshall, who was doing much mischief in that vicinity. Colonel Garfield had been made a brigadier-general, and in this new official capacity he entered into his work.

Colonel Garfield acquainted himself with the situation, and routed Marshall from his entrenched position without a battle by his dextrous management of his forces. The next day, following them up, they had a fierce battle at Middle Creek with a foe several times their number, and gained a Union triumph. The Hiram students were in the thickest of the fight, and proved themselves to have the spirit of their general.

It was midwinter. Heavy rains, even floods, filled the valleys, and snow covered the mountains. Of all roads and regions they were in the worst. They depended on little

30

steamers to take provisions up the Big Sandy river. But it was filled with floating trees and everything to hinder. The colonel and a guide, by the name of Brown, went down the river in a skiff and brought up a boat where the captain said it was impossible to go, the colonel commanding.

On the sides of the mountain the rebels had an encampment from which Garfield dislodged them by taking several hundred men up the cliffs and around the brow of the mountain over ice and snow, where mortal man was never expected to go. He cleaned out the valleys and swept east Kentucky clear of armed rebels. It was at a time when the Union cause was in gloom, and it gave great encouragement to General Buell, President Lincoln and the country.

### GENERAL GARFIELD.

President Lincoln at once commissioned him brigadier-general, and gave him the command of the twentieth brigade, which was in the battle of Shiloh and at the siege of Corinth. General Rosecrans appointed him on his staff, and soon made him chief-of-staff. He was in the great battles of east Tennessee, Chattanooga, Chickamauga and Missionary Ridge, and did eminent service, for which he received the promotion as major-general for gallant and meritorious services. Rosecrans sent him to Washington to report to the war department the exact condition of the army in east Tennessee. About this time he was granted a furlough home, and was afflicted in the loss of his eldest child.

Garfield's congressional district had elected him to Congress. He had shown so much knowledge and ability in his work in the army, that President Lincoln desired him in Congress, and urged him to resign his place in the army and enter Congress. Garfield was now full of the army and its great work. He had mastered the knowledge necessary to the new place, and now commanded great influence in it. He had studied in school, studied teaching, studied theology, studied law, and was now studying military tactics and science with the greatest enthusiasm. In the midst of this came the voices of his home district and his president, asking that he should go into Congress and take up the study of national legislation. In less than two years he had attained his high position in the army, because he was a thorough student, patriot and man. Wherever he was, he was always great. And his greatness was so many-sided that people had only begun to know him when he was cut down by the bullet of the assassin.

## CONGRESSMAN GARFIELD.

General Garfield went into Congress in December, 1863, after three years' service in the army; and went to Congress to begin in earnest a thorough study of political economy—especially finance, taxation, commerce, tariff, manufactures and international law. His study in Congress was intense, and here as elsewhere, he became a master. His powerful frame, massive head and manly voice commanded a place for him everywhere. In his state he was the youngest senator; in the army he was the youngest general; now he was the youngest member in the House. But he soon took his place among those most experienced and greatest, as their peer. He took high moral and patriotic grounds on all questions, and maintained them by great speeches.

In two years he was re-elected to Congress by a heavy majority. In the middle of his second term, President Lincoln was assassinated. The whole country was shocked and aroused. In New York city a great mob took possession of the streets. Two men were shot. "To the World, to the World!" cried some in the mob, and the surge of the maddened people went that way. Just then a strong man mounted some elevation and waved a small flag, as though to still the people. "Another telegram from Washington!" cried out several voices. Everybody stopped and listened. The strong man lifted reverently his eyes to heaven, and in clear, deep, strong tones, said: "Fellow citizens, clouds and darkness are around about Him. His pavilion are dark waters and thick clouds of the skies. Justice and judgment are the habitation of His throne. Mercy and truth shall go before His face. Fellow citizens, God reigns, and the government at Washington still lives!" "The crowd stood riveted to the ground," writes one present, "with awe, gazing at the motionless orator and thinking of God and the security of the government in that hour."

The tumult of the people subsided. A mighty voice had stilled a mighty passion. General Garfield was the providential man who at that moment of danger lifted up his voice over the storm. It was a stroke of genius. Only a mighty master of men and eloquence can do such a thing. It stayed a mob bent on murder and fire.

The great storm of war, the great loss of the president, and the great work of reconstruction in the hands of Congress, only strengthened his powers for greater service. He studied harder than any other member, taking more books out of the congressional library, mostly on the subjects immediately in hand. He rose with the need of each hour, and put on new strength as dangers seemed to thicken. He went on in his work of national legislator through the administration of Presidents Johnson, Grant and Hayes, broadening and enriching his intelligence, holding a commanding position in Congress, and educating the nation in finance, taxation, commerce and international law, till the great republican convention of 1880, at Chicago, put him in nomination for the presidency. His great popularity made the canvass an ovation of popular affection for him.

### PRESIDENT GARFIELD.

The nominating convention at Chicago, the enthusiastic popular canvass, the triumphant election, all indicated that no other man in this country had so large a place in the hearts of the people as General Garfield. His home at Mentor was a republican Mecca; his way to Washington was a triumphal journey; his inauguration was a red-letter day for popular government. Here was a great man, a good man, a kingly man, in person, mind and heart, who had risen from a cabin in the wilderness to the presidential mansion through all the steps of personal struggle and trial, of labor, study, religious devotion, patriotic endeavor, and national discipline and service, to the highest honor the nation could give; and yet he had kept his common-folk simplicity, his humility, frankness, genuineness, heartiness, without seeming to know that he had come to be a great man, or to lose any of the fresh vital love of humanity which had always won him the warmest personal friendship. With his enthusiasms unabated, his noble ambitions yet pure and simple, he went to the office of the president to serve the country and promote the well-being of his kind.

A country that produces such men, that makes it possible for every man to rise as he did according to the measure of his powers, who will obey the conditions, is a country, the worth of which can never be properly estimated. No service rendered to men is better given, than that rendered such a country.

President Garfield's position had its difficulties. His party was not at agreement as to methods. There was a "close corporation" so to speak, within the party, which was managed by a few party leaders, for the most part honored men, who had lost popularity with the other and larger element of the party, who thought this "machine" within the party was a corrupting thing. It was the president's purpose, if possible, to unite these elements in his administration, and at the same time abate the prevailing influence of the "machine" methods. There is but little doubt that he would have succeeded, had not the bullet of the assassin closed his noble career.

### ASSASSINATION.

On the morning of July 2, 1881, the president had arranged to visit New England for a little rest. His wife being at Long Branch, and was to meet him at New York. Senator Blaine, after breakfast, drove to the White House and took the president into his carriage, and took him to the depot. Reaching the station nearly half an hour before train time, they sat in the carriage till a railroad official told them the train was about to start. They left the carriage and went in through the ladies' waiting room which was nearly empty. As they were passing through the room, arm in arm, a strange, thin, wiry-looking man, small and quick, darted up behind them and fired at the back of the president. Recocking his pistol, he fired again in an instant. The president sank to the floor. Mr. Blaine sprang to the assassin who offered little resistance. The woman in charge of the room, ran immediately to the fallen president and held up his head. A physician was summoned, a mattress provided and he was taken to the White House. His wife was summoned and then followed long days of pain and anxiety.

The country was shocked. Sympathy and sorrow were everywhere. Indignation at the wretch who, in dastardly conceit of personal importance, sought to restore a political faction to power, by assassinating the president, made it difficult to keep him from the avenging hands of the populace. No Fourth of July was ever so mournful in this country. All nations sympathized with our suffering president, his family and people. Early in September he was moved to Long Branch; where he lingered till the nineteenth of September, when he died at 10:35 o'clock P.M., 1881.

No words can express the sorrow of the people. He was, indeed, one of the greatest and noblest of American men. It is painful to try to tell the story of so great a life in so short a space.

## The Grave of President Garfield.

After the death of President Garfield, at Long Branch, his body was taken to Washington and laid in state for two days, and then borne to Cleveland and deposited in the Scofield tomb, in Lake View cemetery. Mr. Garfield's home had always been near Cleveland; many of his early neighborhood and school friends were there; Mentor, his chosen country residence, was but one hour's ride by rail from there; some of his strongest political friends had helped to build up the Forest City; he had always watched its growth with the greatest interest; so that Cleveland was more his home than any other city. It was understood among his friends that he had contemplated Lake View cemetery as the final resting place of his mortal remains.

Lake View cemetery is one of the most interesting of the many beautiful cemeteries of the country. It is comparatively new, and is rapidly growing into a delightful resting place of human mortality. It is five and a quarter miles east of the center of Cleveland, on Euclid avenue, one of the finest city streets in the world; three quarters of a mile east of Adelbert college and the Case school of applied science; half a mile southeast of Wade Park, on the side of which, next to the cemetery, is reserved a site for another educational institution. The city already reaches to within a short distance of the cemetery, and will soon enclose it on three sides. The Nickel-plate railroad runs along the north side of it. It is already in the midst of that life and enterprise in which Mr. Garfield felt such an enthusiastic interest. It will soon be in the very presence of great educational institutions, such as he had given much of his life to promote. Education, business, travel, and the homes of the people, are about his resting place. In death, as in life, he is in the midst of the world's great interests, which he loved.

Lake Erie is about two and a half miles from the cemetery, and is visible from all the high part of it. It is an irregular tract of three hundred acres of uneven land—hill and dale—with a pleasant stream of water running through it from the south. The soil is light and gravelly, and the general aspect of the scenery agreeable in every respect.

The Scofield vault, in which the president's body now reposes, is a beautiful Gothic structure of gray sandstone built into the slope of an undulating hill, and facing the stream that runs through the grounds, which just here broadens out into a little lakelet.

Four small granite pillars, two dark and two red, on the front, support the ornamental work of the roof.

The tomb is about fifteen feet wide, and about the same height and depth.

The door is some five or six feet wide. The president's casket is just inside and across the door, on supports about two feet high. It is of bronze, and was sealed at the time his body was put into it, and has not been opened. On it is a large wreath of immortelles, and on the side near the bottom are little sheaves of wheat and baskets of flowers. Behind the casket, and over it, is arched the American flag. Twelve United States soldiers keep guard over it, night and day, taking turns in their watch.

The casket is to rest here, open to the view of the public through the wrought-iron grated gate, which prevents entrance till the monument is completed, affording it a perpetual home.

The Lake View Cemetery Association have contributed a lot of two and a half acres, half a mile from the entrance in the southwest part of the cemetery, near the Mayfield road. The lot is on the highest ground in the cemetery, one hundred and thirty feet above the entrance, and affords a fine view of the lake, the cemetery, the park and college grounds, as well as the country about, and the city towers and spires to the west of it. The lot is valued at one hundred thousand dollars. The monument is to cost one hundred and fifty thousand dollars. Of this sum seventy-five thousand have been contributed by friends of Mr. Garfield in Cleveland. The rest is the free-will offering of friends far and near, much of it in small sums.

Proposals for designs have been made, which are to be opened next May. The monument is to be of granite, and the emblems and statuary of bronze. The monument is to have a receptacle for the president and a vault for the family. The ground is already well along in the process of the grading, and everything looks as though the monument would be completed in a couple of years. When done, it will be one of the finest monuments in the country, and will be a fitting remembrance of our second martyred president.

# CHAPTER XXII.

## CHESTER ALLAN ARTHUR.

### Twenty-first President of the United States.

#### ANCESTRY AND BOYHOOD.

PRESIDENT ARTHUR, now (1884) occupying the executive chair of the republic, was born in Fairfield, Franklin county, Vermont, October 5, 1830, and is in the fifty-fourth year of his age. He is the only son of Vermont who has attained this distinction. Vermont has produced many noted men, and has, from the days of the revolution, taken an active and efficient part in national affairs; has usually been forward and vigorous in the fields of war; strong in Congress; intelligent and high-minded in the conduct of her own public affairs; had a hardy and robust people, independent and vigorous in mind and action; staid, order-loving, law-abiding and truth-seeking. Their patriotism has been intense, and their devotion to the public welfare a strong and steady impulse.

Among such people President Arthur came into being and received his early influences and education. The strong climate and fine scenery did their part in giving vigor to his body and mind, and activity and taste to his imagination.

His father, Reverend William Arthur, was a Baptist clergyman who came to this country from Ireland when eighteen years old. He had had charge of a church in New York city for a number of years; had published a work of considerable merit on

"Family Names," and had held a good place in the ministry of his denomination before his son became much known. He died in 1875.

Chester was the eldest of a family of five children, two sons and three daughters. He fitted himself for college in the Vermont academies, which have done and are still doing excellent service in educating the youth of that state. At the early age of fifteen he entered Union college at Schenectady, New York, where he graduated in the class of 1849, when nineteen years old. During his college course he partly paid his way by teaching a part of the time and continuing his studies. After his graduation, he returned to Vermont and continued teaching for a few years. For a time he was principal of the Pownal academy. But while teaching he had begun the study of law.

### MR. ARTHUR THE LAWYER.

Having saved sufficient money to carry him through his professional studies, he went to New York and entered the office of ex-Judge Culver. Having pursued the prescribed course, he was admitted to the bar, and concluded to accept Mr. Greeley's wholesale advice to the young men of the east to go west, as though young men were no longer needed in the east. After a wide tour through the west with his young friend, H. D. Gardiner, to find the place that needed them and that they needed, in which to grow up to fortune and distinction, they returned to New York city, convinced that the prophetic gift was not theirs to divine the places for the great future cities of the west. The western fever cured, the two young men formed a partnership, opened an office and began the practice of law at the foot of the hill. Little by little their business grew, and they grew with it, till in a few years they were well established in a lucrative practice.

When well established in his profession, he married a daughter of Lieutenant Herndon, of the United States navy, who, with his ship, was lost at sea. His widow was voted a gold medal by Congress for his fidelity. Mrs. Arthur died in 1880, before his election to the vice-presidency.

In 1852, when slaveholders claimed the right to take and hold their slaves wherever they chose to go, a Virginia slave-owner, with eight slaves, went to New York on his way to Texas. While awaiting the sailing of the vessel on which he was expecting to go, a writ of *habeas corpus* was obtained for the slaves, and the law took them in charge. Their case was tried before Judge Paine, Mr. Arthur and William M. Evarts serving them as advocates. It was held by the court that they could not be held as bondmen in New York, nor returned as slaves to Virginia under the fugitive slave law. They were not fugitives from service, but were held by their pretended owner in New York without law. They were liberated. The Virginia legislature sought to recover them, and brought suit in a New York court for that purpose. The case was tried and decision given for the colored people. An appeal was made to the supreme court, and the decision of the court below was sustained. The case gave Mr. Arthur much notoriety, and won him the friendship of the colored people and their friends, and of the friends of humanity, as far as the matter was known.

Another case of a similar kind is recorded to his credit as a man of justice and humanity. A colored girl was ejected from a New York street car after she had paid her fare. Mr. Arthur brought suit for damages, and recovered five hundred dollars for the girl. It brought the whole matter before the public through the press, and resulted in reversing the street railroad order against passengers of color.

As a young man, Mr. Arthur was a whig, and a great admirer of Henry Clay. His Vermont education, perhaps, had something to do with this, as Vermont always stood stoutly for that line of political opinions represented by the federalists, whigs and republicans.

## MR. ARTHUR THE POLITICIAN.

When the convention met at Saratoga which organized the republican party of New York, Mr. Arthur was a delegate. In that party he was, therefore, at home, having assisted in forming it. Its ideas and purposes were his. Its opposition to the extension of slavery, its disbelief in slavery, its recognition of human rights in colored people, its belief in the Union as a permanent national power, under the government of which the states exist; its adhesion to a national currency, and its repudiation of the state rights heresy were all his. On the basis of these ideas he has shaped his political life.

Hence, when the pro-slavery and state rights rebellion broke out he was a national government man by personal affinity and political affiliation, and gave his help to save the Union and redeem it from the slave curse. He was made judge advocate of the second brigade of the state militia.

The governor of New York, in 1860, appointed Mr. Arthur to the position of engineer-in-chief on his staff. He was afterward inspector-general for a time. Later he was quartermaster-general of the militia forces of the state to the close of Governor Morgan's term of office, in 1863. The work of equipping, supplying and transporting the immense number of troops sent to the army by that state tested his business ability. His immense accounts were so systematically kept that they were audited and allowed at Washington without deduction, a thing not very usual then, in the confusion of putting an immense army into the field. His contracts every year reached millions of dollars, and yet his accounts were so exact as to show the most scrupulous integrity in all his dealings. Personally, he profited nothing by his great opportunities to use to his benefit a tariff on his trade. He rejected presents; kept clean hands and just accounts, and made a war record for integrity as creditable as that of bravery on the field. The bravery of an honest conduct of such a great business in one's country's behalf is indeed most worthy, and is to be set down as one of the morally grand things that grand men do.

In 1862, in one of the dark hours of the war, when the loyal governors had a meeting for counsel, Mr. Arthur was invited to sit with them, on account of his great experience in the conduct of army matters. His record was a very honorable and helpful one in the hour of his country's peril.

After his work in the army was over, Mr. Arthur returned

to the practice of law, and gained in a few years a large business, a large portion of which was in collecting claims against the government. He was interested much both in state and national legislation, and drafted many bills in the interest of both. He inclined to politics and to associate with politicians, and hence took a more or less active part in local politics. He had lived long in the city and knew its people and interests and was public spirited. He had skill as an organizer and manager of local partisan matters.

In 1871, Mr. Arthur was appointed by President Grant collector of customs at the port of New York. So satisfactory was his work that he was reappointed four years later. He was continued under President Hayes, and in this showed the large business qualities previously manifested in army affairs.

But now came a break in the smooth current of his affairs. From early in President Grant's administration his party, having come to be powerful, came much under the management of party leaders, and some of them not creditable to the party; greedy, selfish men, who were in the party for place and gain. By such men were soon formed rings of their kind. In a short time these rings came to be managed by single men, these single men playing skillfully into each others hands. At Washington, at each state capital, in each large city, these rings came to hold the party management. They could easily combine, and this combination readily constituted a sort of secret conclave to cut and dry appointments, measures, and the general conduct of state and national affairs. This combination soon came to be a machine for working up the jobs of the ringleaders, who came to be termed "bosses." President Grant's hail-fellow-well-met qualities and natural incompetency for business made him just the ruler under which such a system could easily grow up into a mighty combination. And under him many of the people came to believe such a system had grown up. It was believed by many, that after President Hayes was elected, Grant was made an unconscious agent of this combination, to travel round the world and come home by way of California just in time to receive the enthusiastic welcome from his country and be nominated for a third term in the presidency. Many of the people came to regard this combination as a most intolerable "machine," utterly unrepublican and hostile to pure government and the people's rule.

President Hayes sought to head off this growing state of things and keep his administration free from any complicity with it. So he issued an order against United States officers taking any leading part in political canvasses.

Mr. Arthur was at that time chairman of the republican state committee of New York. His natural talent for management and business made him an efficient man in that place, and much more the agent of the ring "bosses" probably than he realized. He resisted the order of the president, and was removed from the collectorship. He had given entire satisfaction. His accounts were correct. All was as it should be in his office. But he was in a "ring of politicians"; was a ringmaster himself, as many people thought; and this prevalent opinion, no doubt, was shared by President Hayes, and he sought to clear his administration from its evil influence.

Mr. Arthur went back to the practice of law, but not converted to "civil service reform" as practiced by President Hayes. He was still at the head of his ring, now wounded and resolved on maintaining its position. In due time the next presidential election came round, and with it the wandering ex-President Grant, according to the prediction of those who believed he was to be put forward for a third term. The nominating convention came, with the whole combination of "machine" men, resolved on the third term movement. The movement was led by Mr. Roscoe Conkling, of New York, a strong and determined man, and an intimate friend of Mr. Arthur. The third term movement, though urged with a solid combination and great persistency, failed, and Mr. Garfield was nominated. Then the winning party in the convention must be generous, and Mr. Conkling was given the naming of a man for vice-president. He named Chester A. Arthur.

## VICE-PRESIDENT AND PRESIDENT.

Mr. Arthur took an active part in the canvass, especially in his own state, and added much to the well-managed campaign which elected Mr. Garfield and himself.

Mr. Arthur presided with acceptance in the special session of the senate which followed. But the election was accomplished by a divided party. The "civil service reform" part had secured its man for president, who was amiable and conciliatory toward the "machine" part of the party, but Mr. Conkling was imperious and unwilling to accept any lessons in civil service reform, or yield any of his prerogatives as party chief in New York. President Garfield, in spite of himself, was soon in conflict with the imperious New York senator, who, because he could not resist the senate's approval of the president's New York appointments, resigned and went home to engineer his own re-election. Mr. Arthur also went to Albany to secure, if possible, his chief's re-election, who thus put himself in antagonism with the president. The contest at Albany was a very warm one, but the civil service reform sentiment had become too strong to be overcome, and Mr. Conkling was permitted to remain in private life, to which he had voluntarily betaken himself. He had been a sort of idol of his party, many of whom sorrowed over his wrong-headedness, as they called it. It was a needless and willful self-sacrifice, many of his friends thought, and made him exceedingly unpopular. He resisted the popular will to his own political ruin.

This threw Mr. Arthur into the shadow of popular disapprobation. He had been no more willing to learn wisdom from the people than his chief had been. The heat of this conflict was not over when a cracked-brained and conceited would-be politician assassinated President Garfield, and forced by pistol shot the presidency upon Mr. Arthur. A more unfortunate way of coming to a high office never before occurred to its recipient. Many felt that he was unintentionally a participator in the crime in his persistent devotion to Mr. Conkling against the president. Many more lost confidence in him for his opposition to civil service reform, and his devotion to the hitherto prevailing system of ring politics. Many more lost confidence in him on account of his practical rejection of temperance and teetotal principles, and allying himself on the side of the great and destructive liquor selling and drinking system. All these things combined produced a tide of public sentiment against him, greater, perhaps, than any president, except Andrew Johnson, had had to resist. But his humiliation and grief, and every way considerate conduct after the assassination and during the long weeks of watching over the wounded president, won upon the whole people, and made it possible for him to give the country an acceptable presidential service. Yet his service gave evidence that he had not received the lesson which the events plainly taught till the next election gave his state to the opposite party by some two hundred thousand majority. It seemed to many that he threw away a splendid opportunity to crown his life with honor, by his over-devotion to a system of political management and personal self-indulgence almost necessarily corrupt and corrupting. After that election, his course up to the present time (December, 1883), has been far more satisfactory, and it gives evidence of going on peacefully to its close, **March 4, 1885.**

## CHAPTER XXIII.

### AN ANALYSIS

of

### THE AMERICAN GOVERNMENT.

THE original American colonies were separate communities, living on lands which they held by charter from the British Crown, and under governments of their own, sanctioned by the Crown. They had no legal relations with each other.

September 4, 1774, the First Continental Congress met and agreed upon a Bill of Rights, and *united* action to secure their rights under their king. That Congress was re-appointed from year to year, and constituted the government under which the revolution was carried on and independence secured. Under that Congress the colonies were erected into states.

This Continental Congress, as early as 1777, began to provide for a general government of the United States; but it was not effected until 1781, when the Articles of Confederation were adopted. But these were found so inefficient — were so without power of enforcement, so subject to the will, or want of will of each state, that they proved a rope of sand, and the fruits of the revolution would have been lost, had not the *people* unitedly, through their representatives, formed a Constitution with wisdom and power to guide them in "the enjoyment of life, liberty and the pursuit of happiness."

That constitution may well be the perpetual study of the American people who, under its protecting and fostering provisions, have now increased to over fifty millions, and grown to great influence and power.

A brief analysis of these provisions will help to an appreciative understanding of their great value.

### THE PREAMBLE.

"WE, the people of the United States, in order to form a more perfect union, establish justice, insure domestic tranquility, provide for the common defense, promote the general welfare, and secure the blessings of liberty to ourselves and our posterity, do ordain and establish this constitution for the United States of America."

How definite, and yet how Comprehensive! Who ordained and established this constitution? "We, the people." It was not ordained and established by the states. That was the way the "Articles of Confederation" were adopted. The states adopted them one by one. The states elected the Congress that made them. They were understood to be a confederation of states, and in that was their weakness. Now, the people took the matter into their hands, held conventions, and appointed delegates to a representative convention of the people of the United States to form a constitution "for the United States of America." In this preamble, the people gave a name to their government, stated its objects, and ordained and established it. The people are back of the states and control them and hold them to this compact. The states are estopped by "the people of the United States" from having anything to say about changing, abrogating or seceding from the constitution.

The first object named was to "form a more perfect union." The confederation had made a very imperfect union, and it was on the point of falling utterly to pieces. It had no authority, could enforce no law, collect no taxes, coin no money, punish no crimes. These things were all for the states to enforce, and they could do it or not as they chose. Now, under the constitution, a more perfect and vigorous union — one that should have power over all the states to enforce its laws within them, was formed.

The second object was to "establish justice." The states might establish justice among their own citizens, but experience had proved that they would not do it toward those of other states and foreign nations. Justice is wide in its range and must embrace all who have relations with us.

The third object was to "insure domestic tranquility," and peace among the states and the citizens of each state.

The fourth object was to "provide for the common defense." Single states might be unable to resist abuses and attacks from foreign powers. The government would defend each of its children and marshal all the rest in the defense.

The fifth object was to "promote the general welfare." This was a wide and generous object, conferring a great power for usefulness, making the government a mighty hand of helpfulness to bear on and up its people to the attainment of a high civilization.

The sixth object was to "secure the blessings of liberty to ourselves and our posterity." This was a general object involving all in one, which has been realized to a greater degree than by any other people in the world. Grandly have all the objects been realized under this most beneficent of all human governments.

## ARTICLE I.

"SECTION 1. All legislative powers herein granted shall be vested in a Congress of the United States, which shall consist of a Senate and House of Representatives."

This Congress is the law-making power. It was patterned after the English Parliament, which our national fathers thought was the best pattern in the world.

The representatives are chosen by the people, for two years; must be not less than twenty-five years old; "must have been seven years citizens of the United States," and "be inhabitants of the states in which they are chosen." The pay of members of Congress is five thousand dollars per year and mileage at twenty cents each way to and from Washington.

The Senate is composed of two senators from each state, chosen by the legislature, for six years. A senator must be thirty years old, nine years a citizen of the United States, and be an inhabitant of the state in which he is chosen.

The vice-president of the United States is president of the Senate; but the representatives choose their speaker. The salary of vice-president is eight thousand dollars per year.

In cases of impeachment, charges are made by the House of Representatives; but the trials are had before the Senate.

Congress assembles on the first Monday in December of each year.

All bills of revenue must originate in the House of Representatives; but the Senate may propose amendments.

Every bill must have passed both the House and the Senate, and receive the approval of the president before it becomes a law. If the president objects to it, he returns it to the House in which it originated, with his objections. Then if two thirds of both Houses approve it, it becomes a law, without the signature of the president.

Congress has power to raise revenues, pay debts, provide for the defense and general welfare of the United States, to borrow money, to regulate commerce, to establish a uniform rule of naturalization, to coin money, to fix the standard of weights and measures, to provide for the punishment of counterfeiting, to establish post-offices and post roads, to encourage science and the arts by protecting authors and inventors in their rights, to constitute tribunals inferior to the supreme court, to define and punish crimes on the high seas, and against the laws of nations, to declare war, to raise and support armies, to provide for the militia and its use, to exercise exclusive legislation in the District of Columbia and the territories, and to make all laws necessary for carrying these powers into effect.

## ARTICLE II.

"SECTION 1. The executive power shall be vested in a president of the United States of America. He shall hold his office during the term of four years, and together with the vice-president, chosen for the same term, be elected as follows:

"Each state shall appoint, in such manner as the legislature thereof may direct, a number of electors equal to the whole number of senators and representatives to which the state may be entitled in Congress; but no senator or representative, or person holding an office of trust or profit under the United States, shall be appointed an elector."

The duties of the president are to execute the laws of the United States, to command the armies, to make treaties, with the advice of the Senate, to appoint ambassadors, consuls, ministers, judges, and all officers not otherwise provided for. For details, see constitution.

The president's salary is fifty thousand dollars per year.

## ARTICLE III.

"SECTION 1. The judicial power of the United States shall be vested in one supreme court, and in such inferior courts as Congress may from time to time ordain and establish. The judges, both of the supreme and inferior courts, shall hold their offices during good behavior, and shall, at stated times, receive for their services, a compensation which shall not be diminished during their continuance in office."

The supreme court consists of nine members. There are ten circuits in the United States, and a judge in each. There are district courts, at least one in each state. There is also a court of claims.

These constitute the three great divisions of the constitution — the makers, the executors, and the judges of the law. They are so arranged as to be sufficiently independent of each other, and yet so related as to work harmoniously together and to hold each other in check.

The fourth article recognizes the relations of the states to the general government, and to each other, and makes provisions for the territories and new states. Amendments have been made from time to time, as they have been found needful.

This constitution, brief and simple as it is, has proved itself the wisest, profoundest and most practical instrument for the government of a free and intelligent people that has ever been made in this world. Apparently, it has left nothing out, and put nothing in that was not needful. It is worthy of the study of this great people — of all the people — the frequent and oft-repeated study, that they may know by heart the great fundamental law of the nation. It should be their political bible, open on their tables always, for personal and family use. It has been incorporated into this book, and an analysis of it is given in this chapter, to put it into many families, to give it a wide reading and study, in connection with the lives of the great men who have executed it through the first century of its existence. It recognizes all the great principles involved in our government and institutions. It is the solid bottom rock on which they are all founded. It is simple, yet not weak. It is democratic, yet maintains the central power of the whole as a unit, with such force and dignity as to make it commanding over all the parts. It maintains the rights of the individual and the authority of the government with equal ease and force. It is almost a divine balance of these two factions; and in this consists its marvelous excellency. Under it, the states and individuals exist with equal freedom and protection — in what may be called a *dependent independence*.

# The Constitution of the United States.

WE, the people of the United States, in order to form a more perfect union, establish justice, insure domestic tranquility, provide for the common defense, promote the general welfare and secure the blessings of liberty to ourselves and our posterity, do ordain and establish this Constitution for the United States of America.

## ARTICLE I.

SECTION 1. All legislative powers herein granted shall be vested in a Congress of the United States, which shall consist of a Senate and House of Representatives.

SEC. 2. The House of Representatives shall be composed of members chosen every second year by the people of the several states, and the electors in each state shall have the qualifications requisite for electors of the most numerous branch of the State Legislature.

No person shall be a representative, who shall not have attained to the age of twenty-five years, and been seven years a citizen of the United States, and who shall not when elected, be an inhabitant of that state in which he shall be chosen.

Representatives and direct taxes shall be apportioned among the several states which may be included within this union, according to their respective numbers, which shall be determined by adding to the whole number of free persons, including those bound to service for a term of years, and excluding Indians not taxed, three fifths of all other persons. The actual enumeration shall be made within three years after the first meeting of the Congress of the United States, and within every subsequent term of ten years, in such manner as they shall by law direct. The number of representatives shall not exceed one for every thirty thousand, but each state shall have at least one representative; and until such enumeration shall be made, the state of New Hampshire shall be entitled to choose three,

Massachusetts eight, Rhode Island and Providence plantations one, Connecticut five, New York six, New Jersey four, Pennsylvania eight, Delaware one, Maryland six, Virginia ten, North Carolina five, South Carolina five, and Georgia three. When vacancies happen in the representation from any state, the executive authority thereof shall issue writs of election to fill such vacancies.

The House of Representatives shall choose their speaker and other officers: and shall have the sole power of impeachment.

SEC. 3. The Senate of the United States shall be composed of two senators from each state, chosen by the Legislature thereof for six years, and each senator shall have one vote.

Immediately after they shall be assembled in consequence of the first election they shall be divided as equally as may be into three classes. The seats of the senators of the first class shall be vacated at the expiration of the second year; of the second class at the expiration of the fourth year, and of the third class at the expiration of the sixth year, so that one third may be chosen every second year; and if vacancies happen, by resignation or otherwise, during the recess of the Legislature of any state, the executive thereof may make temporary appointments until the next meeting of the Legislature, which shall then fill such vacancies.

No person shall be a senator who shall not have attained to the age of thirty years and been nine years a citizen of the United States, and who shall not, when elected, be an inhabitant of that state for which he shall be chosen.

The vice-president of the United States shall be president of the Senate, but shall have no vote unless they be equally divided.

The Senate shall choose their other officers, and also a president pro tempore, in the absence of the vice-president, or when he shall exercise the office of president of the United States.

The Senate shall have the sole power to try all impeachments. When sitting for that purpose they shall be on oath or affirmation.

When the president of the United States is tried, the chief justice shall preside, and no person shall be convicted without the concurrence of two thirds of the members present. Judgment in cases of impeachment shall not extend further than to removal from office, and disqualification to hold and enjoy any office of honor, trust or profit under the United States, but the party convicted shall, nevertheless, be liable and subject to indictment, trial, judgment and punishment, according to law.

SEC. 4. The times, places and manner of holding elections for senators and representatives shall be prescribed in each state by the Legislature thereof, but the Congress may at any time, by law, make or alter such regulations, except as to the places of choosing senators.

The Congress shall assemble at least once in every year, and such meeting shall be on the first Monday in December, unless they shall by law appoint a different day.

SEC. 5. Each House shall be the judge of the elections, returns and qualifications of its own members, and a majority of each shall constitute a quorum to do business; but a smaller number may adjourn from day to day, and may be authorized to compel the attendance of absent members, in such manner and under such penalties as each House may provide.

Each House may determine the rules of its proceedings, punish its members for disorderly behavior, and with the concurrence of two thirds, expel a member. Each House shall keep a journal of its proceedings, and from time to time publish the same, excepting such parts as may in their judgment require secrecy; and the yeas and nays of the members of either House on any question shall, at the desire of one fifth of those present, be entered on the journal.

Neither House during the session of Congress shall, without the consent of the other, adjourn for more than three days, nor to any other place than that in which the two Houses shall be sitting.

SEC. 6. The senators and representatives shall receive a compensation for their services, to be ascertained by law, and paid out of the Treasury of the United States. They shall, in all cases except treason, felony and breach of the peace, be privileged from arrest during their attendance at the session of their respective Houses, and in going to and returning from the same; and for any speech or debate in either House, they shall not be questioned in any other place.

No senator or representative shall, during the time for which he was elected, be appointed to any civil office under the authority of the United States, which shall have been created, or the emoluments whereof shall have been increased during such time; and no person holding any office under the United States, shall be a member of either House during his continuance in office.

SEC. 7. All bills for raising revenue shall originate in the House of Representatives; but the Senate may propose or concur with amendments, as on other bills. Every bill which shall have passed the House of Representatives and the Senate, shall, before it becomes a law, be presented to the President of the United States. If he approve, he shall sign it, but if not, he shall return it, with his objections to that House in which it shall have originated, who shall enter the objections at large on their journal, and proceed to reconsider it. If, after such reconsideration, two thirds of that House shall agree to pass the bill, it shall be sent, together with the objections, to the other House, by which it shall likewise be reconsidered, and if approved by two thirds of that House, it shall become a law. But in all such cases the votes of both Houses shall be determined by yeas and nays, and the names of the persons voting for and against the bill shall be entered on the journal of each House respectively. If any bill shall not be returned by the President within ten days (Sundays excepted) after it shall have been presented to him, the same shall be a law, in like manner as if he had signed it, unless the Congress by their adjournment prevent its return, in which case it shall not be a law.

Every order, resolution or vote to which the concurrence of the Senate and House of Representatives may be necessary (except on a question of adjournment) shall be presented to the President of the United States; and before the same shall take effect, shall be approved by him, or being disapproved by him, shall be repassed by two thirds of the Senate and House of

Representatives, according to the rules and limitations prescribed in the case of a bill.

SEC. 8. The Congress shall have power to lay and collect taxes, duties, imposts and excises, to pay the debts and provide for the common defense and general welfare of the United States; but all duties, imposts and excises shall be uniform throughout the United States;

To borrow money on the credit of the United States;

To regulate commerce with foreign nations, and among the several states, and with the Indian tribes;

To establish a uniform rule of naturalization, and uniform laws on the subject of bankruptcies throughout the United States;

To coin money, regulate the value thereof, and of foreign coin, and fix the standard of weights and measures;

To provide for the punishment of counterfeiting the securities and current coin of the United States;

To establish post-offices and post roads;

To promote the progress of science and useful arts, by securing for limited times to authors and inventors, the exclusive right to their respective writings and discoveries;

To constitute tribunals inferior to the supreme court;

To define and punish piracies and felonies committed on the high seas, and offenses against the law of nations;

To declare war, grant letters of marque and reprisal, and make rules concerning captures on land and water;

To raise and support armies, but no appropriation of money to that use shall be for a longer term than two years;

To provide and maintain a navy;

To make rules for the government and regulation of the land and naval forces;

To provide for calling forth the militia, to execute the laws of the union, suppress insurrections and repel invasions;

To provide for organizing, arming, and disciplining the militia, and for governing such part of them as may be employed in the service of the United States, reserving to the states respectively the appointment of the officers, and the authority of training the militia, according to the discipline prescribed by Congress;

To exercise exclusive legislation in all cases whatsoever, over such district (not exceeding ten miles square) as may, by cession of particular states, and the acceptance of Congress, become the seat of the Government of the United States, and to exercise like authority over all places purchased by the consent of the legislature of the state in which the same shall be, for the erection of forts, magazines, arsenals, dockyards and other needful buildings,

And to make all laws which shall be necessary and proper for carrying into execution the foregoing powers, and all other powers vested by this constitution, in the government of the United States, or in any department, or office thereof.

Sec. 9. The migration or importation of such persons as any of the states now existing shall think proper to admit, shall not be prohibited by the Congress, prior to the year one thousand eight hundred and eight, but a tax or duty may be imposed on such importation, not exceeding ten dollars for each person.

The privilege of the writ of habeas corpus, shall not be suspended, unless where in cases of rebellion or invasion the public safety may require it.

No bill of attainder or ex post facto law shall be passed.

No capitation or other direct tax shall be laid unless in proportion to the census or enumeration herein before directed to be taken.

No tax or duty shall be laid on articles exported from any state.

No preference shall be given by any regulation of commerce or revenue to the ports of one state over those of another; nor shall vessels bound to or from one state be obliged to enter, clear or pay duties in another.

No money shall be drawn from the treasury, but in consequence of appropriations made by law, and a regular statement and account of the receipts and expenditures of all public money shall be published from time to time.

No title of nobility shall be granted by the United States;

and no person holding any office of profit or trust under them, shall, without the consent of the Congress, accept of any present, emolument, office or title, of any kind whatever, from any king, prince, or foreign state.

SEC. 10. No state shall enter into any treaty, alliance or confederation, grant letters of marque and reprisal, coin money, emit bills of credit, make anything but gold and silver coin a tender in payment of debts, pass any bill of attainder, ex post facto law, or law impairing the obligation of contracts, or grant any title of nobility.

No state shall, without the consent of the Congress, lay any imposts or duties on imports or exports, except what may be absolutely necessary for executing its inspection laws; and the net produce of all duties and imports, laid by any state on imports or exports, shall be for the use of the treasury of the United States; and all such laws shall be subject to the revision and control of the Congress.

No state shall, without the consent of Congress, lay any duty of tonnage, keep troops, or ships of war in time of peace, enter into any agreement or compact with another state, or with a foreign power, or engage in war, unless actually invaded, or in such imminent danger as will not admit of delay.

## ARTICLE II.

SECTION 1. The executive power shall be vested in a president of the United States of America. He shall hold his office during a term of four years, and, together with the vice-president, chosen for the same term, be elected as follows: Each state shall appoint, in such manner as the Legislature thereof may direct, a number of electors equal to the whole number of senators and representatives to which the state may be entitled in the Congress: but no senator or representative or person holding an office of trust or profit under the United States shall be appointed an elector.

The Congress may determine the time of choosing the electors, and the day on which they shall give their votes, which day shall be the same throughout the United States.

No person, except a natural born citizen, or a citizen of the United States at the time of the adoption of this constitution, shall be eligible to the office of president; neither shall any person be eligible to that office who shall not have attained to the age of thirty-five years, and been fourteen years a resident within the United States.

In case of the removal of the president from office, or of his death, resignation or inability to discharge the powers and duties of the said office, the same shall devolve on the vice-president, and the Congress may by law provide for the case of removal, death, resignation, or inability, both of the president and vice-president, declaring what officer shall then act as president, and such officer shall act accordingly, until the disability be removed, or a president shall be elected.

The president shall, at stated times, receive for his services a compensation, which shall neither be increased nor diminished during the period for which he shall have been elected, and he shall not receive within that period any other emolument from the United States, or any of them.

Before he enter on the execution of his office, he shall take the following oath or affirmation: "I do solemnly swear (or affirm) that I will faithfully execute the office of president of the United States, and will to the best of my ability, preserve, protect and defend the Constitution of the United States."

SEC. 2. The president shall be commander in chief of the army and navy of the United States, and of the militia of the several states, when called into the actual service of the United States; he may require the opinion in writing, of the principal officer in each of the executive departments upon any subject relating to the duties of their respective offices, and he shall have power to grant reprieves and pardons for offenses against the United States, except in cases of impeachment.

He shall have power, by and with the advice and consent of the Senate, to make treaties, provided two thirds of the senators present concur; and he shall nominate, and by and with the advice and consent of the Senate, shall appoint ambassadors, other public ministers and consuls, judges of the supreme court, and all other officers of the United States, whose appointments are not herein otherwise provided for, and which shall be established by law; but the Congress may by law vest the appointment of such inferior officers, as they think proper in the president alone, in the courts of law, or in the heads of departments.

The president shall have power to fill up all vacancies that may happen during the recess of the Senate, by granting commissions which shall expire at the end of their next session.

Sec. 3. He shall from time to time give to the Congress information of the states of the Union, and recommend to their consideration such measures as he shall judge necessary and expedient; he may, on extraordinary occasions, convene both Houses, or either of them, and in case of disagreement between them with respect to the time of adjournment, he may adjourn them to such time as he may think proper; he shall receive ambassadors and other public ministers; he shall take care that the laws be faithfully executed, and shall commission all the officers of the United States.

Sec. 4. The president, vice-president, and all civil officers of the United States, shall be removed from office on impeachment for, and conviction of treason, bribery, or other high crimes and misdemeanors.

## ARTICLE III.

Section 1. The judicial power of the United States shall be vested in one supreme court, and in such inferior courts as the Congress may from time to time ordain and establish. The judges, both of the supreme and inferior courts, shall hold their offices during good behavior, and shall, at stated times, receive for their services a compensation which shall not be diminished during their continuance in office.

Sec. 2. The judicial power shall extend to all cases, in law and equity, arising under this constitution, the laws of the United States and treaties made, or which shall be made, under their authority; to all cases affecting ambassadors, other public ministers and consuls; to all cases of admiralty and maritime jurisdiction; to controversies to which the United States shall be a party; to controversies between two or more states; between a state and citizens of another state; between citizens of different states; between citizens of the same state claiming lands under grants of different states, and between a state, or the citizens thereof, and foreign states, citizens or subjects.

In all cases affecting ambassadors, other public ministers and consuls, and those in which a state shall be party, the supreme court shall have original jurisdiction. In all other cases before mentioned the supreme court shall have appellate jurisdiction, both as to law and fact, with such exceptions and under such regulations as the Congress shall make.

The trial of all crimes, except in cases of impeachment, shall be by jury, and such trial shall be held in the state where the said crimes shall have been committed, but when not committed within any state the trial shall be at such place or places as the Congress may by law have directed.

SEC. 3. Treason against the United States shall consist only in levying war against them, or in adhering to their enemies, giving them aid and comfort. No person shall be convicted of treason unless on the testimony of two witnesses to the same overt act, or on confession in open court.

The Congress shall have power to declare the punishment of treason, but no attainder of treason shall work corruption of blood or forfeiture except during the life of the person attained.

## ARTICLE IV.

SECTION 1. Full faith and credit shall be given in each state to the public acts, records and judicial proceedings of every other state, and the Congress may, by general laws, prescribe the manner in which such acts, records and proceedings shall be proved, and the effect thereof.

SEC. 2. The citizens of each state shall be entitled to all privileges and immunities of citizens in the several states.

A person charged in any state with treason, felony or other crime, who shall flee from justice, and be found in another state, shall, on demand of the executive authority of the state from which he fled, be delivered up to be removed to the state having jurisdiction of the crime.

No person held to service or labor in one state, under the laws thereof, escaping into another, shall, in consequence of any law or regulation therein, be discharged from such service or labor, but shall be delivered up on claim of the party to whom such service or labor may be due.

Sec. 3. New states may be admitted by the Congress into this Union; but no new state shall be formed or erected within the jurisdiction of any other state; nor any state be formed by the junction of two or more states, or parts of states, without the consent of the Legislatures of the states concerned as well as of the Congress.

The Congress shall have power to dispose of and make all needful rules and regulations respecting the territory or other property belonging to the United States; and nothing in this constitution shall be so construed as to prejudice any claims of the United States, or of any particular state.

Sec. 4. The United States shall guarantee to every state in this Union a republican form of government, and shall protect each of them against invasion; and on application of the Legislature, or of the executive (when the Legislature cannot be convened), against domestic violence.

## ARTICLE V.

The Congress, whenever two thirds of both Houses shall deem it necessary, shall propose amendments to this constitution, or, on the application of the Legislatures of two thirds of the several states, shall call a convention for proposing amendments, which, in either case, shall be valid to all intents and purposes, as part of this constitution, when ratified by the Legislatures of three fourths of the several states, or by conventions in three fourths thereof, as the one or the other mode of ratification may be proposed by the Congress; provided that no amendment which may be made prior to the year one thousand eight hundred and eight, shall in any manner affect the first and fourth clauses in the ninth section of the first article;

and that no state, without its consent, shall be deprived of its equal suffrage in the Senate.

## ARTICLE VI.

All debts contracted and engagements entered into, before the adoption of this constitution, shall be as valid against the United States under this constitution, as under the confederation.

This constitution, and the laws of the United States, which shall be made in pursuance thereof, and all treaties made, or which shall be made, under the authority of the United States, shall be the supreme law of the land; and the judges in every state shall be bound thereby, anything in the constitution or laws of any state to the contrary notwithstanding.

The senators and representatives before mentioned, and the members of the several State Legislatures, and all executive and judicial officers, both of the United States and the several states, shall be bound by oath or affirmation to support this constitution; but no religious test shall ever be required as a qualification to any office or public trust under the United States.

## ARTICLE VII.

The ratification of the conventions of nine states shall be sufficient for the establishment of this constitution between the states so ratifying the same.

Done in convention by the unanimous consent of the states present, the seventeenth day of September, in the year of our Lord one thousand seven hundred and eighty-seven, and of the independence of the United States of America the twelfth.

In witness whereof we have hereunto subscribed our names.

GEORGE WASHINGTON,
President and Deputy from Virginia.

*New Hampshire.*

JOHN LANGDON.         NICHOLAS GILMAN.

*Massachusetts.*

NATHANIEL GORHAM.         RUFUS KING.

*Connecticut.*
WILLIAM SAMUEL JOHNSON.   ROGER SHERMAN.

*New York.*
ALEXANDER HAMILTON.

*New Jersey.*
WILLIAM LIVINGSTON.   WILLIAM PATERSON.
DAVID BREARLEY.   JONA DAYTON.

*Pennsylvania.*
BENJAMIN FRANKLIN.   THOMAS FITZSIMONS.
THOMAS MIFFLIN.   JARED INGERSOLL.
ROBERT MORRIS.   JAMES WILSON.
GEORGE CLYMER.   GOVERNEUR MORRIS.

*Delaware.*
GEORGE READ.   RICHARD BASSETT.
GUNNING BEDFORD, JR.   JACOB BROOM.
JOHN DICKINSON.

*Maryland.*
JAMES MCHENRY.   DANIEL CARROLL.
DAN OF ST. THOMAS JENIFER.

*Virginia.*
JOHN BLAIR.   JAMES MADISON, JR.

*North Carolina.*
WILLIAM BLOUNT.   HUGH WILLIAMSON.
RICHARD DOBBS SPRAIGHT.

*South Carolina.*
J. RUTLEDGE.   CHARLES PINCKNEY.
CHAS. COTESWORTH PINCKNEY.   PIERCE BUTLER.

*Georgia.*
WILLIAM FEW.   ABRAHAM BALDWIN.

(*Attest.*)   WILLIAM JACKSON, Secretary.

ARTICLES IN ADDITION TO AND AMENDMENT OF THE CONSTITUTION OF THE UNITED STATES OF AMERICA, PROPOSED BY CONGRESS, AND RATIFIED BY THE LEGISLATURES OF THE SEVERAL STATES, PURSUANT TO THE FIFTH ARTICLE OF THE ORIGINAL CONSTITUTION.

## ARTICLE I.

Congress shall make no law respecting an establishment of religion, or prohibiting the free exercise thereof; or abridging the freedom of speech, or of the press, or the right of the people, peaceably to assemble, and to petition the government for a redress of grievances.

## ARTICLE II.

A well-regulated militia being necessary to the security of a free state, the right of the people to keep and bear arms shall not be infringed.

## ARTICLE III.

No soldier shall, in time of peace, be quartered in any house without the consent of the owner, nor in time of war, but in a manner to be prescribed by law.

## ARTICLE IV.

The right of the people to be secure in their persons, houses, papers and effects, against unreasonable searches and seizures, shall not be violated, and no warrants shall issue, but upon probable cause, supported by oath or affirmation, and particularly describing the place to be searched, and the persons or things to be seized.

## ARTICLE V.

No person shall be held to answer for a capital, or other infamous crime, unless on a presentment or indictment of a grand jury, except in cases arising in the land or naval forces, or in the militia, when in actual service in time of war or public danger; nor shall any person be subject, for the same offense to be twice put in jeopardy of life or limb; nor shall be compelled in any criminal case to be a witness against himself, nor be deprived of life, liberty or property, without due process of law; nor shall private property be taken for public use, without just compensation.

## ARTICLE VI.

In all criminal prosecutions the accused shall enjoy the right to a speedy and public trial, by an impartial jury of the state and district wherein the crime shall have been committed, which district shall have been previously ascertained by law, and to be informed of the nature and cause of the accusation; to be confronted with the witnesses against him; to have compulsory process for obtaining witnesses in his favor, and to have the assistance of counsel for his defense.

## ARTICLE VII.

In suits at common law, where the value in controversy shall exceed twenty dollars, the right of trial by jury shall be preserved, and no fact tried by a jury shall be otherwise re-examined in any court of the United States than according to the rules of the common law.

## ARTICLE VIII.

Excessive bail shall not be required, nor excessive fines imposed, nor cruel and unusual punishments inflicted.

## ARTICLE IX.

The enumeration in the constitution of certain rights shall not be construed to deny or disparage others retained by the people.

## ARTICLE X.

The powers not delegated to the United States by the constitution, nor prohibited by it to the states, are reserved to the states respectively, or to the people.

## ARTICLE XI.

The judicial power of the United States shall not be construed to extend to any suit in law or equity, commenced or prosecuted against one of the United States by citizens of another state, or by citizens or subjects of any foreign state.

## ARTICLE XII.

The electors shall meet in their respective states, and vote by ballot for president and vice-president, one of whom, at least, shall not be an inhabitant of the same state with themselves; they shall name in their ballots the person voted for as president, and in distinct ballots the person voted for as vice-president, and they shall make distinct lists of all persons voted for as president, and of all persons voted for as vice-president, and of the number of votes for each, which lists they shall sign and certify, and transmit sealed to the seat of the government of the United States, directed to the president of the Senate. The president of the Senate shall, in the presence of the Senate and House of Representatives, open all the certificates, and the votes shall then be counted. The person having the greatest number of votes for president, shall be the president, if such number be a majority of the whole number of electors appointed; and if no person have such majority, then from the persons having the highest numbers, not exceeding three on the list of those voted for as president, the House of Representatives shall choose immediately, by ballot, the president. But in choosing the president, the vote shall be taken by states, the representation from each state having one vote; a quorum for this purpose shall consist of a member or members from two thirds of the states, and a majority of all the states shall be necessary to a choice. And if the House of Representatives shall not choose a president, whenever the right of choice shall devolve upon them, before the fourth day of March next following, then the vice-president shall act as president, as in the case of death, or other constitutional disability of the president. The person having the greatest number of votes as vice-president, shall be vice-president, if such number be a majority of the whole number of electors appointed, and if no person have a majority, then from the two highest numbers on the list, the Senate shall choose the vice-president; a quorum for the purpose shall consist of two thirds of the whole number of senators, and a majority of the whole number shall be necessary to a choice. But no person constitutionally ineligible to the office of president shall be eligible to that of vice-president of the United States.

## ARTICLE XIII.

SECTION 1. Neither slavery nor involuntary servitude, except as a punishment for crime whereof the party shall have been duly convicted, shall exist within the United States, or any place subject to its jurisdiction.

SEC. 2. Congress shall have power to enforce this article by appropriate legislation.

## ARTICLE XIV.

SECTION 1. All persons born or naturalized in the United States, and subject to the jurisdiction thereof, are citizens of the United States and of the state wherein they reside.

No state shall make or enforce any law which shall abridge the privileges or immunities of citizens of the United States; nor shall any state deprive any person of life, liberty or property without due process of law; nor deny to any person within its jurisdiction the equal protection of its laws.

SEC. 2. Representatives shall be apportioned among the states according to their respective numbers, counting the whole number of persons in each state, excluding Indians not taxed. But when the right to vote at any election for the choice of electors for president and vice-president of the United States, representatives in Congress, the executive and judicial officers of the state, or the members of the Legislature thereof, is denied to any of the male inhabitants of such state, being twenty-one years of age, and citizens of the United States, or in any way abridged, except for participation in rebellion, or other crime, the basis of representation therein shall be reduced in the proportion which the number of such male citizens shall bear to the whole number of male citizens twenty-one years of age in such state.

Sec. 3. No person shall be a senator or representative in Congress, or elector of president or vice-president, or hold any office, civil or military, under the United States, or under any state, who, having previously taken an oath, as a member of Congress, or an officer of the United States, or a member of any state Legislature, or as an executive or judicial officer of any state, to support the Constitution of the United States, shall have engaged in insurrection or rebellion against the same, or given aid or comfort to the enemies thereof. But Congress may, by a vote of two thirds of each House, remove such disability.

Sec. 4. The validity of the public debt of the United States, authorized by law, including debts incurred for payment of pensions and bounties for services in suppressing insurrection or rebellion, shall not be questioned. But neither the United States, nor any state shall assume or pay any debt or obligation incurred in aid of insurrection or rebellion against the United States, or any claim for the loss or emancipation of any slave; but all such debts, obligations and claims shall be held illegal and void.

Sec. 5. Congress shall have power to enforce, by appropriate legislation, the provisions of this article.

## ARTICLE XV.

Section 1. The right of the citizens of the United States to vote shall not be denied or abridged by the United States, or by any state on account of race, color, or previous condition of servitude.

Sec. 2. The Congress shall have power to enforce this article by appropriate legislation.

www.ingramcontent.com/pod-product-compliance
Lightning Source LLC
Chambersburg PA
CBHW031944290426
44108CB00011B/664